THE
WORKS
Of the REVEREND
WILLIAM LAW, M.A.,

Sometime Fellow of *Emmanuel* College, *Cambridge*.

In Nine Volumes.

Volume VII.

I. The Spirit of Prayer; or, the Soul Rising out of the Vanity of Time, into the Riches of Eternity. In Two Parts.

II. The Way to Divine Knowledge; being several Dialogues between Humanus, Academicus, Rusticus, and Theophilus.

Wipf & Stock
PUBLISHERS
Eugene, Oregon

Wipf and Stock Publishers
199 West 8th Avenue, Suite 3
Eugene, Oregon 97401

Vol. 7-The Spirit of Prayer; The Way to Divine Knowledge,
By Law, William
Copyright© by Law, William
ISBN: 1-57910-621-8
Publication date 3/12/2001
Previously published by G. Moreton, Safety, 1892

THE SPIRIT of PRAYER;

OR,

The SOUL rising out of the VANITY of TIME, INTO THE RICHES of ETERNITY.

In TWO PARTS.

PART I.

By *WILLIAM LAW*, M.A.

LONDON:
Printed for M. RICHARDSON, in *Pater-noster-Row.* 1749.

THE SPIRIT OF PRAYER.

Chapter I.

Treating of some Matters preparatory to the Spirit of Prayer.

THE greatest Part of Mankind, nay of Christians, may be said to be asleep; and that particular Way of Life, which takes up each Man's Mind, Thoughts, and Actions, may be very well called his particular Dream. This Degree of Vanity is equally visible in every Form and Order of Life. The Learned and the Ignorant, the Rich and the Poor, are all in the same State of Slumber, only passing away a short Life in a different kind of Dream. But why so? It is because Man has an Eternity within him, is born into this World, not for the Sake of living here, not for any Thing this World can give him, but only to have Time and Place, to become either an eternal Partaker of a Divine Life with God, or to have an hellish Eternity among fallen Angels: And therefore, every Man who has not his Eye, his Heart, and his Hands, continually governed by this twofold Eternity, may be justly said to be fast asleep, to have no awakened Sensibility of Himself. And a Life devoted to the Interests and Enjoyments of this World, spent and wasted in the Slavery of earthly Desires, may be truly called a Dream, as having all the Shortness, Vanity, and Delusion of a Dream; only with this great Difference, that when a Dream is over, nothing is lost but Fictions and Fancies; but when the Dream of Life is ended *only* by Death, all that Eternity is lost for which we were brought into Being. Now there is no Misery in this World, nothing that makes either the Life or Death of Man to be full of Calamity, but this Blindness and Insensibility of his State, into which he so willingly, nay obstinately plunges himself. Every Thing that has the Nature of Evil and Distress in it takes its Rise from hence. Do but suppose a Man to know himself, that he comes into this World on no other Errand, but to rise out of the Vanity of Time into the Riches of Eternity; do but suppose him to govern his inward Thoughts and outward Actions by this View of himself, and then to him every Day has lost all its Evil; Prosperity and Adversity have no

Difference, because he receives and uses them both in the same Spirit; Life and Death are equally welcome, because equally Parts of his Way to Eternity. For poor and miserable as this Life is, we have all of us free Access to all that is Great, and Good, and Happy, and carry within ourselves a *Key* to all the Treasures that Heaven has to bestow upon us.—We starve in the midst of Plenty, groan under Infirmities, with the Remedy in our own Hand; live and die without knowing and feeling any Thing of the *One, only Good*, whilst we have it in our Power to know and enjoy it in as great a Reality, as we know and feel the Power of this World over us: For Heaven is as near to our Souls, as this World is to our Bodies; and we are created, we are redeemed, to have our Conversation in it. God, the only *Good* of all intelligent Natures, is not an absent or distant God, but is more present *in* and *to* our Souls, than our own Bodies; and we are Strangers to Heaven, and without God in the World, for this only Reason, because we are void of that Spirit of Prayer, which alone can, and never fails to unite us with the *One, only* Good, and to open Heaven and the Kingdom of God within us. A Root set in the finest Soil, in the best Climate, and blessed with all that Sun, and Air, and Rain can do for it, is not in so sure a Way of its Growth to Perfection, as every Man may be, whose Spirit aspires after all that, which God is ready and infinitely desirous to give him. For the *Sun* meets not the springing Bud that stretches towards him with half that Certainty, as God, the Source of all Good, communicates himself to the Soul that longs to partake of Him.

We are all of us, by Birth, the Offspring of God, more nearly related to him than we are to one another; for *in him we live, and move, and have our Being*. The first Man that was brought forth from God had the Breath and Spirit of *Father, Son, and Holy Ghost*, breathed into him, and so he became a living Soul. Thus was our first Father born of God, descended from Him, and stood in Paradise in the Image and Likeness of God. He was the Image and Likeness of God, not with any Regard to his outward Shape or Form, for no Shape has any Likeness to God; but he was in the Image and Likeness of God, because the Holy Trinity had breathed their own Nature and Spirit into him. And as the Deity, *Father, Son*, and *Holy Spirit*, are always in Heaven, and make Heaven to be everywhere, so this Spirit, breathed by them into Man, brought Heaven into Man along with it; and so Man was in Heaven, as well as on Earth, that is, in Paradise, which signifies an heavenly State, or Birth of Life.*

---

* *Spirit of Prayer*, Part II., page 61.

Adam had all that Divine Nature, both as to an heavenly *Spirit*, and heavenly *Body*, which the Angels have: But as he was brought forth to be a Lord and Ruler of a new World, created out of the *Chaos* or *Ruins* of the Kingdom of fallen Angels; so it was necessary that he should also have the Nature of this new created World in himself, both as to its *Spirit* and *Materiality*. Hence it was, that he had a Body taken from this new created Earth, not such dead Earth as we now make *Bricks* of, but the *blessed* Earth of Paradise, that had the Powers of Heaven in it, out of which the *Tree of Life* itself could grow. Into the Nostrils of this outward Body, was the Breath or *Spirit* of this World breathed; and in this Spirit and Body of this World, did the inward celestial Spirit and Body of *Adam* dwell: It was the *Medium* or *Means* through which he was to have Commerce with this World, become visible to its Creatures, and rule over it and them. Thus stood our first Father; an Angel both as to Body and Spirit (as he will be again after the Resurrection) yet dwelling in a Body and Spirit taken from this new created World, which however was as inferior to him, as subject to him, as the Earth and all its Creatures were. It was no more alive in him, no more brought forth its Nature within him, than *Satan* and the Serpent were alive in him at his first Creation. And herein lay the Ground of *Adam's* Ignorance of Good and Evil; it was because his outward Body, and the outward World (in which alone was Good and Evil) could not discover their own Nature, or open their own Life within him, but were kept inactive by the Power and Life of the celestial Man within it. And this was Man's first and great Trial; a Trial, not imposed upon him by the mere Will of God, or by Way of Experiment; but a Trial necessarily implied in the Nature of his State: He was created an Angel, both as to Body and Spirit; and this Angel stood in an outward Body, of the Nature of the outward World; and therefore, by the Nature of his State, he had his Trial, or *Power* of choosing, whether he would live as an Angel, using only his outward Body as a Means of opening the Wonders of the outward World to the Glory of his Creator; or whether he would turn his Desire to the opening of the bestial Life of the outward Worldling himself, for the Sake of *knowing the Good and Evil* that was in it. The Fact is certain, that he lusted after the Knowledge of this Good and Evil, and made use of the Means to obtain it. No sooner had he got this Knowledge, by the opening the bestial Life and Sensibility within him, but in that Day, nay, in that Instant, *he died;* that is, his heavenly Spirit with its heavenly Body were both extinguished in him; but his Soul, an immortal Fire that could not die, became a poor Slave in Prison of bestial Flesh and Blood. See here the Nature and Necessity of our Redemption; it is to redeem the first Angelic Nature that departed from *Adam;* it is to make that heavenly Spirit and Body which *Adam* lost, to be alive again in all the human Nature; and this is called *Regeneration.* See also the true Reason why only the *Son,* or *eternal Word* of God, could be our Redeemer; it is because He alone, by whom all Things were at first made, could be able to bring to Life again that celestial Spirit and Body which had departed from *Adam.* See also why our blessed Redeemer said, ' Except a Man be born ' again, of Water and the Spirit, he cannot enter into the King- 'dom of Heaven.' He must be born again of the *Spirit,* because *Adam's* first heavenly *Spirit* was lost: He must be born again of *Water,* because that heavenly Body which *Adam* lost, was formed out of the heavenly Materiality, which is called *Water.* Thus in the *Revelation* of St. *John,* the heavenly Materiality, out of which the Bodies of the Angels and also of *Adam* were formed, is called a *glassy Sea,* as being the nearest and truest Representation of it that can be made to our Minds. The Necessity of our regaining our first heavenly Body, is the Necessity of our eating the Body and Blood of Christ. The Necessity of having again our first heavenly Spirit, is declared by the Necessity of our being baptized by the Holy Ghost. Our *Fall* is nothing else, but the Falling of our Soul from this celestial Body and Spirit into a *bestial* Body and Spirit of this World. Our rising out of our fallen State, or Redemption, is nothing else but the regaining our first angelic Spirit and Body, which in Scripture is called our *inward,* or *new Man, created again in Christ Jesus.* See here, lastly, the true Ground of all the Mortifications of Flesh and Blood, required in the Gospel; it is because this *bestial Life* of this outward World should not have been opened in Man; it is his Separation from God, and Death to the Kingdom of Heaven; and therefore, all its *Workings, Appetites,* and *Desires,* are to be restrained and kept under, that the first heavenly Life, to which *Adam* died, may have Room to rise up in us.

But to return. That *Adam* was thus an Angel at his first Creation, dwelling in an outward Body and outward World, incapable of receiving any Impressions from them, and able to rule them at his Pleasure; that all outward Nature was a State of Life *below* him, in Subjection to him; that neither Sun, nor Stars, nor Fire, nor Water, nor Earth, nor Stones, could act upon him, or hurt him, is undeniably plain from hence; because his first and great Sin, which cost him his angelical Life, and took from him his Crown of Glory, consisted in this, that he lusted to know, and took the Means of knowing, what Good and Evil are in the bestial Life of this World : For this plainly demonstrates, that before his Sin, whilst he stood in the first State of his Creation, that he was an Angel in Nature and Power, that neither his *own outward* Body, nor any Part of outward Nature, had any Power in him or upon him ; for had his own outward Body, or any Element of outward Nature, had any Power to act upon him, to make any Impressions, or raise any Sensations in him, he could not have been ignorant of Good and Evil in this World. Therefore, seeing that his eating of the forbidden Tree, was that alone which opened this Knowledge in him, it is a Demonstration, that in his first State he was in this World as an Angel, that was put into the Possession of it only to rule as a superior Being over it ; that he was to have no Share of its Life and Nature, no Feeling of Good or Evil from it, but to act in it as a heavenly Artist, that had Power and Skill to open the Wonders of God in every Power of outward Nature. An Angel, we read, used at a certain Time to come down into a *Pool* at *Jerusalem;* the Water stirred by the Angel gave forth its Virtues, but the Angel felt no Impressions of *Weight*, or *Cold* from the Water. This is an Image of *Adam's* first Freedom from, and Power over all outward Nature. He could wherever he went, do as this Angel did, make every Element, and elementary Thing, discover all the Riches of God that were hidden in it, without feeling any Impressions of any kind from it. This was to have been the Work both of *Adam* and his Offspring, to make all the Creation show forth the Glory of God, to spread Paradise over all the Earth, till the Time came, that all the Good in this World was to be called back to its first State, and all the Evil in every Part left to be possessed by the Devil and his Angels. But since He fell from this first State into an *Animal* of this World, his Work is changed, and he must now labour with Sweat to *till* the cursed Earth, both for Himself and the Beasts upon it.

Let us now consider some plain and important Truths, that follow from what has been said above.

First, It is plain that the Sin and fall of *Adam* did not consist in this, *viz.*, that he had only committed *a single Act of Disobedience*, and so might have been just as He was before, if God had pleased to overlook this *single Act* of Disobedience, and not to have brought a Curse upon him and his Posterity for it.— Nothing of this is the Truth of the Matter, either on the Part of God, or on the Part of Man.

Secondly, It is plain also, that the Command of God, not to lust after, and eat of the forbidden Tree, was not an *arbitrary*

Command of God, given at Pleasure, or as a mere Trial of Man's Obedience; but was a most kind and loving *Information* given by the God of Love to his new-born Offspring, concerning the State He was in, with Regard to the outward World: Warning him to withdraw all Desire of entering into a *Sensibility* of its Good and Evil; because such Sensibility could not be had, without his immediate dying to that Divine and heavenly Life which he then enjoyed. 'Eat not,' says the God of Love, 'of the Tree 'of Knowledge of Good and Evil, for in the Day thou eatest 'thereof thou wilt surely die.'

As if it had been said, 'I have brought Thee into this Paradise, 'with such a Nature as the Angels have in Heaven. By the 'Order and Dignity of thy Creation, every Thing that lives and 'moves in this World is made subject to Thee, as to their 'Ruler. I have made Thee in thy outward Body of this World, 'to be for a Time a little lower than the Angels, till Thou hast 'brought forth a numerous Offspring, fit for that Kingdom which 'They have lost. The World around Thee, and the Life which 'is newly awakened in it, is much lower than Thou art; of a 'Nature quite inferior to thine. It is a gross, corruptible State 'of Things, that cannot stand long before me; but must for 'awhile bear the Marks of those Creatures, which first made Evil 'to be known in the Creation. The Angels, that first inhabited 'this Region, where Thou art to bring forth a new Order of 'Beings, were great and powerful Spirits, highly endowed with 'the Riches and Powers of their Creator. Whilst they stood (as 'the Order of Creation requires) in Meekness and Resignation, 'under their Creator, nothing was impossible to them; there was 'no End of their glorious Powers throughout their whole King-'dom. Perpetual Scenes of Light, and Glory, and Beauty, were 'rising and changing through all the Height and Depth of their '*glassy Sea*, merely at their Will and Pleasure. But finding what 'Wonders of Light and Glory they could perpetually bring forth; 'how all the *Powers* of Eternity, treasured up in their *glassy Sea*, 'unfolded themselves, and broke forth in ravishing Forms of 'Wonder and Delight, merely in Obedience to their Call; they 'began to admire and even adore themselves, and to fancy 'that there was *some Infinity of Power hidden* in themselves, 'which they supposed was kept under, and suppressed, by that 'Meekness, and Subjection to God, under which they acted. 'Fired and intoxicated with this proud Imagination, they boldly 'resolved, with all their eternal Energy and Strength, to take 'their Kingdom, with all its Glories, to themselves, by eternally 'abjuring all Meekness and Submission to God. No sooner did 'their eternal potent Desires fly in this Direction of a Revolt

'from God, but in the Swiftness of a Thought Heaven was lost;
'and they found themselves dark Spirits, stripped of all their
'Light and Glory. Instead of Rising up above God (as they
'hoped) by breaking off from Him, there was no End of their
'eternal Sinking into new Depths of Slavery, under their own
'self-tormenting Natures. As a Wheel going down a Mountain,
'that has no bottom, must continually keep on its Turning, so
'are they whirled down by the Impetuosity of their own wrong
'turned Wills, in a continual Descent from the Fountain of all
'Glory, into the bottomless Depths of their own dark, fiery,
'working Powers. In no Hell, but what their own natural
'Strength had awakened; bound in no Chains, but their own
'unbending, hardened Spirits; made such, by their renouncing,
'with all their eternal Strength, all Meekness, and Subjection to
'God. In that Moment, the beautiful Materiality of their King-
'dom, their *glassy Sea* in which they dwelt, was by the wrathful
'rebellious Workings of these apostate Spirits broken all into
'Pieces, and became a black Lake, a horrible Chaos of Fire and
'Wrath, Thickness and Darkness, a Height and Depth of the
'confused, divided, fighting Properties of Nature. My creating
'*Fiat* stopped the Workings of these rebellious Spirits, by divid-
'ing the Ruins of their wasted Kingdom, into an Earth, a Sun,
'Stars, and separated Elements. Had not this Revolt of Angels
'brought forth that disordered *Chaos*, no such Materiality as this
'outward World is made of had ever been known. Gross com-
'pacted Earth, Stones, Rocks, wrathful Fire here, dead Water
'there, fighting Elements, with all their gross Vegetables and
'Animals, are Things not known in Eternity, and will be only
'seen in Time, till the great Designs are finished, for which Thou
'art brought forth in Paradise. And then, as a Fire awakened
'by the Rebel Creature, began all the Disorders of Nature, and
'turned that glassy Sea into a Chaos, so a *last Fire*, kindled at
'my Word, shall thoroughly purge the Floor of this World. In
'those purifying Flames, the Sun, the Stars, the Air, the Earth
'and Water, shall part with all their Dross, Deadness, and Divi-
'sion, and all become again that first, heavenly Materiality, a
'*glassy Sea* of everlasting Light and Glory, in which Thou and
'thy Offspring shall sing Hallelujahs to all Eternity. Look not
'therefore, thou Child of Paradise, thou Son of Eternity, look
'not with a longing Eye after any Thing in this outward World.
'There are the Remains of the fallen Angels in it; Thou hast
'nothing to do in it, but as a Ruler over it. It stands before
'Thee, as a Mystery big with Wonders; and Thou, whilst an
'Angel in Paradise, hast Power to open and display them all.
'It stands not in thy Sphere of Existence; it is, as it were, but a

'Picture, and transitory Figure of Things; for all that is not
'Eternal, is but as an Image in a Glass, that seems to have a
'Reality, which it has not. The Life which springs up in this
'Figure of a World, in such an infinite Variety of Kinds and
'Degrees, is but as a Shadow; it is a Life of such Days and Years,
'as in Eternity have no Distinction from a Moment. It is a life
'of such Animals and Insects, as are without any Divine Sense,
'Capacity, or Feeling. Their Natures have nothing in them,
'but what I commanded this new modelled *Chaos*, this Order of
'Stars and fighting Elements, to bring forth.

'Now *Adam*, observe, I will open to Thee a great Mystery.
'The heavenly Materiality of the Angels' Kingdom before their
'Revolt was a *glassy Sea*, a Mirror of beauteous Forms, Figures,
'Virtues, Powers, Colours, and Sounds, which were perpetually
'springing up, appearing and changing in an infinite Variety, to
'the Manifestation of the Wonders of the Divine Nature, and
'to the Joy of all the Angelical Kingdom. This heavenly
'Materiality had its Fruits and Vegetables, much more real
'than any that grow in Time, but as different from the Grossness
'of the Fruits of this World, as the heavenly Body of an Angel
'is different from the Body of the grossest Beast upon Earth.
'In this angelical Kingdom, the *one* Element (which is now in
'four Parts) was then a fruitful Mother of Wonders, continually
'bringing forth new *Forms* and *Figures of Life;* not Animals,
'Beasts, or Insects, but beautiful *Figures*, and *ideal* Forms of
'the endless Divisibility, and Degrees of Life, which only broke
'forth as delightful Wonders of the Depth of the Riches of the
'Divine Nature, and to tune the Voices of Angels with Songs of
'Praise to the infinite Source of Life. And hence, O *Adam*, is
'that endless infinite Variety both of the animal and vegetable
'Life in this perishable World. For no Fruits of Vegetables
'could have sprung up in the divided Elements, but because
'they are the divided Parts of that one heavenly Materiality, or
'*glassy Sea*, in which angelical Fruits had formerly grown forth.
'No animal Life could have arose from Stars, Air, and Water,
'but because they are all of them the gross Remains of that one
'Element, in which the *Figures* and *Images* of Life had once
'risen up in such an infinite Variety of Degrees and Kinds.
'Hence it was, that when my creating *Fiat* spoke to these new
'ranged Stars, and Elements, and bid Life awake in them all
'*according to its Kind*, they all obeyed my Word, and every
'Property of Nature strove to bring forth, after the *Kind* and
'*Manner* as it had done in the Region of Eternity. This, my
'Son, is the Source and Original of all that infinite Variety, and
'Degrees of Life, both of Animals and Vegetables, in this

'World. It is because all outward Nature, being fallen from
'Heaven, must yet, as well as it can, do and work as it had done
'in Heaven.
   'In Heaven, all Births and Growths, all Figures and spiritual
'Forms of Life, though infinite in Variety, are yet all of a
'heavenly Kind, and only so many Manifestations of the Good-
'ness, Wisdom, Beauty, and Riches of the Divine Nature. But
'in this new modelled *Chaos*, where the Disorders that were
'raised by *Lucifer* are not wholly removed, but Evil and Good
'must stand in Strife, till the last purifying Fire, here every
'Kind and Degree of Life, like the World from whence it
'springs, is a Mixture of Good and Evil in its Birth.
   'Therefore, my Son, be content with thy angelical Nature, be
'content, as an Angel in Paradise, to eat Angels' Food, and to
'rule over this mixed, imperfect, and perishing World, without
'partaking of its corruptible, impure, and perishing Nature.
'Lust not to know *how* the Animals feel the Evil and Good
'which this Life affords them; for if Thou couldst feel what
'they feel, Thou must be as they are; Thou canst not have
'their *Sensibility*, unless Thou hast their Nature: Thou canst
'not at once be an Angel and an earthly Animal. If the bestial
'Life is raised up in Thee, the same Instant the heavenly Birth
'of thy Nature must die in Thee. Therefore turn away thy
'Lust and Imagination from a Tree, that can only help Thee to
'the Knowledge of such Good and Evil, as belongs only to the
'Animals of this outward World; for nothing but the bestial
'Nature can receive Good or Evil from the Stars and Elements;
'they have no Power, but over that Life which proceeds from
'them. Eat therefore only the Food of Paradise; be content
'with Angels' Bread; for if Thou eatest of this Tree, it will
'unavoidably awaken and open the bestial Life within Thee;
'and in that Moment, all that is heavenly must die, and cease to
'have any Power in Thee. And Thou must fall into a Slavery
'for Life, under the divided fighting Powers of Stars and
'Elements. Stripped of thy angelical Garment, that hid thy
'outward Body under its Glory, Thou wilt become more naked
'than any Beast upon Earth, be forced to seek from Beasts a
'Covering, to hide Thee from the Sight of thine own Eyes. A
'shameful, fearful, sickly, wanting, suffering, and distressed
'Heir of the same speedy Death in the Dust of the Earth, as
'the poor Beasts, whom Thou wilt thus have made to be thy
'Brethren.'
   This Paraphrase I leave to the Reflection of the Reader, and
proceed to show,
   Thirdly, That the Misery, Distress, and woeful Condition,

which *Adam* by his Transgression brought upon Himself, and all his Posterity, was not the Effect of any *severe vindictive* Wrath *in* God, calling for Justice to his offended Sovereignty, and inflicting Pains and Punishments suitable to the Greatness of his just Indignation, and Anger at the disobedient Creature.

If *Adam*, contrary to the Will of God, and for the Sake of some new-fancied Knowledge, had broken both his own Legs, and put out both his Eyes, could it with any Show of Truth and Reason have been said, that God, in the Severity of his Wrath at so heinous an Offence, had punished *Adam* with *Lameness* and *Blindness* ? And if it be further supposed, that God seeing *Adam* lying in this lame and blind Condition, came and spoke kindly to him, informing him of a *Secret of Love*, which He had in Heaven, which He promised to send him immediately by his highest Messenger of Love ; assuring him, that by the Use of this heavenly *Secret* or *Divine Power*, his Legs and Eyes should, in some Course of Time, be infallibly restored to him, even in a better State than they were in at the first ; must it not be still more unreasonable and absurd, to charge anything of this *Lameness* and *Blindness* upon a *Wrath* in God kindled against *Adam?* Nay, is it not clear, in the Highest Degree, that in all this Matter *Adam* had nothing from God, but the Overflowings of mere Love and Goodness, and that he had no Lameness and Blindness, but from his own voluntary Acts upon himself?

This is a simple, but clear Representation of the Case, how Matters stood betwixt God and our first Father, when by his own Act and Deed he extinguished that Divine Life, in which God had created him. *Adam* had no more Hurt, no more Evil done to Him, at his Fall, than the very Nature of his *own Action* brought along with it upon himself. He lusted to have the *Sensibility* of that Good and Evil, which the Beasts of this World have. He was told, that it could not be had without the Loss of his heavenly Life ; because such Loss was as necessarily implied in the Nature of the Thing itself, as Blindness is implied in the Extinction of Eyes. However, he ventured to make the Trial, and chose to eat of That, which could and did open this *Sensibility* of earthly Good and Evil in him. No sooner was this Sensibility opened in him, but he found it to be a *Subjection* and *Slavery* to all outward Nature, to Heat and Cold, to Pains and Sickness, Horror of Mind, disturbed Passions, Misery, and Fears of Death. Which is in other Words only saying, that he found it to be an Extinction of that Divine, angelical Nature, which till then had kept him insensible, and incapable of any hurtful Impressions, from any or all the Powers of this World. Therefore, to charge his miserable State, as a Punishment inflicted upon him by the severe Wrath of an incensed God, is the same Absurdity, as in the former supposed Lameness and Blindness. Because the whole Nature of all that miserable Change, both as to *Body* and *Soul*, which then came upon him, was neither more, nor less, than what was necessarily implied in that which he chose to do to himself. And therefore it had nothing of the Nature of a Punishment inflicted from *without*, but was only that which his own Action had done in and to himself: Just as the Man that puts out his own Eyes, has only that Darkness and Blindness, which his own Action has brought forth in himself.

From this short, yet plain and true Account of this Matter, we are at once delivered from a Load of Difficulties that have been raised about the *Fall* of Man, and *Original Sin*. It has been a great Question, How the Goodness of God could punish so *small* and *single* an Act of *Disobedience* in *Adam*, with so great a Punishment? Here the *Sovereignty* of God has been appealed to, and has set the Matter right; and from this Sovereignty, thus asserted, came forth the Systems of absolute *Election*, and absolute *Reprobation*. But for our Comfort it appears, that the Question here put concerns neither God nor Man, that it relates not at all to the Matter, and has no Existence, but in the Brains of those that formed it. For the Action in which *Adam's* Sin consisted, was such an Act, as in *itself* implied *all that miserable Change* that came upon him, and so was not a *small*, or *single* Act of *Disobedience*, nor had the least Punishment, of any kind, inflicted by God upon it. All that God did on this Transgression was mere Love, Compassion, and Relief administered to it. All the Sovereignty that God here showed, was a Sovereignty of Love to the fallen Creature. So that all the *Volumes* on this Question may be laid aside, as quite beside the Point. Another, and the greatest Question of all, and which *Divines* of all Sorts have been ever solving, and yet never have solved, is this; *How it can consist with the Goodness of* God, *to impute the Sin of* Adam *to all his Posterity?* But here, to our Comfort again, it may be said, that this Question is equally a vain Fiction with the other, and has nothing to do with the Procedure of God towards Mankind. For there is *no Imputation* of the Sin of *Adam* to his Posterity, and so no Foundation for a Dispute upon it. How absurd would it be to say, that God *imputes* the Nature, or the Body and Soul of *Adam* to his Posterity? for have they not the Nature of *Adam* by a natural Birth from him, and not by Imputation from God? Now this is all the Sin that *Adam's* Posterity have from him, they have only their Flesh and Blood, their Body and Soul from him, by a Birth from him, and not *imputed* to them from God. Instead therefore of the former Question, which is quite beside the Matter, it should have been asked thus, How it was consistent with the Goodness of God, *that* Adam *could not generate Children of a* Nature *and* Kind *quite superior to himself?* This is the only Question that can be asked with relation to God; and yet it is a Question whose Absurdity confutes itself. For the only Reason why Sin is found in all the Sons of *Adam*, is this, it is because *Adam* of earthly Flesh and Blood, cannot bring forth a holy Angel out of himself, but must beget children of the same Nature and Condition with himself. And therefore here again it may be truly said, that all the laborious Volumes on God's imputing *Adam's* Sin to his Posterity, ought to be considered as waste Paper.*

But further, As it is thus evident from the Nature of *Adam's* Transgression, that all his Misery came from the Nature of his own Action, and that nothing was inflicted upon him, from a Wrath or Anger in God at him, so is it still much more so, from a Consideration of the Divine Nature. For it is a glorious and joyful Truth, (however suppressed in various Systems of Divinity) that from Eternity to Eternity, no Spark of Wrath ever was, or ever will be in the holy Triune God. If a Wrath of God was anywhere, it must be everywhere, if it burned once, it must burn to all Eternity. For everything that is in God himself is boundless, incapable of any Increase or Diminution, without Beginning, and without End. It is as good Sense, as consistent with the Divine Nature, to say that God, moved by a Wrath *in* and *from* Himself, began the Creation, as that a Wrath in God ever punished any Part of it. Nature and Creature is the only *Source* from whence, and the *Seat* in which, Wrath, Pain, and Vexation can dwell. Nor can they ever break forth either in *Nature* or *Creature*, but so far as either this, or that, has lost its State in God. This is as certain, as that Storms and Tempests, Thunder and Lightnings, have no Existence in Heaven. God, considered in Himself, is as infinitely separate from all Possibility of doing Hurt, or willing Pain to any Creature, as He is from a Possibility of suffering Pain or Hurt from the Hand of a Man. And this, for this plain Reason, because He is in himself, in his holy Trinity, nothing else but the boundless Abyss of all that is Good, and Sweet, and Amiable, and therefore stands in the utmost Contrariety to every Thing that is not a Blessing, in an eternal Impossibility of willing and intending a Moment's Pain or Hurt to any Creature. For from this unbounded Source of Goodness and Perfection, nothing but

---

* See *Appeal to all that Doubt, &c.*, page 198. *Letter to the Bishop of London*, page 70.

infinite Streams of Blessing are perpetually flowing forth upon all Nature and Creature, in a more incessant Plenty, than Rays of Light stream from the Sun. And as the *Sun* has but one Nature, and can give forth nothing but the Blessings of Light, so the holy Triune God has but *one* Nature and Intent towards all the Creation, which is, to pour forth the Riches and Sweetness of his Divine Perfections, upon every Thing that is capable of them, and according to its Capacity to receive them.

The Goodness of God breaking forth into a Desire *to communicate Good*, was the Cause and the Beginning of the Creation. Hence it follows, that to all Eternity, God can have no *Thought*, or *Intent* towards the Creature, but *to communicate Good;* because He made the Creature for this sole End, to receive Good. The first Motive towards the Creature is unchangeable; it takes its Rise from God's Desire *to communicate Good;* and it is an eternal Impossibility, that anything can ever come from God, as his *Will* and *Purpose* towards the Creature, but *that same Love and Goodness*, which first created it: He must always *will* that to it, which He *willed* at the Creation of it. This is the amiable Nature of God, He is *the Good*, the unchangeable, overflowing Fountain of Good, that sends forth nothing but Good to all Eternity. He is *the Love* itself, the unmixed, unmeasurable Love, doing nothing but from Love, giving nothing but Gifts of Love, to every Thing that He has made; requiring nothing of all his Creatures, but the Spirit and Fruits of that Love, which brought them into Being. Oh, how sweet is this Contemplation of the Height and Depth of the Riches of Divine Love! With what Attraction must it draw every thoughtful Man, to return Love for Love to this overflowing Fountain of boundless Goodness? What Charms has that Religion, which discovers to us our Existence in, Relation to, and Dependence upon this Ocean of Divine Love! View every Part of our Redemption, from *Adam's* first Sin, to the Resurrection of the Dead, and you will find nothing but successive Mysteries of that first Love, which created Angels and Men. All the Mysteries of the Gospel are only so many Marks and Proofs of God's desiring to make his Love triumph, in the Removal of Sin and Disorder from all Nature and Creature.*

But to return, and consider further the Nature of *Adam's* Fall, We have seen that it consisted of no *arbitrary Punishment* inflicted on him by a Wrath raised *in* God, but was only such a State of Misery, as his own Action necessarily brought upon him. Let us now see what happened to his Soul, a little more

---

* *Spirit of Love*, Part II., pages 1—18, 71.

distinctly, and how it differed from what it was before his Fall, in its heavenly State.

The Angels that kept their State, and those that fell from it, were at first of one and the same Nature; the Angels that fell, did not lose all their Nature, for then they must have fallen into *nothing;* they only lost the heavenly and Divine Part of it, and therefore there is something still remaining in them, that is also in the holy Angels, and which is common to both of them. Now this which they did not lose, because it cannot be lost, is a certain *Root of Life,* or *Ground* of their Existence, which when once in Being, cannot be broken, and in which the unceasing Eternity, or Immortality of their Nature consists, a *Root* or first Ground of Life, equally capable of a Heavenly Birth, or of a Birth and Growth into Hell. Now that there is this *Root* of Life in Angels, and that it is something quite distinct from their heavenly Nature, is very plain from hence, that the Devils have lost their *heavenly*, and yet have kept their *eternal* and *immortal* Nature; therefore that in which their Eternity and Immortality consists, must be something entirely distinct from their heavenly Nature, and must be also the same with *that*, in which the Eternity and Immortality of the holy Angels consists. For the fallen Angels have no other *eternal Root* in them, but that which they had before their Fall, and which they brought from Heaven; and therefore *that* which is, and must be eternal and undying in their Nature, is the *same eternal Root* of Life, which is in the Angels that kept their State. And consequently, the only Difference betwixt an Angel and a Devil, is this, that in the Angel its eternal *Root* of Life *generates* a Birth of the *Light* and holy *Spirit* of God in it; and in a Devil, this eternal Root of Life has lost *this Birth*, and the Power of bringing it forth again. Now here is to be truly seen the real Difference betwixt the Soul of *Adam* before, and after his Fall. Before his Fall, it had the Nature of an Angel of God, in which the Divine Birth of the Light and holy Spirit of God sprung up, but when contrary to the Will, and Command of God, a bestial Life was awakened in him, the heavenly Life was necessarily extinguished. The Soul therefore having lost that heavenly Birth which made it like an Angel of God, had nothing remaining in it, but that eternal and immortal *Root* of Life, which is the very Essence of a fallen Angel. But here we must observe a great and happy Difference, betwixt the Soul of *Adam*, though dead to all that was heavenly, and the Soul of a Devil. The Angels that extinguished the Birth of Heaven in themselves, fell directly into the horrible Depths of their own strong self-tormenting Nature, or their *own Hell*, and that for these two Reasons.

First, Because there was nowhere else for them to fall into, but into this tormenting Sensibility of their own fiery, wrathful, darkened Nature.

Secondly, Because their Revolt from God was an Attempt, and Intent to be higher and greater by awakening, and trusting to their own *natural Powers*, than they had hitherto been by Submission to God. They would have a Greatness that sprung only from *themselves*, and therefore they found *That* which they sought, they found themselves left to all the *Greatness* that was in themselves, and that was *their Hell, viz.*, a fiery Strength of a self-tormenting Nature, because separate from the one Source of Light and Love, of Peace and Joy.

But *Adam*, though his Soul was as entirely dead to Heaven, as the Souls of the Devils were, yet fell not into *their Hell*, for these two Reasons.

First, Because his Angelical Man dwelt in a Body taken from this outward World, which Body did not die at his Transgression, therefore his Soul that had lost his Heavenly Light, did not fall directly into the Devil's Hell, but it fell into a Body of Earthly Flesh and Blood, which being capable of the Enjoyments and Satisfactions of this Life, could, whilst it lasted, keep the Soul insensible of its own fallen State, and hellish Condition.

Secondly, because *Adam* not aspiring to be *above*, or *without* God by his own proud Strength, but only lusting to enter in a *Sensibility* of the Good and Evil of the bestial Life of this World, he found *only That* which he sought, and fell into no *other State* or Misery, than that bestial Life, which his own Actions and Desires had opened in him. And therefore this outward World stood him in great Stead, it prevented his immediate Falling into the State of Fallen Angels.

But then, as there was nothing that kept him out of the Hell of Fallen Angels, but his *Body* of Earthly Flesh and Blood, and as this was now as *mortal* in him, as it was in the Beasts, and lay at the Mercy of a thousand Accidents, that could every Moment take it from him, so he was in his fallen State, standing as it were on the Brink of Hell, liable every Moment to be pushed into it.*

See here the *deep* Ground and *absolute* Necessity of that new Birth, of *Word*, *Son*, and *Spirit* of God, which the Scripture speaks so much of. It is because our Soul, as fallen, is quite dead to, and separate from the Kingdom of Heaven, by having lost the Light and Spirit of God in itself; and therefore it is,

---

* See *Grounds and Reasons of Regeneration*, pages 6—12, 39—48.

and must be incapable of entering into Heaven, till by this new Birth, the Soul gets again its first Heavenly Nature.

If thou hast nothing of this Birth when thy Body dies, then thou hast only that *Root* of Life in Thee, which the Devils have, thou art as far from Heaven, and as incapable of it, as they are; thy Nature is their Nature, and therefore their Habitation must be thine. For nothing can possibly hinder thy Union with Fallen Angels, when thou diest, but a Birth of *That* in thy Soul, which the Fallen Angels have *lost*.

How pitiable therefore, or rather how hurtful is that *Learning*, which uses all its Art of Words, to avoid and lose the true Sense of our Saviour's Doctrine concerning the new Birth, which is necessary to fallen Man, by holding, that the Passages asserting the new Birth, are only a *figurative*, strong Form of Words concerning *something*, that is not *really* a Birth, or Growth of a new Nature, but may, according to the best Rules of *Criticism*, signify, either our *Entrance* into the Society of Christians, by the Rite of Baptism, or such a new Relation, as a Scholar may have with his Master, who by a Conformity to Terms of Union, or by copying his Ways and Manners, may, by a *Figure of Speech*, be said to be born again of him.

Now let it here be observed, that no Passage of Scripture is to be called, or esteemed as a *figurative* Expression, but where the *literal* Meaning cannot be allowed, as implying something that is either *bad* in itself, or *impossible*, or *inconsistent* with some plain and undeniable Doctrines of Scripture. Now that this is not the Case here, is very evident. For who will presume to say, that for the Soul of fallen Man to be born again of the Son, or Light, and Holy Spirit of God, is in the *literal* Sense of the Words, a Thing *bad* in itself, or *impossible*, or *inconsistent* with any plain and undeniable Doctrines of Scripture? The *Critics* therefore, who, in this Matter, leave the literal Meaning of the Words, and have Recourse to a figurative Sense, are without Excuse, and have nothing they can urge as a Reason for so doing, but their own Skill in Words. But it may be further added as a just Charge against these *Critics*, that their fixing these Passages to a figurative Meaning, is not only without any Ground, or Reason for so doing, but is also a *bad* Meaning, *impossible* to be true, and utterly *inconsistent* with the most plain, and fundamental Doctrines of Scripture. Now that this is the Case here, may in Part be seen by the following Instance.

Let it be supposed, that a human Body had lost the *Light*, and *Air* of this World, and was in a State of Death, because both these were quite extinguished in it. Must it not be said, that this human Body cannot see, or enter again into the Life of this World, unless the Light and Air of this World get again a *new Birth* in it: Is there here any Occasion, or any Room to form a Doubt, how these Words are to be understood, or any Possibility to mistake the Meaning of them? What a *Philosopher* would he be, who for fear of being called an *Enthusiast*, should here deny the *literal* Meaning of a new Birth of *Light* and *Air*, aud think himself sufficiently justified in flying from it, because in his great Reading, he had seen the Words, *Birth, Light* and *Air*, sometimes, and upon some Occasions, used only in a *figurative* Sense?

Now this is exactly, and to a Tittle the Case of the Soul, as fallen, and lying in the same State of Death to the Kingdom of God, till a *new Birth* of the Light and Spirit of God be again brought forth in it. And therefore the *Necessity* of understanding these Words in their literal Meaning, the Absurdity of flying to a *figurative* Sense of the new Birth, and the *Impossibility* of that being the true one, is equally plain, and certain in both these Cases.

Now that the Soul, as fallen, is in this *real State* of Death, is a Doctrine not only plain from the whole Tenor of Scripture, but affirmed in all Systems of Divinity. For all hold, and teach, that Man *unredeemed*, must at the Death of his Body have fallen into a State of Misery, like that of the fallen Angels. But how can this be true, unless it be true, that the Life of Heaven was extinguished in the Soul, and that Man had really lost that Light, and Spirit of God, which alone can make any Being capable of living in Heaven? All therefore that I have here, and elsewhere said, concerning the Death of the Soul by its Fall, and its wanting a *real* new Birth of the Son, and Holy Spirit of God in it, in order to its Salvation, cannot be denied, but by giving up this great, fundamental Doctrine, namely, 'That Man in his fallen State, and unredeemed, must have been 'eternally lost.' For it cannot be true, that the Fall of Man unredeemed, would have kept him for ever out of Heaven, but because his Fall had absolutely put an End to the Life of Heaven in his Soul.

On the other Hand, it cannot be true that Jesus Christ is his Redeemer, and does deliver him from his fallen State, unless it be true, that Jesus Christ helps him to a new Birth of that Light and Spirit of God, which was extinguished by his Fall. For nothing could possibly be the Redemption, or Recovery of Man, but *Regeneration* alone. His Misery was his having lost the Life and Light of Heaven from his Soul, and therefore nothing in all the Universe of Nature, but a new Birth of that which he had lost, could be his Deliverance from his fallen State.

And therefore if Angels after Angels had come down from Heaven to assure him, that God had no Anger at him, he would still have been in the same *helpless State ;* nay, had they told him, that God had Pity and Compassion towards him, he had yet been *unhelped ;* because in the Nature of the Thing, nothing could make so much as a Beginning of his Deliverance, but that which made a Beginning of a new Birth in him, and nothing could fully effect his Recovery, but which perfectly finished the new Birth of all that heavenly Life which he had lost.

The Gospel tells us of a certain Man who fell among Thieves, who stripped him, and wounded him, and left him half dead ; that first a *Priest,* then a *Levite* coming that Way, both of them avoided the poor Man, by passing on the other Side.

Here it is plain, that this Priest and Levite left the poor Man in the *same helpless* State in which they found him. Let it now be supposed, that instead of going on the other Side of the Road, they had come up to him, and poured *Oil* and *Wine* into his Wounds, only in a *figurative* Sense of the Words, that is, that they had spoken such Words to him, Words so *soft,* so oily, and reviving, that in a just *Figure* of Speech, they might be called a *pouring of Wine and Oil* into his Wounds. Now had they done this, must it not still be said, that the poor Man's Wounds and Nakedness were still left in their first *helpless* State? And all for this plain Reason, because the poor Man was naked, and wounded, not in a *figurative* Sense of the Words, but *really* and *truly,* and therefore could have no Help or Benefit, but from real Oil and Wine really poured into his Wounds. And for the same plain Reason, the fallen Soul, *really* dead to the Kingdom of Heaven, can have no Help but by a new Birth of the Light and Spirit of Heaven, *really* brought forth again in it. When *Adam* lay in his Death Wounds to the Kingdom of God, had the highest Order of *Archangels,* or *Seraphims* come by that Way, they could only have done as the Priest and Levite did, go on the other Side ; or if they had come up to him, and done all they could for him, it could only have been such a *Good* or *Relief* to him, as by a *Figure* of Speech might be so called.

For as *Adam* had extinguished the Light and Spirit of God in himself, so no one could be the *good Samaritan* to him, or pour that Wine and Oil into his Wounds, which they wanted, but He who was the *Author* and *Source* of Light and Life to every Being that lives in Heaven.

One would wonder how any Persons, that believe the great Mystery of our Redemption, who adore the Depths of the Divine

Goodness, in that the Son of God, the second Person in the Trinity, became a Man himself, in order to make it *possible* for Man by a *Birth* from him to enter again into the Kingdom of God, should yet seek to, and contend for, not a *real*, but a figurative Sense of a new Birth in Jesus Christ. Is there any Thing more inconsistent than this? Or can any Thing strike more directly at the Heart of the whole Nature of our Redemption? God became Man, took upon him a Birth from the fallen Nature. But why was this done? Or wherein lies the adorable Depth of this Mystery? How does all this manifest the Infinity of the Divine Love towards Man? It is because nothing less than this mysterious Incarnation (which astonishes Angels) could open a *Way*, or begin a *Possibility*, for fallen Man to be *born again* from above, and made again a *Partaker* of the Divine Nature. It was because Man was become so dead to the Kingdom of Heaven, that there was no Help for him through all Nature. No Powers, no Abilities of the highest Order of Creatures, could kindle the least Spark of Life in him, or help him to the least Glimpse of that heavenly Light which he had lost. Now when all Nature and Creature stood round about *Adam* as unable to help him, as he was to help himself, and all of them *unable* to help him, for *this Reason*, because *that* which he had lost, was the *Life* and *Light* of Heaven, how glorious, how adorable is that Mystery, which enables us to say, that when Man laid thus incapable of any Relief from all the *Powers* and *Possibilities* of Nature, that then the Son, the Word of God, entered by a Birth into this fallen Nature, that by this mysterious Incarnation all the fallen Nature might be *born again* of him according to the *Spirit*, in the *same Reality*, as they were born of *Adam* according to the *Flesh*? Look at this Mystery in this true Light, in this plain Sense of Scripture, and then you must be forced to fall down before it, in Adoration of it. For all that is great and astonishing in the Goodness of God, all that is glorious and happy with Regard to Man, is manifestly contained in it.

But tell me, I pray, what becomes of all this, what is there left in any Part of this Mystery, if this *new Birth*, for the Sake of which God became Man, is not really a new Birth in the Thing itself, is not, as the Scripture affirms, a real Birth of the Son and Spirit of God in the Soul, but something or other, this or that, which the *Critics* say, may be called a new Birth, by a certain Figure of Speech? Is not *this* to give up all our Redemption at once, and a turning all the Mysteries of our Salvation into mere empty, unmeaning Terms of Speech? He that should deny the *Reality* of the Resurrection, upon Pretence, that by the Rules of Criticism, it needs not signify a real coming out of a State of Natural Death, might have more to say for himself both from Reason and Scripture, than he that denies the Reality of the new Birth in Christ Jesus. For this new Birth is not a *Part*, but the *Whole* of our Salvation. Every Thing in Religion, from the Beginning to the End of Time, is only for the Sake of it. Nothing does us any Good, but either as it helps forward our Regeneration, or as it is a true Fruit or Effect of it.

All the glad Tidings of the Gospel, all the Benefits of our Saviour, however variously expressed in Scripture, all centre in this one Point, that He is become our Light, our Life, our Resurrection, our Holiness and Salvation; that we are in Him new Creatures, *created again* unto Righteousness, born again of Him, from above, of the Spirit of God. Every Thing in the Gospel is for the Sake of this new Creature, this new Man in Christ Jesus, and nothing is regarded without it. What Excuse therefore can be made for that Learning, which, robbing us of the true Fruits of the Tree of Life, leaves us nothing to feed upon, but the dry Dust of Words?

'I am the Vine, Ye are the Branches.' Here Christ, our second *Adam*, uses this Similitude to teach us, that the new Birth that we are to have from Him is *real*, in the most strict and literal Sense of the Words, and that there is the same *Nearness* of Relation, betwixt Him and his true Disciples, that there is betwixt the *Vine* and its Branches, that He does all that in us, and for us, which the Vine does to its Branches. Now the Life of the Vine must be really derived into the Branches, they cannot be Branches, till the Birth of the Vine is brought forth in them. And therefore as sure as the Birth of the Vine must be brought forth in the Branches, so sure is it, that we must be born again of our second *Adam*. And that unless the Life of the Holy Jesus be in us by a Birth from Him, we are as dead to Him, and the Kingdom of God, as the Branch is dead to the Vine, from which it is broken off.

Again our Blessed Saviour says, 'Without me, ye can do 'Nothing.' The Question is, when, or how a Man may be said to be *without* Christ? Consider again the Vine and its Branches: A Branch can then only be said to be without its Vine, when the Vegetable Life of the Vine is no longer *in it*. This is the only Sense, in which we can be said to be *without* Christ; when He is no longer in us, as a Principle of a heavenly Life, we are then without Him, and so *can do Nothing*, that is, Nothing that is good or holy. A Christ not *in us*, is the same Thing as a Christ *not ours*. If we are only *so far* with Christ, as to own and receive the History of his Birth, Person, and Character, if this is all that we have of Him, we are as much *without* Him, as much left to ourselves, as little helped by Him, as those evil Spirits which cried out, 'We know Thee, who thou art, the Holy 'One of God.' For those evil Spirits, and all the fallen Angels, are totally *without* Christ, have no Benefit from Him, for this *one* and *only* Reason, because Christ is not *in Them;* Nothing of the Son of God is *generated,* or *born* in them. Therefore every Son of *Adam*, that has not *something* of the Son of God *generated*, or born *within* Him, is as much *without Christ*, as destitute of all Help from Him, as those evil Spirits who could only make an *outward Confession* of Him.

It is the Language of Scripture, that *Christ in us* is our Hope of Glory? that Christ formed in us, living, growing, and raising his own Life and Spirit in us, is our only Salvation. And indeed all this is plain from the Nature of the Thing; for since the *Serpent, Sin, Death* and *Hell*, are all essentially *within* us, the very *Growth* of our Nature, must not our Redemption be equally *inward*, an inward *essential Death* to this State of our Souls, and an inward Growth of a contrary Life within us? If *Adam* was only an *outward Person*, if his whole Nature was not our Nature, born in us, and derived *from Him into us*, it would be Nonsense to say, that his Fall is our Fall. So in like manner, if Christ, our second *Adam*, was only an *outward* Person, if He entered not as *deeply* into our Nature as the first *Adam* does, if we have not *as really* from Him a new inward, spiritual Man, as we have outward Flesh and Blood from *Adam*, what Ground could there be to say, that our Righteousness is from Him, as our Sin is from *Adam?*

Let no one here think to charge me with Disregard to the Holy Jesus, who was born of the *Virgin Mary*, or with setting up an *inward* Saviour in Opposition to that outward Christ, whose History is recorded in the Gospel. No: It is with the utmost Fulness of Faith and Assurance, that I ascribe all our Redemption to that blessed and mysterious Person, that was then born of the *Virgin Mary*, and will assert no inward Redemption but what wholly proceeds from, and is effected by that Life-giving Redeemer, who died on the Cross for our Redemption.

Was I to say, that a *Plant* or *Vegetable* must have the Sun *within* it, must have the Life, Light, and Virtues of the Sun incorporated *in it*, that it has no Benefit from the Sun, till the Sun is thus *inwardly* forming, generating, quickening, and raising up a Life of the Sun's Virtues in it, would this be setting up an *inward* Sun, in Opposition to the outward one? Could any Thing be more ridiculous than such a Charge? For is not all that is here said of an inward Sun in the Vegetable, so much said of a Power and Virtue derived from the Sun in the Firmament? So in like manner, all that is said of an inward Christ, inwardly formed, and generated in the Root of the Soul, is only so much said of an *inward Life*, brought forth by the *Power* and *Efficacy* of that Blessed Christ, that was born of the *Virgin Mary*.

Chapter II.

Discovering the true Way of turning to God, and of finding the Kingdom of Heaven, the Riches of Eternity in our Souls.

THOU hast seen, dear Reader, the Nature and Necessity of *Regeneration*, be persuaded therefore fully to believe, and firmly to settle in thy Mind this most certain Truth, that all our Salvation consists in the *Manifestation of the Nature, Life, and Spirit of Jesus Christ, in our inward new Man*. This alone is Christian Redemption, this alone delivers from the Guilt and Power of Sin, this alone redeems, renews, and regains the first Life of God in the Soul of Man. Every Thing besides this, is *Self*, is *Fiction*, is *Propriety*, is *own Will*, and however coloured, is only thy *old Man, with all his Deeds*. Enter therefore with all thy Heart into this Truth, let thy Eye be always upon it, do every Thing in View of it, try every Thing by the Truth of it, love Nothing but for the Sake of it. Wherever thou goest, whatever thou dost, at Home, or Abroad, in the Field, or at Church, do all in a Desire of Union with Christ, in Imitation of his Tempers and Inclinations, and look upon all as Nothing, but that which exercises, and increases the Spirit and Life of Christ in thy Soul. From Morning to Night keep Jesus in thy Heart, long for Nothing, desire Nothing, hope for Nothing, but to have all that is within Thee changed into the Spirit and Temper of the Holy Jesus. Let this be thy *Christianity*, thy *Church*, and thy *Religion*. For this new Birth in Christ thus firmly believed, and continually desired, will do every Thing that thou wantest to have done in Thee, it will dry up all the Springs of Vice, stop all the Workings of Evil in thy Nature, it will bring all that is Good into Thee, it will open all the Gospel within Thee, and thou wilt know what it is to be taught of God. This longing Desire of thy Heart to be *one* with Christ will soon put a stop to all the

Vanity of thy Life, and nothing will be admitted to enter into thy Heart, or proceed from it, but what comes from God and returns to God : thou wilt soon be, as it were, tied and bound in the Chains of all holy Affections and Desires, thy *Mouth* will have a *Watch* set upon it, thy *Ears* would willingly hear nothing that does not tend to God, nor thy *Eyes* be open, but to see, and find Occasions of doing Good. In a Word, when this Faith has got both thy *Head* and thy *Heart*, it will then be with thee, as it was with the *Merchant* who found a *Pearl of great Price*, it will make thee gladly to *sell all that thou hast, and buy it*. For all that had seized and possessed the Heart of any Man, whatever the *Merchant* of this World had got together, whether of Riches, Power, Honour, Learning, or Reputation, loses all its Value, is counted but as *Dung*, and willingly parted with, as soon as this glorious Pearl, the new Birth in Christ Jesus, is discovered and found by him. This therefore may serve as a *Touchstone*, whereby every one may try the Truth of his State ; if the old Man is still a *Merchant* within thee, trading in all sorts of worldly Honour, Power, or Learning, if the Wisdom of this World is not Foolishness to thee, if earthly Interests, and sensual Pleasures, are still the Desire of thy Heart, and only covered under a *Form* of Godliness, a *Cloak* of Creeds, Observances, and Institutions of Religion, thou mayest be assured, that the *Pearl of great Price* is not yet found by thee. For where Christ is born, or his Spirit rises up in the Soul, *there all Self* is denied, and obliged to turn out ; *there* all carnal Wisdom, Arts of Advancement, with every Pride and Glory of this Life, are as so many *heathen Idols* all willingly renounced, and the Man is not only content, but rejoices to say, that *his Kingdom is not of this World.*

But thou wilt perhaps say, How shall this great Work, the Birth of Christ, be effected in me? It might rather be said, since Christ has an infinite Power, and also an infinite Desire to save Mankind, how can anyone miss of this Salvation, but through his *own unwillingness* to be saved by Him? Consider, how was it, that the *Lame* and *Blind*, the *Lunatic* and *Leper*, the *Publican* and *Sinner*, found Christ to be their Saviour, and to do *all That* for them, which they wanted to be done to them? It was because they had a real Desire of having *That* which they asked for, and therefore in true *Faith* and *Prayer* applied to Christ, that his Spirit and Power might enter into them, and heal That which they wanted, and desired to be healed in them. Every one of these said in *Faith and Desire*, 'Lord, if thou wilt, 'thou canst make me whole.' And the Answer was always this, 'According to thy Faith, so be it done unto Thee.' This is Christ's Answer *now*, and thus it is done to every one of us at this Day, as *our Faith is, so is it done unto us*. And here lies the whole Reason of our falling short of the Salvation of Christ, it is because we have *No Will* to it.

But you will say, Do not all Christians desire to have Christ to be their Saviour? Yes. But here is the Deceit; all would have Christ to be their Saviour in the *next World*, and to help them into Heaven when they die, by his Power, and Merits with God. But this is not *willing* Christ to be thy Saviour; for his Salvation, if it is had, must be had in this World; if He saves Thee, it must be done in this Life, by changing and altering *all that is within Thee*, by helping thee to a new Heart, as He helped the Blind to see, the Lame to walk, and the Dumb to speak. For to have Salvation from Christ, is nothing else but to be made like unto Him; it is to have his Humility and Meekness, his Mortification and Self-denial, his Renunciation of the Spirit, Wisdom, and Honours of this World, his Love of God, his Desire of doing God's Will, and seeking only his Honour. To have these Tempers formed and begotten in thy Heart, is to have Salvation from Christ. But if thou *willest not* to have these Tempers brought forth in thee, if thy Faith and Desire does not seek, and cry to Christ for them in the *same Reality*, as the Lame asked to walk, and the Blind to see, then thou must be said to be *unwilling* to have Christ to be thy Saviour.

Again, Consider, How was it, that the carnal *Jew*, the deep-read *Scribe*, the learned *Rabbi*, the Religious *Pharisee*, not only did not receive, but *crucified* their Saviour? It was because they *willed*, and *desired* no such Saviour as He was, no such *inward Salvation* as He offered to them. They desired no Change of their own Nature, no inward Destruction of their own natural Tempers, no Deliverance from the Love of themselves, and the Enjoyments of their Passions; they liked their Sate, the Gratifications of their Old Man, their *long Robes*, their *broad Phylacteries*, and *Greetings* in the Markets. They wanted not to have their *Pride* and *Self-love* dethroned, their Covetousness and Sensuality to be subdued by a new Nature from Heaven derived into them. Their only Desire was the Success of *Judaism*, to have an *outward* Saviour, a *temporal* Prince, that should establish their *Law* and Ceremonies over all the Earth. And therefore they crucified their Dear Redeemer, and would have none of his Salvation, because it all consisted in a Change of their Nature, in a *new Birth* from above, and a Kingdom of Heaven to be opened *within* them by the Spirit of God.

Oh Christendom, look not only at the *old Jews*, but see thyself in this Glass. For at this Day (Oh sad Truth to be told!) at this Day, a Christ *within* us, an *inward* Saviour raising a *Birth* of his own Nature, Life, and Spirit within us, is rejected as gross *Enthusiasm*, the learned *Rabbies* take Counsel against it. The Propagation of *Popery*, the Propagation of *Protestantism*, the Success of some *particular* Church, is the *Salvation* which Priests and People are chiefly concerned about.

But to return. It is manifest, that no one can fail of the Benefit of Christ's Salvation, but through an *unwillingness* to have it, and from the same Spirit and Tempers which made the *Jews* unwilling to receive it. But if thou wouldst still further know, how this great Work, the *Birth* of Christ, is to be effected in thee, then let this joyful Truth be told thee, that this great Work is *already* begun in every one of us. For this Holy Jesus, that is to be formed in thee, that is to be the Saviour and new Life of thy Soul, that is to raise thee out of the Darkness of Death into the Light of Life, and give thee Power to become a Son of God, is already *within* thee, living, stirring, calling, knocking at the Door of thy Heart, and wanting nothing but thy own *Faith* and *good Will*, to have as real a Birth and Form in thee, as He had in the Virgin *Mary*. For the eternal *Word*, or Son of God, did not then first begin to be the Saviour of the World, when He was Born in *Bethlehem* of *Judea*; but that Word which became Man in the Virgin *Mary*, did, from the Beginning of the World, enter as a *Word* of Life, a *Seed* of Salvation, into the first Father of Mankind, was inspoken into him, as an ingrafted Word, under the Name and Character of a *Bruiser of the Serpent's Head.* Hence it is, that Christ said to his Disciples, ' the Kingdom of God is within you '; that is, the Divine Nature is within you, given unto your first Father, into the Light of his Life, and from him, rising up in the Life of every Son of *Adam*. Hence also the holy Jesus is said to be the ' Light, which ' lighteth every Man that cometh into the World.' Not as He was born at *Bethlehem*, not as He had an human Form upon Earth; in these Respects he could not be said to have been the Light of every Man that cometh into the World; but as He was that *eternal Word*, by which all Things were created, which was the *Life* and *Light* of all Things, and which had as a *second* Creator entered again into fallen Man, as a Bruiser of the Serpent; in this respect it was truly said of our Lord, when on Earth, that ' He was that Light which lighteth every Man, that cometh into ' the World.' For He was really and truly all this, as He was the *Immanuel*, the God *with us*, given unto *Adam*, and in him to all his Offspring. See here the Beginning and glorious Extent of the *Catholic Church* of Christ, it takes in all the World. It is God's unlimited, universal Mercy to all Mankind; and every human Creature, as sure as he is born of *Adam*, has a Birth of the Bruiser of the Serpent within him, and so is infallibly in Covenant with God through Jesus Christ. Hence also it is, that the Holy Jesus is appointed to be Judge of all the World, it is because all Mankind, all Nations and Languages have in him, and through him been put into Covenant with God, and made capable of resisting the Evil of their fallen Nature.

When our blessed Lord conversed with the Woman at *Jacob's* Well, he said unto her, ' If thou knewest the Gift of God, and ' who it is that talketh with thee, thou wouldest have asked of ' Him, and He would have given Thee living Water.' How happy (may anyone well say) was this Woman of *Samaria*, to stand so near this *Gift of* God, from whom she might have had living water, had she but vouchsafed to have asked for it! But, dear Christian, this Happiness is thine; for this Holy Jesus, *the Gift of* God, first given unto *Adam*, and in him to all that are descended from him, is the *Gift of* God *to* Thee, as sure as thou art born of *Adam ;* nay, hast thou never yet owned him, art thou wandered from him, as far as the Prodigal Son from his Father's House, yet is he still with Thee, he is the Gift of God to Thee, and if thou wilt turn to Him, and ask of Him, he has living Water for Thee.

Poor Sinner! consider the Treasure thou hast within Thee, the Saviour of the World, the eternal Word of God lies hid in Thee, as a Spark of the Divine Nature, which is to overcome Sin and Death, and Hell within Thee, and generate the Life of Heaven again in thy Soul. Turn to thy Heart, and thy Heart will find its Saviour, its God within itself. Thou seest, hearest, and feelest nothing of God, because thou seekest for Him *abroad* with thy outward Eyes, thou seekest for Him in Books, in Controversies, in the Church, and outward Exercises, but *there* thou wilt not find Him, till thou hast *first* found Him in thy Heart. Seek for Him in thy Heart, and thou wilt never seek in vain, for there He dwells, there is the Seat of his Light and Holy Spirit.

For this turning to the Light and Spirit of God within Thee, is thy *only true* turning unto God, there is no other Way of finding Him, but in that Place where he dwelleth in Thee. For though God be everywhere present, yet He is only present to Thee in the deepest, and most central Part of thy Soul. Thy natural *Senses* cannot possess God, or unite Thee to Him, nay thy inward Faculties of *Understanding*, *Will*, and *Memory*, can only reach after God, but cannot be the *Place* of his Habitation in Thee. But there is a *Root*, or *Depth* in Thee, from whence all these Faculties come forth, as Lines from a *Centre*, or as Branches from the Body of the Tree. This Depth is called the *Centre*, the *Fund* or *Bottom* of the Soul. This Depth is the

Unity, the *Eternity*, I had almost said, the *Infinity* of thy Soul; for it is so infinite, that nothing can satisfy it, or give it any Rest, but the infinity of God. In this *Depth* of the Soul, the Holy Trinity brought forth its own living Image in the first created Man, bearing in Himself a living Representation of Father, Son, and Holy Ghost, and this was his Dwelling in God and God in him. This was the Kingdom of God *within* Him, and made Paradise *without* Him. But the Day that *Adam* did eat of the forbidden earthly Tree, in that Day he absolutely died to this Kingdom of God *within Him*. This *Depth* or *Centre* of his Soul having lost its God, was shut up in Death and Darkness, and became a Prisoner in an earthly Animal, that only excelled its Brethren, the Beasts, in an upright Form, and serpentine Subtilty. Thus ended the Fall of Man. But from that Moment that the God of Mercy inspoke into *Adam* the Bruiser of the Serpent, from that Moment all the Riches and Treasures of the Divine Nature came again into Man, as a *Seed* of Salvation sown into the *Centre* of the Soul, and only lies hidden there in every Man, till he desires to rise from his fallen State, and to be born again from above.

Awake then, thou that Sleepest, and Christ, who from all Eternity has been espoused to thy Soul, shall give Thee Light. Begin to search and dig in thine own Field for this *Pearl of Eternity*, that lies hidden in it; it cannot cost Thee too much, nor canst thou buy it too dear, for it is *All*, and when thou hast found it, thou wilt know, that all which thou hast sold or given away for it, is as mere a Nothing, as a Bubble upon the Water.

But if thou turnest from this heavenly Pearl, or tramplest it under thy Feet, for the sake of being Rich, or Great, either in Church or State, if Death finds Thee in *this Success*, thou canst not then say, that though the *Pearl* is lost, yet *something* has been gained instead of it. For in that parting Moment, the *Things*, and the *Sounds* of this World, will be exactly alike; to have had an *Estate*, or only to have *heard* of it, to have lived at *Lambeth* twenty Years, or only to have twenty Times *passed by* the Palace, will be the *same Good*, or the same *Nothing* to Thee.

But I will now show a little more distinctly, what this *Pearl of Eternity* is. *First*, It is the *Light* and *Spirit* of God within Thee, which has hitherto done Thee but little Good, because all the Desire of thy Heart has been after the Light and Spirit of this World. Thy Reason, and Senses, thy Heart and Passions, have turned all their Attention to the poor Concerns of this Life, and therefore thou art a Stranger to this Principle of

Heaven, this Riches of Eternity within Thee. For as God is not, cannot be truly found by any Worshippers, but those who worship Him in *Spirit* and in *Truth,* so this Light and Spirit, though always within us, is not, cannot be found, felt, or enjoyed, but by those whose whole Spirit is turned to it.

When Man first came into Being, and stood before God as his own Image and Likeness, this *Light* and *Spirit* of God was as *natural* to him, as truly the Light of his Nature, as the *Light and Air* of this World is natural to the Creatures that have their Birth in it. But when Man, not content with the Food of Eternity, did eat of the earthly Tree, this Light and Spirit of Heaven was no more *natural* to him, no more rose up as a Birth of his Nature, but instead thereof, he was left solely to the Light and Spirit of this World. And this is *that Death,* which God told *Adam,* he should surely die, in the Day that he should eat of the forbidden Tree.

But the Goodness of God would not leave Man in this Condition. A Redemption from it was immediately granted, and the Brusier of the Serpent brought the Light and Spirit of Heaven *once more* into the human Nature, not as it was in its first State, when Man was in Paradise, but as a *Treasure hidden* in the Centre of our Souls, which should discover, and open itself by Degrees, in such Proportion, as the *Faith* and *Desires* of our Hearts were turned to it. This Light and Spirit of God thus freely restored again to the Soul, and lying in it as a *secret Source* of Heaven, is called *Grace, Free Grace,* or the *Supernatural* Gift, or Power of God in the Soul, because it was something that the Natural Powers of the Soul could no more obtain. Hence it is, that in the greatest Truth, and highest Reality, every *stirring* of the Soul, every *Tendency* of the Heart towards God and Goodness, is *justly* and *necessarily* ascribed to the *Holy Spirit,* or the *Grace* of God. It is because this *first Seed* of Life, which is sown into the Soul, as the *Gift* or *Grace* of God to fallen Man, is itself the *Light* and *Spirit* of God, and therefore every *Stirring,* or *Opening* of this Seed of Life, every awakened Thought or Desire that arises from it, must be called the *Moving,* or the *Quickening* of the Spirit of God; and therefore that new Man which arises from it, must of all Necessity be said to be *solely the Work and Operation of* God. Hence also we have an easy and plain Declaration of the true Meaning, solid Sense, and certain Truth, of all those Scriptures, which speak of the *Inspiration* of God, the Operation of the *Holy Spirit,* the Power of the *Divine Light,* as the *sole* and *necessary* Agents in the Renewal and Sanctification of our Souls, and also as being Things *common* to all Men. It is because this

Seed of Life, or Bruiser of the Serpent, is *common* to all Men, and has in all Men a *Degree* of Life, which is in itself so much of the *Inspiration*, or Life of God, the *Spirit* of God, the *Light* of God, which is in every Soul, and is its Power of becoming born again of God. Hence also it is, that all Men are exhorted not to *quench*, or *resist*, or *grieve* the Spirit, that is, this *Seed of the Spirit and Light of* God that is in *all* Men, as the only Source of Good. Again, *the Flesh lusteth against the Spirit, and the Spirit against the Flesh*. By the Flesh and its Lustings, are meant the *mere human Nature*, or the *natural Man*, as He is by the Fall; by the *Spirit* is meant the *Bruiser of the Serpent*, that Seed of the Light and Spirit of God, which lies as a Treasure hidden in the Soul, in order to bring forth the Life that was lost in *Adam*. Now as the Flesh has its Life, its Lustings, whence all sorts of Evil are truly said to be inspired, quickened, and stirred up in us, so the Spirit being a *Living* Principle *within us*, has its *Inspiration*, its *Breathing*, its *Moving*, its *Quickening*, from which alone the Divine Life, or the Angel that died in *Adam*, can be born in us.

When this *Seed* of the Spirit, *common* to all Men, is not resisted, grieved, and quenched, but its *Inspirations* and *Motions* suffered to grow and increase in us, to unite with God, and get Power over all the Lusts of the Flesh, then we are born again, the Nature, Spirit, and Tempers of Jesus Christ are opened in our Souls, the Kingdom of God is come, and is found within us. On the other Hand, when the Flesh, or the *Natural* Man has resisted and quenched this Spirit or Seed of Life within us, then the works of the Flesh, Adultery, Fornication, Murders, Lying, Hatred, Envy, Wrath, Pride, Foolishness, worldly Wisdom, carnal Prudence, false Religion, hypocritical Holiness, and serpentine Subtilty, have set up their Kingdom within us.

See here in short, the State of Man as redeemed. He has a *Spark* of the Light and Spirit of God, as a *Supernatural Gift* of God given into the Birth of his Soul, to bring forth by Degrees a *New Birth* of that Life which was Lost in Paradise. This Holy Spark of the Divine Nature within Him, has a natural, strong, and almost infinite Tendency, or Reaching after that eternal Light and Spirit of God, from whence it came forth. It came forth from God, it came *out* of God, it *partaketh* of the Divine Nature, and therefore it is always in a State of Tendency and Return to God. And all this is called the *Breathing*, the *Moving*, the *Quickening* of the Holy Spirit within us, which are so many Operations of this Spark of Life tending towards God. On the other Hand, The Deity as considered in itself, and *without* the Soul of Man, has an *infinite, unchangeable* Tendency of Love, and Desire towards the Soul of Man, to unite and communicate its own Riches and Glories to it, just as the Spirit of the *Air without* Man, unites and communicates its Riches and Virtues to the Spirit of the Air that is *within* Man. This Love, or Desire of God towards the Soul of Man, is so great, that He gave his only begotten Son, the Brightness of his Glory, to take the human Nature upon Him, in its fallen State, that by this mysterious Union of God and Man, all the Enemies of the Soul of Man might be overcome, and every human Creature might have a Power of being born again according to that Image of God, in which he was first created. The Gospel is the History of this Love of God to Man. Inwardly he has a *Seed* of the Divine Life given into the Birth of his Soul, a Seed that has all the *Riches of Eternity* in it, and is always wanting to come to the Birth in him, and be alive in God. Outwardly he has Jesus Christ, who as a *Sun* of Righteousness, is always casting forth his enlivening Beams on this *inward Seed*, to kindle and call it forth to the Birth, doing that to this Seed of Heaven in Man, which the Sun in the Firmament is always doing to the vegetable Seeds in the Earth.

Consider this Matter in the following Similitude. A *Grain* of Wheat has the *Air* and *Light* of this World inclosed, or incorporated in it: This is the Mystery of its Life, this is its Power of Growing, by this it has a strong continual Tendency of uniting again with that *Ocean* of Light and Air, from whence it came forth, and so it helps to kindle its own Vegetable Life.

On the other Hand, That great *Ocean* of Light and Air, having its own *Offspring* hidden in the Heart of the Grain, has a perpetual strong Tendency to unite, and communicate with it again. From this Desire of Union on *both Sides*, the Vegetable Life arises, and all the Virtues and Powers contained in it.

But here let it be well observed, that this Desire on both Sides cannot have its Effect, till the *Husk* and gross Part of the Grain falls into a State of Corruption and Death, till this begins, the Mystery of Life hidden in it, cannot come forth. The Application here may be left to the Reader. I shall only observe, that we may here see the true Ground, and absolute Necessity, of that dying to ourselves, and to the World, to which our Blessed Lord so constantly calls all his Followers. An universal Self-Denial, a perpetual Mortification of the Lust of the Flesh, the Lust of the Eyes, and the Pride of Life, is not a Thing imposed upon us by the *mere Will* of God, is not required as a *Punishment*, is not an Invention of dull and *monkish* Spirits, but has its *Ground* and *Reason* in the Nature of the Thing, and is as absolutely necessary to make Way for the New Birth, as the Death of the *Husk* and gross Part of the Grain, is necessary to make Way for its Vegetable Life.

But *Secondly*, This *Pearl of Eternity* is the *Wisdom* and *Love* of God within Thee. In this Pearl of thy Serpent Bruiser, all the Holy Nature, Spirit, Tempers, and Inclinations of Christ, lie as in a Seed in the Centre of thy Soul, and Divine Wisdom and heavenly Love will grow up in Thee, if thou givest but true Attention to God present in thy Soul. On the other Hand, There is hidden also in the Depth of thy Nature the *Root*, or *Possibility* of all the hellish Nature, Spirit, and Tempers of the fallen Angels. For Heaven and Hell have each of them their *Foundation* within us, they come not into us from *without*, but spring up in us, according as our *Will* and *Heart* is turned either to the Light of God, or the Kingdom of Darkness. But when this Life, which is in the midst of these two Eternities, is at an End, either an Angel, or a Devil will be found to have a *Birth* in us.

Thou needest not therefore run here, or there, *saying, Where is Christ? Thou needest not say, Who shall ascend into Heaven, that is, to bring down Christ from above? Or who shall descend into the Deep, to bring up Christ from the Dead?* For behold the *Word*, which is the Wisdom of God, is in thy Heart, it is there as a Bruiser of thy Serpent, as a Light unto thy Feet and Lanthorn unto thy Paths. It is there as an *Holy Oil*, to soften and overcome the wrathful fiery Properties of thy Nature, and change them into the humble Meekness of Light and Love. It is there as a *speaking Word* of God in thy Soul; and as soon as thou art ready to hear, this eternal speaking Word will speak Wisdom and Love in thy inward Parts, and bring forth the Birth of Christ, with all his Holy Nature, Spirit, and Tempers, within Thee. Hence it was (that is, from this Principle of Heaven, or Christ in the Soul) hence I say it was, that so many eminent Spirits, Partakers of a Divine Life, have appeared in so many Parts of the heathen World; glorious Names, Sons of Wisdom, that shone, as Lights hung out by God, in the midst of idolatrous Darkness. These were the Apostles of a *Christ within*, that were awakened and commissioned by the *inward Bruiser* of the Serpent, to call Mankind from the blind Pursuits of Flesh and Blood, to know themselves, the Dignity of their Nature, the Immortality of their Souls, and the Necessity of Virtue to avoid eternal Shame and Misery. These *Apostles*, though they had not the *Law*, or *written Gospel* to urge upon their Hearers, yet having turned to God, they found, and preached the Gospel, that was written in their Hearts. Hence one of them could say this Divine Truth, *viz.*, That *such only are Priests and*

Prophets, who have God in themselves. Hence also it is, that in the Christian Church, there have been in all Ages, amongst the most illiterate, both Men and Women, who have attained to a deep Understanding of the Mysteries of the Wisdom and Love of God in Christ Jesus. And what wonder? Since it is not Art or Science, or Skill in Grammar or Logic, but the Opening of the Divine Life in the Soul, that can give true Understanding of the Things of God. This Life of God in the Soul, which for its Smallness at first, and Capacity for great Growth, is by our Lord compared to a Grain of Mustard Seed, may be, and too generally is suppressed and kept under, either by worldly Cares, or Pleasures, by vain Learning, Sensuality, or Ambition. And all this while, whatever Church, or Profession any Man is of, he is a mere *Natural* Man, *unregenerate, unenlightened* by the Spirit of God, because this Seed of Heaven is choked, and not suffered to grow up in him. And therefore his *Religion* is no more from Heaven than his *fine Breeding;* his *Cares* have no more Goodness in them than his *Pleasures;* his Love is worth no more than his *Hatred;* his Zeal for this, or against that Form of Religion, has only the Nature of any other worldly Contention in it. And thus it is, and must be with every mere natural Man, whatever Appearances he may put on, he may, if he pleases, know himself to be the Slave, and Machine of his own corrupt Tempers and Inclinations, to be enlightened, inspired, quickened and animated by Self-love, Self-esteem, and Self-seeking, which is the only Life, and Spirit of the mere natural Man, whether he be *Heathen, Jew,* or *Christian.*

On the other Hand, Wherever this Seed of Heaven is suffered to take Root, to get Life and Breath in the Soul, whether it be in Man, or Woman, young or old, there this new born inward Man is justly said to be *inspired, enlightened, and moved* by the Spirit of God, because his whole Birth and Life is a Birth from above, of the Light and Spirit of God; and therefore all that is in him, has the Nature, Spirit, and Tempers of Heaven in it. As this regenerate Life grows up in any Man, so there grows up a true and real Knowledge of the whole Mystery of Godliness in himself. All that the Gospel teaches of Sin and Grace, of Life and Death, of Heaven and Hell, of the New and Old Man, of the Light and Spirit of God, are Things not got by *Hearsay*, but inwardly known, felt and experienced in the Growth of his own new born Life. He has then an *Unction* from above which teaches him all Things, a Spirit that *knows what it ought to pray for*, a Spirit that *prays without ceasing*, that is risen with Christ from the Dead, and has all its Conversation in Heaven, a Spirit that has *Groans and Sighs that cannot be uttered*, that travaileth and groaneth with the whole Creation, to be delivered from Vanity, and have its glorious Liberty in that God, from whom it came forth.

Again, *Thirdly*, This *Pearl* of Eternity is the *Church*, or Temple of God *within Thee*, the consecrated Place of Divine Worship, where alone thou canst worship God in *Spirit, and in Truth*. *In Spirit*, because thy Spirit is that alone in Thee, which can unite, and cleave unto God, and receive the Workings of his Divine Spirit upon Thee. *In Truth*, because this *Adoration* in Spirit, is that *Truth* and *Reality*, of which all outward *Forms* and *Rites*, though instituted by God, are only the *Figure* for a Time, but this Worship is Eternal. Accustom thyself to the Holy Service of this inward Temple. In the midst of it is the Fountain of Living Water, of which thou mayest drink, and live for ever. There the Mysteries of thy Redemption are celebrated, or rather opened in Life and Power. There the Supper of the Lamb is kept; the *Bread that came down from Heaven, that giveth Life to the World*, is thy true Nourishment: all is done, and known in real Experience, in a living Sensibility of the Work of God on the Soul. There the Birth, the Life, the Sufferings, the Death, the Resurrection and Ascension of Christ, are not merely remembered, but inwardly found, and enjoyed as the real States of thy Soul, which has followed Christ in the Regeneration. When once thou art well grounded in this *inward Worship*, thou wilt have learnt to live unto God *above Time*, and *Place*. For every Day will be *Sunday* to thee, and wherever thou goest, thou wilt have a *Priest*, a *Church*, and an *Altar* along with Thee. For when God has all that He should have of thy Heart, when renouncing the Will, Judgment, Tempers and Inclinations of thy *old Man*, thou art wholly given up to the Obedience of the Light and Spirit of God within Thee, to *Will* only in his Will, to *Love* only in his Love, to be *Wise* only in his Wisdom, then it is, that every Thing thou doest is as a Song of Praise, and the common Business of thy Life is a conforming to God's Will on Earth, as Angels do in Heaven.

Fourthly, and *Lastly*, This *Pearl* of Eternity is the *Peace* and *Joy* of God within Thee, but can only be found by the Manifestation of the Life and Power of Jesus Christ in thy Soul. But Christ cannot be thy Power and thy Life, till in Obedience to his Call, *thou deniest thyself, takest up thy daily Cross, and followest Him*, in the Regeneration. This is peremptory, it admits of no Reserve or Evasion, it is the one Way to Christ and Eternal Life. But be where thou wilt, either *here,* or at *Rome,* or *Geneva,* if *Self* is undenied, if thou livest to thine *own Will*, to the Pleasures of thy natural Lust and Appetites, Senses and Passions, and in Conformity to the vain Customs, and Spirit of this World, thou art dead whilst thou livest, the Seed of the Woman is crucified within Thee, Christ can profit thee Nothing, thou art a Stranger to all that is holy and heavenly within Thee, and utterly incapable of finding the *Peace* and *Joy* of God in thy Soul. And thus thou art *Poor*, and *Blind*, and *Naked*, and *Empty*, and livest a miserable Life in the Vanity of Time ; whilst all the Riches of Eternity, the Light and Spirit, the Wisdom and Love, the Peace and Joy of God are within Thee. And thus it will always be with Thee, there is no Remedy, go where thou wilt, do what thou wilt, all is shut up, there is no open Door of Salvation, no Awakening out of the Sleep of Sin, no Deliverance from the Power of thy corrupt Nature, no Overcoming of the World, no Revelation of Jesus Christ, no Joy of the New Birth from above, till dying to thy Self and the World, thou turnest to the Light, and Spirit, and Power of God in thy Soul. All is fruitless, and insignificant, all the Means of thy Redemption are at a Stand, all outward Forms are but a dead Formality, till this Fountain of Living Water is found within Thee.

But thou wilt perhaps say, How shall I discover this Riches of Eternity, this Light, and Spirit, and Wisdom, and Peace of God, treasured up within me ? Thy *first Thought* of Repentance, or *Desire* of turning to God, is thy *first Discovery* of this Light and Spirit of God within Thee. It is the Voice and Language of the *Word* of God within Thee, though thou knowest it not. It is the Bruiser of thy Serpent's Head, thy Dear *Immanuel*, who is beginning to preach *within* Thee, that same which He first preached in public, saying, ' Repent, for the Kingdom of Heaven ' is at Hand.' When therefore but the smallest Instinct or Desire of thy Heart calls Thee towards God, and a newness of Life, give it Time and Leave to speak ; and take care thou refuse not Him that speaketh. For it is not an Angel from Heaven that speaks to Thee, but it is the eternal *speaking Word* of God in thy Heart, that Word which at first created Thee, is thus beginning to create Thee a *second Time* unto Righteousness, that a new Man may be formed again in Thee in the Image and Likeness of God. But above all Things, beware of taking this *Desire* of Repentance to be the Effect of thy own Natural *Sense* and *Reason*, for in so doing thou losest the *Key* of all the Heavenly Treasure that is in Thee, thou shuttest the Door against God, turnest away from Him, and thy Repentance (if thou hast any) will be only a vain, unprofitable Work of thy own Hands, that will do Thee no more Good, than a *Well* that is without Water. But if thou takest this *awakened Desire* of turning to God, to be, as in Truth it is, the coming of Christ in thy Soul, the *Working*,

Redeeming Power of the Light and Spirit of the Holy Jesus within Thee, if thou dost reverence and adhere to it, as such, this *Faith will save Thee, will make Thee whole;* and by thus believing in Christ, though thou wert dead, yet shalt thou live.

Now all depends upon thy right Submission and Obedience to this speaking of God in thy Soul. Stop therefore all Self-activity, listen not to the Suggestions of thy own Reason, run not on in thy own Will, but be retired, silent, passive, and humbly attentive to this new risen Light within Thee. Open thy Heart, thy Eyes, and Ears, to all its Impressions. Let it enlighten, teach, frighten, torment, judge, and condemn Thee, as it pleases, turn not away from it, hear all it says, seek for no Relief out of it, consult not with Flesh and Blood, but with a Heart full of Faith and Resignation to God, pray only this Prayer, that God's Kingdom may come, and his Will be done in thy Soul. Stand faithfully in this State of Preparation, thus given up to the Spirit of God, and then the Work of thy Repentance will be wrought in God, and thou wilt soon find, that He that is in Thee, is much greater than all that are against Thee.

But that thou mayest do all this the better, and be more firmly assured, that this *Resignation* to, and *Dependence* upon the working of God's Spirit within Thee, is right and sound, I shall lay before Thee two great, and infallible, and fundamental Truths, which will be as a Rock for thy Faith to stand upon.

First, That through all the whole Nature of Things, nothing can *do*, or *be* a real Good to thy Soul, but the *Operation of God* upon it. *Secondly*, That all the Dispensations of God to Mankind, from the Fall of *Adam*, to the Preaching of the Gospel, were only for this *one End*, to fit, prepare, and dispose the Soul for the *Operation* of the Spirit of God upon it. These two great Truths well and deeply apprehended, put the Soul in its right State, in a continual Dependence upon God, in a Readiness to receive all Good from Him, and will be a continual Source of Light in thy Mind. They will keep Thee safe from all Errors, and false Zeal in Things, and Forms of Religion, from a Sectarian Spirit, from Bigotry, and Superstition; they will teach Thee the true Difference between the Means and End of Religion; and the Regard thou showest to the *Shell*, will be only so far, as the *Kernel* is to be found in it.

Man, by his Fall, had broken off from his true *Centre*, his proper Place in God, and therefore the Life and Operation of God was no more in Him. He was fallen from a Life in God into a Life of *Self*, into an animal Life of Self-love, Self-esteem, and Self-seeking in the poor perishing Enjoyments of this

World. This was the *Natural State* of Man by the Fall. He was an Apostate from God, and his natural Life was all Idolatry, where *Self* was the great Idol that was worshipped instead of God. See here the whole Truth in short. All Sin, Death, Damnation, and Hell, is nothing else but this Kingdom of *Self*, or the various Operations of Self-love, Self-esteem, and Self-seeking, which separate the Soul from God, and end in eternal Death and Hell.

On the other Hand, All that is *Grace, Redemption, Salvation, Sanctification, Spiritual Life,* and the *New Birth,* is nothing else but so much of the Life, and Operation of God found again in the Soul. It is Man come back again into his *Centre* or *Place* in God, from whence he had broken off. The Beginning again of the Life of God in the Soul, was then first made, when the Mercy of God inspoke into *Adam* a *Seed* of the Divine Life, which should bruise the Head of the Serpent, which had wrought itself into the human Nature. Here the Kingdom of God was again within us, though only as a *Seed*, yet small as it was, it was yet a *Degree* of the Divine Life, which if rightly cultivated, would overcome all the Evil that was in us, and make of every fallen Man a new-born Son of God.

All the Sacrifices and Institutions of the ancient Patriarchs, the *Law* of *Moses*, with all its Types, and Rites, and Ceremonies, had this *only End ;* they were the Methods of Divine Wisdom for a Time, to keep the Hearts of Men from the Wanderings of Idolatry, in a State of *Holy Expectation* upon God, they were to keep the *first Seed* of Life in a State of Growth, and make Way for the further Operation of God upon the Soul ; or, as the Apostle speaks, to be as a *Schoolmaster unto Christ*, that is, till the Birth, the Death, the Resurrection and Ascension of Christ, should conquer Death and Hell, open a new Dispensation of God, and baptize Mankind afresh with the Holy Ghost, and Fire of Heaven. Then, that is, on the Day of *Pentecost*, a *new Dispensation* of God came forth ; which on God's Part, was the Operation of the Holy Spirit in Gifts and Graces upon the whole Church ; and on Man's Part, it was the Adoration of God in *Spirit* and *in Truth*. Thus all that was done by God, from the Bruiser of the Serpent given to *Adam*, to Christ's sitting down on the right Hand of God, was all for this End, to remove all that stood between God and Man, and to make Way for the *immediate* and *continual* Operation of God upon the Soul; and that Man, baptized with the Holy Spirit, and born again from Above, should absolutely renounce *Self*, and wholly give up his Soul to the Operation of God's Spirit, to know, to love, to will, to pray, to worship, to preach, to exhort, to use all the Faculties of his Mind, and all the outward Things of this World, as enlightened, inspired, moved and guided by the Holy Ghost, who by this last Dispensation of God, was given to be a Comforter, a Teacher, and Guide to the Church, who should abide with it for ever.

This is Christianity, a spiritual Society, not because it has no worldly Concerns, but because all its Members, as such, are born of the Spirit, kept alive, animated and governed by the Spirit of God. It is constantly called by our Lord the Kingdom of God, or Heaven, because all its *Ministry* and *Service*, all that is done in it, is done in Obedience and Subjection to *that Spirit*, by which Angels live, and are governed in Heaven.* Hence our blessed Lord taught his Disciples to pray, that this Kingdom might come, that so God's Will might be done on Earth, as it is in Heaven; which could not be, but by that same Spirit, by which it is done in Heaven. The short is this: The Kingdom of *Self* is the Fall of Man, or the great Apostasy from the Life of God in the Soul; and everyone wherever he be, that lives unto *Self*, is still under the Fall and great Apostasy from God. The Kingdom of Christ is the Spirit and Power of God dwelling and manifesting itself in the Birth of a new inward Man; and no one is a Member of this Kingdom, but *so far* as a true Birth of the Spirit is brought forth in him. These two Kingdoms take in all Mankind, he that is not of one, is certainly in the other; Dying to one is Living to the other.

Hence we may gather these following Truths: *First*, Here is shown the true Ground and Reason of what was said above, namely, That when the *Call* of God to Repentance first arises in thy Soul, thou art to be *retired, silent, passive*, and humbly attentive to this new risen Light within thee, by wholly stopping, or disregarding the Workings of thy own Will, Reason, and Judgment. It is because all these are false Counsellors, the sworn Servants, bribed Slaves of thy fallen Nature, they are all Born and Bred in the Kingdom of *Self;* and therefore if a new Kingdom is to be set up in thee, if the Operation of God is to have its Effect in thee, all these natural Powers of *Self* are to be silenced and suppressed, till they have learned Obedience and Subjection to the Spirit of God. Now this is not requiring thee to become a *Fool*, or to give up thy Claim to Sense and Reason, but is the shortest Way to have thy Sense and Reason delivered from Folly, and thy whole rational Nature strengthened, enlightened, and guided by that Light, which is Wisdom itself.

A Child that obediently denies his own Will, and own Reason,

---

* *Way to Divine Knowledge, &c.*, page 77.

to be guided by the Will and Reason of a truly wise and understanding Tutor, cannot be said to make himself a Fool, and give up the Benefit of his rational Nature, but to have taken the shortest Way to have his own Will and Reason made truly a Blessing to him.

Secondly, Hence is to be seen the true Ground and Necessity of that universal Mortification and Self-denial with regard to all our Senses, Appetites, Tempers, Passions and Judgments. It is because all our whole Nature, as fallen from the Life of God, is in a State of Contrariety to the Order and End of our Creation, a continual Source of disorderly Appetites, corrupt Tempers, and false Judgments. And therefore every Motion of it is to be mortified, changed and purified from its *natural State*, before we can enter into the Kingdom of God. Thus when our Lord says, 'Except a Man hateth his Father and 'Mother, yea, and his own Life, he cannot be my Disciple'; it is because our best Tempers are yet *carnal*, and full of the *Imperfections* of our fallen Nature. The Doctrine is just and good; not as if *Father* and *Mother* were to be hated; but *that Love*, which an unregenerate Person, or *natural Man*, has towards them, is to be *hated*, as being a blind *Self-love*, full of all the *Weakness* and *Partiality*, with which fallen Man loves, honours, esteems, and cleaves to himself. This Love, *born* from corrupt Flesh and Blood, and *polluted* with Self, is to be *hated* and *parted* with, that we may love them with a Love *born* of God, with such a Love, and on such a Motive, as Christ has loved us. And then the *Disciple* of Christ far exceeds all others in the Love of Parents. Again, Our *own Life* is to be *hated;* and the Reason is plain, it is because there is nothing lovely in it. It is a *Legion* of Evil, a monstrous Birth of the *Serpent*, the *World*, and the *Flesh;* it is an *Apostasy* from the *Life* and *Power* of God in the Soul, a Life that is *Death* to Heaven, that is pure unmixed *Idolatry*, that lives wholly to *Self*, and not to God; and therefore *all this own Life* is to be absolutely *hated*, all this Self is to be *denied* and *mortified*, if the Nature, Spirit, Tempers and Inclinations of Christ are to be brought to Life in us. For it is as impossible to live to both these Lives at once, as for a *Body* to move two contrary Ways at the same Time. And therefore all these Mortifications and Self-denials have an absolute Necessity in the Nature of the Thing itself.

Thus when our Lord further says, unless a Man forsaketh *all that he hath, he cannot be my Disciple;* the Reason is plain, and the Necessity absolute. It is because *all* that the *natural* Man has, is in the Possession of *Self-love*, and therefore *this Possession* is to be absolutely *forsaken*, and parted with. All that he has, is to be put into other Hands, to be given to Divine Love, or this *natural Man* cannot be changed into a *Disciple* of Christ. For Self-love in *all that it has*, is earthly, sensual, and devilish, and therefore must have *all* taken away from it ; and then to the *natural* Man *all* is lost, he has *nothing* left, all is laid down at the Feet of Jesus. And then all Things are common, as soon as *Self-love* has lost the Possession of them. And then the Disciple of Christ, *though having nothing, yet possesseth all Things*, all that the *natural* Man has *forsaken*, is restored to the *Disciple* of Christ an *hundred-fold*. For Self-love, the greatest of all *Thieves*, being now cast out, and all that he had stolen and hidden, thus taken from him, and put into the Hands of Divine Love, every *Mite* becomes a large Treasure, and Mammon opens the Door into everlasting Habitations. This was the Spirit of the *first Draught* of a Christian Church at *Jerusalem*, a Church made truly after the Pattern of Heaven, where the Love that reigns in Heaven reigned in it, where Divine Love broke down all the selfish Fences, the Locks and Bolts of *me, mine, my own, &c.*, and laid all Things common to the Members of this new Kingdom of God on Earth.

Now though many Years did not pass after the Age of the Apostles, before *Satan* and *Self* got footing in the Church, and set up Merchandize in the House of God, yet this *one Heart*, and *one Spirit*, which then first appeared in the *Jerusalem* Church, is that *one Heart* and *Spirit* of Divine Love, to which *all are* called, that would be true Disciples of Christ. And though the Practice of it is lost as to the Church in general, yet it ought not to have been lost ; and therefore every Christian ought to make it his great Care and Prayer, to have it restored in himself. And then, though born in the Dregs of Time, or living in *Babylon*, he will be as truly a Member of the first heavenly Church at *Jerusalem*, as if he had lived in it, in the Days of the Apostles. This Spirit of Love, born of that celestial Fire, with which Christ baptizes his true Disciples, is alone that Spirit, which can enter into Heaven, and therefore is that Spirit which is to be born in us, whilst we are on Earth. For no one can enter into Heaven, till he is made heavenly, till the Spirit of Heaven is entered into him. And therefore all that our Lord has said of denying and dying to *Self*, and of his parting with all that he has, are Practices absolutely necessary from the Nature of the Thing.

Because all turning to Self is so far turning *from* God, and so much as we have of Self-love, so much we have of a hellish, earthly Weight, that must be taken off, or there can be no Ascension into Heaven. But thou wilt perhaps say, If *all Self-*

love is to be renounced, then all Love of our Neighbour is renounced along with it, because the Commandment is, only *to love our Neighbour as ourselves*. The Answer here is easy, and yet no Quarter given to Self-love. There is but *one only* Love in Heaven, and yet the Angels of God love one another in the *same manner*, as they love themselves. The Matter is thus: The one supreme, unchangeable *Rule* of Love, which is a *Law* to all intelligent Beings of all Worlds, and will be a Law to all Eternity, is this, *viz., That God alone is to be loved for himself,* and *all other Beings only* in *Him, and for Him.* Whatever intelligent Creature lives not under this Rule of Love, is so far fallen from the Order of his Creation, and is, till He returns to this eternal Law of Love, an *Apostate* from God, and incapable of the Kingdom of Heaven.

Now if God alone is to be loved for *Himself,* then no Creature is to be loved for *itself;* and so all *Self-love* in every Creature is absolutely condemned.

And if all created Beings are only to be loved *in* and *for* God, then my Neighbour is to be loved, *as* I love myself, and I am only to love myself, as I love my Neighbour, or any other created Being, that is, only *in* and *for* God. And thus the Command of loving our Neighbour as ourselves, stands firm, and yet all Self-love is plucked up by the Roots. But what is loving any Creature, only *in,* and *for* God? It is when we love it only as it is God's *Work, Image,* and *Delight,* when we love it merely as it is God's, and belongs to him, this is loving it *in* God, and when all that we wish, intend, or do to it, is done from a Love of God, for the Honour of God, and in Conformity to the Will of God, this is loving it *for* God. This is the *one Love* that is, and must be the Spirit of all Creatures that live united to God. Now this is no speculative Refinement, or finespun Fiction of the Brain, but the simple Truth, a first Law of Nature, and a necessary Band of Union between God and the Creature. The Creature is not in God, is a Stranger to Him, has lost the Life of God in itself, whenever its Love does not thus begin and end in God.

The Loss of this Love, was the *Fall* of Man, as it opened in him a Kingdom of *Self,* in which Satan, the World, and the Flesh, could all of them bring forth their own Works.* If therefore Man is to rise from his Fall, and return to his Life in God, there is an absolute Necessity that *Self,* with all his Brood of gross Affections, be deposed, that his first Love in and for which he was created, may be born again in him. Christ came

---

* *Spirit of Prayer,* Part II., pages 12—22.

into the World to *save Sinners*, to destroy the Works of the Devil. Now *Self* is not only the Seat and Habitation, but the very *Life* of Sin. The Works of the Devil are all wrought in *Self*, it is his peculiar *Workhouse*, and therefore Christ is not come as a Saviour from Sin, as a Destroyer of the Works of the Devil in any of us, but *so far* as Self is beaten down, and overcome in us. If it is literally true, what our Lord said, *That his Kingdom was not of this World*, then it is a Truth of the same Certainty, that no one is a Member of this Kingdom, but he that in the literal Sense of the Words renounces the Spirit of this World. Christians might as well part with half the Articles of their Creed, or but half believe them, as really to refuse, or but by halves enter into these Self-denials.

For all that is in the *Creed*, is only to bring forth this Dying and Death to all and every Part of the old Man, that the Life and Spirit of Christ may be formed in us.

Our Redemption is *this new Birth;* if this is not done, or doing in us, we are still unredeemed. And though the Saviour of the World is come, He is not come in us, He is not received by us, is a Stranger to us, is not ours, if his Life is not within us. His Life is not, cannot be within us, but so far as the Spirit of the World, Self-love, Self-esteem, and Self-seeking, are renounced, and driven out of us.

Thirdly, Hence we may also learn the true Nature and Worth of all *Self-denials* and *Mortifications*. As to their Nature, considered in themselves, they have nothing of *Goodness* or *Holiness*, nor are any real Parts of our Sanctification, they are not the true *Food* or *Nourishment* of the Divine Life in our Souls, they have no *Quickening, Sanctifying Power* in them; their only Worth consists in this, that they remove the Impediments of Holiness, break down that which stands between God and us, and make Way for the *Quickening, Sanctifying* Spirit of God to operate on our Souls. Which Operation of God is the *one only* Thing that can raise the Divine Life in the Soul, or help it to the smallest Degree of real Holiness, or Spiritual Life. As in our Creation, we had only that *Degree* of a Divine Life, which the Power of God derived into us; as then all that we had, and were, was the *sole Operation* of God in the Creation of us; so in our Redemption, or regaining that first Perfection, which we have lost, all must be again the Operation of God; *every Degree* of the Divine Life restored in us, be it ever so small, must and can be nothing else but so much of the Life and Operation of God found again in the Soul. All the Activity of Man in the Works of Self-denial has no Good in itself, but is only to open an Entrance for the *one only* Good, the Light of God, to operate upon us.

Hence also we may learn the Reason, why many People not only lose the Benefit, but are even the worse for all their Mortifications. It is because they mistake the whole Nature and Worth of them. They practise them for their *own Sakes*, as Things good in themselves, they think them to be *real* Parts of Holiness, and so *rest* in them, and look no *further*, but grow full of Self-esteem, and Self-admiration, for their own Progress in them. This makes them Self-sufficient, morose, severe Judges of all those that fall short of their Mortifications.

And thus their *Self-denials* do only *that* for them, which *Indulgences* do for other People, they withstand and hinder the Operation of God upon their Souls, and instead of being *really* Self-denials, they strengthen and keep up the Kingdom of *Self*.

There is no avoiding this fatal Error, but by deeply entering into this great Truth, that all our own Activity and Working has no Good in it, can do no Good to us, but as it leads and turns us in the best Manner to the Light and Spirit of God, which alone brings Life and Salvation into the Soul. 'Stretch forth thy ' Hand,' said our Lord to the Man ' that had a withered Hand ;' he did so, and ' it was immediately made whole as the other.'

Now had this Man any Ground for Pride, or a high Opinion of himself, for the Share he had in the Restoring of his Hand? Yet just such is our Share in the Raising up of the Spiritual Life within us. All that we can do by our own Activity, is only like this Man's stretching out his Hand ; the rest is the Work of Christ, the only Giver of Life to the withered Hand, or the dead Soul. We can only then do living Works, when we are so far born again, as to be able to say with the Apostle, 'Yet not I, but 'Christ that liveth in me.' But to return, and further show, how the Soul that feels the Call of God to Repentance is to behave under it, that this stirring of the Divine Power in the Soul may have its full Effect, and bring forth the Birth of the new Man in Christ Jesus. We are to consider it (as in Truth it is) as the *Seed* of the Divine Nature within us, that can only grow by its *own Strength*, and *Union* with God. It is a Divine Life, and therefore can grow from nothing but Divine Power. When the Virgin *Mary* conceived the Birth of the holy Jesus, all that she did towards it herself, was only this single Act of Faith and Resignation to God ; 'Behold the Handmaid of the Lord, be it 'unto me according to thy Word.' This is all that we can do towards the Conception of that new Man that is to be born in ourselves. Now this Truth is easily consented to, and a Man thinks he believes it, because he consents to it, or rather, does not deny it. But this is not enough, it is to be apprehended in a deep, full, and practical Assurance, in such a Manner as a Man knows and believes that he did not create the *Stars*, or cause Life to rise up in himself. And then it is a Belief, that puts the Soul into a right State, that makes room for the Operation of God upon it. His Light then enters with full Power into the Soul, and his holy Spirit moves and directs all that is done in it, and so Man lives again in God as a new Creature. For this Truth thus firmly believed, will have these two most excellent Effects: *First*, It will keep the Soul fixed, and continually turned towards God, in Faith, Prayer, Desire, Confidence, and Resignation to Him, for all that it wants to have done in it, and to it; which will be a continual Source of all Divine Virtues and Graces. The Soul thus turned to God must be always receiving from Him. It stands at the true Door of all Divine Communications, and the Light of God as freely enters into it, as the Light of the *Sun* enters into the *Air*. *Secondly*, It will fix and ground the Soul in a true and lasting Self-denial. For by thus knowing and owning our own *Nothingness* and Inability, that we have no other Capacity for Good, but that of receiving it from God alone, *Self* is wholly denied, its Kingdom is destroyed; no room is left for spiritual Pride and Self-esteem; we are saved from a Pharisaical Holiness, from wrong Opinions of our own Works and good Deeds, and from a Multitude of Errors, the most dangerous to our Souls, all which arise from the *Something* that we take ourselves to be either in Nature or Grace. But when we once apprehend but in some good Degree, the *All* of God, and the *Nothingness* of ourselves, we have got a Truth, whose Usefulness and Benefit no Words can express. It brings a Kind of Infallibility into the Soul in which it dwells; all that is vain, and false, and deceitful, is forced to vanish and fly before it. When our Religion is founded on this Rock, it has the Firmness of a Rock, and its Height reaches unto Heaven. The World, the Flesh, and the Devil, can do no hurt to it; all Enemies are known, and all disarmed by this great Truth dwelling in our Souls. It is the Knowledge of the *All* of God, that makes *Cherubims* and *Seraphims* to be Flames of Divine Love. For where this *All* of God is truly known, and felt in any Creature, there its whole Breath and Spirit is a Fire of Love, nothing but a pure disinterested Love can arise up in it, or come from it, a Love that begins and ends in God. And where this Love is born in any Creature, there a Seraphic Life is born along with it. For this pure Love introduces the Creature into the *All* of God; all that is in God is opened in the Creature, it is united with God, and has the Life of God manifested in it.

There is but *one Salvation* for all Mankind, and that is the *Life* of God in the Soul. God has but *one Design* or Intent towards all Mankind, and that is to *introduce* or *generate* his own Life, Light, and Spirit in them, that all may be as so many Images, Temples, and Habitations of the Holy Trinity. This is God's good Will to all *Christians, Jews,* and *Heathens.* They are all *equally* the Desire of his Heart, his Light continually *waits* for an Entrance into *all* of them, his *Wisdom crieth, she putteth forth her Voice*, not here, or there, but everywhere, in all the Streets of all the Parts of the World.

Now there is but *one possible* Way for Man to attain this Salvation, or Life of God in the Soul. There is not one for the *Jew,* another for a *Christian,* and a Third for the *Heathen.* No; God is one, human Nature is one, Salvation is one, and the *Way* to it is one ; and that is, the Desire of the Soul turned to God. When this *Desire* is alive and breaks forth in any Creature under Heaven, then the *lost Sheep* is found, and the *Shepherd* has it upon his Shoulders. Through *this Desire* the Poor *prodigal Son* leaves his *Husks* and *Swine,* and hastes to his Father : it is because of *this Desire,* that the Father sees the Son, while yet *afar off,* that he runs out to meet him, falls on his Neck, and kisses him. See here how plainly we are taught, that no sooner is this Desire *arisen,* and in *Motion* towards God, but the *Operation* of God's Spirit answers to it, cherishes and welcomes its *first Beginnings,* signified by the Father's seeing, and having Compassion on his Son, whilst yet *afar off,* that is, in the first Beginnings of his Desire. Thus does *this Desire* do all, it brings the Soul to God, and God into the Soul, it unites with God, it co-operates with God, and is one Life with God. Suppose this *Desire* not to be alive, not in Motion either in a *Jew,* or a *Christian,* and then all the Sacrifices, the Service, the Worship either of the *Law,* or the *Gospel,* are but *dead* Works, that bring *no Life* into the Soul, nor beget any *Union* between God and it. Suppose this Desire to be awakened, and fixed upon God, though in Souls that never heard either of the Law or Gospel, and then the Divine Life, or Operation of God, enters into them, and the new Birth in Christ is formed in those who never heard of his Name. And these are they ' that shall come ' from the East, and from the West, and sit down with Abraham, ' and Isaac, in the Kingdom of God.'

Oh my God, just and good, how great is thy Love and Mercy to Mankind, that Heaven is thus everywhere open, and Christ thus the *common* Saviour to all that turn the Desire of their Hearts to thee ! Oh sweet Power of the *Bruiser* of the Serpent, born in every Son of Man, that stirs and works in every Man, and gives every Man a Power, and Desire, to find his Happiness in God ! O holy Jesus, heavenly *Light, that lightest every Man that cometh into the World*, that redeemest every Soul that follows thy Light, which is *always within Him!* O holy Trinity, immense Ocean of Divine Love in which all Mankind live, and move, and have their Being! None are separated from Thee, none live out of thy Love, but all are embraced in the Arms of thy Mercy, all are Partakers of thy Divine Life, the Operation of thy holy Spirit, as soon as their Heart is turned to Thee! Oh plain, and easy, and simple Way of Salvation, wanting no Subtleties of Art or Science, no borrowed Learning, no Refinements of Reason, but all done by the simple natural Motion of every Heart, that truly longs after God. For no sooner is the finite Desire of the Creature in motion towards God, but the infinite Desire of God is united with it, co-operates with it. And in this united Desire of God and the Creature, is the Salvation and Life of the Soul brought forth. For the Soul is shut out of God, and imprisoned in its own dark Workings of Flesh and Blood, merely and solely, because it desires to live to the Vanity of this World. This *Desire* is its Darkness, its Death, its Imprisonment, and Separation from God.

When therefore the *first Spark* of a Desire after God arises in thy Soul, cherish it with all thy Care, give all thy Heart into it, it is nothing less than a Touch of the Divine *Loadstone*, that is to draw Thee out of the Vanity of Time into the Riches of Eternity. Get up therefore and follow it as gladly, as the *Wise men of the East* followed the *Star* from Heaven that appeared to them. It will do for Thee, as the Star did for them, it will lead Thee to the Birth of Jesus, not in a Stable at *Bethlehem* in *Judea*, but to the Birth of Jesus in the *dark Centre* of thy own fallen Soul.

I shall conclude this *first Part*, with the Words of the heavenly Illuminated, and blessed *Jacob Behmen*.

' It is much to be lamented, that we are so blindly led, and the
' Truth withheld from us through imaginary Conceptions; for if
' the *Divine Power* in the inward Ground of the Soul was
' manifest, and working with its Lustre in us, then is the whole
' Triune God present in the *Life* and *Will* of the Soul; and the
' Heaven, wherein God dwells, is opened in the Soul, and *There*,
' in the Soul, is the *Place* where the Father begets his Son, and
' where the Holy Ghost proceeds from the Father and the Son.

' Christ says, "I am the Light of the World, he that followeth
' me, walketh not in Darkness." He directs us only to himself,
' He is the Morning Star, and is generated and rises in us, and
' shines in the Darkness of our Nature. O how great a Triumph
' is there in the Soul, when he arises in it! then a Man knows,
' as he never knew before, that he is a Stranger in a foreign Land.'

A PRAYER.

OH heavenly Father, infinite, fathomless Depth of never-ceasing Love, save me from myself, from the disorderly Workings of my fallen, long corrupted Nature, and let my Eyes see, my Heart and Spirit feel and find, thy Salvation in Christ Jesus.

O God, who madest me for thyself, to show forth thy Goodness in me, manifest, I humbly beseech Thee, the Life-giving Power of thy holy Nature within me; help me to such a true and living Faith in Thee, such Strength of Hunger and Thirst after the Birth, Life, and Spirit of thy Holy Jesus in my Soul, that all that is within me, may be turned from every inward Thought, or outward Work, that is not Thee, thy Holy Jesus, and heavenly working in my Soul. *Amen.*

FINIS.

THE SPIRIT of PRAYER;

OR,

The SOUL rising out of the VANITY of TIME, INTO THE RICHES of ETERNITY.

PART THE SECOND.

In several DIALOGUES between ACADEMICUS, RUSTICUS and THEOPHILUS. At which HUMANUS was present.

By *WILLIAM LAW*, M.A.

LONDON:
Printed for J. RICHARDSON, in *Pater-noster-Row*. 1750.

THE FIRST DIALOGUE

BETWEEN

Academicus, Rusticus, and *Theophilus.*
At which *Humanus* was present.

ACAD. Well met, honest *Rusticus.* I can now tell you with much Pleasure, that we shall soon see a *Second Part* of the Spirit of Prayer. And as soon as I get it, I will come and read it to you.

Rust. I have often told you, *Academicus,* that I wondered at your Eagerness and Impatience to see more of this Matter. As to my Part, I have no such Thrift within me, and should make no Complaint, if it never came out.

Acad. My Friend *Rusticus,* you cannot read; and that is the Reason, that you are not in my State of Impatience, to see another Book.

Rust. Indeed, *Academicus,* you quite mistake the Matter. The First Part of the Spirit of Prayer you read to me more than three or four times, and that is the Reason, why I am in no State of Eagerness after a Second Part. I have found in the First Part, all that I need to know of God, of Christ, of myself, of Heaven, of Hell, of Sin, of Grace, of Death, and of Salvation: That all these Things have their *Being,* their *Life,* and their *Working,* in my own Heart: That God is always in me, that Christ is always within me; that he is the inward *Light* and *Life* of my Soul, a *Bread* from Heaven, of which I may always eat; a *Water* of eternal *Life* springing up in my Soul, of which I may always drink. O my Friend, these Truths have opened a new Life in my Soul: I am brought home to myself; the Veil is taken off from my Heart; I have found my God; I know that his Dwelling-place, his Kingdom, is within me. What need we then call out for Books written only with Pen and Ink, when such a Book as this, so full of Wonders, is once opened in our own Hearts? My Eyes, my Ears, my Thoughts, are all turned inwards, because all that God, and Christ, and Grace, are doing for me, all that the Devil, the World, and the Flesh, are working against me, are only to be known, and found there. What need then of so much News from abroad, since all that concerns either *Life* or *Death*, are all transacting, and all at work, within me?

How could I be said to have felt these great Truths, to be sensible of these Riches of Eternity treasured up in my Soul, to know what a great Good the Divine Nature is in me, and to me, if instead of turning all the Desire and Delight of my Heart towards them, I only felt a Longing and Desire to read more concerning the Spirit of Prayer? No, *Academicus*, another, and a better Fire is kindled within me; my Heart is in motion, and all that is within me tends towards God; and I find that nothing concerns me more, than to keep my Heart from wandering after anything else. I now know to what it is that I am daily to die, and to what it is that I am daily to live; and therefore look upon every Day as lost, that does not help forwards both this Death, and this Life, in me. I have not yet done half, what the First Part of the Spirit of Prayer directs me to do, and therefore have but little Occasion to call out for a Second.

Theop. Indeed, *Academicus*, I must own, that honest *Rusticus*, as you called him, has spoken well. Your Education has so accustomed you to the Pleasure of reading Variety of Books, that you hardly propose any other End in reading, than the Entertainment of your Mind: Thus the Spirit of Prayer has only awakened in you a Desire to see another Part upon the same Subject. This Fault is very common to others, as well as Scholars, and even to those who only delight in reading good Books.

Philo for this twenty Years has been collecting and reading all the *spiritual* Books he can hear of. He reads them, as the *Critics* read Commentators and Lexicons, to be nice and exact in telling you the *Style*, *Spirit*, and *Intent* of this or that spiritual Writer, how one is more accurate in this, and the other in that. *Philo* will ride you forty Miles in Winter to have a Conversation about spiritual Books, or to see a Collection larger than his own. *Philo* is amazed at the Deadness and Insensibility of the Christian World, that they are such Strangers to the inward Life and spiritual Nature of the Christian Salvation; he wonders how they can be so zealous for the outward Letter and Form of Ordinances, and so averse to that spiritual Life, that they all point at, as the one thing needful. But *Philo* never thinks how wonderful it is, that a Man who knows Regeneration to be the Whole, should yet content himself with the Love of Books upon the new Birth, instead of being born again himself. For all that is changed in *Philo*, is his Taste for Books. He is no more dead to the World, no more delivered from himself, is as fearful of Adversity, as fond of Prosperity, as easily provoked, and pleased with Trifles, as much governed by his *own* Will, Tempers, and Passions, as unwilling to deny his Appetites, or enter into War with himself, as he was *twenty Years* ago. Yet all is well with *Philo;* he has no Suspicion of himself; he dates the Newness of his Life, and the Fulness of his Light, from the time that he discovered the Pearl of Eternity in spiritual Authors.

All this, *Academicus*, is said on your Account, that you may not lose the Benefit of this Spark of the Divine Life that is kindled in your Soul, but may conform yourself suitably to so great a Gift of God.

It demands at present an Eagerness of another Kind, than that of much reading, even upon the most spiritual Matters.

Acad. I thank you, *Theophilus*, for your good Will towards me ; but did not imagine my Eagerness after such Books to be so great and dangerous a Mistake. And if I do not yet entirely give into what you say, it is because a Friend of yours has told us (and as I thought by way of Direction) that he has been a diligent Reader of all the spiritual Authors, from the apostolical *Dionysius* down to the illuminated *Guion*, and celebrated *Fenelon* of *Cambray:* And therefore it would never have come into my Head, to suspect it to be a Fault, or dangerous, to follow his Example.

Theoph. I have said nothing, my Friend, with a Design of hindering your Acquaintance with all the truly spiritual Writers. I would rather in a right Way help you to a true Intimacy with them : For they are Friends of God, entrusted with his Secrets, and Partakers of the Divine Nature : And he that converses rightly with them, has a Happiness, that can hardly be over-valued.

My Intention is only to abate, for a time, a Spirit of Eagerness after much reading, which in your State has more of Nature than Grace in it ; which seeks Delight in a Variety of new Notions, and rather gratifies Curiosity, than reforms the Heart.

Suppose you had seen an Angel from Heaven, who had discovered to you a Glimpse of its own internal Brightness, and of that glorious Union in which it lived with God, opening more of itself to the inward Sight of your Mind, than you could either forget or relate. Suppose it had told you with a piercing Word, and living Impression, that all its own angelic and heavenly Brightness was hid in yourself, concealed from you under a bestial Covering of Flesh and Blood ; that this Flesh and Blood was become the Master of it, would not suffer it to breathe, or stir, or come to Life in you. Suppose it had told you, that all your Life had been spent in helping this Flesh and Blood to more and more Power over you, to hinder you from knowing and feeling this Divine Life within you. Suppose it had told you, that to this Day you had lived in the grossest *Self-idolatry*, loving, serving, honouring, and adoring yourself instead of loving, serving, and adoring God with all your Heart, and Soul, and Spirit: That all your Intentions, Projects, Cares, Pleasures, and Indulgences, had been only so much Labour to bring you to the Grave in a total Ignorance of that great Work, for which alone you were born into the World.

Suppose it had told you, that all this Blindness and Insensibility of your State, was obstinately and wilfully brought upon yourself, because you had boldly slighted and resisted all the daily inward and outward Calls of God to your Soul, all the Teachings, Doings, and Sufferings, of a Son of God to redeem you. Suppose it left you with this *Farewell*, O Man awake; thy Work is great, thy Time is short, I am thy last Trumpet; the *Grave* calls for thy Flesh and Blood, thy Soul must enter into a new Lodging. To be born again, is to be an Angel: Not to be born again is to become a Devil.

Tell me now, *Academicus,* what would you expect from a Man who had been thus awakened, and pierced by the Voice of an Angel? Could you think he had any Sense left, if he was not cast into the deepest Depth of Humility, Self-dejection, and Self-abhorrence? Casting himself, with a broken Heart, at the Feet of the Divine Mercy, desiring nothing but that, from that Time, every Moment of his Life might be given unto God, in the most perfect Denial of every Temper, Will, and Inclination, that nourished the Corruption of his Nature: Wishing and praying from the Bottom of his Heart, that God would lead him into and through everything inwardly and outwardly, that might destroy the evil Workings of his Nature, and awaken all that was holy and heavenly within him; that the Seed of Eternity, the Spark of Life, that he had so long quenched and smothered under earthly Rubbish, might breathe, and come to Life, in him.

Or would you think he was enough affected with this angelic Visit, if all that it had awakened in him, was only a Longing and eager Desire to hear the same, or another Angel talk again?

Acad. Oh *Theophilus,* you have said enough: For all that is within me consents to the Truth and Justness of what you have said. I now feel in the strongest Manner, that I have been rather amused, than edified, by what I have read.

Theoph. A spiritual Book, *Academicus*, is a Call to as real and total a Death to the Life of corrupt Nature, as that which *Adam* died in Paradise, was to the Life of Heaven. He indeed died at once totally to the Divine Life in which he was created: But as our Body of Earth is to last to the End of our Lives; so to the End of our earthly Life, every Step we take, every Inch of our Road, is to be made up of Denial, and dying to ourselves; because all our Redemption consists in our regaining that first Life of Heaven in the Soul, to which *Adam* died in Paradise. And therefore the one single Work of Redemption, is the one single Work of Regeneration, or the raising up of a Life, and Spirit, and Tempers, and Inclinations, contrary to that Life and Spirit which we derive from our earthly fallen Parents. To think therefore of anything, but the continual, total Denial of our earthly Nature, is to overlook the very one thing on which all depends. And to hope for anything, to trust or pray for anything, but the *Life of God*, or a *Birth* of Heaven, in our Souls, is as useless to us, as placing our Hope and Trust in a graven Image. Thus saith the Christ of God the one Pattern, and Author of our Salvation: 'If any Man 'will be my Disciple, let him deny himself, hate his own Life, 'take up his daily Cross, and follow me.' And again: 'Unless 'a Man be born again from above, of Water and the Spirit, he 'cannot see, or enter into, the Kingdom of God.'

Now is your time, *Academicus*, to enter deeply into this great Truth. You are just come out of the Slumber of Life, and begin to see with new Eyes the Nature of your Salvation. You are charmed with the Discovery of a Kingdom of Heaven hidden within you, and long to be entertained more and more with the Nature, Progress, and Perfection of the new Birth, or the Opening of the Kingdom of God in your Soul.

But my Friend, stop a little. It is indeed great Joy, that the *Pearl of great Price* is found; but take notice, that it is not yours, you can have no Possession of it, till, as the Merchant did, *you sell all that you have*, and buy it. Now *Self* is all that you have, it is your sole Possession; you have no Goods of your *own*, nothing is yours but *this Self*. The Riches of *Self* are your *own Riches;* but *all this Self* is to be parted with before the Pearl is yours. Think of a lower Price, or be unwilling to give thus much for it, plead in your Excuse, that you keep the Commandments, and then you are that very rich young Man in the Gospel, who went away sorrowful from our Lord, when he had said, 'If thou wilt be perfect,' that is, if thou wilt obtain the Pearl, 'sell all that thou hast, and give to 'the Poor'; that is, die to all thy *Possession of Self*, and then thou hast given all that thou hast to the Poor ; all that thou hast is devoted and used for the Love of God and thy Neighbour. This selling all, *Academicus*, is the Measure of your dying to *Self;* all of it is to be given up; it is an *apostate* Nature, a *stolen* Life, brought forth in Rebellion against God : it is a continual Departure from him. It corrupts everything it touches ; it defiles everything it receives ; it turns all the Gifts and Blessings of God into Covetousness, Partiality, Pride, Hatred, and Envy. All these Tempers are born, and bred, and nourished, in *Self;* they have no other Place to live in, no Possibility of Existence, but in that Creature which is fallen from a Life in God, into a Life in *Self*.

Acad. Pray, Sir, tell me more plainly, what this Self is, since so much depends upon it.

Theoph. It is Hell, it is the Devil, it is Darkness, Pain, and Disquiet. It is the one only Enemy of Christ, the great Antichrist. It is the•Scarlet Whore, the fiery Dragon, the old Serpent, the devouring Beast, that is mentioned in the Revelation of St. *John.*

Acad. You rather terrify than instruct me, by this Description.

Theoph. It is indeed a very frightful Matter ; it contains everything that Man has to dread and hate, to resist and avoid. Yet be assured, my Friend, that, careless and merry as the World is, every Man that is born into it, has all these Enemies to overcome *within* himself. And every Man, till he is in the Way of Regeneration, is more or less governed by them. No Hell in any remote Place, no Devil that is separate from you, no Darkness or Pain that is not within you, no Antichrist either at *Rome* or *England*, no furious Beast, no fiery Dragon, without, or apart from you, can do you any Hurt. It is your own Hell, your own Devil, your own Beast, your own Antichrist, your own Dragon, that lives in your own Heart's Blood, that alone can hurt you.

Die to this Self, to this inward Nature ; and then all outward Enemies are overcome. Live to this Self, and then, when this Life is out, all that is within you, and all that is without you, will be nothing else but a mere seeing and feeling this Hell, Serpent, Beast, and fiery Dragon.

See here, *Academicus*, the twofold Nature of every Man. He has *within* him a redeeming Power, the *Meekness* of the heavenly Life, called the *Lamb of God.* This seed is surrounded, or encompassed, with the *Beast* of fleshly Lusts, the *Serpent* of Guile and Subtlety, and the *Dragon* of fiery Wrath. This is the great Trial, or Strife of human Life, whether a Man will live to the

Lusts of the *Beast*, the Guile of the *Serpent*, the Pride and Wrath of the *fiery Dragon*, or give himself up to the Meekness, the Patience, the Sweetness, the Simplicity, the Humility, of the *Lamb of God.*

This is the Whole of the Matter between God and the Creature. On one Side, Fire and Wrath, awakened first by the rebellious Angels; and on the other Side, the Meekness of the Lamb of God, the Patience of Divine Love coming down from Heaven, to stop and overcome the Fire and Wrath that is broken out in Nature and Creature. Your Father *Adam* has introduced you into the Fire and Wrath of the fallen Angels, into a World from whence Paradise is departed. Your Flesh and Blood is kindled in that Sin, which first brought forth a murdering *Cain*. But, dear Soul, be of good Comfort, for the *Meekness*, the *Love*, the *Heart*, the *Lamb* of God, is become Man, has set himself in the Birth of thy own Life, that in him, and with him, and by a Birth from him, Heaven and Paradise may be again opened both within thee, and without thee, not for a Time, but to all Eternity.

Once more, *Academicus*. Every Man in this World stands *essentially* in Heaven, and in Hell, both as to that which is within him and that which is without him: For Man and the World are both in the *same* fallen State. The *Curse* in the Earth is that *same thing* in outward Nature, that the *Loss* of the Divine Life was to the Soul of *Adam*. The whole World, in all its Nature, is nothing else but a *real Mixture* of Heaven and Hell. The Sun and the Water of this World, are what keep under and overcome the Darkness, Wrath, and Fire of Hell, and carry on the vegetable and animal Life that are in it. The Light of the Sun blesses all the Workings of the Elements, and the cool softening Essence of the Water, keeps under the Fire and Wrath of Nature. In all *animal* Creatures, the Birth of *Light* in their own Life, and the *Water* of their own Blood, both produced by the Light of the Sun, and the Water of outward Nature, bring forth an Order of earthly Creatures, that can enjoy the Good that is in this World, in Spite of the Wrath of Hell, and the Malice of Devils.

But Man has more than all this; for being at first created an Angel, and intended by the Mercy of God to be an Angel again, he has the *Light* of Heaven, and the *Water* of eternal Life, both given to *Adam* in that *Seed of the Woman*, which was to *bruise* the Head of the Serpent that is, to overcome the Curse, the Fire, and Wrath, or Hell, that was awakened in the fallen Soul. So that Man has not only, in common with the other Animals, the Light and Water of outward Nature, to quench the Wrath of his own Life in this mixed World, but he has the Meekness, the Light, the Love, the Humility of the Holy Jesus, as a Seed of

Life born in his Soul, to bring forth that first Image of God, in which *Adam* was created. This, my Friend, is the true Ground of all true Religion : It means nothing, it intends nothing, but to overcome that *earthly Life*, which overcame *Adam* in the Fall, that made him a Prisoner of Hell, and a Slave to the corrupt Workings of earthly Flesh and Blood. And therefore you may see, and know with a mathematical Certainty, that the one thing necessary for every fallen Soul, is to die to all the Life that we have from this World, and the Life of Heaven may be born again in him. The Life of this World is the Life of the *Beast*, the *Scarlet Whore*, the old *Serpent* and the *fiery Dragon*.

Hence it is that Sin rides in Triumph over Church and State, and from the Court to the Cottage all is over-run with Sensuality, Guile, Falseness, Pride, Wrath, Envy, Selfishness, and every form of Corruption. Everyone swims away in this Torrent, but he who hears and attends to the *Voice* of the Son of God *within* him, calling him to die to this Life, to take up his Cross, and follow him. Much learned Pains has been often taken to prove *Rome*, or *Constantinople*, to be the Seat of the Beast, the Antichrist, the Scarlet Whore, *&c*. But, alas! they are not at such a Distance from us, they are the Properties of fallen human Nature, and are all of them alive in our own Selves, till we are dead or dying to all the Spirit and Tempers of this World. They are everywhere, in every Soul, where the heavenly Nature, and Spirit of the Holy Jesus is not. But when the human Soul turns from itself, and turns to God, dies to itself, and lives to God in the Spirit, Tempers, and Inclinations of the Holy Jesus, loving, pitying, suffering, and praying for all its Enemies, and overcoming all Evil with Good, as this Christ of God did ; then, but not till then, are these Monsters separate from it. For Covetousness and Sensuality of all kinds, are the very devouring *Beast;* Religion governed by a worldly, trading Spirit, and gratifying the partial Interest of Flesh and Blood, is nothing else but the *Scarlet Whore ;* Guile, and Craft, and Cunning, are the very Essence of the *old Serpent ;* Self-Interest and Self-Exaltation are the whole Nature of *Antichrist*. Pride, Persecution, Wrath, Hatred and Envy, are the very Essence of the *fiery Dragon.*

This, *Academicus*, is the fallen human Nature, and this is the *old Man*, which is alive in everyone, though in various Manners, till he is born again from above. To think therefore of anything in Religion, or to pretend to real Holiness, without totally dying to this old Man, is building Castles in the Air, and can bring forth nothing, but *Satan* in the Form of an Angel of Light. Would you know, *Academicus*, whence it is, that so many false Spirits have appeared in the World, who have deceived themselves and others with false Fire, and false Light, laying Claim to Inspirations, Illuminations, and Openings of the Divine Life, pretending to do Wonders under extraordinary Calls from God? It is this; they have turned to God without turning from themselves; would be alive in God, before they were dead to their own Nature; a thing as impossible in itself, as for a Grain of Wheat to be alive before it dies.

Now Religion in the Hands of Self, or corrupt Nature, serves only to discover Vices of a worse kind, than in Nature left to itself. Hence are all the disorderly Passions of religious Men, which burn in a worse Flame than Passions only employed about worldly Matters: Pride, Self-Exaltation, Hatred, and Persecution, under a Cloak of religious Zeal, will sanctify Actions, which Nature, left to itself, would be ashamed to own.

You may now see, *Academicus*, with what great Reason I have called you, at your first setting out, to this great Point, the *total dying to Self*, as the only Foundation of a solid Piety. All the fine Things you hear or read of an inward and spiritual Life in God, all your Expectations of the Light and Holy Spirit of God, will become a false Food to your Soul, till you only seek for them through Death to Self.

Observe, Sir, the Difference which Clothes make in those, who have it in their Power to dress as they please: Some are all for Show, Colours, and Glitter; others are quite fantastical and affected in their Dress; Some have a grave and solemn Habit; others are quite simple and plain in their whole manner. Now all this Difference of Dress, is only an outward Difference, that covers the same poor Carcase, and leaves it full of all its own Infirmities. Now all the Truths of the Gospel, when only embraced and possessed by the *old Man*, make only such superficial Difference, as is made by Clothes. Some put on a solemn, formal, prudent, outside Carriage; others appear in all the Glitter and Show of religious Colouring, and spiritual Attainments; but under all this outside Difference, there lies the poor fallen Soul, imprisoned, unhelped, in its own fallen State. And thus it must be, it is not possible to be otherwise, till the spiritual Life begins at the true Root, grows out of *Death*, and is born in a broken Heart, a Heart broken off from all its own natural Life. Then Self-hatred, Self-contempt, and Self-denial, are as suitable to this new-born Spirit, as Self-love, Self-esteem, and Self-seeking, are to the unregenerate Man. Let me, therefore, my Friend, conjure you, not to look forward, or cast about for spiritual Advancement, till you have rightly taken this *first* Step in the spiritual Life. All your future Progress depends upon it: For this Depth of Religion goes no deeper than the Depth of your Malady: For Sin has its Root in the Bottom of your Soul, it comes to Life with your Flesh and Blood, and breathes in the Breath of your natural Life; and therefore, till you die to Nature, you live to Sin ; and whilst this Root of Sin is alive in you, all the Virtues you put on, are only like fine painted Fruit hung upon a bad Tree.

Acad. Indeed, *Theophilus,* you have made the Difference between true and false Religion as plain to me, as the Difference between Light and Darkness. But all that you have said, at the same time, is as new to me, as if I had lived in a Land, where Religion had never been named. But pray, Sir, tell me how I am to take this *first Step,* which you so much insist upon.

Theop. You are to turn wholly from yourself, and to give up yourself wholly unto God, in this or the like twofold Form of Words or Thoughts:

'Oh my God, with all the Strength of my Soul, assisted by
'thy Grace, I desire and resolve to resist and deny all my own
'Will, earthly Tempers, selfish Views, and Inclinations ; every-
'thing that the Spirit of this World, and the Vanity of fallen
'Nature, prompts me to. I give myself up wholly and solely
'unto Thee, to be all thine, to have, and do, and be, inwardly
'and outwardly, according to thy good Pleasure. I desire to
'live for no other Ends, with no other Designs, but to accom-
'plish the Work which thou requirest of me, an humble, obedient,
'faithful, thankful Instrument in thy Hands to be used as thou
'pleasest.'

You are not to content yourself, my Friend, with now and then, or even many times, making this Oblation of yourself to God. It must be the daily, the hourly Exercise of your Mind ; till it is wrought into your very Nature, and becomes an essential State and Habit of your Mind, till you feel yourself as habitually turned from all your own Will, selfish Ends, and earthly Desires, as you are from Stealing and Murder ; till the whole Turn and Bent of your Spirit points as constantly to God, as the Needle touched with the Loadstone does to the North. This, Sir, is your first and necessary Step in the spiritual Life; this is the Key to all the Treasures of Heaven ; this unlocks the sealed Book of your Soul, and makes room for the Light and Spirit of God to arise up in it. Without this, the spiritual Life is but spiritual Talk, and only assists Nature to be pleased with an Holiness that it has not.

The Necessity of this first Step, and the Folly of pretending to succeed without it, is thus represented by our blessed Lord : ' What Man intending to build a house,' *&c.*

All our Ability and Preparation to succeed in this great Affair, lie in this *first Step*. You may perhaps think this an hard Saying. But do not go away sorrowful, like the young Man in the Gospel, because he had great Possessions. For, my Friend, you little think what a Deliverance you will have from all Hardships, and what a Flow of Happiness is found even in this Life, as soon as the Soul is *thus* dead to *Self*, freed from its own Passions, and wholly given up to God ; of which I shall speak to you by and by. I have told you the Price of the new Birth. I shall now leave you to consider, whether you will be so wise a Merchant, as to give up all the Wealth of the old Man for this heavenly Pearl. I do not expect your Answer now, but will stay for it till To-morrow.

But pray, Gentlemen, who is this *Humanus ?* I do not remember to have seen him before : He seems not willing to speak, yet is often biting his Lips at what is said.

Rust. This *Humanus*, Sir, is my Neighbour ; but so ignorant of the Nature of the Gospel, that he is often trying to persuade me into a Disbelief of it. I say ignorant (though he is a learned man) because I am well assured, that no Man ever did, or can oppose the Gospel, but through a total Ignorance of what it is in itself: For the Gospel, when rightly understood, is irresistible; it brings more good News to the human Nature, than Sight to the Blind, Limbs to the Lame, Health to the Sick, or Liberty to the condemned Slave. But this Neighbour of mine has never yet been in Sight of the Truth, as it is in the Gospel ; he knows nothing of the Grounds and Reason of it, but what he has picked up out of Books, that have been written against it, and for it. He often makes use of one Maxim of the Gospel, to overthrow it, and wonders that so plain and honest a Man as I am, will not submit to it. He says, if it be a Truth, as the Gospel saith, ' That the Tree must be known by its Fruit, and that a good Tree ' cannot bring forth corrupt Fruit,' we need only look at the Lives of Christians, the Craft of Priests, the Wars, Contentions, Hatreds, Sects, Parties, Heresies, Divisions, Outrages, and Persecutions, which Christianity has brought forth, we need only look at this, to have all our Senses and Reason assure us, that the Gospel must be a bad Tree.

But this is enough concerning the Man. He comes with me at his own earnest Desire, which has lately seized him, and upon his own strict Promise, not to interrupt our Conversation ; but to be a silent Hearer, till it is all over. And therefore, if you please, Sir, I beg our Conversation may for awhile turn upon the chief Points asserted in the Spirit of Prayer, for two Reasons ; first, that *Academicus* may see what Reasons I had for saying, that Book had given me a sufficient Instruction ; and also that

Humanus, hearing these great Points, may hear the whole Ground and Nature, the Necessity and Blessedness of the Christian Redemption, set forth in such a Degree of Light, and Truth, and Amiableness, as he had no Notion of before.

Theoph. Your Neighbour is welcome, and I pray God to give him an Heart attentive to those Truths, which have made so good an Impression upon you. The first Point that you desire us to speak to, is concerning the Original of this temporal World. How God was moved to create it, upon the Fall of a whole Host, or Kingdom of Angels, who, by their Revolt from God, lost the Divine Light, and awakened in themselves, and the Region in which they dwelt, the dark, wrathful Fire of Hell: For Hell is nothing else, but Nature departed, or excluded, from the Beams of Divine Light. The *Materiality* of their Kingdom was *spiritual*, and the Light that glanced through it, that filled its Transparency with an Infinity of glorious Wonders, was the Son of God, the Brightness of the Father's Glory. The *Spirit* that animated the inward Life of those glorious Angels, and that moved with its sweet Breath, through all this *glassy Sea*, opening and changing new Scenes in the Mirror of Divine Wisdom, was the *Holy Spirit* of God, that eternally proceeds from the Father and the Son. Thus did these celestial Spirits live, move, and have their Being, in God. All was Heaven, and they all were so many created Gods, eternally sinking down, and rising up, into new Heights and Depths of the Riches of the Divine Nature. With this Degree of Glory and Happiness was the whole Extent of the Place of this World filled, before the Angels fell: and to this Degree of Happiness, and heavenly Glory, will the whole Place of this World be again raised, when the Love of God shall have finished the great Work of the Redemption of Mankind. Heaven again, and Angels again, raised out of the Misery of Time, to sing eternal Praises to the Holy Trinity, and to the Lamb that has overcome Sin, and Death, and Hell, and turned all the Wrath, and Misery and Darkness of this World, into an Heaven never more to be changed. Oh *Rusticus*, what Sentiments do these Things raise in you?

Rust. Indeed, Sir, they almost make me to forget, that I am in the Body. You have set me upon a Mountain, from which, whether I look backwards, or forwards, or downwards, all is equally surprising: backwards, a Breach made in Heaven, the first Opening of Hell and Darkness, and a new Creation out of the Ruins of the fallen Angels; forwards, Time and all temporal Nature rising again into its first Eternity; downwards, a Globe of Earth, the Seat of War between Heaven and Hell, where Men are born to partake of the dreadful Strife, and have only the little Span of Life, either to overcome with God, or be overcome by the Devil. Oh, Sir, what great things are these? I wish that all the World, as well as my Neighbour *Humanus*, were forced to be silent Hearers of them. But pray, Sir, go on.

Theoph. When God saw the *Darkness that was upon the Face of the Deep*, and the whole angelic Habitation become a Chaos of Confusion, the *Spirit of God moved upon the Face of the Waters;* that is, the Spirit of God began to operate again in this outward Darkness, that covered this once transparent *glassy Sea;* for from a glassy Sea it was become a Deep covered with Darkness, which was soon to take another Nature; to have its Fire and Wrath converted into Sun and Stars; its Dross and Darkness into a Globe of Earth; its Mobility and Moisture into Air and Water; when the Spirit of God began to move and operate in it. But before this Chaos had entered into this new Order, God said, 'Let there be Light; and there was Light.' This Light, my Friend, was not the present Light of this World, which now governs the Night and the Day; for the Sun, the Moon, and Stars, were not created till the fourth Day. But the Light which God then spoke forth, was a Degree of Heaven, that was commanded to glance into the darkened Deep, which penetrated through all the Depth of the Chaos, and intermixed itself through every Part; not turning the Whole into a Region of Light, but only by its quickening Virtue fitting, disposing, and preparing every Part to take that Change, which every following Day of the Creation was to bring forth, in and out of this darkened Deep: For Darkness is Death, and Light is Life. This was the Nature and Work of that first Light, which God called forth on the first Day: It was God's baptizing the dead *Chaos* with the Spirit of Life, that it might be capable of a Resurrection into a new Creation.

See here the Uniformity of the Divine Procedure, with regard both to fallen Nature and Creature. When the Creature (Man) was fallen, his Redemption was begun by God's speaking a *Seed* of Light, called the Seed of the Woman, into the Birth of his Life. This alone could qualify him for the new Creation in Christ Jesus. When *Nature* was fallen, its Restoration was begun in the same Manner: Light was commanded to enter into it, or rather to rise up in it: This was its Power or Possibility of coming out of its fallen State.

Marvel not, *Rusticus*, that I call this first Light of the first Day, a Degree of Heaven: For Light is natural, essential, and inseparable from heaven; it belongs only to Heaven; and wherever else it is, it is only there as a Gift from Heaven. And therefore so much as there is of Light in this World, so much there is of Heaven in it. Darkness is natural, essential, and inseparable from Hell; and can be nowhere else, but where Hell can in some Degree open and discover itself. And wherever, and in what Degree, Darkness can show itself; there, and in the same Degree, is the Nature of Hell known and felt. This World is made up of Light and Darkness, not only as it consists of Day and Night, but because every earthly thing is itself a *Mixture* of Light and Darkness. The Darkness is the Evil, and the Light is the Good, that is in everything. If the Darkness was predominant in Vegetables, they would all be rank Poison; if in Animals, they would be all as so many wrathful venomous Serpents of Hell. If the Light did quite suppress the Darkness in Vegetables, they would be like the Fruits which were to have been Man's Food in Paradise.

Rust. These Things, *Theophilus*, strike a most amazing Light into all the Mysteries both of Nature and Grace. But they do not more enlighten, than they edify the Mind. They are all reforming Truths; they have the Nature of Alteratives, they purge the Heart of all its Dross; they force it to drop all its Pretentions to earthly things, as the poor deceitful Baits of fallen Nature; and to long for nothing, but to have That first Heaven and Life in God, for which Angels and Men were at first created. But I want to show to my Friend *Humanus*, as it were in one View, that Chain of Truths, which follows from what you have said: Though I had rather you would do it.

Theoph. Agreed: And I will set them in order thus. First, That the Place of this World is the very Place, or Region, which belonged to *Lucifer*, and his Angels. Secondly, That everything that we see in this World, all its Elements, the Stars, the Firmament, &c., are nothing else but the invisible Things of the fallen World, made visible in a new and lower State of Existence. Thirdly, That before the Rebellion of the Angels there was nothing but God, and Heaven, and heavenly Beings. Light, and Love, and Joy, and Glory, with all the Wonders thereof, were the only things seen and felt by the Angels. Darkness and Fire, with every Quality thereof, were absolutely unknown to the Angels; they had no more Suspicion of them, than of the Possibility of Sickness, Pains, Heat, and Cold. All they aimed at, was at being higher in the Glories, and Powers, and Light, of that Heaven in which they lived. But their turning to their own Strength to effect this, was their whole turning from God, and a falling into Nature without God, which was the first Discovery of *Darkness*, Wrath, and Fire, and Pain, and Torment. Fourthly, Hence it appears, that *Darkness* is the *Ground* of the Substance, or Materiality of Nature; *Fire* is its Life; and *Light*

The Spirit of Prayer.

is its glorious Transmutation into the Kingdom of Heaven; and *Spirit* is the Opener of all its Wonders. All that can be conceived, is either God, or Nature, or Creature; God is the Holy Trinity *without*, or *before* Nature; but Nature is the Manifestation of the Holy Trinity in a triune Life of *Fire, Light*, and *Spirit*.

Fifthly. Here we see the plain and true Original of all Evil, without any Perplexity, or Imputation upon God: That Evil is nothing else but the Wrath, and Fire, and Darkness of Nature broken off from God: That the Punishment, the Pain, or the Hell of Sin, is no designedly prepared, or arbitrary Penalty inflicted by God, but the natural and necessary State of the Creature, that leaves, or turns from God. Sixthly, That the Will of the Creature is the only Opener of all Evil or Good in the Creature; the Will stands between God and Nature, and must in all its Workings unite either with God, or Nature: The Will totally resigned, and given up to God, is one Spirit with God, and God dwelleth in it; the Will turned from God, is taken Prisoner in the Wrath, Fire, and Darkness of Nature.

Seventhly. Here we see, *how* and *why* a Creature can lose, and die to all its Happiness and Perfection, and, from a beauteous Angel become a deformed Devil. It is because Nature has no Beauty, Happiness, or Perfection, but solely from the *Manifestation* or *Birth* of the Holy Trinity in it. God manifested in Nature, is the only Blessing, Happiness, and Perfection of Nature. Therefore the Creature, that in the Working of its Will is turned from God, must have as great a Change brought forth in it, as that of Heaven into Hell, forced to live, but to have no other Life, but that of its own gnawing Worm left to itself.

Eighthly. Hence we see the deep Ground, and absolute Necessity, of the Christian Redemption, by a Birth from above, of the Light and Spirit of God, demonstrated in the most absolute Degree of Certainty. It is because all Nature is in itself nothing, but an *hungry wrathful Fire* of Life, a tormenting Darkness, unless the Light and Spirit of God kindle it into a Kingdom of Heaven. And therefore the fallen Soul can have no *possible Relief*, or Redemption, it must be, to all Eternity, an *hungry, dark, fiery, tormenting* Spirit of Life, unless the Light, or Son, and Spirit of God, be born again in it.

Hence also it follows, that in all the Possibility of Things, there is and can be but one Happiness, and one Misery. The one Misery, is Nature and Creature left to itself; the one Happiness, is the Life, the Light, and Spirit of God, manifested in Nature and Creature. This is the true Meaning of those

Words of our Lord, 'There is but one that is good, and that is 'God.'

Ninthly. Hence it is also seen, that there is and can be but *one true* Religion for the fallen Soul, and that is, the Dying to *Self*, to *Nature* and *Creature;* and a turning with all the *Will,* the *Desire,* and *Delight* of the Soul to God. Sacrifices, Oblations, Prayers, Praises, Rites, and Ceremonies, without this, are but as sounding Brass, and tinkling Cymbals. Nay, Zeal, and Constancy, and Warmth, and Fervour, in the Performance of these religious Practices, is not the Matter; for Nature and Self-love can do all this. But these religious Practices are then only Parts of true Religion, when they mean nothing, seek nothing, but to keep up a continual Dying to Self, and all worldly things, and turn all the Will, Desire, and Delight of the Soul to God alone. *Lastly,* There is and can be only *one* Salvation for the fallen Soul, and that is Heaven opened again in the Soul, by the Birth of such a Life, Light, and Spirit, as is born in Angels. For *Adam* was created to possess that Heaven from which the Angels fell; but nothing can enter into Heaven, but the angelic Life, which is born of Heaven. The Loss of this angelic Life was the Fall of *Adam,* or that Death which he died, on the Day he did eat of the earthly Fruit; therefore the Regeneration, or new Birth of his first angelic Life, is the one only Salvation of the fallen Soul. Ask not therefore, whether we are saved by Faith, or by Works? for we are saved by neither of them. Faith and Works are at first only *preparatory* to the new Birth; afterwards they are the true *genuine Fruits* and Effects of it. But the new Birth, a Life from Heaven, the new Creature, called *Christ in us,* is the one only Salvation of the fallen Soul. Nothing can enter into Heaven, but this Life which is born of, and comes from Heaven.

Rust. I thank you, *Theophilus,* for setting these awakening Truths in so strong a Light. And I think it is not possible for my Friend *Humanus* to be unaffected with them.

They must needs open in him a new Way of thinking about Religion, and show him the deep and solid Ground of the absolute Necessity of the Christian Redemption, and incline him to be a willing Hearer of that which follows.

Theoph. I hope it will be so, *Rusticus;* and what I would here, and through every Point we speak of, observe to your Friend *Humanus,* is this: That the Christian Religion is the *one only* true *Religion of Nature,* deeply and necessarily founded in the *Nature* of Things; that its Doctrines are not founded in an *arbitrary Appointment* of God, but have their *natural* and *necessary* Reason, why they cannot be otherwise, as has here been shown in the one great Point of Regeneration, which is the Whole of Man's Salvation, and the one only thing intended by all Revelation, from the Fall of Man to the End of the World. Now the true Ground of the one true Religion of Nature cannot be known, or seen into, but by going back to the Beginning of Things, and showing how they came into their present State. We must find out, *why* and *how* Religion came to be necessary, and on *what* its Necessity is founded. Now this cannot be done, unless we find out, what *Sin*, and *Evil*, and *Death*, and *Darkness*, are in themselves; and how they came into Nature and Creature. For this alone can show us, what Religion is *true*, is *natural*, is *necessary*, and alone sufficient to remove all Evil, Sin, and Disorder, out of the Creation. For this Reason, we began with the Grounds and Reasons of the Creation of this World, showing how it came to be as it is. But this could not be done, but by going so far back as the Fall of Angels. For it was their Revolting from God, that brought *Wrath*, and *Fire*, and *Thickness*, and *Darkness*, and *Death*, into Nature and Creature; and so gave occasion to this new Creation, and to its being in such a State, and of such a Nature, as it is.

For who does not see, that this first Deadness, Thickness, Wrath, Fire, and Darkness, caused by the Angels' Sin, are the very *Materials* out of which this World is made? For are not the Fire, the Air, the Water, the Earth, the Rocks and Stones of this World, the Rage of Heat and Cold, the Succession of Day and Night, the Wrath of Storms and Tempests, an undeniable and daily Proof of all this? Now when we thus see what Sin, and Evil, and Death, and Darkness, are in Nature, and how they came into it, then we see also, how and what they are, and how they came into the Creature; because the Creature has its Form, its Being, in and out of Nature. They came into Nature, or rose up in it, by Nature's being broken off from God, and so losing the Light and Spirit of God, which made it to be a Kingdom of Heaven; we see also, that when this disordered Nature was to be taken out of its fallen State by a new Creation, that, to do this, the *Spirit of God moved*, or entered again into the Darkness of the Waters, and the *Light* of God was called into it. A plain Proof, that the Malady of Nature, was nothing else but *its Loss of the Light* and *Spirit* of God working in it. This shows us also, that the fallen Creature is to be restored, or put into a Way of Recovery, in *one and the same* Way as fallen Nature; *viz.*, by the *Spirit*, and *Light* of God *entering* into it again, and bringing forth a new Birth, or Creation in Christ Jesus. Just as the Spirit and Light entering into the *Chaos*, created or turned the Angels' ruined Kingdom into a Paradise on Earth. God help him, who can see no Light or Truth here! Your Friend *Humanus* lays claim to a Religion of Nature and Reason : I join with him, with all my Heart. No other Religion can be right, but that which has its Foundation in Nature. For the God of Nature can require nothing of his Creatures, but what the *State* of their Nature calls them to. Nature is his great Law, that speaks his whole Will both in Heaven and on Earth ; and to obey Nature, is to obey the God of Nature, to please him, and live to him, in the highest Perfection. God indeed has many *After-laws;* but it is after his Creatures have fallen from Nature, and lost its Perfection. But all these After-laws have no other End or Intention, but to repair Nature, and bring Men back to their first natural State of Perfection. What say you now, *Academicus*, to all these Matters?

Acad. You, Sir, and *Rusticus*, both of you know, how these Matters have affected me, ever since I read the Book called *The Appeal to all that Doubt, &c.* From that Time, I have stood upon new Ground ; I have seen things in such a Newness of Light and Reality, as makes me take my former Knowledge for a Dream. A Dream I may justly call it, since all my Labour was taken up in searching into a Seventeen hundred Years History of Doctrines, Disputes, Decrees, Heresies, Schisms, and Sects, wherever to be found, in *Europe, Asia,* and *Africa.* From this goodly Heap of Stuff crowded into my Mind, I have been settling Matters betwixt all the present Christian Divisions both at home and abroad, according to the best Rules of Criticism ; having little or no other Idea of a religious Man, than that of a stiff Maintainer of certain Points against all those that oppose them. And in this respect, I believe I may say, that I only swam away in the common Torrent.

And in this laborious Dream I had in all Likelihood ended my Days, had not that Book, and some others of the like kind, shown me, that Religion lay nearer home, was not to be dug out of Disputes, but lay hid in myself, like a Seed, which, for want of its proper Nourishment, could not come to the Birth. But however, though Matters stand thus with myself, and I seem to be entered into a Region of Light, yet I must not forget to tell you, what some of my learned Friends object to all this. They say, that in those Books, there are many Things asserted, which have not the *plain Letter* of Scripture to support them ; and therefore Men of sober Learning, are cautious of giving into Opinions, not strictly grounded on the plain Letter of Scripture, however fine and plausible they may seem to be.

Theoph. Is there not some Reason, *Academicus*, to take this Objection of your learned Friends to be a mere Pretence? For what is more fully grounded upon the plain Letter of Scripture, than the Doctrine of a real Regeneration, a new Birth of the *Word*, the *Son*, and *Holy Spirit* of God, really brought forth in the Soul? And yet this *plain Letter* of Scripture, upon the most important of all Points, the very *Life*, and *Essence*, and whole Nature of our Redemption, is not only *overlooked*, but openly *opposed*, by the Generality of Men of sober Learning. But this Point, has not only the plain Letter of Scripture for it, but what the Letter asserts, is absolutely required by the whole Spirit and Tenor of the New Testament. All the Epistles of the Apostles proceed upon the supposed Certainty of this one great Point.

A Son of God, united with, and born in our Nature, that his Nature may have a Birth in us; an Holy Spirit, breathing in the Birth and Life of our Souls, quickening the dead Life of fallen *Adam*, is the Letter and Spirit of the Apostles' Writings; grounded upon the plain Letter of our Lord's own Words, that unless we are born again from above, of the Son, Word, Water, and Spirit of God, we cannot enter or see the Kingdom of Heaven.

Again: Is it not the plain Letter of Scripture, that *Adam* died the Day that he did eat of the earthly Tree? Have we not the most solemn Asseveration of God for the Truth of this? Was not the Change which *Adam* found in himself a Demonstration of the Truth of this Fact? Instead of the Image and Likeness of God in which he was created, the Beauty of Paradise, he was stripped of all his Glory, confounded at the shameful Deformity of his own Body, afraid of being seen, and unable to see himself uncovered; delivered up a Slave to a Rage of all the Stars and Elements of this World, not knowing which Way to look, or what to do in a World, where he was dead to all that he formerly felt, and alive only to a new and dreadful Feeling of Heat and Cold, Shame and Fear, and horrible Remorse of Mind, at his sad Entrance into a World, whence Paradise, and God, and his own Glory, were departed. Death enough surely!

Death in its highest Reality, much greater in its Change, than when an Animal of earthly Flesh and Blood is only changed into a cold lifeless Carcase.

A Death, that in all Nature had none like it, none equal to it, none of the same Nature with it, but that which the Angels died, when, from Angels of God, they became living Devils, serpentine, hideous Forms, and Slaves to Darkness. Say that the Angels lost no Life, that they did not die a real Death, because they are yet alive in the Horrors of Darkness, and then you may say, with the same Truth, that *Adam* did not die, when he lost God, and Paradise, and the first Glory of his Creation, because he afterwards lived and breathed in a World which was outwardly, in all its Parts, full of the same Curse that was within himself. But further, not only the plain Letter of the Text, and the Change of State, which *Adam* found in himself, demonstrated a *real Death* to his former State; but the whole Tenor of Scripture absolutely requires it; all the System of our Redemption proceeds upon it. For tell me, I pray, What need of a Redemption, if *Adam* had not lost his first State of Life? What Need of the Deity to enter again into the human Nature, not only as acting, but taking a Birth in it, and from it? What need of all this mysterious Method, to bring the Life *from above* again into Man, if the Life from above had not been *lost?* Say that *Adam* did not die, and then tell me, what Sense or Reason there is in saying, that the Son of God became Man, and died on the Cross to restore to him the Life that he had lost? It is true indeed, that *Adam*, in his Death to the Divine Life, was left in the Possession of an earthly Life. And the Reason is plain why he was so: For his great Sin consisted in his Desire and Longing to enter into the Life of this World, to know its Good and Evil, as the Animals of this World do; it was his choosing to have a Life of this World after this *new Manner*, and his entering upon the Means of attaining it, that was his Death to the Divine Life. And therefore it is no Wonder, that after his Death to Heaven and Paradise, he found himself *still alive* as an earthly Animal. For the Desire of this earthly Life was his *great Sin*, and the *Possession* of this earthly Life was the proper Punishment and Misery that belonged to his Sin; and therefore it is no Wonder that *that Life*, which was the proper Punishment, and real Discovery of the Fruits of his Sin, should subsist, after his Sin had put an End to the Life of Paradise and God in him. But wonderful it is to a great Degree, that any Man should imagine, that *Adam* did not die on the Day of his Sin, because he had as good a Life left in him, as the Beasts of the Field have.

For is this *the Life* or is *the Death* that such Animals die, the Life and Death with which our Redemption is concerned? Are not all the Scriptures full of a Life and Death of a much higher Kind and Nature? And do not the Scriptures make Man the perpetual Subject to whom this *higher* Life and Death belong? What Ground or Reason therefore can there be to think of the Death of an Animal of this World, when we read of the Death, that *Adam* was assuredly to die the Day of his Sin? For does not all that befel him on the Day of his Sin, show that he lost a much greater Life, suffered a more dreadful

Change, than that of giving up the Breath of this World ? For in the Day of his Sin, this Angel of Paradise, this Lord of the new Creation, fell from the Throne of his Glory (like *Lucifer* from Heaven) into the State of a poor, darkened, naked, distressed Animal of gross Flesh and Blood, unable to bear the odious Sight of that which his new-opened Eyes forced him to see ; inwardly and outwardly feeling the Curse awakened in himself, and all the Creation, and reduced to have only the Faith of the Devils, to *believe* and *tremble.* Proof enough, surely, that *Adam* was dead to the Life, and Light, and Spirit of God ; and that, with this Death, all that was *Divine* and *heavenly* in his Soul, his Body, his Eyes, his Mind, and Thoughts, was quite at an End. Now *this* Life to which *Adam* then died, is *that* Life which all his Posterity are in want of, and cannot come out of that State of that Death into which he fell, but by having *this first* Life of Heaven born again in them. Now is there any Reason to say, that Mankind, in their Natural State, are not dead to that first Life in which *Adam* was created, because they are alive to this World ? Yet this is as well as to say, that *Adam* did not die a real Death, because he had afterwards an earthly Life in him. How comes our Lord to say, that ' unless ' ye eat the Flesh, and drink the Blood, of the Son of Man, ye ' have no Life in you ?' Did he mean, ye have no earthly Life in you ? How comes the Apostle to say, ' He that hath the Son ' of God has Life, but he that hath not the Son of God hath ' not Life ?' Does he mean the Life of this World ? No. But both Christ and his Apostle assert this great Truth, that all Mankind are in the State of *Adam's first Death,* till they are made alive again, by a Birth of the *Son,* and *Holy Spirit* of God brought forth in them. So plain is it, both from the express Letter, and Spirit of Scripture, that *Adam* died a *real Death* to the Kingdom of God in the Day of his Sin. Take away this Death, and all the Scheme of our Redemption has no Ground left to stand upon.

Judge now, *Academicus,* Who leaves the Letter of Scripture, your learned Friends, or the Author of the *Appeal?* They leave it, they oppose it, in that which is the *very Life* of Christianity.

For without the *Reality* of a new Birth, founded on the Certainty of a *real Death* in the Fall of *Adam,* the Christian Scheme is but a Skeleton of empty Words, a Detail of strange Mysteries between God and Man, that do nothing, and have nothing to do.

On the other hand, look now at the things set forth in the *Appeal,* concerning the Fall of Angels, the Nature and Effects of their Revolt, and the Creation of this World as deduced therefrom. They neither *leave,* nor *oppose* any Letter, or Doctrine of

Scripture. They add nothing to Religion, but the *full Proof* of all its Articles; they intend nothing but to open the *original Ground*, and true Reason, of the Christian Redemption, and the absolute Necessity of its being such, as the Gospel declares. Now the *Letter* of Scripture does not do this in open Words; it sets not forth the *why*, and *how* things are, either in Nature or Grace; it teaches not the *Ground* or *Philosophy* of the Christian Faith; it contents itself with bare *Facts* and *Doctrines*, and calls for *simple* Faith and Obedience. No Wonder therefore, that when the *natural* and *necessary* Ground of the Christian Redemption is *opened*, that the Letter of Scripture is not *Step* by *Step* appealed to, for everything that is said. And yet many things may be sufficiently grounded on Scripture, that are not so expressed in the *Letter*. The *Sadducees* denied, that there was any Resurrection at all; and this they did, because they could not find it in the *express Letter* of the Five Books of *Moses*. And yet it seems, that the Resurrection was *plainly* and *strongly* taught there: For thus saith our Lord,—That the Dead shall rise again, *Moses* showed at the Bush, when he said, 'The Lord 'is the God of Abraham, Isaac, *&c*. For he is not the God of 'the Dead, but of the Living.'* This shows us that a thing may be fully and sufficiently proved from Scripture, which is not plainly expressed in the Letter. And thus stands the Matter with regard to those great, and edifying Truths set forth in the *Appeal*. They are *truly scriptural*, they have their *Ground* and *Authority* from Scripture, though not so open and express in the Letter, as Matters of Faith and necessary Doctrine are. For is not the Fall of Angels a Scripture-Truth? Is not the Desolation which their Fall brought into Nature, and the very Place of this World a Scripture-Truth? What else can be meant by *Darkness upon the Face of the Deep?* What Darkness, or what Deep, but in the Place of this World? What Darkness, or State of the Deep, but that, which God was about to raise out of its disordered State? And does not the Letter of Scripture show, that out of *this Darkness and Waters*, and State of the Deep, the Spirit and Light of God entering into them, brought forth the Earth, the Stars, the Sun, and all the Elements, into a Form of a new World?

To ask for a particular Text of Scripture, saying in so many express Words, that the Place of this World is the very Place and Extent of the Kingdom of the fallen Angels, is quite ridiculous, and without the least Ground in Reason, as is enough shown in the *Appeal*. For does not our Lord expressly call the *Devil*,

---

* Luke xx. 37, 38.

a Prince of this World? But how could this Name belong to him, but because he is here in his own *first Region* and *Territories*, and has still some Power, till all the Evil that he has raised in it, shall be entirely separated from it? For was not this World raised out of the *Materials* of the fallen Angels' Kingdom, and was not the Wrath, and Fire, and Darkness *of their Fall*, still in some Degree remaining in every Part of this World, they could have *no more* Power in it, than they have in Heaven; they must be as entirely incapable of seeing or entering into it, as they are of seeing or entering into the Kingdom of Heaven: For they have nothing but Evil in their Nature; they can touch nothing, move nothing, see nothing, feel nothing, taste nothing, act in nothing, but *that very* Evil, Darkness, Fire, and Wrath, and Disorder, which they first awakened and kindled both in themselves, and their Kingdom. And therefore it is a Truth of the utmost Certainty, that they can be nowhere, but where there is something of *that* Evil still subsisting which they brought forth. And this may pass for Demonstration (if there be any such thing) that the Scriptures themselves *demonstrate* the Place of this World, to be the *very* Place and Region in which the Angels fell. And they still are *here*, because their Kingdom is not *wholly* delivered from all the Evil they had raised in it, but is to stand for a Time, only in a State of Recovery, where they themselves must see, in spite of all the Rage and Malice of their fiery Darts, that the *Mystery* of a Lamb of God, born upon Earth, will raise Creatures of Flesh and Blood, amidst the Ruins of their spoiled Kingdom, to be an Host of Angels in Heaven restored, and themselves plunged into an Hell, that is cut off from everything, but their *own* Wrath, Fire, and Darkness. And all this, *Academicus*, to make it known through all the Regions of Eternity, that *Pride* can degrade the highest Angels into Devils, and *Humility* raise fallen Flesh and Blood to the Thrones of Angels. This, this is the *great End* of God's raising a new Creation, out of a fallen Kingdom of Angels; for *this End* it stands in its State of War, a War betwixt the Fire and Pride of fallen Angels, and the Meekness and Humility of the Lamb of God: It stands its Thousands of Years in this Strife, that the last Trumpet may sound *this great* Truth, through all Heights and Depths of Eternity, 'That Evil can have no Beginning, but from Pride; 'nor any End, but from Humility.'

Oh *Academicus*, what a Blindness there is in the World! What a Stir is there amongst Mankind about *Religion*, and yet almost all seem to be afraid of *That*, in which alone is *Salvation!*

Poor Mortals! What is the one Wish and Desire of your Hearts? What is it that you call Happiness, and matter of

Rejoicing? Is it not when everything about you helps you to stand upon *higher Ground,* gives full Nourishment to *Self-esteem,* and gratifies every *Pride* of Life? And yet *Life* itself is the *Loss* of everything, unless *Pride* be *overcome.* Oh stop awhile in Contemplation of this great Truth. It is a Truth as unchangeable as God; it is written and spoken through all Nature; Heaven and Earth, fallen Angels, and redeemed Men, all bear Witness to it. The Truth is this: *Pride must die in you,* or *nothing of Heaven* can live in you. Under the Banner of this Truth, give up yourselves to the meek and humble Spirit of the Holy Jesus, the Overcomer of all Fire, and Pride, and Wrath. This is the one Way, the one Truth, and the one Life. There is no other open Door into the Sheepfold of God. Everything else is the *Working* of the Devil in the *fallen Nature* of Man. Humility must sow the Seed, or there can be no Reaping in Heaven. Look not at Pride only as an unbecoming Temper; not at Humility only as a decent Virtue; for the one is Death, and the other is Life; the one is all Hell, and the other is all Heaven.

So much as you have of Pride, so much you have of the fallen Angel alive in you; so much as you have of true Humility, so much you have of the Lamb of God within you. Could you see with your Eyes what *every Stirring* of Pride does to your Soul, you would beg of everything you meet, to tear the Viper from you, though with the Loss of an Hand, or an Eye. Could you see what a sweet, Divine, transforming Power there is in Humility, what an heavenly Water of Life it gives to the fiery Breath of your Soul, how it expels the Poison of your fallen Nature, and makes room for the Spirit of God to live in you, you would rather wish to be the *Footstool* of all the World, than to want the smallest Degree of it. Excuse, *Academicus,* this little Digression, if it be such, for the Subject we were upon, forced me into it.

Acad. Indeed, Sir, the Lesson you have here given, is the same that the whole Nature of the Fall of Angels, and the whole Nature of the Redemption of Man, daily reads to every Creature; and he, who alone can redeem the World, has plainly shown us, wherein the Life and Spirit of our Redemption must consist, when he saith, 'Learn of me, for I am meek 'and lowly of Heart.' Now if this Lesson is unlearnt, we must be said to have *left* our Master, as those Disciples did, 'who 'went back, and walked no more with him.'* But if you please, *Theophilus,* we will now break off till the Afternoon.

Theoph. Give me Leave first, *Academicus,* but just to mention

---

* John vi.

one Point more, to show you still further, how unreasonably your Friends object to the *Appeal* the Want of the plain Letter of Scripture. Now let it be supposed, that the Account of the Fall of Angels, the Creation, *&c.*, given in the *Appeal*, has not Scripture *enough ;*—Take then the contrary Opinion, which is that of your Friends; *viz.*, That all Worlds, and all Things, are created *out of nothing*.

Show me now, *Academicus*, I do not say a Text, but the *least Hint* of Scripture, that by all the Art of commenting, can so much as be drawn to look that way. It is a *Fiction*, big with the grossest Absurdities, and *contrary* to everything that we know, either from Nature or Scripture, concerning the Rise and Birth, and Nature of Things, that have begun to be. *Adam* was not created out of nothing ; for the Letter of *Moses* tells us in the plainest Words, *out of what* he was created or formed, both as to his inward, and his outward Nature. It tells us also as expressly *out of what*, *Eve*, the next Creature, was created. But from the Time of *Adam* and *Eve*, the Creation of every human Creature is a Birth out of its Parents' Body and Soul, or whole Nature. And to show us how *all things*, or Worlds, as well as all living Creatures, are not created *out of nothing*, St. *Paul* appeals to this very Account, that *Moses* gives of the Woman's being formed *out of the Man ;* But ' all things ' (says he) ' are out of God.'* Here this *Fiction* of a Creation *out of nothing*, is by the plain and open Letter of Scripture, absolutely removed from the whole System of created things, or things which begin to be ; for St. *Paul's* Doctrine is, that *all things* come into Being, *out of God*, in the same Reality, as the Woman was formed or created *out of* Man. So again, ' There is to us ' but one God, out of whom are all things ;'† for so you know the *Greek* should be translated, not of, but *out of* God ; not of, but *out of* the Man. The *Fiction* therefore, which I speak of, is not only without, but expressly *contrary* to, the plain Letter of Scripture. For everything that we see, every Creature that has Life, is by the Scripture-account, a *Birth* from *something else*. And here, Sir, you are to take Notice of a *Maxim* that is not deniable, that the Reason why *any* thing proceeds from a *Birth*, is the Reason why *every* thing *must* do so. For a *Birth* would not be in Nature, but because Birth is the *only* Procedure of Nature. Nature itself is a *Birth* from God, the *first Manifestation* of the hidden, inconceivable God, and is so far from being *out of* nothing, that it is the Manifestation of *all that* in God, which was before unmanifest. As Nature is the first

---

* 1 Cor. ix. 12. † 1 Cor. viii. 6.

Birth, or Manifestation of God, or Discovery of the Divine Powers, so all Creatures are the *Manifestation* of the Powers of Nature, brought into a Variety of Births, by the Will of God, *out of* Nature. The first Creatures that are the nearest to the Deity, are *out of* the highest Powers of Nature, by the Will of God, willing that Nature should be manifested in the Rise and Birth of Creatures *out of* it. Nature, directed and governed by the Wisdom of God, goes on in the Birth of one thing *out of* another. The spiritual Materiality of Heaven brings forth the Bodies, or heavenly Flesh and Blood of Angels, as the Materiality of this World brings forth the Birth of gross Flesh and Blood. The spiritual Materiality of Heaven, so far as the Extent of the Kingdom of fallen Angels reached, has by various Changes occasioned by their Fall, gone through a Variety of *Births*, or *Creations*, till some of it came down to the Thickness of *Air* and *Water*, and the Hardness of *Earth* and *Stones*. But when things have stood in this State their appointed Time, the last purifying Fire, kindled by God, will take away all *Thickness*, *Hardness*, and *Darkness*, and bring all the divided Things and Elements of this World back again, to be that first *glassy Sea*, or heavenly *Materiality*, in which the Throne of God is set, as was seen by St. *John*, in the Revelation made to him.

But the Fiction of the Creation *out of nothing*, is not only contrary to the Letter and Spirit of the Scripture-account of the Rise and Birth of Things, but is in itself full of the grossest Absurdities, and horrid Consequences. It *separates* everything from God, it leaves *no Relation* between God and the Creature, nor any *Possibility* for any *Power*, *Virtue*, *Quality*, or *Perfection* of God, to be in the Creature : For if it is created *out of nothing*, it cannot have *something* of God in it. But I here stop : For, as you know, we have agreed, if God permit, to have hereafter one Day's entire Conversation on the Nature and End of the Writings of *Jacob Behmen*, and the right Use and Manner of reading them, as preparatory to a *New Edition* of his Works, so this and some other Points shall be adjourned to that Time. In the Afternoon, we will proceed only on such Matters, as may further set the Christian Redemption in its true and proper Light before your Friend *Humanus*.

Acad. I am very glad, *Theophilus*, that I have mentioned these Objections to you, though they were of no Weight with me, since you have thereby had an Occasion of giving so full an Answer to them. The Master stands now in this plain and easy Point of Light.

In the *Appeal* we have a System of uniform Truths, concerning the Fall of Angels, their spoiled and darkened Kingdom, and the Creation of this World as raised out of it. We have the Creation and Fall of Man, his Regeneration, and the Manner of it, all opened and explained according to the *Letter and Tenor* of Scripture, from their deepest Ground, in such a manner, as to give Light and Clearness into all the Articles of the Christian Faith; to expel all Difficulties and Absurdities that had crept into it; and the whole Scheme of our Redemption is proved to be absolutely necessary, both from Scripture, and all that is seen and known in Nature and Creature.

On the other hand, the Opinion which is, and must be received, if the Account in the *Appeal* is rejected, appears to be a *Fiction*, that has no Sense, no Reason, no Fact, no Appearance in Nature, nor one single Letter of Scripture, to support it, but stands in the utmost Contrariety to all that the Scripture saith of the Creation of everything, and is in itself full of the grossest Absurdities, raising Darkness and Difficulties in all Parts of Religion, that can never be removed from it. For a Creation that has nothing of God in it, can explain nothing that relates to God: For a Creation out of nothing, has no better Sense in it, than a Creation *into nothing*. My Friends, for this time, Adieu.

The End of the First DIALOGUE.

THE
SECOND DIALOGUE.

THEOPH. Let us now speak of *Adam* in his first Perfection, created by God to be a Lord and Ruler of this new-created World, to people it with an Host of angelic Men, till Time had finished its Course, and all things were fitted to be restored to that State, from which they were fallen by the Revolt of Angels.

For the Restoration of all things to their first glorious State, by making the Good to overcome the Evil, was the End which God proposed by the State and Manner of this new Creation.

Adam was the chosen Instrument of God, to conduct this whole Affair, to keep up this new-made World in the State in which God had created it, not *to till the Earth*, which we now plough, but to keep *That*, which is now called the *Curse* of the Earth, *covered, hid,* and *overcome,* by that Paradise in which he was created. For this End, he was created in a twofold Nature, of the Powers of Heaven, and the Powers of this World. Inwardly, he had the celestial Body and Soul of an Angel, and he had this angelic Nature united to a Life and Body taken from the Stars and Elements of this outward World. As Paradise overcame, and concealed all the Wrath of the Stars and Elements, and kept that *Evil,* which is called the *Curse,* from being known or felt, so *Adam's* angelic, heavenly Nature, which was the Paradise of God within him, kept him quite ignorant of the Properties of that earthly Nature that was under it. He knew, and saw, and felt nothing in himself, but a Birth of Paradise, that is, a Life, Light, and Spirit of Heaven: For he had no Difference from an Angel in Heaven, but that this World was joined to him, and put under his Feet. And this was done, because he was created by God to be the *restoring Angel*, to do all that in this outward World, which God would have to be done in it, before it could be restored to its first State. And therefore he must have the Nature of all this World in him, because he was to act in it, and upon it, as its *restoring Angel;* and yet with such Distinction from it, with such Power upon it, and over it, as the Light has upon and over Darkness. Does not now the whole Spirit of the Scriptures consent to this Account of *Adam's* first Perfection? Do not all the chief Points of our Redemption demand this Perfection in *Adam unfallen?* How else could his *Fall* bring on the Necessity of the Gospel-Redemption of a new Birth from above, of the *Word* and Holy Spirit of God? For had he not had this Perfection of Nature at first, his Redemption could not have consisted in the Revival of this Birth and Perfection in him. For had it been something less than the Loss of an angelic and heavenly Life, that had happened to him by his Fall, had it been only *some Evil*, that related to a Life of this World, nothing else but *some Remedy* from this World, could have been his Redemption. But since it is the Corner-stone of the Gospel, that nothing less than the *eternal Word*, which was Man's Creator, could be his Redeemer, and that by a new Birth from above, it is a Demonstration, that he was at first created an Angel, born from above, and such a Partaker of the Divine Life, as the Angels are; and that his Fall was a real Death or Extinction of his angelic Life.

Now the Letter of *Moses* is express for this first Perfection of *Adam*. God said, 'Let us make Man in our own Image, 'after our Likeness.' How different is this from the Creation of the Animals of this World? What can you think or say higher of an Angel? Or what Perfection can an Angel have, but that of being in the Image and after the Likeness of God? But now what an Absurdity would it be, to hold that *Adam* was created in the Image and Likeness of God, and yet had not in him so much as the Image and Likeness of an Angel? Again, was not Paradise lost, was not *Evil* and the *Curse* awakened in all the Elements, as soon as *Adam* fell? And does not this prove, beyond all Contradiction, that *Adam* was created by God, as I said above, to be the *restoring Angel;* to have Power over all the outward World; to keep all its Evil from being known or felt; till the Fall of Angels from Heaven had been repaired by a Race of angelic Men born on Earth? But how could he do, and be all this, for which he was created by God, how could he keep up the Life of Heaven and Paradise in himself, and this new World, unless the Life of Heaven had been his own Life? Or how could he be the Father of an Offspring that were to have no Evil, nor so much as the Knowledge of what was Good and Evil in this World? Could anything but an heavenly Man bring forth an heavenly Offspring? Or could he be said to have the Life of this World opened in him in his Creation, who was to bring forth a Race of Beings, insensible of the Good and Evil in this World? For everything that has the Life of this World opened in it, is under an absolute Necessity of knowing and feeling its Good and Evil.

Secondly, That *Adam,* when he first entered into the World, had the Nature and Perfection of an Angel, is further plain from *Moses,* who tells us, that he was made at first both Male and Female in one Person ; and that *Eve,* or the Female Part of him, was aftewards taken out of him. Now this Union of the Male and Female in him, was the *Purity,* or *Virgin Perfection* of his Life, and is the very Perfection of the angelic Nature. This we are assured of from our Lord himself, who, in Answer to the Question of the *Sadducees,* said unto them ; 'Ye do err, not 'knowing the Scriptures, and the Power of God ; for in the Resur- 'rection they neither marry, nor are given in Marriage, but are 'as the Angels in Heaven.'* Or, as in St. *Luke,* 'for they are ' equal to the Angels of God.' Here we have a twofold Proof of the angelic Perfection of *Adam :* (1.) Because we are told, that that State in which he was created, neither Male nor Female, but with both Natures in his one Person, is the very Nature and Perfection of the Angels of God in Heaven. (2.) Because everyone who shall have a Part in this Resurrection, shall then have this angelic Perfection again ; to be no more Male or Female, or a Part of the Humanity, but such perfect, complete, undivided Creatures, as the Angels of God are. But now this Perfection could not belong to the Humanity after the Resurrection, but because it belonged to the first Man before his Fall : For nothing will be restored, but that which was first lost ; nothing rise again, but that which should not have died ; nor anything be united, but that which should not have been parted. The short is this : Man is *at last* to have a Nature equal to that of the Angels. This Equality consists in this, that as they have, so the Humanity will have, both Male and Female Nature in one Person.

But the Humanity was thus created at first, Male and Female in one Person, therefore the Humanity had at *first* a Nature and Perfection equal to that of the Angels. Thus is the Letter of *Moses* much more plain for the angelic Perfection of *Adam* in his Creation, than it is for the Resurrection of the Dead ; and yet we have our Lord's Word for it, that *Moses* sufficiently proved the Resurrection of the Dead. What say you, *Academicus,* to this Matter ?

Acad. I will here just mention what my good old *Tutor* says : The Author of the *Appeal,* says he, founds all his Scheme of Regeneration or Redemption on a supposed *threefold Life,* in which *Adam* was created. His sole Proof of this threefold Life is taken from this Text of *Moses :* 'God breathed into Man the

---

* Matt. xxii. 29, 30.

'Breath of Lives, and Man became a living Soul.' From this Phrase, *The Breath of Lives*, the *Appeal*, without any Authority from the Text, observes thus; 'Here the highest, and most 'Divine Original is not darkly, but openly, absolutely, and in the 'strongest Form of Expression, ascribed to the Soul,' *&c*. A vain Assertion, says my Tutor; for the *Breath of Life* or Lives is used by *Moses* only as a Phrase for *animal Life*. This is plainly seen, *Gen*. vii. *ver*. 21. 'And all Flesh died,—all in 'whose Nostrils was the Breath of Lives.'

Behold, says he, the very Phrase, which the *Appeal* takes to be so full a Proof of the high Dignity, and threefold Life of God in the Soul, here made use of to denote the Life of every kind of Animal.—And therefore, says he, if this *Phrase* proves the Soul of *Adam* to be a *Mirror of the Holy Trinity*, it proves the same of every Breath in the Nostrils of every Creature.

Theoph. To make short work, *Academicus*, with your Tutor's Confutation, as he thinks, of the capital Doctrine of the *Appeal*, I shall only quote the whole Period, as it stands in the *Appeal*. '*God breathed* into him *the Breath of Lives* (Spiraculum vitarum) '*and Man became a living Soul.* Here, says the *Appeal*, the 'Notion of a Soul, created *out of nothing*, is in the plainest, 'strongest Manner, rejected by the first written Word of God; 'and no *Jew* or *Christian* can have the least Excuse for falling 'into *such* an Error: Here the *highest and most Divine* Original 'is not darkly, but openly, absolutely ascribed to the Soul. It 'came forth as a Breath of Life, or Lives, out of, and from the 'Mouth of God; and therefore did not come out of the *Womb* 'of *nothing*, but is what it is, and has what it has in itself, '*from*, and *out of, the* first and highest of all Beings.'* Here, *Academicus*, behold the Falseness and Weakness of your Tutor's Observation.—The *Appeal*, you plainly see, proves only from the Text of *Moses*, the high Original of the Soul; and only for this Reason, because it is the *Breath of God*, breathed into Man. The *Appeal* makes no Use of the Expression, the *Breath of Lives*, takes no Notice of it, deduces nothing from it, but *solely* considers the *Act* of God, as *breathing* the Spirit of the Soul from himself; and from this *Act* of God, the high Birth and Dignity of the Soul is most justly affirmed. And the *Appeal* makes this Observation *solely* to prove, that the Soul is not created *out of nothing*. This is the one, sole, open, and declared Intent of the *Appeal*, in all this Paragraph. But your Tutor, overlooking all this, though nothing else is there, makes the Author of the *Appeal* to affirm the threefold Life of God in the Soul, merely

---

* *Appeal*, page 2.

from the Phrase of the *Breath of Lives*, when there is not one single Word about it. For the *Appeal* not only has not the least Hint in this Place of any such Matter, to be proved from the *Breath of Lives*, but through the whole Book there is not the smallest Regard paid to this Expression, nor any Argument ever deduced from it. How strange is all this in your good old Tutor!

The Matter is plainly this ; the Author of the *Appeal* looks wholly to the *Action* of God, *breathing* his own Spirit into *Adam ;* and from this Breathing, he justly affirms the *Divine Nature* of the Soul ; all his Argument is deduced from thence. Now if your Tutor, or anyone else, could show, that God *breathed* his own Spirit into every Animal, and with this Intent, that it might come forth in his own Image and Likeness, then the Distinction and high Birth of the Soul, pleaded for by the *Appeal*, would indeed be lost. But till then, the *Appeal* must, and therefore will for ever, stand unconfuted in its Assertion of the Dignity and Divine Birth of the Soul.

Again ; behold, *Academicus*, a still further Weakness chargeable upon your Tutor. You have seen, that his Reasoning upon the *Breath of Lives*, is meddling with something that the *Appeal* meddles not with, makes no Account of : But your Tutor has conjured it up for his own Use ; and yet see what a poor Use he makes of it. He affirms that *Moses* uses only the *Breath of Lives*, as a Phrase for animal Life. How does he prove this? Why, truly from this Reason, because *Moses* uses the same Phrase when he speaks of the Lives of all Animals.

Now does not every *Englishman* know, that we make use of the same *four Letters* of the Alphabet, when we say the *Life* of a Man, the Life of a Beast, and the Life of a Plant ? That we use the same *five Letters*, when we say the *Death* of a Man, the Death of a Beast, and the Death of a Plant? But will it thence follow, that the Life and Death of Men, and Beasts, and Plants, are of the same Nature and Degree, and have the same Good and Evil in them ? Yet this is full as well, as to conclude, that the Breath of Life in Man, and the Breath of Life in Animals, is of the same *Nature* and *Degree*, has the same *Goodness* and *Excellence* in it, because the same Words, made up of the same Letters, express them both. Your Tutor therefore, *Academicus*, and not the Author of the *Appeal*, is the Person that reasons weakly from the Phrase of *the Breath of Lives :* For that Author never so much as offers to argue from it. His Proof of the threefold Life of God in the Soul, so far as it is deduced from the Text of *Moses*, lies wholly in this ; that it is the Breath and Spirit of the triune God, breathed forth from this triune Deity into Man. This, sure, is no small Proof of its having the triune

The Spirit of Prayer.

Nature of God in it. And this threefold Life of the Soul, thus plainly deducible from the Letter of *Moses*, is shown to be absolutely certain, from every chief *Doctrine* and Institution, nay, from the *whole Nature* of our Redemption: And all the Gospel is shown to set its Seal to this great Truth, the *threefold Life* of God in the Soul. Nay, everything in Nature, Fire, and Light, and Air; everything that we know of Angels, of Devils, of the animal Life of this World; are all in the plainest and strongest manner, from the Beginning to the End of the *Appeal*, made so many Proofs of the threefold Life of the triune God in the Soul. Thus says the *Appeal; No* Omnipotence *can make you a Partaker of the Life of this outward World, without having the Life of this outward World born in your own creaturely Being;* the Fire, and Light, and Air of this World, must have their Birth in your own creaturely Being, or you cannot possibly live in, or have a Life from *outward Nature*. And therefore no Omnipotence can make you a Partaker of the beatific Life, or Presence of the Holy Trinity, unless that Life stands in the same triune State within you, as it does without you.* Again: Search to Eternity, says the *Appeal*, why no Devil or Beast can possibly enter into Heaven, and there can only this one Reason be assigned for it, because neither of them have the *triune* holy Life of God in them.† But enough of this Mistake of your good old Tutor. *Rusticus* will I am afraid chide you for being the Occasion of this long Digression from the Point we were speaking to.

Rust. Truly, Sir, I do not know what to make of these great Scholars; they seem to have more Love for the Shadow of an Objection, than for the most substantial Truths. I think I here see a great Reason, why our Saviour chose poor and illiterate Fishermen to be his Apostles. St. *Paul* was the only Man that had some Learning, and he was a Persecutor of Christ, till such time as God made *as it were Scales* to fall from his Eyes;—And then he became a powerful Apostle. But let us return to your Account of the first created Perfection of Man, and the Degree of his falling from it. It is one of the best Doctrines that I ever heard in my Life. It not only stirs up everything that is good, and makes me hate everything that is evil, in me; but it gives so good a Sense, so sound a Meaning to every Mystery of the Gospel, that it makes everything our Saviour has done for us, and everything he requires of us, to be equally necessary and beneficial to us. But suppose now our Fall not to be a Change of Nature, not a *Death* to our first Life, but only a single Sin or Mistake in the first Man; What a Difficulty is there in sup-

---

* *Appeal*, page 51. † *Ibid.*, page 53.

posing so great a Scheme of Redemption to set right a single Mistake in one single Creature? Again, What could Man have to do with Angels and Heaven, if he had not, at his Creation, had the Nature of Heaven and Angels in him? But pray, Sir, begin again just where you left off.

Theoph. I was indeed, *Rusticus*, at that Time just going to say, that *Adam* had lost much of his first Perfection before his *Eve* was taken out of him; which was done to prevent worse Effects of his Fall, and to prepare a means for his Recovery, when his Fall should become total, as it afterwards was, upon the eating of the earthly Tree of Good and Evil.

'It is not good that Man should be alone,' saith the Scripture: This shows, that *Adam* had altered his first State, had brought some *Beginning* of Evil into it, and had made *that* not to be good, which God saw to be good, when he created him. And therefore as a less Evil, and to prevent a greater, God divided the first perfect human Nature into two Parts, into a Male and a Female Creature; and this, as you shall see by and by, was a wonderful Instance of the Love and Care of God towards this new Humanity. It was at first, the total Humanity in one Creature, who should in that State of Perfection, have brought forth his own Likeness out of himself, in such *Purity* of Love, and such *Divine Power*, as he himself was brought forth by God: The Manner of his own Birth from God, was the Manner that his own Offspring should have had a Birth from him; all done by the pure Power of a Divine Love. Man stood no longer in the Perfection of his first State, as a birth of Divine Love, than whilst he loved himself *only* as God loved him, as in the *Image*, and *after the Likeness of God.* This *Purity* of Love, and Delight in the Image of God, would have carried on the Birth of the Humanity, in the same manner, and by the same Divine Power, as the first Man was brought forth: For it was only a Continuation of the same generating Love that gave Birth to the first Man. But *Adam* turned away his Love from the Divine Image, which he should only have loved, and desired to propagate out of himself. He gazed upon this outward World, and let in an adulterate Love into his Heart, which desired to know the Life that was in this World. This impure Desire brought the Nature of this World into him. His first Love and Divine Power, had no Strength left in it; it was no longer a Power of bringing forth a Divine Birth from himself. His first Virginity was lost by an *adulterate* Love, which had turned its desire into this World. This State of *Inability*, is that which is called his falling into a deep Sleep: And in this Sleep, God divides this overcome Humanity into a Male and Female.

The first Step therefore towards the Redemption or Recovery of Man, *beginning* to fall, was the taking his *Eve* out of him, that so he might have a *second Trial* in Paradise; in which if he failed, another effectual Redeemer might arise out of the *Seed of the Woman.* Oh my Friends, what a wonderful Procedure is there to be seen in the Divine Providence, turning all Evil, as soon as it appears, into a further Display and Opening of new Wonders of the Wisdom and Love of God! Look back to the first Evil, which the Fall of Angels brought forth. The Darkness, Wrath, and Fire, of fallen Nature, were immediately taken from them, and turned into a new Creation, where those apostate Angels were to see all the Evil that they had raised in their Kingdom, turned against them, and made the Ground of a new Race of Beings, which were to possess those Thrones which they had lost. Look now at *Adam* brought into the World in such angelic Nature, as he, and all his redeemed Sons, will have after the Resurrection; an Angel at first, and an Angel at last; with Time, and Misery, and Sin, and Death, and Hell, all of them felt, and all overcome betwixt the two glorious Extremes. When this first human Angel, through a *false, impure* Love, lost the Divine Power of generating his own Likeness out of himself, God took Part of his Nature from him, that so the Eye of his Desire, which was turned to the Life of this World, might be directed to that Part of his Nature which was taken from him. And this is the Reason of my saying before, that this was chosen as a less Evil, and to avoid a greater; for it was a less Degree of falling from his first Perfection, to love the Female Part of his own divided Nature, than to turn his Love towards that, which was so much lower than his own Nature. And thus, at *that Time, Eve* was an *Help*, that was truly and properly *meet* for him, since he had lost his first Power of being himself the Parent of an angelic Offspring, and stood with a longing Eye, looking towards the Life of this World.

But the most glorious Effect of this Division into Male and Female is yet to come. For when *Adam* and *Eve* had joined in the eating of the Tree of Good and Evil, and so were totally fallen from God and Paradise, into the Misery and Slavery of the bestial Life of this World; when this greatest of all Evils had thus happened to these two divided Parts of the Humanity; when all the Angel was lost, and nothing but a shameful, frightened Animal of this World, was to be seen in this divided Male and Female; then in, and by, and through this Division, did God open and establish the glorious Scheme of an *universal* Redemption to these fallen Creatures, and all their Offspring, by the mysterious *Seed* of the *Woman.*

Had *Adam* stood in his first State of Perfection, as a Birth of Divine Love, and loving only the Divine Image and Likeness in himself, this Love would have been itself the fruitful Parent of an holy Offspring ; no *Eve* had been taken out of him, nor any Male or Female ever known in human Nature : All his Posterity had been in him secured, and the earthly Tree of Good and Evil had never been seen in Paradise. But though he lost this first generating Power of Divine Love, and stood as a barren Tree, yet seeing God's Purpose of raising an Offspring from *Adam*, to possess the Thrones of fallen Angels, must go on and succeed, therefore that *Adam* might yet have an Offspring, God took from him that, which is called the Female Part of his Nature, that by this means, both a *Posterity*, and a *Saviour*, might proceed from him : For through this Division of Man, God would, in a wonderful Manner, do *that* which *Adam* should have done, before he was divided.

For out of this Female Part, and after the Fall, God would raise, without the Help of *Adam*, that same glorious angelic Man, which *Adam* should have brought forth before and without his *Eve ;* which glorious Man is therefore called the Second *Adam :* 1. As having in his Humanity that very Perfection, which the First *Adam* had in his Creation. 2. Because he was to do all that for Mankind, by a Birth of Redemption from him, which they should have had by a Birth of Nature from *Adam*, had he kept his first State of Perfection. What say you, *Academicus*, to all this ?

Acad. Truly, Sir, there seems to be so much Light, and Truth, and Scripture, for all this Account that you have given of these Matters, as must even force one to consent to it. But then all our Systems of Divinity, to which learned Men are chained, are quite silent of these Matters. I never before heard of this *gradual Fall* of *Adam*, nor this angelic State of his first Creation, and Power of bringing forth his own Offspring, and therefore can hardly believe it so strongly as I would, and as the Truth seems to demand of me.

Rust. Pray, Sir, let me speak to *Academicus :* He seems to be so hampered with Learning, that I can hardly be sorry, that I am not a great Scholar.

Can anything be more punctually related in Scripture than the *gradual Fall* of *Adam ?* Do not you see, that he was created first with both Natures in him ? Is it not expressly told you, that *Eve* was not taken out of him, till such Time as it was *not good* for him to be as he then *was*, and yet God saw that it was good when he created him ? Is it not plain therefore, that he had fallen from the Goodness of his first Creation, and therefore his Fall was not at once, nor total, till his eating of the earthly Tree ? Again, as to his being an *Angel* at his first Creation, because of both Natures in him, is it not sufficiently plain from his being designed to be an Angel of the same Nature at last, in the Resurrection? For this is an Axiom that cannot be shaken, that *Nothing can rise higher*, than its *first created Nature;* and therefore an Angel at last, must have been an Angel at first. Do you think it possible for an Ox in Tract of Time to be changed into a rational Philosopher? Yet this is as possible, as for a Man that has only by his Creation the Life of this World in him, to be changed into an Angel of Heaven. The Life of this World can reach no further than this World; no Omnipotence of God can carry it further; and therefore, if Man is to be an Angel at the last, and have the Life of Heaven in him, he must of all Necessity, in his Creation, have been created an Angel, and had his Life kindled from Heaven; because no Creature can possibly have any other Life, or higher Degree of Life, than that which his Creation brought forth in him.

Theoph. Marvel not, *Academicus*, at that which has been said of the first Power of *Adam*, to generate in a Divine Manner an holy Offspring, by the Power of that Divine Love which gave Birth to himself; for he was born of that Love for no other End, than to multiply Births of it ; and whilst his Love continued to be *one* with that Love, which brought him into Being, nothing was impossible to it. For Love is the great Creating *Fiat* that brought forth every Thing, that is distinct from God, and is the only working Principle that stirs, and effects every Thing that is done in Nature and Creature. Love is the *Principle* of Generation from the highest to the lowest of Creatures; it is the first Beginning of every Seed of Life ; every Thing has its Form from it; every Thing that is born is born in the Likeness, and with the Fruitfulness, of that same Love that generates and bears it ; and this is its own Seed of Love within itself, and is its Power of fructifying in its Kind.

Love is the holy, heavenly, magic Power of the Deity, the first *Fiat* of God; and all Angels, and eternal Beings, are the first Births of it. The Deity delights in beholding the ideal Images, which rise up and appear in the Mirror of his own eternal Wisdom. This Delight becomes a loving Desire to have living Creatures in the Form of these Ideas; and this loving Desire is the *generating* heavenly Parent, out of which Angels, and all eternal Beings are born. Every Birth in Nature is a Consequence of this first prolific Love of the Deity, and generates from that which began the first Birth. Hence it is, that through all the Scale of Beings, from the Top to the Bottom of Nature, Love is the *one Principle* of Generation of every Life ; and every Thing generates from the same Principle, and by the same Power, by which itself was generated. Marvel not therefore, my Friend, that *Adam*, standing in the *Power* of his first Birth, should have a Divine Power of bringing forth his own Likeness. But I must now tell you, that the greatest Proof of this glorious Truth is yet to come: For I will show you that all the Gospel bears Witness to that heavenly Birth, which we should have had from *Adam* alone.—This Birth from *Adam* is still the one Purpose of God, and must be the *one Way* of all those, that are to rise with Christ to an Equality with the Angels of God. All must be Children of *Adam*; for all that are born of Man and Woman, must lay aside this polluted Birth, and be born again of a second *Adam*, in that same Perfection of an holy angelic Nature, which they should have had from the first *Adam*, before his *Eve* was separated from him. For it is an undeniable Truth of the Gospel, that we are called to a new Birth, different in its whole Nature, from that which we have from Man and Woman, or there is no Salvation; and therefore it is certain from the Gospel, that the Birth which we have from *Adam*, divided into Male and Female, is not the Birth that we should have had, because it is the one Reason, why we are under a Necessity of being born again of a Birth from a second *Adam*, who is to generate us again in that Purity and Divine Power, in and by which we should have been born of the first angelic *Adam*.

A Divine Love in the first pure and holy *Adam*, united with the Love of God, willing him to be the Father of an holy Offspring, was to have given Birth to a Race of Creatures from him. But *Adam* fulfilled not this Purpose of God; he awakened in himself a false Love, and so all his Offspring were forced to be born of Man and Woman, and thereby to have such *impure* Flesh and Blood as cannot enter into the Kingdom of Heaven. Is not this Proof enough, that this Birth from *Adam* and *Eve* is not the *first Birth* that we should have had? Will anyone say, How could *Adam* have such a Power to bring from a Birth in such a *Spiritual* Way, and so contrary to the present State of Nature? The whole Nature of the Gospel is a full Answer to this Question. For are we not all to be born again in the *same Spiritual* Way, and are we not, merely by a Spiritual Power, to have a Birth of heavenly Flesh and Blood? The Strangeness of such a Power in the first *Adam*, is only just so strange, and hard to be believed, as the same Power in the second *Adam*; who is called the second *Adam* for no other Reason, but because he stands in the *Place* of the first, and is to do *That*, which the first should have done. And therefore our having from him a new heavenly Flesh and Blood raised in us by a *Spiritual Power*, superior to the common Way of Birth in this World, is the strongest of Proofs, that we should have been born of *Adam* in the *same Spiritual* Power, and so contrary to the Birth of Animals into this World. For all that we have from the second *Adam*, is a Proof that we should have had the same from *Adam* the first:—A Divine *Love* in *Adam* the first, was to have brought forth an holy Offspring. A Divine *Faith* now takes its Place, in the second Birth, and is to generate a new Birth from the second *Adam*, is to eat his Flesh, and drink his Blood, by the same Divine Power, by which we should have had a Birth of the angelic Flesh and Blood of our first Parent. Thus, *Academicus*, is this Birth from *Adam alone* no Whimsy, or Fiction, or fine-spun Notion, but the very Birth that the Gospel absolutely requires, as the Substance of our Redemption. There is no Room to deny it, without denying the whole Nature of our Redemption. On the other hand, the Birth that we have from *Adam* divided into *Male* and *Female*, is through all Scripture declared to be the Birth of *Misery*, of *Shame*, of *Pollution*, of *sinful* Flesh and Blood; and is only a Ground and Reason, why we must be born again of other Flesh and Blood, before we can enter into the Kingdom of Heaven. This Truth therefore, that we were to have had an heavenly Birth from *Adam*, depends not upon this, or that particular Text of Scripture, but is affirmed by the whole Nature of our Redemption, and the whole Spirit of Scripture, representing our Birth from this World as shameful, as that of the wild Ass's Colt, and calling for a new Birth from above, as absolutely necessary, if Man is to have a Place among the Angels of God. And therefore it may be affirmed, that so sure as it is from Scripture, that Christ is become our second *Adam*, to help us to *such* a Birth, so sure is it from Scripture, that we should have had the *same Birth* from our first Parent, who, if not fallen, could have wanted no Redeemer of his Offspring, and therefore must have brought forth that *same Birth*, which we have from Christ, but could not have from the Birth of Man and Woman. I shall now only just mention to you a Passage much to the Matter in Hand, taken from the second Epistle of St. *Clemens*, a Bishop of *Rome*, who lived in the very Time of the Apostles. He relates, that Christ being asked, when his Kingdom should come, gave this Answer: 'When two 'Things shall become one, and that which is outward be as that 'which is inward, the Male with the Female, and neither Man 'nor Woman.' There wants no Comment here: I shall only observe, that the Meaning of the Words, *When that which is outward shall be as that which is inward*, seems plainly to be this, when the outward Life or Birth is come to be as the inward angelic Life is, then the Birth will be one, the Male and Female in one, and then the Kingdom of God is come. These Words were in the next Century quoted by *Clemens* of *Alexandria*, though with some Alteration. The same Author also relates another Answer given by our Lord, to much the same Question, put by *Salome*, where our Lord's Answer was thus: 'When ye 'shall have put off, or away, the Garment of Shame and Ignominy, 'and when two shall become one, the Male and the Female 'united, and neither Man nor Woman.' The Garment of Shame and Ignominy, is plainly that Clothing of Flesh and Blood, at the Sight of which both *Adam* and *Eve* were ashamed.

Acad. I am fully satisfied, *Theophilus*, with the Account you have given of the first Perfection, and Divine State of our first Parent. And I think nothing can be plainer, than that we were to have been born of him to the same heavenly Birth, which we now are to receive from Christ, our second *Adam*. But I must still say, that I am afraid, your critical Adversaries will here find some Pretence, to charge you with a Tendency, at least, to that Heresy, which held Marriage to be unlawful, since you here hold that it came in by *Adam's* falling from his first Perfection.

Theoph. I own, my Friend, that there is no knowing when one is safe from Men of that Stamp. But as for me, my Eye is only upon Truth; and wherever that leads, there I follow; they, if they please, may persecute it with Objections. Here is not the least Pretence for the Charge you speak of: For here is no more Condemnation of Marriage, as *unlawful*, than there is a Condemnation of God, for keeping up the State, and Life of this World. The Continuation of the World, though fallen, is a glorious Proof and Instance of the Goodness of God, that so a Race of new-born Angels may be brought forth in it. Happy therefore is it, that we have such a World as this to be born into, since we are only born, to be born again to the Life of Heaven. Now Marriage has the Nature of this fallen World; but it is God's appointed Means of raising the Seed of *Adam* to its full Number. Honourable therefore is Marriage in our fallen State, and happy is it for Man to derive his Life from it, as it helps him to a Power of being eternally a Son of God.

Nor does this Original of Marriage cast the smallest Reflection upon the *Sex*, as if they brought *all*, or *any* Impurity into the human Nature. No, by no means. The Impurity lies in the *Division*, and that which *caused it*, and not in either of the divided Parts. And the female Part has this Distinction, though not to boast of, yet to take Comfort in, that the Saviour of the World is called the *Seed of the Woman*, and had his Birth only from the female Part of our divided Nature. But *Rusticus*, I see, wants to speak.

Rust. Indeed, Sir, I do. But it is only to observe to you, what a System of solid, harmonious, and great Truths are here opened to our View, by this Consideration of the first angelic State of *Adam*, and his falling from it into an earthly animal Life of this World ; created at first an human Angel, with an Host of Angels in his Loins, and then falling from this State, with this particular Circumstance, that he had not only undone himself, but had also involved an innocent, and almost numberless Posterity in the same Misery, who now must all be born of him in his fallen Condition. Thus looking at this Creation of so noble and high a Creature, and his Fall, as introducing so extensive a Train of Misery, how worthy of God, how becoming a Love and Wisdom that are infinite, does all the stupendous Mystery of our Redemption appear ! It was to restore an Angel, big with an angelic Offspring, an Angel that God had created to carry on the great Work of this new Creation, to bring Time with all its Conquests back into Eternity, an Angel in whom, and with whom, were fallen an innocent, numberless Posterity, that had not yet begun to breathe.

What a Sense and Reasonableness does this State of Things give to all those Passages of Scripture, which bring a God incarnate from Heaven, to remedy this sad Scene of Misery, that was opened on Earth ! What less than God, could awaken again the dead angelic Life? What less than God's entering into the human Birth itself, and becoming one of it, and with it, could generate again the Life of God in every human Birth? The *Scripture* saith, ' God so loved the World ;'—' God spared ' not his only Son ;'—' Christ laid down his Life for us ;' *&c.* How glorious a Sense is there in all these Sayings, when it is considered, that all this was done for so high and Divine a Creature, created by God for such great Ends, and full of a Posterity, that was to have filled an Heaven restored ? In this Light, every Part of our Redemption gives a Glory, a Wisdom, and Goodness to God, which far surpasses every other View we can possibly take of them: Whereas if you *lessen* this angelic Dignity of the first Man, if you suppose his Fall to be *less* than that of falling, with all his Posterity, from an *angelic* Life, into the *earthly, animal Life* of this World, Slaves to Sin and Misery, all the Fabric of our Redemption is full of such Wonders, as can only be wondered at. Thus, if you consider this World, and Man its highest Inhabitant made out of nothing, and with only the Breath of this earthly Life breathed into his Nostrils, what is there to call for this great Redemption from Heaven ?

Again, if you consider the Fall of Man, only as a *single Act* of

Disobedience to a *positive, arbitrary* Command of God, this is to make all the Consequences of his Fall inexplicable. For had the first Sin been only a *single Act* of Disobedience, it had been more worthy of Pardon, than any other Sin, merely because it was the first, and by a Creature that had as yet no Experience. But to make the first single Act of Disobedience, not only *unpardonable*, but the Cause of such a Curse and Variety of Misery entailed upon all his Posterity, from the Beginning to the End of Time; and to suppose, that so much Wrath was raised in God at this single Act of Disobedience, that nothing could make an Atonement for it, but the stupendous Mystery of the Birth, Sufferings, and Death, of the Son of God; is yet further impossible to be accounted for. In this Case, the supposed Wrath, and Goodness of God, are equally inexplicable.—And from hence alone, have sprung up the detestable Doctrines, about the *Guilt* and *Imputation* of the first Sin, and the several Sorts of partial, absolute Elections, and Reprobations, of some to eternal Happiness, and others to be Firebrands of Hell to all Eternity. Detestable may they well be called, since if *Lucifer* could truly say, that God from all Eternity determined, and created him to be *that* wicked hellish Creature that he is, he might then add, *Not unto him*, but *unto his Creator*, must all his Wickedness be ascribed. How innocent, how tolerable is the Error of Transubstantiation, when compared with this absolute Election and Reprobation! It indeed cannot be reconciled to our Senses and Reason, but then it leaves God, and Heaven, possessed of all that is holy and good; but this Reprobation-Doctrine, not only overlooks all Sense and Reason, but confounds Heaven and Hell, takes all Goodness from the Deity, and leaves us nothing to detest in the Sinner, but God's eternal irresistible Contrivance to make him to be such.

But now, when we take this Matter of the Creation, and Fall of Man, as Truth, and Fact, and Scripture, plainly represent it, every Thing that can awaken in ourselves a Love, and Desire to be like unto God, is to be found in it. Whilst Man stood in his first Perfection, unturned from God, this World was under his Feet; Paradise was the Element in which he lived; the *Spirit* of God was his Life; the *Son* of God was his Light; he was in the World, as much above it, and with as full Distinction from it, as incapable of being hurt by it, as an Angel, that only comes with a Divine Commission into it. The whole World was a Gift, put into his Hands; the Standing, or Fall of it was left to him; as his Will and Mind should *work*, so should either Paradise, or a cursed Earth overcome. God, by this new Creation, had so altered the wrathful State of *Lucifer's* fallen

Kingdom, that the Evil that had been raised in it, was hid and overcome by the Good. It was thus created, and put into this new State, for this sole End, that a human Angel might keep Paradise alive, and bring forth a paradisaical Host of Angels, in the very Place, where the fallen Angels had brought forth their Evil. But all these great Things, depended upon *Adam's* conforming to the Designs of God, and living in this World in such a State, as God had created him in. He could not conform to the Designs of God any other Way, than by the *Rectitude* of his *Will*, willing that which God willed, both in the Creation of him, and the World.

Whilst his Will stood thus inclined, the new Creation was preserved, himself was an Angel, and the World a Paradise. No Evil would have been known either in Plant, or Fruit, or Animal, nor could have been known, but by the *declining Will*, and Desire of Man calling it forth. His first *longing Look* towards the Knowledge of the Life of this World, was the first *loosening* of the Reins of Evil.—It began to have Life, and a Power of stirring, as soon as his Desire began to be earthly; hence the Curse, or Evil, hid in the Earth, could begin to show itself, and got a *Power* of giving forth an *evil* Tree, whose Fruit was the Key to the Knowledge of Good and Evil; a Tree which could not have grown, had he willed nothing, but that which God willed in the Creation of him.

He was not the Creator of this bad Tree, no more than he was the Creator of the good Trees, that grew in Paradise. But as the heavenly *Rectitude* of his Will *kept up* the heavenly Powers of Paradise in the Earth, so when his Will began to be earthly, it opened a Passage for the natural Evil; that was hid in the Earth, to bring forth a Tree in its own Likeness. The Earth as now, had then a natural Power of bringing forth a Tree of its own Nature, *viz.*, Good and Evil, but Paradise was that heavenly Power, which hindered it from bringing forth *such* Productions: But when the *Keeper* of Paradise turned a Wish from God, and Paradise, after a bad Knowledge, then Paradise lost some of its Power, and the Curse, or Evil, hid in the Earth, could give forth a bad Tree. But see now the Goodness, and Compassion of God towards this mistaken Creature; for no sooner had *Adam*, by the abuse of his Power and Freedom, given *occasion* to the Birth of this evil Tree, but the God of Love informs him of the *dreadful* Nature of it, *commands* him not to eat of it, assuring him, that *Death* was hid in it, that Death to his angelic Life, would be found in the Day that he should eat of it. A plain Proof, if anything can be plain, that this Tree came not from God, was not according to *his own Will* and *Purpose* towards *Adam*, but from such a natural Power in the Earth, as could not show itself, till the *strong Will and Desire* of *Adam*, beginning to be earthly, worked with *That*, which was the *Evil* hid in the Earth. But pray, *Theophilus*, do you now speak again.

Theoph. The short of the Matter then, my Friend, is this: Neither *Adam*, nor any other Creature, has at its *Creation*, or Entrance into Life, any *arbitrary Trial* imposed upon it by God. The *natural* State of every intelligent Creature is its *one only* Trial; and it cannot sin, but by departing from that Nature, or falling from that State in which it was created. *Adam* was created an human Angel in Paradise, and he had no *other Trial* but this, whether he would live in Paradise, as an Angel of God, insensible of the Life, or the Good and Evil, of this earthly World. This was the Tree of Life, and the Tree of Death, that must stand before him; and the Necessity of his choosing either the one, or the other, was a Necessity founded in his own happy Nature.

The true Account therefore of the Fall of *Adam*, is a *gradual* Declension, or Tendency of his Will, from the Life of Paradise into the Life of this World, till he was at last wholly fallen into it, and swallowed up by it. The first Beginning of his Lust towards this World, was the first Beginning of his Fall, or Departure from the Life of Heaven and Paradise; and his eating of the earthly Tree, was his last and finishing Step of his Entrance into, and under the full Power of this World. This was the true Nature of his Fall. On the other hand, all that we see on the Part of God, is a *gradual* Help, administered by God to this falling Creature, suitable to *every Degree* of his falling, till at last, in the Fulness of his Fall, an *universal* Redeemer of him, and his Posterity, was given by a Second *Adam*, to regenerate again the whole Seed of *Adam* the First.

Thus, the first Degree of his Lust towards this World had *some Stop* put to it, by the taking his *Eve* out of him; that so his Desire into the Life of this World, might be in some measure lessened. When his Lust into this World still went on, and gave Occasion to the Birth of the evil Tree, a suitable Remedy was here given by God; for God laid a *Prohibition* upon it, and declared the *Death* that must be received from it. When he was further so overcome by his lusting Desire, as to eat of the Tree that had the Nature of this World in it, and so lost his first Life, and angelic Clothing, then God, even then all Goodness and Mercy to him, only told him of the *Curse* and *Misery* that was opened in Nature; that himself and Posterity must be sweating, labouring Animals, in a fallen World, till their sickly, shameful, naked, new-gotten Bodies mixed and mouldered in the Corruption of that Earth, whose Fruits they had chosen to know, instead of those of Paradise.

Now all this is nothing of a *Penalty wrathfully* inflicted by God, but was the *natural State of Adam*, as soon as his own Lust had led him out of an heavenly Paradise, into the earthly Life of this World. God brings no Misery upon him, but only *shows* the Misery that he had *opened* in himself, by not keeping to the State in which he was created. And no sooner had God informed this miserable Pair of the State they had brought upon themselves, but, in that Moment, his eternal Love *begins a Covenant* of Redemption, that was to begin in them, and in and through them extend itself to all their Posterity. A Beginning of a new Birth, called the *Seed of the Woman*, as the Remains of the first Breath of Life, was treasured up, or preserved in the Light of their Life, which, as an *Immanuel*, or *God with them*, should be born in all their Posterity, and be their Power of becoming again such Sons of God, as should fulfil the first Designs of the Creation of *Adam*, and fill Heaven again with that Host of Angels which it had lost. Thus from the Creation of *Adam*, through all the Degrees of his Fall to the Mystery of his Redemption, everything tells you, that God is Love. Nay the very Possibility of his having so great a Fall, gives great Glory to the Goodness and Love of God towards him. He was created an Angel, and therefore had the highest Perfection of an Angel, which is a *Freedom* of Willing. Secondly. He was created to be the *restoring* Angel of this new Creation. Now these two Things, which were his highest Glory, and greatest Marks of the Divine Favour, were the only *Possibility* of his falling. Had he not had an angelic Freedom of Will, he could not have had a false Will; had he not had *all Power* given unto him over this World, he could not have fallen into it? It was this Divine and high Power over it, that opened a Way for his Entrance, or falling into it.— Thus, *Academicus*, from this View of Man, we come to the utmost Certainty of a threefold Nature or Life in him. 1. He is the Son of a fallen Angel. 2. He is the Son of a Male and Female of this bestial World. 3. He is a Son of the Lamb of God, and has a Birth of Heaven again in his Soul. Hence we see also, that all that we have to fear, to hate, and renounce; all that we have to love, to desire, and pray for; is *all within* ourselves. No Man can be miserable, but by falling a Sacrifice to his own *inward Passions* and Tempers; nor anyone happy, but by overcoming himself. How ridiculous would a Man seem to you, who should torment himself, because the Land in *America* was not well tilled? Now everything that is not within you, that has not its Birth and Growth in your own Life, is at the same

Distance from you, is as foreign to your own Happiness or Misery, as an *American* Story. Your Life is all that you have; and nothing is a Part of it, or makes any Alteration in it, but the Good or Evil that is in the Workings of your own Life. Hence you may see why our Saviour, who, though he had all Wisdom, and came to be the Light of the World, is yet so short in his Instructions, and gives so small a Number of Doctrines to Mankind, whilst every Moral Teacher, writes Volumes upon every single Virtue. It is because he knew what they knew not, that our whole Malady lies in this, that the *Will* of our Mind, the *Lust* of our Life, is turned into this World; and that nothing can relieve us, or set us right, but the *turning* the Will of our Mind, and the Desire of our Hearts to God, and that Heaven which we had lost. And hence it is, that he calls us to nothing, but a *total Denial* of ourselves, and the *Life* of this World, and to a Faith in him, as the Worker of a new Birth and Life in us. Did we but receive his short Instructions with true Faith, and Simplicity of Heart, as the Truth of God, we should not want anyone to comment or enlarge upon them. A Traveller that has taken a wrong Road, does not want an Orator to discourse to him on the Nature of Roads, but to be told, in short, which is his right Way. Now this is our Case; it was not a *Number* of things that brought about our Fall; *Adam* only took up a *wrong Will;* that Will brought him, and us into our present State, or *Road of Life;* and therefore our Saviour uses not a Number of Instructions to set us right; he only tells us to renounce the *false Will*, which brought *Adam* into the *Life* of this World, and to take up that Will, which should have kept him in Paradise. Observe now, my Friend, the great Benefit that we have from the foregoing Account of Man's original Perfection, and the Nature of his Fall. It opens the true Ground of our Religion, and the absolute Necessity of it; it forces us to know, that our whole natural Life is a mistaken Road, and that Christ is alone our true Guide out of it. It teaches us every Reason for renouncing ourselves, and loving the whole Nature of our Redemption, as the greatest Joy and Desire of our Hearts. We are not only compelled, as it were, to hunger after it, to run with Eagerness into its Arms, but are also delivered from all Mistakes about it, from all the Difficulties and Perplexities, which divided Sects and Churches have brought into it. For, from this View of things, we see, not uncertainly, but with the fullest Assurance, that our *Will*, and our *Heart* is all; that nothing else either finds or loses God; and that all our Religion is only the Religion of the Heart. We see with open Eyes, that as a *Spirit of Longing* after the Life of this World, made *Adam* and us to be the poor

Pilgrims on Earth that we are, so the *Spirit of Prayer*, or the longing Desire of the Heart after Christ, and God, and Heaven, breaks all our Bonds asunder, casts all our Cords from us, and raises us out of the Miseries of Time, into the Riches of Eternity. Thus seeing and knowing our first and our present State, everything calls us to Prayer; and the Desire of our Heart becomes the Spirit of Prayer. And when the Spirit of Prayer is born in us, then Prayer is no longer considered, as only the Business of this or that Hour, but is the continual Panting or Breathing of the Heart after God. Its Petitions are not picked out of Manuals of Devotion; it loves its own Language, it speaks most when it says least. If you ask what its Words are, they are *Spirit*, they are *Life*, they are *Love*, that unite with God.

Acad. I apprehend, Sir, that what you here say of the Spirit of Prayer, will be taken by some People for a Censure upon *Hours* and *Forms* of Prayer; though I know you have no such Meaning.

Rust. Pray let me speak again to *Academicus:* His Learning seems to be always upon the Watch, to find out some Excuse for not receiving the whole Truth. Does not *Theophilus* here speak of the *Spirit of Prayer*, as a *State* of the Heart, which is become the *governing* Principle of the Soul's Life? And if it is a living State of the Heart, must it not have its Life in itself, independent of every outward Time and Occasion? And yet must it not, at the same time, be that alone which disposes and fits the Heart to rejoice and delight in Hours, and Times, and Occasions of Prayer? Suppose he had said, that *Honesty* is an *inward living* Principle of the Heart, a Rectitude of the Mind, that has all its Life and Strength *within* itself: Could this be thought to censure all Times and Occasions of performing outward Acts of Honesty? Now the *Spirit* of Prayer differs from all outward Acts and Forms of Prayer, just as the *Honesty of the Heart*, or a living Rectitude of Mind, differs from outward and occasional Acts of Honesty. And yet should a Man overlook, or disregard Times and Occasions of outward Acts of Honesty, on Pretence that true Honesty was an inward living Principle of the Heart, who would not see, that such a one had as little of the inward Spirit, as of the outward Acts of Honesty? St. *John* saith, 'If any Man hath this World's Goods, and seeth 'his Brother hath need, and shutteth up his Bowels of Com-'passion to him, how dwelleth the Love of God in him?' Just so, and with the same Truth, it may be said, If a Man overlooks, neglects, or refuses, Times and Hours of Prayer, *how dwelleth the Spirit of Prayer* in him? And yet, its own Life and Spirit is vastly superior to, independent of, and stays for no particular Hours, or Forms of Words. And in this Sense it is truly said, that it has its own Language, that it wants not to pick Words out of Manuals of Devotion, but is always speaking forth Spirit and Life, and Love towards God. But pray, *Theophilus*, do you go on, as you intended.

Theoph. I shall only add, before we pass on to another Point, that, from what has been said of the first State and Fall of Man, it plainly follows, that the *Sin* of all Sins, or the *Heresy* of all Heresies, is a *worldly Spirit*. We are apt to consider this Temper only as an Infirmity, or pardonable Failure; but it is indeed the great *Apostasy* from God and the Divine Life. It is not a single Sin, but the whole Nature of all Sin, that leaves no Possibility of coming out of our fallen State, till it be totally renounced with all the Strength of our Hearts. Every Sin, be it of what kind it will, is only a Branch of the worldly Spirit that lives in us. 'There is but one that is good,' saith our Lord, 'and that is God.' In the same Strictness of Expression it must be said, there is but *one Life* that is good, and that is the Life of God and Heaven. Depart in the least Degree from the Goodness of God, and you depart into Evil; because nothing is good but his Goodness.

Choose any Life, but the Life of God and Heaven, and you choose Death; for Death is nothing else but the Loss of the Life of God. The Creatures of this World have but *one Life*, and that is the Life of this World: This is their *one Life*, and *one Good*. Eternal Beings have but *one Life*, and *one Good*, and that is the Life of God. The Spirit of the Soul is in itself nothing else but a Spirit breathed forth from the Life of God, and for this only End, that the Life of God, the Nature of God, the Working of God, the Tempers of God, might be manifested in it. God could not create Man to have a Will of his own, and a Life of his own, different from the Life and Will that is in himself; this is more impossible than for a good Tree to bring forth corrupt Fruit. God can only delight in his own Life, his own Goodness, and his own Perfections; and therefore cannot love or delight, or dwell, in any Creatures, but where his own Goodness and Perfections are to be found. Like can only unite with Like, Heaven with Heaven, and Hell with Hell; and therefore the Life of God must be the Life of the Soul, if the Soul is to unite with God. Hence it is, that all the Religion of fallen Man, all the Methods of our Redemption, have only this *one End*, to take from us that *strange* and *earthly* Life we have gotten by the Fall, and to kindle again the Life of God and Heaven in our Souls: Not to deliver us from that gross and sordid Vice called *Covetousness*, which Heathens can condemn, but to take the *whole Spirit* of this World entirely from us, and that for this necessary Reason, because 'All that is in the World, the Lust of the Flesh, the 'Lust of the Eyes, and the Pride of Life, is not of the Father,' that is, is not that Life, or Spirit of Life, which we had from God by our Creation, 'but is of this World,' is brought into us by our Fall from God into the Life of this World. And therefore a worldly Spirit is not to be considered, as a single Sin, or as something that may consist with some real Degrees of Christian Goodness, but as a State of *real Death* to the Kingdom and Life of God in our Souls. Management, Prudence, or an artful Trimming betwixt God and Mammon, are here all in vain; it is not only the Grossness of an outward, visible, worldly Behaviour, but the *Spirit*, the *Prudence*, the *Subtlety*, the *Wisdom* of this World, that is our *Separation* from the Life of God.

Hold this therefore, *Academicus*, as a certain Truth, that the *Heresy* of all Heresies is a *worldly Spirit*. It is the whole Nature and Misery of our Fall; it keeps up the Death of our Souls, and, so long as it lasts, makes it impossible for us to be born again from above. It is the greatest Blindness and Darkness of our Nature, and keeps us in the grossest Ignorance both of Heaven and Hell. For though they are both of them within us, yet we feel neither the one, nor the other, so long as the Spirit of this World reigns in us. Light, and Truth, and the Gospel, so far as they concern Eternity, are all empty Sounds to the worldly Spirit. His own Good, and his own Evil, govern all his Hopes and Fears; and therefore he can have no Religion, or be further concerned in it, than so far as it can be made serviceable to the Life of this World. *Publicans* and *Harlots* are all born of the Spirit of this World; but its highest Birth, are the *Scribes*, and *Pharisees*, and *Hypocrites*, who turn Godliness into Gain, and serve God for the Sake of Mammon; these live, and move, and have their Being, in and from the Spirit of this World.—Of all Things therefore, my Friend, detest the Spirit of this World, or there is no Help; you must live and die an *utter Stranger* to all that is Divine and heavenly. You will go out of the World in the same Poverty and Death to the Divine Life, in which you entered into it. For a worldly, earthly Spirit can know nothing of God; it can know nothing, feel nothing, taste nothing, delight in nothing, but with earthly Senses, and after an earthly Manner. 'The natural Man,' saith the Apostle, 'receiveth not the Things of the Spirit of God, 'they are Foolishness unto him. He cannot know them, 'because they are spiritually discerned'; that is, they can only be discerned by *that Spirit*, which he has not. Now the true

Ground and *Reason* of this, and the absolute Impossibility for the natural Man to receive and know them, how polite, and learned, and acute soever he be, is this; it is because all *real* Knowledge is *Life*, or a living *Sensibility* of the Thing that is known. There is no Light in the Mind, but what is the Light of *Life;* so far as our Life reaches, so far we understand, and *feel*, and know, and no further. All after this, is only the Play of our Imagination, amusing itself with the *dead Pictures* of its own Ideas. Now this is all that the natural Man, who has not the Life of God in him, can possibly do with the Things of God. He can only contemplate them, as Things *foreign* to himself, as so many *dead Ideas*, that he receives from Books, or Hearsay; and so can learnedly dispute and quarrel about them, and laugh at those as Enthusiasts, who have a living Sensibility of them. He is only the worse for his *hearsay, dead Ideas* of Divine Truths; they become a bad Nourishment of all his natural Tempers: He is proud of his Ability to discourse about them, and loses all Humility, all Love of God and Man, through a vain and haughty Contention for them. His *Zeal* for Religion is Envy and Wrath; his *Orthodoxy* is Pride and Obstinacy; his *Love* of the Truth is Hatred and Ill-will to those who dare to dissent from him. This is the constant Effect of the Religion of the natural Man, who is under the Dominion of the Spirit of this World. He cannot know more of Religion, nor make a better Use of his Knowledge, than this comes to; and all for this plain Reason, because he stands at the *same Distance* from a *living Sensibility* of the Truth, as the Man that is born blind, does from a *living Sensibility* of Light. Light must first be the *Birth* of his own Life, before he can enter into a *real* Knowledge of it. Yet so ignorant is the natural Man with all his learned Acuteness, that he does not so much as know, that there is, and must be, this great *Difference* between real Knowledge, and dead Ideas of Things; and that a Man cannot know anything, any further than as his *own Life* opens the Knowledge of it in himself.

The Measure of our Life is the Measure of our Knowledge; and as the Spirit of our Life works, so the Spirit of our Understanding conceives. If our Will works with God, though our natural Capacity be ever so mean and narrow, we get a real Knowledge of God, and heavenly Truths; for everything must feel that in which it lives.

But if our Will works with Satan, and the Spirit of this World, let our Parts be ever so bright, our Imaginations ever so soaring, yet all our living Knowledge, or real Sensibility, can go no higher or deeper, than the *Mysteries* of Iniquity, and the

Lusts of Flesh and Blood. For where our Life is, there, and there only, is our Understanding; and that for this plain Reason, because as Life is the *Beginning* of all Sensibility, so it is and must be the *Bounds* of it; and no Sensibility can go any further than the Life goes, or have any other *Manner* of Knowledge, than as the Manner of its Life is. If you ask what *Life* is, or what is to be understood by it? It is in itself nothing else but a *working Will;* and no Life could be either good or evil, but for this Reason, because it is a *working Will*: Every Life, from the highest Angel to the lowest Animal, consists in a working Will; and therefore as the Will works, as that is with which it unites, so has every Creature its *Degree*, and *Kind*, and *Manner* of Life; and consequently as the Will of its Life works, so it has its *Degree*, and *Kind*, and *Manner* of Conceiving and Understanding, of Liking and Disliking. For nothing feels, or tastes, or understands, or likes, or dislikes, but the Life that is in us. The Spirit that leads our Life, is the Spirit that forms our Understanding. The Mind is our Eye, and all the Faculties of the Mind see everything according to the State the Mind is in. If *selfish Pride* is the Spirit of our Life, everything is only seen, and felt, and known, through this Glass. Everything is dark, senseless, and absurd to the proud Man, but that which brings Food to this Spirit. He understands nothing, he feels nothing, he tastes nothing, but as his Pride is made *sensible* of it, or capable of being *affected* with it. His *working Will*, which is the Life of his Soul, lives and works only in the Element of Pride; and therefore what suits his Pride, is his *only Good;* and what contradicts his Pride, is *all* the Evil that he can feel or know. His Wit, his Parts, his Learning, his Advancement, his Friends, his Admirers, his Successes, his Conquests, all these are the *only* God and Heaven, that he has any *living* Sensibility of. He indeed can talk of a Scripture-God, a Scripture-Christ, and Heaven; but these are only the ornamental Furniture of his Brain, whilst Pride is the God of his Heart. We are told, that 'God resisteth the Proud, and giveth Grace to the Humble.' This is not to be understood, as if God, by an *arbitrary Will*, only chose to deal thus with the proud and humble Man. Oh no. The true Ground is this, The *Resistance* is on the Part of Man. Pride resisteth God, it rejects him, it turns from him, and chooses to worship and adore something else instead of him; whereas Humility leaves all for God, falls down before him, and opens all the Doors of the Heart for his Entrance into it. This is the only Sense, in which God resisteth the Proud, and giveth Grace to the Humble. And thus it is in the true Ground and Reason of every Good and Evil that rises up in us;

we have neither Good nor Evil, but as it is the *natural* Effect of the *Workings* of our own Will, either with, or against God; and God only interposes with his Threatenings and Instructions, to *direct* us to the right Use of our Wills, that we may not blindly work ourselves into Death, instead of Life. But take now another Instance like that already mentioned. Look at a Man whose *working Will* is under the Power of *Wrath*. He sees, and hears, and feels, and understands, and talks wholly from the *Light* and *Sense* of Wrath. All his Faculties are only so many Faculties of Wrath; and he knows of no Sense or Reason, but that which his enlightened Wrath discovers to him. I have appealed, *Academicus*, to these Instances, only to illustrate and confirm that great Truth, which I before asserted, namely, that the *working of our Will*, or the State of our Life, governs the State of our Mind, and forms the *Degree* and *Manner* of our Understanding and Knowledge; and that as the *Fire* of our Life burns, so is the Light of our Life kindled: And all this only to show you the utter *Impossibility* of *knowing* God, and Divine Truths, till your *Life* is Divine, and wholly dead to the Life and Spirit of this World; since our Light and Knowledge can be no better, or higher, than the State of our Life and Heart is. Tell me now, do you feel the Truth of all this? I say feel, because no Truth is possessed, till you have a feeling and living Sensibility of it.

Acad. Oh! Sir, you have touched every String of my Heart; and I now wish, with the *Psalmist*, that I had the Wings of a Dove, that I might fly away, and be at Rest; fly away from the Spirit of this World, to be at Rest in the sweet Tranquillity of a Life born again of God. You know, Sir, that in the Morning you told me of a certain *first Step*, that all Necessity must be the *Beginning* of a spiritual Life; you gave me till To-morrow to speak my Mind and Resolution about it. But you have now extorted my Answer from me, I cannot stay a Moment longer: With all the Strength that I have, I turn from every Thing that is not God, and his holy Will; with all the Desire, Delight, and Longing of my Heart, I give up myself wholly to the Life, Light, and Holy Spirit of God; pleased with nothing in this World, but as it gives Time, and Place, and Occasions, of doing and being *that*, which my heavenly Father would have me to do, and be; seeking for no Happiness from this earthly fallen Life, but that of *overcoming* all its Spirit and Tempers. But I believe, *Theophilus*, that you had something further to say.

Theoph. Indeed, *Academicus*, there is hardly any knowing, when one has said enough of the evil Effects of a *worldly Spirit*. It is the Canker that eats up all the Fruits of our other good

Tempers; it leaves no Degree of Goodness in them, but transforms all that we are, or do, into its own earthly Nature. The *Philosophers* of old, began all their Virtue in a total Renunciation of the Spirit of this World. They saw with the Eyes of Heaven, that Darkness was not more contrary to Light, than the Wisdom of this World was contrary to the Spirit of Virtue; therefore they allowed of no Progress in Virtue, but so far as a Man had overcome himself, and the Spirit of this World.

This gave a Divine Solidity to all their Instructions, and proved them to be Masters of true Wisdom. But the Doctrine of the Cross of Christ, the last, the highest, the most finishing Stroke given to the Spirit of this World, that speaks more in *one Word* than all the Philosophy of voluminous Writers, is yet professed by those, who are in more Friendship with the World, than was allowed to the Disciples of *Pythagoras, Socrates, Plato*, or *Epictetus*.

Nay, if those ancient Sages were to start up amongst us with their Divine Wisdom, they would bid fair to be treated by the Sons of the Gospel, if not by some Fathers of the Church, as dreaming Enthusiasts.

But, *Academicus*, this is a standing Truth, The World can only love its own, and Wisdom can only be justified of her Children. The Heaven-born *Epictetus* told one of his Scholars, That *then* he might *first* look upon himself, as having made *some true* Proficiency in Virtue, when the World took him for a *Fool;* an Oracle like that, which said, *The Wisdom of this World is Foolishness with God.*

If you were to ask me, What is the Apostasy of these last Times, or whence is all the Degeneracy of the present Christian Church? I should place it all in a *worldly Spirit*. If here you see open Wickedness, there only Forms of Godliness; if here superficial Holiness, political Piety, crafty Prudence, there haughty Sanctity, partial Zeal, envious Orthodoxy; if almost everywhere you see a *Jewish* Blindness, and Hardness of Heart, and the Church trading with the Gospel, as the old *Jews* bought and sold Beasts in their Temple; all these are only so many Forms and proper Fruits of the worldly Spirit. This is the great *Net*, with which the Devil becomes a Fisher of Men; and be assured of this, my Friend, that every Son of Man is in this *Net*, till through and by the Spirit of Christ, he breaks out of it.

I say the *Spirit* of Christ, for nothing else can deliver him from it. Trust now to any Kind, or Form of religious Observances, to any Number of the most plausible Virtues, to any Kinds of Learning, or Efforts of human Prudence, and then I will tell you what your Case will be; you will overcome *one*

Temper of the World, *only* and *merely* by cleaving to another. For nothing leaves the World, nothing renounces it, nothing can possibly overcome it, but singly and solely the Spirit of Christ. Hence it is, that many learned Men, with all the rich Furniture of their Brain, live and die Slaves to the Spirit of this World; and can only differ from gross Worldlings, as the *Scribes* and *Pharisees* differ from *Publicans* and *Sinners*: It is because the Spirit of Christ, is not the *one only* thing that is the *Desire* of their Hearts; and therefore their Learning only works in, and with the Spirit of this World, and becomes itself, no small Part of the *Vanity of Vanities.* Would you further know, *Academicus,* the evil Nature and Effects of a worldly Spirit, you need only look at the blessed Power and Effects of the *Spirit of Prayer;* for the one goes downwards with the same Strength, as the other goes upwards; the one betroths and weds you to an earthly Nature, with the same Certainty, as the other espouses, and unites you to Christ, and God, and Heaven. The Spirit of Prayer, is a *pressing forth* of the Soul out of this earthly Life; it is a stretching with all its Desire after the Life of God; it is a leaving, as far as it can, all its *own Spirit,* to receive a Spirit from above, to be one Life, one Love, one Spirit with Christ in God. This Prayer, which is an emptying itself of all its own Lusts, and natural Tempers, and an opening itself for the Light and Love of God to enter into it, is the Prayer in *the Name of Christ,* to which nothing is denied. For the Love which God bears to the Soul, his eternal, never-ceasing Desire to enter into it, to dwell in it, and open the Birth of his Holy Word, and Spirit in it, stays no longer, than till the Door of the Heart opens for him. For nothing does, or can keep God out of the Soul, or hinder his holy Union with it, but the *Desire* of the Heart turned from him. And the Reason of it is this; it is because the *Life* of the Soul is in itself nothing else but a *working Will;* and therefore wherever the Will works or goes, there, and there only, the Soul lives, whether it be in God, or the Creature.

Whatever it desires, that is the *Fuel* of its Fire; and as its Fuel is, so is the Flame of its Life. A Will, given up to earthly Goods, is at Grass with *Nebuchadnezzar,* and has one Life with the Beasts of the Field: For earthly Desires keep up the *same Life* in a Man and an Ox. For the one only Reason, why the Animals of this World have no Sense or Knowledge of God, is this; it is because they cannot form any other than earthly Desires, and so can only have an earthly Life. When therefore a Man wholly turns his working Will to earthly Desires, he dies to the Excellence of his natural State, and may be said only to live, and move, and have his Being, in the Life of this World, as the Beasts have.—Earthly Food, &c., only desired and used for the Support of the earthly Body, is suitable to Man's present Condition, and the Order of Nature: But when the Desire, the Delight, and Longing of the Soul is set upon earthly Things, then the Humanity is degraded, is fallen from God; and the Life of the Soul is made as *earthly* and *bestial*, as the Life of the Body: For the Creature can be neither higher nor lower, neither better nor worse, than as the Will worketh: For you are to observe, that the Will has a Divine and *magic* Power; what it desires, that it takes, and of that it *eateth* and *liveth*. Wherever, and in whatever, the *working* Will chooses to *dwell* and *delight*, that becomes the Soul's *Food*, its *Condition*, its *Body*, its *Clothing*, and *Habitation*: For all these are the true and certain Effects and Powers of the working Will.

Nothing does, or can go with a Man into Heaven, nothing follows him into Hell, but *that* in which the Will dwelt, with which it was fed, nourished, and clothed, in this Life. And this is to be noted well, that Death can make no Alteration of this State of the Will; it only takes off the outward, worldly Covering of Flesh and Blood, and forces the Soul to see, and feel, and know, what a Life, what a State, *Food, Body,* and *Habitation,* its own working Will has brought forth for it. Oh *Academicus*, stop awhile, and let your Hearing be turned into Feeling. Tell me, is there anything in Life that deserves a Thought, but how to keep this *Working* of our Will in a right State, and to get that *Purity* of Heart, which alone can see, and know, and find, and possess God? Is there anything so frightful as this worldly Spirit, which turns the Soul from God, makes it an House of Darkness, and feeds it with the Food of Time, at the Expense of all the Riches of Eternity?

On the other hand, what can be so desirable a Good as the *Spirit of Prayer*, which empties the Soul of all its own Evil, separates Death and Darkness from it, leaves *Self, Time,* and the *World,* and becomes one Life, one Light, one Love, one Spirit with Christ, and God, and Heaven?

Think, my Friends, of these Things, with something more than Thoughts; let your hungry Souls eat of the Nourishment of them as a Bread of Heaven; and desire only to live, that with all the *Working* of your Wills, and the *whole Spirit* of your Minds, you may live and die united to God: And thus let this Conversation end, till God gives us another Meeting.

The End of the Second DIALOGUE.

THE
THIRD DIALOGUE.

*R*UST. I have brought again with me, Gentlemen, my silent Friend, *Humanus*, and upon the same Condition of being silent still. But though his Silence is the same, yet he is quite altered. For this twenty Years I have known him to be of an even cheerful Temper, full of Good-nature, and even quite calm and dispassionate in his Attacks upon Christianity, never provoked by what was said either against his Infidelity, or in Defence of the Gospel. He used to boast of his being free from those four Passions and Resentments, which, he said, were so easy to be seen, in many or most Defenders of the Gospel-Meekness. But now he is morose, peevish, and full of Chagrin, and seems to be as uneasy with himself, as with every Body else: whatever he says, is rash, satirical, and wrathful. I tell him, but he will not own it, that his Case is this: The Truth has touched him; but it is only so far, as to be his *Tormentor*. It is only as welcome to him, as a *Thief* that has taken from him all his Riches, Goods, and Armour, wherein he trusted. The Christianity he used to oppose is vanished; and therefore all the Weapons he had against it, are dropped out of his Hands. It now appears to stand upon another Ground, to have a deeper Bottom, and better Nature, than what he imagined; and therefore he, and his Scheme of Infidelity, are quite disconcerted. But though his Arguments have thus lost all their Strength, yet his *Heart* is left in the State it was; it stands in the same Opposition to Christianity as it did before, and yet without any Ideas of his Brain to support it. And this is the true Ground of his present, uneasy, peevish State of Mind. He has nothing now to subsist upon, but the resolute *Hardness* of his Heart, his *Pride* and *Obstinacy*. These he cannot give up by the Force of his Reason; his Heart cannot bear the Thoughts of such a Sacrifice; and yet he feels and knows, that he has no Strength left, but in a settled Hardness, Pride, and Obstinacy, to continue as he is.—These, I own, are severe and hard Words: But, hard as they are, I am sure *Humanus* knows, that they proceed from the Softness and Affection of my Heart towards him, from a compassionate Zeal to show him where his Malady lies, and the Necessity of overcoming himself, before he can have the Blessing of Light, and Truth, and Peace. Though it is with some Reluctance, yet I have chosen thus to make my Neighbour known both to himself, and to you, that you may speak of such Matters as may give the best Relief to the State he is in.

Theoph. Indeed, *Rusticus*, I much approve of the Spirit you have here shown, with regard to your Friend, and hope he will take in good Part all that you have said. As for me, I embrace him with the utmost Tenderness of Affection. I feel and compassionate the trying State of his Heart, and have only this one Wish, that I could pour the heavenly Water of Meekness, and the Oil of Divine Love, into it. Let us force him to know, that we are the Messengers of Divine Love to him; that we seek not ourselves, nor our own Victory, but to make him victorious over his own Evil, and become possessed of a new Life in God. His Trial is the greatest and hardest that belongs to human Nature: And yet it is absolutely necessary to be undergone.

Nature must become a Torment and Burden to itself, before it can willingly give itself up to that Death, through which alone it can pass into Life. There is no true and real *Conversion*, whether it be from Infidelity, or any other Life of Sin, till a Man comes to know, and feel, that nothing less than his *whole* Nature is to be parted with, and yet finds in himself no *Possibility* of doing it. This is the Inability that can bring us at last to say, with the Apostle, 'When I am weak, then am I strong.' This is the Distress that stands near to the Gate of Life; this is the Despair by which we lose all our own Life, to find a new one in God. For here, in this Place it is, that *Faith*, and *Hope*, and true Seeking to God and Christ, are born.—But till all is Despair in ourselves, till all is lost that we had any Trust in as our own; till then, Faith and Hope, and turning to God in Prayer, are only things learnt and practised by *Rule* and *Method;* but they are not born in us, are not *living* Qualities of a new Birth, till we have done feeling any Trust or Confidence in ourselves. Happy therefore is it for your Friend *Humanus*, that he is come thus far, that everything is taken from him on which he trusted, and found Content in himself. In this State, one *Sigh* or *Look*, or the least *Turning* of his Heart to God for Help, would be the Beginning of his Salvation. Let us therefore try to improve this happy Moment to him, not so much by Arguments of Reason, as by the Arrows of that Divine Love which overflows all Nature and Creature.

For *Humanus*, though hitherto without Christ, is still within the Reach of Divine Love: He belongs to God; God created him for himself, to be an Habitation of his own Life, Light, and Holy Spirit; and God has brought him and us together, that the lost Sheep may be found, and brought back to its heavenly Shepherd.

Oh *Humanus*, Love is my *Bait;* you must be caught by it; it will put its Hook into your Heart, and force you to know, that of all strong Things, nothing is so strong, so irresistible, as Divine Love.

It brought forth all the Creation ; it kindles all the Life of Heaven ; it is the Song of all the Angels of God. It has redeemed all the World ; it seeks for every Sinner upon Earth ; it embraces all the Enemies of God ; and from the Beginning to the End of Time, the one Work of Providence, is the one Work of Love.

Moses and the Prophets, Christ and his Apostles, were all of them Messengers of Divine Love. They came to kindle a Fire on Earth, and that Fire was the Love which burns in Heaven. Ask what God is? His Name is Love ; he is the Good, the Perfection, the Peace, the Joy, the Glory, and Blessing, of every Life. Ask what Christ is? He is the *universal Remedy* of all Evil broken forth in Nature and Creature. He is the *Destruction* of Misery, Sin, Darkness, Death, and Hell. He is the *Resurrection and Life* of all fallen Nature. He is the unwearied Compassion, the long-suffering Pity, the never-ceasing Mercifulness of God to every Want and Infirmity of human Nature.

He is the Breathing forth of the Heart, Life, and Spirit of God, into all the dead Race of *Adam.* He is the Seeker, the Finder, the Restorer, of all that was lost and dead to the Life of God. He is the Love, that, from *Cain* to the End of Time, prays for all its Murderers ; the Love that willingly suffers and dies among Thieves, that Thieves may have a Life with him in Paradise ; the Love that visits Publicans, Harlots, and Sinners, and wants and seeks to forgive, where most is to be forgiven.

Oh, my Friends, let us surround and encompass *Humanus* with these Flames of Love, till he cannot make his Escape from them, but must become a willing Victim to their Power. For the universal God is universal Love ; all is Love, but that which is hellish and earthly. All Religion is the Spirit of Love ; all its Gifts and Graces are the Gifts and Graces of Love ; it has no Breath, no Life, but the Life of Love. Nothing exalts, nothing purifies, but the Fire of Love ; nothing changes Death into Life, Earth into Heaven, Men into Angels, but Love alone. Love breathes the *Spirit* of God ; its Words and Works are the *Inspiration* of God. It speaketh not of itself, but the *Word*, the eternal Word of God speaketh in it ; for all that Love speaketh, that God speaketh, because Love is God. Love is Heaven revealed in the Soul ; it is Light, and Truth ; it is infallible ; it has no Errors, for all Errors are the Want of Love. Love has no more of Pride, than Light has of Darkness ; it stands and bears all its Fruits from a Depth, and Root of Humility. Love is of no Sect or Party; it neither makes, nor admits of any Bounds ; you may as easily inclose the Light, or shut up the Air of the World into one Place, as confine Love to a Sect or Party. It lives in the *Liberty*, the *Universality*, the *Impartiality* of Heaven. It believes in one, holy, catholic God, the God of all Spirits ; it unites and joins with the catholic Spirit of the one God, who unites with all that is good, and is meek, patient, well-wishing, and long-suffering over all the Evil that is in Nature and Creature. Love, like the Spirit of God, rideth upon the Wings of the Wind ; and is in Union and Communion with all the Saints that are in Heaven and on Earth. Love is quite pure ; it has no By-ends ; it seeks not its own ; it has but *one Will*, and that is, to give itself into everything, and overcome all Evil with Good. Lastly, Love is the *Christ* of God ; it comes down from Heaven ; it regenerates the Soul from above ; it blots out all Transgressions ; it takes from Death its Sting, from the Devil his Power, and from the Serpent his Poison. It heals all the Infirmities of our earthly Birth ; it gives Eyes to the Blind, Ears to the Deaf, and makes the Dumb to speak ; it cleanses the Lepers, and casts out Devils, and puts Man in Paradise before he dies. It lives wholly to the Will of him, of whom it is born; its Meat and Drink is, to do the Will of God. It is the Resurrection and Life of every Divine Virtue, a fruitful Mother of true Humility, boundless Benevolence, unwearied Patience, and Bowels of Compassion. This, *Rusticus*, is the Christ, the Salvation, the Religion of Divine Love, the true Church of God, where the Life of God is found, and lived, and to which your Friend *Humanus* is called by us. We direct him to nothing but the inward Life of Christ, to the Working of the Holy Spirit of God, which alone can deliver him from the Evil that is in his own Nature, and give him a Power to become a Son of God.

Rust. My Neighbour has infinite Reason to thank you, for this lovely Draught you have given of the Spirit of Religion ; he cannot avoid being affected with it. But pray let us now hear, how we are to enter into this Religion of Divine Love, or rather what God has done to introduce us into it, and make us Partakers again of his Divine Nature.

Theoph. The first Work, or Beginning of this redeeming Love of God, is in that *Immanuel*, or God with us, treasured up, or preserved in the first *Adam*, as the *Seed of the Woman*, which in him, and all his Posterity, should bruise the Head, and overcome the Life of the Serpent in our fallen Nature. This is Love indeed, because it is universal, and reaches every Branch of the human Tree, from the first to the last Man, that grows from it. Miserably as Mankind are divided, and all at War with one another, everyone *appropriating* God to themselves, yet they all have but one God, who is the Spirit of all, the Life of all, and the Lover of all. Men may divide themselves, to have God to themselves; they may hate and persecute one another for God's sake; but this is a blessed Truth, that neither the Hater, nor the Hated, can be divided from the one, holy, catholic God, who with an unalterable Meekness, Sweetness, Patience, and Goodwill towards all, waits for all, calls them all, redeems them all, and comprehends all in the outstretched Arms of his catholic Love. Ask not therefore how we shall enter into this Religion of Love and Salvation? for it is itself entered into us, it has taken Possession of us from the Beginning. It is *Immanuel* in every human Soul; it lies as a Treasure of Heaven, and Eternity in us; it cannot be divided from us by the Power of Man; we cannot lose it ourselves; it will never leave us nor forsake us, till with our last Breath we die in the Refusal of it. This is the open Gate of our Redemption; we have not far to go to find it. It is every Man's own Treasure; it is a Root of Heaven, a Seed of God, sown into our Souls by the *Word* of God; and, like a small Grain of Mustard-seed, has a Power of growing to be a Tree of Life. Here, my Friend, you should, once for all, mark and observe, *where* and *what* the true Nature of Religion is; for here it is plainly shown you, that its *Place* is within; its Work and Effect is *within;* its Glory, its Life, its Perfection, is all within; it is merely and solely the raising a new Life, new Love, and a new Birth, in the inward Spirit of our Hearts. Religion (which is solely to restore Man to his first and right State in God) had its Beginning, and first Power, from the *Seed of the Woman*, the Treader on the Serpent's Head; and therefore all its Progress, from its Beginning to its last finished Work, is, and can be nothing else, but the growing Power and Victory of the *Seed of the Woman*, over all the Evil brought by the Serpent into human Nature. For the Seed of the Woman is the Spirit, and Power, and Life of God, given or breathed again into Man, to be the Raiser and Redeemer of that first Life, which he had lost. This was the *spiritual* Nature of Religion in its first Beginning, and this alone is its *whole Nature* to the End of Time; it is nothing else, but the Power, and Life, and Spirit of God, as *Father*, *Son*, and *Holy Spirit*, working, creating, and reviving Life in the fallen Soul, and driving all its Evil out of it. This is the true Rock, on which the Church of Christ is built; this is the *one Church* out of which there is no Salvation, and against which the Gates of Hell can never prevail.

Here therefore we are come to this firm Conclusion, that let Religion have ever so many *Shapes, Forms,* or *Reformations,* it is no true Divine *Service,* no proper *Worship* of God, has no Good in it, can do no Good to Man, can remove no Evil out of him, raise no Divine Life in him, but so far as it *serves, worships, conforms,* and *gives* itself up to this *Operation* of the holy, triune God, as living and dwelling in the Soul. Keep close to this Idea of Religion, as an inward, spiritual Life in the Soul; observe all its Works within you, the Death and Life that are found there; seek for no Good, no Comfort, but in the inward Awakening of all that is holy and heavenly in your Heart; and then, so much as you have of this inward Religion, so much you have of a real Salvation. For Salvation is only a Victory over Nature; so far as you resist and renounce your own vain, selfish, and earthly Nature, so far as you overcome all your own natural Tempers of the old Man, so far God enters into you, lives, and operates in you, he is in you the Light, the Life, and the Spirit, of your Soul; and you are in him that new Creature, that worships him in Spirit, and in Truth. For Divine Worship or Service is, and can be only performed by being *like-minded* with Christ; nothing worships God, but the Spirit of Christ his beloved Son, in whom he is well pleased. This is as true, as that 'no Man hath known 'the Father, but the Son, and he to whom the Son revealeth 'him.' Look now at anything as Religion, or Divine Service, but a strict, unerring Conformity to the Life and Spirit of Christ, and then, though every Day was full of Burnt-offerings, and Sacrifices, yet you would be only like those Religionists, who 'drew near to God with their Lips, but their Hearts were far 'from him.'

For the Heart is always far from God, unless the Spirit of Christ be alive in it. But no one has the living Spirit of Christ, but he who in all his Conversation walketh, as he walked. Consider these Words of the Apostle, ' My little Children, of whom ' I travail in Birth, till Christ be formed in you.' This is the Sum total of all, and, if this is wanting, all is wanting. Again, says he, ' He is not a Jew, which is one outwardly.—Circumcision is ' nothing, and Uncircumcision is nothing, but the new Creature ' is all.' Nay, see how much further he carries this Point, in the following Words: ' Though I speak with the Tongues of Men ' and Angels, though I have the Gift of Prophecy, though I have ' all Faith, so that I could remove Mountains,' *&c.,* ' and have not ' Charity' (that is, have not the Spirit of Christ) 'it profiteth me ' nothing.' For by *Charity* here, the Apostle means neither more nor less, but strictly that same Thing, which, in other Places, he calls the *new Creature, Christ formed in us*, and our being led by the Spirit of Christ. According to the Apostle, nothing avails but the *new Creature*, nothing avails but the Spirit of Charity here described; therefore this Charity, and the new Creature, are only two different Expressions of *one* and the *same* Thing, viz., the *Birth*, and *Formation* of Christ in us. Thus saith he, 'If any Man has not the Spirit of Christ, he is none of his;' nay, though he could say of himself (as our Lord says many will) Have I not prophesied in the Name of Christ, cast out Devils, and done many wonderful Works? yet such a one not being *led by the Spirit of Christ*, is that very Man, whose high State the Apostle makes to be a mere Nothing, because he has not that Spirit of Charity, which is the Spirit of Christ. Again, 'There 'is no Condemnation to those, who are in Christ Jesus;' therefore to be in Christ Jesus, is to have that Spirit of Charity, which is the Spirit, and Life, and Goodness of all Virtues. Now here you are to observe, that the Apostle no more rejects *all outward* Religion, when he says *Circumcision is nothing*, than he rejects *Prophesying*, and *Faith*, and *Alms-giving*, when he says they *profit nothing;* he only teaches this solid Truth, that the Kingdom of God is within us, and that it all consists in the State of our Heart; and that therefore all outward Observances, all the most specious Virtues, profit nothing, are of no Value, unless the hidden Man of the Heart, the new Creature, led by the Spirit of Christ, be the Doer of them.

Thus, says he, 'They who are led by the Spirit of God, are 'the Sons of God.' And therefore none else, be they who, or where, or what they will, Clergy, or Laity, none are, or can be, Sons of God, but they who give up themselves entirely to the Leading and Guidance of the Spirit of God, desiring to be moved, inspired, and governed solely by it.

Again, 'We are of the Circumcision, who worship God in 'Spirit'; and to show, that this is not a vain Pretence, he says in another Place, 'The Manifestation of the Spirit is given to 'every Man to profit withal.' Therefore *no Profit* from anything else; all Preaching and Hearing is vain, and all Preachers and Hearers stand chargeable with the Vanity of their religious Performances, who think of Preaching or Hearing *profitably*, any other Way, or by any other Power, than in and by the Holy Spirit of God dwelling and working in them. Thus again, 'If 'the Spirit of him, who raised Jesus from the Dead, dwell in you, 'he also shall quicken your mortal Bodies by his Spirit, which 'dwelleth in you.' In vain therefore is Life expected, either for Body or Soul, but by the Holy Spirit dwelling in them. Again,

'Through him we both have Access by one Spirit to the Father'; therefore this *one Spirit* is the one only Way to God, and Salvation. Thus does all Scripture bring us to this Conclusion, that all Religion is but a dead Work, unless it be the Work of the Spirit of God; and that Sacraments, Prayers, Singing, Preaching, Hearing, are only so many Ways of being fervent in the Spirit, and of giving up ourselves more and more to the inward working, enlightening, quickening, sanctifying Spirit of God within us; and all for this End, that the Curse of the *Fall* may be taken from us, that Death may be swallowed up in Victory, and a true, real, Christ-like Nature formed in us, by the same Spirit, by which it was formed in the Holy Virgin *Mary*. Now for the true Ground, and absolute Necessity, of this turning wholly and solely to the Spirit of God, you need only know this plain Truth; namely, that the Spirit of God, the Spirit of *Satan*, or the Spirit of this World, are, and must be, the one or the other of them, the *continual* Leader, Guide, and Inspirer, of everything that lives in Nature. There is no going out from some one of these; the Moment you cease to be moved, quickened, and inspired by God, you are infallibly moved and directed by the Spirit of *Satan*, or the World, or by both of them. And the Reason is, because the Soul of Man is a *Spirit*, and a *Life*, that in its whole Being is nothing else but a *Birth* both of God and Nature; and therefore, every Moment of its Life, it must live in some Union and Conjunction, either with the Spirit of God governing Nature, or with the Spirit of Nature fallen from God, and working in itself. As Creatures therefore, we are under an absolute Necessity of being under the Motion, Guidance, and Inspiration, of some Spirit, that is more and greater than our own. All that is put in our own Power, is only the Choice of our *Leader;* but led and moved we must be, and by that Spirit, to which we give up ourselves, whether it be to the Spirit of God, or the Spirit of fallen Nature. To seek therefore to be always under the Inspiration and Guidance of God's Holy Spirit, and to act by an immediate Power from it, is not proud Enthusiasm, but as sober and humble a Thought, as suitable to our State, as to think of renouncing the World, and the Devil: For they never are, or can be, renounced by us, but so far as the Spirit of God is living, breathing, and moving in us: And that for this plain Reason, because nothing is contrary to the Spirit of *Satan*, and the World, nothing works, or can work, contrary to it, but the Spirit of Heaven.

Hence our Lord said, 'He that is not with me, is against me; and 'he that gathereth not with me, scattereth;' plainly declaring, that not to be with him, and led by his Spirit is to be led by the Spirit of *Satan*, and the World. Ask now, what Hell is? It is Nature destitute of the Light and Spirit of God, and full only of its own Darkness; nothing else can make it to be Hell. Ask what Heaven is? It is Nature quickened, enlightened, blessed, and glorified, by the Light and Spirit of *God* dwelling in it. What Possibility therefore can there be, of our dividing from Hell, or parting with all that is hellish in us, but by having the Life, Light, and Spirit of God living and working in us? And here again, my Friends, you may see in the greatest Clearness, why nothing is available, nothing is Salvation, but the new Birth of a Christlike Nature; it is because everything else but this Birth, and Life of the Spirit, is only the Spirit of *Satan*, or the Spirit of this World. Have you anything to object to these things?

Acad. Truly, Sir, all Objections are over with me; you have taken from me every Difficulty or Perplexity that I had, either about Religion, or the Providence of God. I can now look back into the first Origin of Things with Satisfaction: I have seen how the World and Man began to be, in a Way highly worthy of the Divine Wisdom, and how they both came into their present Condition, and how they both are to rise out of it, and return back to their first State in a glorious Eternity. It now appears to me with the utmost Clearness, that to look for Salvation in anything else, but the Light of God *within* us, the Spirit of God working *in us*, the Birth of Christ *really* brought forth *in us*, is to be as carnally minded, as ignorant of God, and Man, and Salvation, as the Jews were, when their Hearts were wholly set upon the Glory of their *Temple-service*, and a temporal Saviour to defend it, by a temporal Power. For everything but the Light and Spirit of God bringing forth a Birth of Christ in the Soul, everything else, be it what it will, has and can have no more of Salvation in it, than a temporal fighting Saviour. For what is said of the Impossibility of the Blood of Bulls and of Goats to take away Sins, must with the same Truth be said of all other outward creaturely Things; they are all at the same Distance from being the Salvation of the Soul, and in the same Degree of Inability to take away Sins, as the Blood of Bulls and Goats.

And all this for this plain Reason, because the Soul is a Spirit breathed forth from God himself, which therefore cannot be blessed but by having the Life of God in it; and nothing can bring the Life of God into it, but only the Light and Spirit of God. Upon this Ground I stand in the utmost Certainty, looking wholly to the Light and Spirit of God for an inward Redemption from all the inward Evil that is in my fallen Nature. All that I now want to know is this, what I am to do, to procure this continual Operation of the Spirit of God within me. For I seem to myself, not to know this enough; and I am also afraid of certain Delusions, which I have heard many have fallen into, under Pretences of being led by the Spirit of God. Pray therefore, *Theophilus*, give me some Instructions on this Head.

Rust. Pray, Gentlemen, let an unlearned Man speak a Word here. Suppose, *Academicus*, you had a longing earnest Desire, to be governed by a *Spirit* of *Plainness* and *Sincerity* in your whole Conversation. Would this put you upon asking for *Art*, and *Rules*, and *Methods*, or consulting some learned Man, or Book, to direct you, and keep you from Delusion? Would you not know and feel in yourself, that your own earnest Desire, and Love of Sincerity and Plainness, and your own inward Aversion to everything that was contrary to it, must be the one only possible Way of attaining it, and that you must have it in that Degree, as you loved and liked to act by it? Now there is no more of *Art*, or any *Secret* required to bring and keep you under the Direction of the Spirit of God, than under the Spirit of Plainness and Sincerity. The longing earnest Desire of the Heart, brings you into the safe Possession of the one, as it does of the other. For it has been enough proved, that the *Spirit of Prayer* forms the Spirit of our Lives, and every Man lives as the Spirit of Prayer leads him. Nay every Prayer for the Holy Spirit, is the Spirit itself praying in you. For nothing can turn to God, desire to be united to him, and governed by him, but the Spirit of God. The Impossibility of praying for the Spirit of God in vain, is thus shown by our blessed Lord: 'If ye, 'being evil, know how to give good Gifts unto your Children, 'how much more shall your heavenly Father give the Holy Spirit 'to those that ask for it?' But I here stop.

Acad. I do not know how to understand what *Rusticus* has said. For do not all good Christians daily pray for the Spirit of God? yet how few are led by it? Pray, *Theophilus*, do you speak here.

Theoph. People may be daily at the Service of the Church, and read long Prayers at home, in which are many Petitions for the Holy Spirit, and yet live and die, led and governed by the Spirit of the World; because all these Prayers, whether we hear them read by others, or read them ourselves, may be done in Compliance only to Duties, Rules, and Forms of Religion, as Things we are taught not to neglect; but, being only done thus, they are not the true, real Working of the Spirit of the Heart, nor make any real Alteration in it. But you are to observe, that *Rusticus* spoke of the *Spirit of Prayer*, which is the Heart's own Prayer, and which has all the Strength of the Heart in it. And this is the Prayer that must be affirmed to be *always* effectual ; it never returns empty ; it eats and drinks that, after which it hungers and thirsts ; and nothing can possibly hinder it from having that, which it prays for. This we are assured of from these Words of Truth itself ; ' Blessed are they that hunger and ' thirst after Righteousness, for they shall be filled.' But this Blessedness could not belong to Hungering, if the truly Hungry and Thirsty, could ever be sent empty away. Every Spirit necessarily reaps that which it sows, it cannot possibly be otherwise, it is the unalterable Procedure of Nature. Spirit is the first Power of Nature, everything proceeds from it, is born of it, yields to it, and is governed by it. If the Spirit soweth to the Flesh, it reapeth that Corruption which belongs to the Flesh ; if it soweth to the Spirit, it reapeth the Fruits of the Spirit, which are eternal Life. *The Spirit of Prayer* therefore is the Opener of all that is good within us, and the Receiver of all that is good without us ; it unites with God, is one Power with him ; it works with him, and drives all that is not God, out of the Soul. The Soul is no longer a Slave to its natural Impurity and Corruption, no longer imprisoned in its own Death and Darkness, but till the Fire from Heaven, the Spirit of Prayer, is kindled in it.

Then begins the Resurrection, and the Life ; and all that which died in *Adam* comes to Life in Christ. Ask not therefore, *Academicus*, what you are to do to obtain the Spirit of God, to live in it, and be led by it ? For your Power of having it, and your Measure of receiving it, are just according to that *Faith* and Earnestness with which you desire to be led by it. For the hungry Spirit of Prayer is *that Faith*, to which all Things are possible, to which all Nature, though as high as Mountains, and as stiff as Oaks, must yield and obey. It heals all Diseases, breaks the Bands of Death, and calls the Dead out of their Graves. Look at the small *Seeds* of Plants, shut up in their own dead Husks, and covered with thick Earth, and see how they grow. What do they do ? They *hunger* and *thirst* after the Light and Air of this World. Their Hunger eats that which they hunger after, and this is their Vegetation. If the Plant ceases to hunger, it withers and dies, though surrounded with the Air and Light of this World.

This is the true Nature of the spiritual Life ; it is as truly a Growth or *Vegetation*, as that of Plants ; and nothing but its *own Hunger* can help it to the true Food of its Life. If this hunger of the Soul ceases, it withers and dies, though in the midst of Divine Plenty. Our Lord, to show us that the new Birth s really a State of spiritual Vegetation, compares it to a small Grain of Mustard-seed, from whence a great Plant arises. Now every Seed has a Life in itself, or else it could not grow. What is this Life? It is nothing else but an *Hunger* in the Seed, after the Air and Light of this World; which Hunger, being met and fed by the Light and Air of Nature, changes the Seed into a living Plant. Thus it is with the *Seed* of Heaven in the Soul? it has a Life in itself, or else no Life could arise from it. What is this Life? It is nothing else but Faith, or an *Hunger* after God and Heaven; which no sooner stirs, or is suffered to stir, but it is met, embraced, and quickened, by the *Light* and *Spirit* of God and Heaven; and so a new Man in Christ, is formed from the Seed of Heaven, as a new Plant from a Seed in the Earth. Let us suppose now, that the *Seed* of a Plant had *Sense* and *Reason*, and that, instead of continually hungering after, and drawing in the Virtue of the Light and Air of our outward Nature, it should amuse, and content its Hunger with *reasoning* about the Nature of Hunger, and the different Powers and Virtues of Light and Air; must not such a Seed of all Necessity wither away, without ever becoming a living Plant? Now this is no false Similitude of the *Seed* of Life in Man: Man has a Power of drawing all the Virtue of Heaven into himself, because the *Seed* of Heaven is the *Gift* of God in his Soul, which wants the Light and Spirit of God to bring it to the Birth, just as the Seed of the Plant wants the Light and Air of this World; it cannot possibly grow up in God, but by taking in Light, Life, and Spirit from Heaven, as the Creatures of Time take in the Light, and Life, and Spirit of this World. If therefore the Soul, instead of *hungering* after Heaven, instead of eating the Flesh and Blood of the Christ of God, contents and amuses this *Seed* of Life with *Ideas*, and *Notions*, and Sounds, must not such a Soul of Necessity wither, and die, without ever becoming a living Creature of Heaven? Wonder not therefore, *Academicus*, that *all the Work* of our Salvation and Regeneration is, by the Scripture, *wholly* confined to the Operation of the Light and Spirit of God, *living* and *working* in us. It is for the same Reason, and on the same Necessity, that the Life and Growth of the Creatures of this World, must be *wholly* ascribed to the Powers of this World, living and working in them. Nor does all this, in the least Degree, make a Man a *Machine*, or without any Power with regard to his Salvation. He must grow in God, as the *Plants* grow in this World, from a Power that is not his own, as they grow from the Powers of outward Nature. But he differs entirely from the Plants in this, that an *uncontrollable* Will, which is his own, must be the Leader and Beginner of his Growth either in God, or Nature. It is strictly true, that all Man's Salvation depends upon himself; and it is as strictly true, that *all the Work* of his Salvation, is *solely* the Work of God in his Soul. All his Salvation depends upon himself, because his *Will-Spirit* has its Power of Motion in itself. As a Will, it can only receive that which it willeth; everything else is absolutely shut out of it. For it is the unalterable Nature of the Will, that it cannot possibly receive anything into it, but that which it *willeth;* its Willing is its only Power of receiving; and therefore there can be no possible Entrance for God or Heaven into the Soul, till the *Will-Spirit* of the Soul desires it; and thus all Man's Salvation depends upon himself. On the other hand, nothing can create, effect, or bring forth, a Birth or Growth of the Divine Life in the Soul, but that *Light* and *Spirit* of God, which brings forth the Divine Life in Heaven, and all heavenly Beings. And thus the *Work* of our Salvation is wholly and solely the Work of the Light and Spirit of God, dwelling and operating in us. Thus, *Academicus,* you see that God is all; that nothing but *his Life* and *working Power* in us, can be our Salvation; and yet that nothing but the *Spirit of Prayer* can make it *possible* for us to have it, or be capable of it. And therefore neither you, nor any other human Soul, can be *without* the Operation of the Light and Spirit of God in it, but because its *Will-Spirit*, or its Spirit of *Prayer*, is turned towards something else; for we are always in Union with *that*, with which our Will is united. Again: Look, *Academicus,* at the Light and Air of this World, you see with what a Freedom of Communication they *overflow, enrich,* and *enliven* every Thing; they enter everywhere, if not hindered by *something* that withstands their Entrance. This may represent to you the *ever-overflowing* free Communication of the Light and Spirit of God, to every human Soul. They are everywhere; we are encompassed with them; our Souls are as near to them, as our Bodies are to the Light and Air of this World; nothing shuts them out of us, but the Will and Desire of our Souls, turned from them, and *praying* for something else. I say, *praying* for something else; for you are to notice this, as a certain Truth, that every Man's Life is a *continual State* of Prayer; he is no Moment free from it, nor can possibly be so. For all our natural Tempers, be they what they will, Ambition, Covetousness, Selfishness, Worldly-mindedness, Pride, Envy, Hatred, Malice, or any other Lust whatever, are all of them in reality, only so many different *Kinds*, and *Forms* of a *Spirit of Prayer*, which is as inseparable from the Heart, as Weight is from the Body. For every natural Temper is nothing else, but a Manifestation of the Desire and Prayer of the Heart, and shows us, how it *works* and wills. And as the Heart worketh, and willeth, *such*, and no other, is its Prayer. All else is only *Form*, and *Fiction*, and empty beating of the Air. If therefore the working Desire of the Heart is not habitually turned towards God, if this is not our Spirit of Prayer, we are *necessarily* in a State of Prayer towards something else, that carries us from God, and brings all kind of Evil into us. For this is the Necessity of our Nature; pray we must, as sure as our Heart is alive; and therefore when the State of our Heart is not a Spirit of Prayer to God, we pray *without ceasing* to some, or other Part of the Creation. The Man whose Heart habitually tends towards the Riches, Honours, Powers, or Pleasures of this Life, is in a *continual* State of Prayer towards all these Things. His Spirit stands always *bent* towards them; they have his Hope, his Love, his Faith, and are the many Gods that he worships: And though when he is upon his Knees, and uses Forms of Prayer, he directs them to the God of Heaven; yet these are in Reality the God of his Heart, and, in a sad Sense of the Words, he really worships them in Spirit, and in Truth. Hence you may see, *Academicus*, how it comes to pass, that there is so much Praying, and yet so little of true Piety amongst us. The *Bells* are daily calling us to Church, our *Closets* abound with *Manuals* of Devotion, yet how little Fruit! It is all for this Reason, because our Prayers are not *our own;* they are not the Abundance of *our own* Heart; are not *found* and *felt* within us, as we feel our own Hunger and Thirst; but are only so many *borrowed Forms* of Speech, which we use at certain Times and Occasions. And therefore it is no Wonder that little Good comes of it. What Benefit could it have been to the *Pharisee*, if, with an Heart inwardly full of its own Pride and Self-exaltation, he had outwardly hung down his Head, smote upon his Breast, and borrowed the *Publican's* Words, 'God 'be merciful to me a Sinner?' What greater Good can be expected from our Praying in the Words of *David*, or Singing his Psalms seven times a Day, if our Heart has no more of the Spirit of *David* in it, than the Heart of the *Pharisee* had of the Spirit of the humble *Publican?*

Acad. O *Theophilus*, Truth and Reason force me to consent to what you say; and yet I am afraid of following you: For you here seem to condemn Forms of Prayer in public, and *Manuals* of Devotion in private. What will become of Religion, if these are set aside or disregarded?

Theoph. Dear *Academicus*, abate your Fright. Can you think, that I am against your praying in the Words of *David*, or breathing his Spirit in your Prayers, or that I would censure your singing his Psalms seven times a Day? Remember how very lately I put into your Hands the *Book* called, *A Serious Call to a Devout*

Life, &c., and then think how unlikely it is, that I should be against Times and Methods of Devotion. At three several Times, we are told, our Lord prayed, repeating the *same Form of Words;* and therefore a set Form of Words are not only consistent with, but may be highly suitable to, the most Divine Spirit of Prayer. If your own Heart, for Days and Weeks, was unable to alter, or break off from inwardly thinking and saying, ' Hallowed be thy Name, thy Kingdom come, thy Will be done;' if at other times, for Weeks and Months, it stood always inwardly in another Form of Prayer, unable to vary, or depart from saying, 'Come, Lord Jesus, come quickly, with all thy holy Nature, 'Spirit, and Tempers, into my Soul, that I may be born again of 'Thee, a new Creature;' I should be so far from censuring such a *Formality* of Prayer, that I should say, Blessed and happy are they, whose Hearts are tied to such a Form of Words. It is not therefore, Sir, a set Form of Words that is spoken against, but an *heartless* Form, a Form that has no Relation to, or Correspondence with, the State of the Heart that uses it. All that I have said is only to teach you the true Nature of Prayer, that it is only the Work of the Heart. and that the Heart only prays in Reality (whatever its Words are) for that which it habitually *wills, likes, loves,* and *longs* to have. It is not therefore the using the Words of *David*, or any other Saint, in your Prayers, that is censured, but the using them without that State of Heart, which first spoke them forth, and the trusting to them, because they are a good Form, though in our Hearts we have nothing that is like them. It would be good to say incessantly with holy *David*, 'My Heart is athirst for God. — As the Hart desireth the 'Water-brooks, so longeth my Soul after Thee, O God.' But there is no Goodness in saying daily these Words, if no *such Thirst* is felt, or desired in the Heart. And, my Friend, you may easily know, that dead Forms of Religion, and Numbers of repeated Prayers, keep Men content with their State of Devotion, because they make use of such holy Prayers; though their Hearts, from Morning to Night, are in a State quite contrary to them, and join no further in them, than in liking to use them at certain times.

Acad. I acquiesce, *Theophilus*, in the Truth of what you have said, and plainly see the Necessity of condemning what you have condemned; which is not the Form, but the *heartless* Form. But still I have a Scruple upon me: I shall be almost afraid of going to Church, where there are so many good Prayers offered up to God, as suspecting they may not be the Prayers or Language of my own Heart, and so become only a *Lip-labour*, or, what is worse, an *Hypocrisy* before God.

The Spirit of Prayer.

Theoph. I do not, *Academicus,* dislike your Scruple at all; for you do well to be afraid of saying anything of yourself, or to God, in your Prayers, which your Heart does not truly say. It is also good for you to think, that many of the Prayers of the Church may go faster, and higher, than your Heart can in Truth go along with them. For this will put you upon a right Care over yourself, and so to live, that, as a true Son of your Mother the Church, your Heart may be able to speak her Language, conform to her Service, and find the Delight of your Soul in the Spirit of her Prayers. But this will only then come to pass, when the Spirit of Prayer is the Spirit of your Heart; then every good Word, whether in a Form, or out of a Form, whether heard, or read, or thought, will be as suitable to your Heart, as gratifying to it, as Food is to the hungry, and Drink to the thirsty Soul. But till the Spirit of the Heart is thus renewed, till it is *emptied* of all earthly Desires, and stands in an *habitual* Hunger and Thirst after God (which is the true Spirit of Prayer) till then, all our Forms of Prayer will be, more or less, but too much like *Lessons* that are given to *Scholars;* and we shall mostly say them, only because we dare not neglect them. But be not discouraged, *Academicus;* take the following Advice, and then you may go to Church without any Danger of a mere Lip-labour or Hypocrisy, although there should be an *Hymn,* or a *Psalm,* or a *Prayer,* whose Language is higher than that of your own Heart. Do this: Go to the Church, as the *Publican* went into the Temple; stand *inwardly* in the Spirit of your Mind, in that *Form* which he outwardly expressed, when he cast down his Eyes, smote upon his Breast, and could only say, God be merciful to me a Sinner! Stand unchangeably (at least in your Desire) in *this Form* and State of Heart; it will sanctify every Petition that comes out of your Mouth; and when anything is read, or sung, or prayed, that is more exalted and fervent than your Heart is, if you make this an Occasion of a further *sinking down* in the Spirit of the *Publican,* you will then be helped, and highly blessed, by those Prayers and Praises, which seem only to fit, and belong to, a better Heart than yours.

This, my Friend, is a Secret of Secrets; it will help you to reap where you have not sown, and be a continual Source of Grace in your Soul. This will not only help you to receive Good from those Prayers, which seem too good for the State of your Heart, but will help you to find Good from everything else: For everything that inwardly stirs in you, or outwardly happens to you, becomes a real Good to you, if it either finds or excites in you this humble Form of Mind: For nothing is in vain, or without Profit, to the humble Soul; like the Bee, it takes its

Honey even from bitter Herbs; it stands always in a State of Divine Growth; and everything that falls upon it, is like a Dew of Heaven to it. Shut up yourself therefore in this *Form* of Humility, all Good is enclosed in it; it is a Water of Heaven, that turns the Fire of the fallen Soul, into the Meekness of the Divine Life, and creates that Oil, out of which the Love to God and Man gets its Flame. Be inclosed therefore always in it; let it be as a Garment wherewith you are always covered, and the Girdle with which you are girt; breathe nothing but in and from its Spirit; see nothing but with its Eyes; hear nothing but with its Ears; And then, whether your are in the Church, or out of the Church; hearing the Praises of God, or receiving Wrongs from Men, and the World, all will be Edification, and every Thing will help forward your Growth in the Life of God.

Acad. Indeed, *Theophilus*, this Answer to my Scruple is quite Good: I not only like, but I love it much: it gives as well an Unction to my Heart, as a Light to my Mind. All my Desire now is, to live no longer to the World, to myself, my own natural Tempers and Passions, but wholly to the Will of the blessed and adorable God, moved and guided by his Holy Spirit.

Theoph. This Resolution, *Academicus*, only shows that you are just come to yourself; for everything short of this earnest Desire to live wholly unto God, may be called a most dreadful Infatuation or Madness, an Insensibility that cannot be described. For what else is our Life, but a *Trial* for the greatest Evil, or Good, that an Eternity can give us? What can be so dreadful, as to die possessed of a wicked immortal Nature, or to go out of this World with Tempers, that must keep us for ever burning in our *own Fire*, and Brimstone? What has God not done to prevent this? His redeeming Love began with our Fall, and kindles itself as a Spark of Heaven in every fallen Soul. It calls every Man to Salvation, and every Man is forced to hear, though he will not obey his Voice. God has so loved the World, that his only Son hung and expired, bleeding on the Cross, not to atone his *own* Wrath against us, but to extinguish our *own Hell* within us, to pour his heavenly Love into us, to show us that Meekness, Suffering, and Dying to our own Fallen Nature, is the *one, only possible* Way, for fallen Man to be alive again in God. Are we yet Sons of Pride, and led away with Vanity? Do the Powers of Darkness rule over us? Do impure evil Spirits possess and drive on our Lives? Has Sin lost all its Power of frightening us? Is Remorse of Conscience no longer felt? Are Falsehood, Guile, Debauchery, Profaneness, Perjury, Bribery, Corruption, and Adultery, no longer seeking to hide themselves in Corners, but openly entering all our high Places, giving Battle to every Virtue, and laying

Claim to the Government of the World? Are we thus near being swallowed up by a Deluge of Vice and Impiety? All this is not come upon us, because God has left us too much without Help from Heaven, or too much exposed us to the Powers of Hell; but it is because we have rejected and despised the *whole Mystery* of our Salvation, and trampled under Foot the precious Blood of Christ, which alone has that omnipotence, that can either bring Heaven into us, or drive Hell out of us. O *Britain, Britain,* think that the Son of God saith unto thee, as he said, 'O Jerusalem, Jerusalem, how often would I have gathered thy 'Children, as a Hen gathereth her Chickens under her Wings, 'and ye would not! Behold, your House is left unto you desolate.' And now let me say, What aileth thee, O *British* Earth, that thou *quakest*, and the Foundations of thy Churches that they *totter?* Just *that same* aileth thee, as ailed *Judah's* Earth, when the Divine Saviour of the World, dying on the Cross, was *reviled, scorned,* and *mocked,* by the inhabitants of *Jerusalem;* then the *Earth quaked, the Rocks rent,* and the Sun refused to give its Light. Nature again declares for God; the Earth, and the Elements can no longer bear our Sins: *Jerusalem's* Doom for *Jerusalem's* Sin, may well be feared by us. Oh ye miserable *Pens* dipped in *Satan's* Ink, that dare to publish the Folly of believing in Jesus Christ, where will you hide your guilty Heads, when Nature dissolved, shall show you the Rainbow, on which the crucified Saviour shall sit in Judgment, and every Work receive its Reward? O tremble! ye *apostate* Sons that come out of the Schools of Christ, to fight *Lucifer's* Battles, and do that for him, which neither he, nor his Legions can do for themselves. Their inward Pride, Spite, Wrath, Malice and Rage against God, and Christ, and human Nature, have no *Pens* but yours, no *Apostles* but you. They must be forced to work in the Dark, to steal privately into impure Hearts, could they not beguile you into a fond *Belief,* that you are *Lovers* of Truth, *Friends* of Reason, *Detectors* of Fraud, great *Geniuses,* and *Moral Philosophers,* merely, and solely, because ye blaspheme Christ, and the Gospel of God. Poor deluded Souls, rescued from Hell by the Blood of Christ, called by God to possess the Thrones of fallen Angels, permitted to live only by the Mercy of God, that ye may be born again from above! my Heart bleeds for you. Think, I beseech you, in time, what Mercies ye are trampling under your Feet. Say not that *Reason,* and your intellectual Faculties, stand in your Way; that these are the *best Gifts,* that God has given you, and that these suffer you not to come to Christ. For all this is as vain a Pretence, and as gross a Mistake, as if ye were to say, that you had nothing but your *Feet* to carry you to Heaven. For your *Heart* is the best and greatest *Gift* of God to you; it is the highest, greatest, strongest, and noblest *Power* of your Nature; it forms your whole Life, be it what it will; all Evil, and all Good, comes from it; your Heart alone has the Key of Life and Death; it does all that it will; Reason is but its *Plaything*, and whether in Time or Eternity, can only be a *mere Beholder* of the *Wonders* of Happiness, or *Forms* of Misery, which the right, or wrong *Working* of the Heart is entered into.

I will here give you an infallible *Touch-stone*, that will try all to the Truth. It is this: Retire from the World, and all Conversation, only for *one Month*; neither write, nor read, nor debate anything in private with yourself; stop all the former Workings of your Heart and Mind; and, with all the Strength of your Heart, stand all this Month as continually as you can, in this following Form of Prayer to God. Offer it frequently on your Knees; but, whether sitting, standing, or walking, be always inwardly longing, and earnestly praying this *one Prayer* to God: ' That, of his great Goodness, he would make known to you, and ' take from your Heart, every *Kind*, and *Form*, and *Degree* of ' Pride, whether it be from evil Spirits, or your own corrupt ' Nature; and that he would awaken in you the deepest *Depth* ' and *Truth* of all that Humility, which can make you capable of ' his Light, and Holy Spirit.' Reject every Thought, but that of wishing, and praying in this Manner from the Bottom of your Heart, with such Truth and Earnestness, as People in Torment, wish and pray to be delivered from it. Now if you dare not, if your Hearts will not, cannot give themselves up in this manner to the Spirit of this Prayer, then the *Touch-stone* has done its Work, and you may be as fully assured, both what your Infidelity is, and from what it proceeds, as you can be of the plainest Truth in Nature. This will show you, how vainly you appeal to your *Reason*, and *Speculation*, as the Cause of your Infidelity; that it is full as false and absurd, as if *Thieves* and *Adulterers* should say, that their Theft and Adultery was entirely owing to their bodily *Eyes*, which showed them external Objects, and not to anything that was *wrong* or *bad* in their Hearts. On the other hand, if you can, and will give yourselves up in *Truth* and *Sincerity* to this Spirit of Prayer, I will venture to affirm, that if you had twice as many evil Spirits in you, as *Mary Magdalen* had, they will all be cast out of you, and you will be forced with her, to weep with Tears of Love, at the feet of the holy Jesus.

But here, my Friends, I stop, that we may return to the Matter we had in hand.

Rust. You have made no Digression, *Theophilus*, from our main Point, which was to recommend Christianity to poor *Humanus.* He must, I am sure, have felt the Death-blows, that you have here given to the Infidel Scheme. Their *Idol* of Reason, which is the vain God, that they worship in vain, is here like *Dagon* fallen to the Ground, never to rise up again. *Humanus* is caught by your *Bait* of Love, and I daresay he wants only to have this Conversation ended, that he may try himself to the Truth, by this Divine *Touch-stone*, which you have put into his Hands.

Acad. Give me leave, Gentlemen, to add one Word to this Matter. *Theophilus* has here fairly pulled *Reason* out of its usurped Throne, and shown it to be a powerless, idle *Toy*, when compared to the royal Strength of the Heart, which is the kingly Power, that has all the Government of Life in its Hands. But if *Humanus*, or anyone else, would see *Reason* fully maintained in all its *just Rights*, and yet entirely disarmed of all its Pretences to a Religion of *its own*, and the Truth of the Gospel fully proved to every Man, learned, or unlearned, from the known State of his own Heart; if he would see all this set forth in the strongest, clearest Light, he need only read about an hundred Pages of a *Book** published about twelve Years ago, to which no Answer has, nor, it may be, ever will be given by any Patron of Reason, and Infidelity. And if Part of that Book (as I have often wished) beginning at Page 70 to 117, was printed by itself, and known and read in every Part of the Kingdom, all Christians, though no Scholars, would have Learning enough both to see the *deep, true*, and *comfortable* Foundation of their Gospel Faith, and the miserable Folly, and Ignorance of those, who would set up a Religion of human Reason instead of it. But now, *Theophilus*, I beg we may return to that very Point concerning Prayer, where we left off. I think my Heart is entirely devoted to God, and that I desire nothing but to live in such a State of Prayer, as may best keep me under the Guidance and Direction of the Holy Spirit. Assist me therefore, my dear Friend, in this important Matter; give me the fullest Directions, that you can; and if you have any *Manual* of Devotion, that you prefer, or any Method that you would put me in, pray let me know it.

Rust. I beg leave to speak a Word to *Academicus*. I am glad, Sir, to see this Fire of Heaven, thus far kindled in your Soul; but wonder that you should want to know, how you are to keep

---

* A Demonstration of the Gross and Fundamental Errors of a late Book, called, *A Plain Account of the Nature, &c., of the Sacrament of the Lord's Supper.*

up its Flame, which is like wanting to know, how you are to *love* and *desire* that, which you do love and desire. Does a blind, or sick, or lame Man want to know, how he shall *wish* and *desire* Sight, Health, and Limbs? or would he be at a Loss, till some *Form* of Words taught him how to long for them? Now you can have no Desire or Prayer for any *Grace*, or Help from God, till you in some Degree as surely feel the *Want* of them, and desire the *Good* of them, as the sick Man feels the Want, and desires the Good of Health. But when this is your Case, you want no more to be told how to pray, than the thirsty Man wants to be told, what he shall ask for. Have you not fully consented to this Truth, that the Heart only can pray, and that it prays for nothing but *that*, which it *loves, wills*, and *wishes* to have? But can *Love* or *Desire* want *Art*, or *Method*, to teach it to be, that which it is? If from the Bottom of your Heart you have a sincere, warm Love for your most valuable Friend, would you want to buy a Book, to tell you, what Sentiments you feel in your Heart towards this Friend, what Comfort, what Joy, what Gratitude, what Trust, what Honour, what Confidence, what Faith, are all alive, and stirring in your Heart towards him? Ask not therefore, *Academicus*, for a Book of Prayers; but ask your Heart what is *within* it, what it *feels*, how it *stirs*, what it *wants*, what it would have altered, what it desires? and then, instead of calling upon *Theophilus* for Assistance, stand in the same Form of Petition to God.

For this turning to God according to the inward *Feeling, Want*, and *Motion* of your own Heart, in Love, in Trust, in Faith of having from him all that you want, and wish to have, this turning thus unto God, whether it be with, or without Words, is the best Form of Prayer in the World.—Now no Man can be ignorant of the State of his own Heart, or a Stranger to those Tempers, that are alive and stirring in him, and therefore no Man can want a Form of Prayer; for what should be the Form of his Prayer, but that which the Condition, and State of his Heart demands? If you know of no Trouble, feel no Burden, want nothing to be altered, or removed, nothing to be increased or strengthened in you, how can you pray for anything of this Kind? But if your Heart knows its own Plague, feels its inward Evil, knows what it wants to have removed, will you not let your Distress form the Manner of your Prayer? or will you pray in a Form of Words, that have no more Agreement with your State, than if a Man walking above-ground, should beg every Man he met, to pull him out of a deep Pit. For Prayers not formed according to the *real State* of your Heart, are but like a Prayer to be pulled out of a deep Well, when you are not in it. Hence you may see, how unreasonable it is to make a Mystery of Prayer, or an Art, that needs so much Instruction; since every Man is, and only can be, directed by his *own inward* State and Condition, when, and how, and what he is to pray for, as every Man's *outward* State shows him what he outwardly wants. And yet it should seem, as if a Prayer-Book was highly necessary, and ought to be the Performance of great Learning and Abilities, since only our learned Men and Scholars make our Prayer-Books.

Acad. I did not imagine, *Rusticus*, that you would have so openly declared against *Manuals* of Devotion, since you cannot but know, that not only the most learned, but the most pious Doctors of the Church, consider them as necessary Helps to Devotion.

Rust. If you, *Academicus*, were obliged to go a long Journey on *Foot*, and yet through a Weakness in your Legs could not set one Foot before another, you would do well to get the best travelling *Crutches* that you could.

But if, with sound and good Legs, you would not stir one Step, till you had got *Crutches* to hop with, surely a Man might show you the Folly of not walking with your own Legs, without being thought a declared Enemy to Crutches, or the Makers of them. Now a *Manual* is not so good an Help, as *Crutches*, and yet you see Crutches are only proper, when our Legs cannot do their Office. It is, I say, not so good an Help as Crutches, because that which you do with the Crutches, is that *very same* Thing, that you should have done with your Legs; you *really* travel; but when the Heart cannot take one Step in Prayer, and you therefore read your Manual, you do not do that *very same* Thing, which your Heart should have done, that is, *really* pray. A fine Manual therefore is not to be considered as a Means of praying, or as something that puts you in a State of Prayer, as Crutches help you to travel; but its chief Use, as a Book of Prayers to a dead and hardened Heart that has no Prayer of its own, is to show it, what a *State* and *Spirit* of Prayer it *wants*, and at what a sad Distance it is from feeling all that Variety of humble, penitent, grateful, fervent, resigned, loving Sentiments, which are described in the Manual, that so, being touched with a View of its own miserable State, it may begin its own Prayer to God for Help. But I have done. *Theophilus* may now answer your earnest Request.

Theoph. Your earnest Desire, *Academicus*, to live in the Spirit of Prayer, and be truly governed by it, is a most excellent Desire; for to be a Man of Prayer is that which the Apostle means by *living in the Spirit, and having our Conversation in Heaven.* It is to have done, not only with the confessed Vices, but with the allowed Follies and Vanities of this World. To tell such a soul of the *Innocence* of Levity, that it needs not run away from idle Discourse, vain Gaiety, and trifling Mirth, as being the harmless Relief of our heavy Natures, is like telling the *Flame*, that it needs not always be ascending upwards. But here you are to observe, that this Spirit of Prayer is not to be taught you by a Book, or brought into you by an *Art* from without, but must be an inward Birth, that must arise from your own *Fire* and *Light* within you, as the Air arises from the Fire and Light of this World. For the Spirit of every Being, be it what or where it will, or be its Spirit of what Kind it will, is only the Breath or Spirit that proceeds from its own Fire and Light. In vegetative, sensitive, and intellectual Creatures, it is all in the same Manner; Spirit is the *third Form* of its Life, and is the Birth that proceeds from the other *two;* and is the Manifestation of their Nature and Qualities. For such as the Fire and Light are, such and no other, neither higher nor lower, neither better nor worse, is the *Spirit* that proceeds from them. Now the Reason why all, and every Life does, and must stand in this Form, is wholly and solely from hence, because the Deity, the one Source and Fountain of all life, is a *triune* God, whose *third Form* is, and is called, the Spirit of God, proceeding from the Father, and the Son.

The *painful* Sense and Feeling of what you are, kindled into a working State of Sensibility by the Light of God within you, is the *Fire* and *Light* from whence your Spirit of Prayer proceeds. In its first kindling nothing is found or felt, but Pain, Wrath, and Darkness, as is to be seen in the first kindling of every Heat or Fire. And therefore its first Prayer is nothing else but a Sense of Penitence, Self-condemnation, Confession, and Humility. It feels nothing but its own Misery, and so is all Humility. This Prayer of Humility is met by the Divine Love, the Mercifulness of God embraces it; and then its Prayer is changed into Hymns, and Songs, and Thanksgivings. When this State of Fervour has done its Work, has melted away all earthly Passions and Affections, and left no Inclination in the Soul, but to delight in God alone, then its Prayer changes again. It is now come so near to God, has found such Union with him, that it does not so much pray as live in God. Its Prayer is not any particular Action, is not the Work of any particular Faculty, not confined to Times, or Words, or Place, but is the Work of his whole Being, which continually stands in Fulness of Faith, in Purity of Love, in absolute Resignation, to do, and be, what and how his Beloved pleases. This is the last State of the Spirit of Prayer, and is its highest Union with God in this Life.

Each of these foregoing States has its Time, its Variety of Workings, its Trials, Temptations, and Purifications, which can only be known by Experience in the Passage through them. The *one* only and *infallible* Way to go safely through all the Difficulties, Trials, Temptations, Dryness, or Opposition, of our own evil Tempers, is this: It is to expect nothing from ourselves, to trust to nothing in ourselves, but in everything expect, and depend upon God for Relief. Keep fast Hold of this *Thread*, and then let your Way be what it will, Darkness, Temptation, or the Rebellion of Nature, you will be led through all, to an Union with God: For nothing hurts us in any State, but an Expectation of something in it, and from it, which we should only expect from God. We are looking for our *own* Virtue, our *own* Piety, our *own* Goodness, and so live on and on in our *own* Poverty and Weakness; To-day pleased and comforted with the seeming Strength and Firmness of our own pious Tempers, and fancying ourselves to be *somewhat;* To-morrow, fallen into our own *Mire*, we are dejected, but not humbled; we grieve, but it is only the Grief of Pride, at the seeing our Perfection not to be such as we vainly imagined. And thus it will be, till the *whole Turn* of our Minds is so changed, that we as fully see and know our *Inability* to have any Goodness of *our own*, as to have a Life of our own.

For since nothing is, or can be, good in us, but the Life of God manifested in us, how can this be had but from God alone? When we are happily brought to this Conviction, then we have done with all Thought of being our own Builders; the whole Spirit of our Mind is become a mere *Faith*, and *Hope*, and *Trust* in the sole Operation of God's Spirit, looking no more to any other Power, to be formed in Christ new Creatures, than we look to any other Power for the Resurrection of our Bodies at the last Day. Hence may be seen, that the Trials of every State are its greatest Blessings; they do that for us, which we most of all want to have done, they force us to know our own *Nothingness*, and the *All* of God.

People who have long dwelt in the Fervours of Devotion, in an high Sensibility of Divine Affections, practising every Virtue with a kind of Greediness, are frightened, when *Coldness* seizes upon them, when their Hymns give no Transport, and their Hearts, instead of flaming with the Love of every Virtue, seem ready to be overcome by every Vice. But here, keep *fast Hold* of the Thread I mentioned before, and all is well. For this *Coldness* is the Divine *Offspring*, or genuine Birth, of the former Fervour; it comes from it as a good Fruit, and brings the Soul nearer to God, than the Fervour did. The Fervour was good, and did a good Work in the Soul; it overcame the earthly Nature, and made the Soul delight in God, and spiritual Things; but its Delight was too much an *own Delight,* a fancied Self-holiness, and occasioned Rest and Satisfaction in Self, which if it had continued uninterrupted, undiscovered, an earthly Self had only been changed into a spiritual Self. Therefore I called this Coldness, or Loss of Fervour, its Divine *Offspring,* because it brings a Divine Effect, or more fruitful Progress in the Divine Life. For this Coldness overcomes, and delivers us from spiritual Self, as Fervour overcame the earthly Nature. It does the Work that Fervour did, but in an higher Degree, because it gives up more, sacrifices more, and brings forth more Resignation to God, than Fervour did; and therefore it is more in God, and receives more from him. The devout Soul therefore is always safe in every State, if it makes everything an Occasion either of rising up, or falling down into the Hands of God, and exercising Faith, and Trust, and Resignation to him. Fervour is good, and ought to be loved; but Tribulation, Distress, and Coldness, in their Season are better, because they give Means and Power of exercising an *higher* Faith, a *purer* Love, and *more perfect* Resignation to God, which are the best State of the Soul. And therefore the pious Soul that eyes only God, that means nothing but being his alone, can have no Stop put to its Progress; Light and Darkness equally assist him; in the Light he looks up to God; in the Darkness he lays hold on God; and so they both do him the same Good.

This little Sketch, *Academicus,* of the Nature and Progress of the Spirit of Prayer, may show you, that a *Manual* is not so great a Matter as you imagined.

The best Instruction that I can give you, as helpful, or preparatory to the Spirit of Prayer, is already fully given, where we have set forth the original Perfection, the miserable Fall, and the glorious Redemption of Man. It is the true Knowledge of these great Things that can do all for you, which human Instruction can do. These Things must fill you with a Dislike of your present State, drive all earthly Desires out of your Soul, and create an earnest Longing after your first Perfection. For Prayer cannot be taught you, by giving you a Book of Prayers, but by awakening in you a true Sense and Knowledge of what you are, and what you should be; that so you may see, and know, and feel, what Things you want, and are to pray for. For a Man does not, cannot pray for anything, because a fine Petition for it is put into his Hands, but because his *own* Condition is a *Reason* and *Motive* for his asking for it. And therefore it is, that the *Spirit of Prayer,* in the First Part, began with a full Discovery and Proof of these high and important Matters, at the Sight of which the World, and all that is in it, shrinks into nothing, and everything past, present, and to come, awakens in our Hearts a continual Prayer, and longing Desire, after God, Christ, and Eternity.

Acad. I perceive then, *Theophilus*, that you direct me entirely to my *own* Prayer in my private Devotions, and not to the Use of any Book. But surely you do not take this to be right in general, that the common People, who are unlearned, and mostly of low Understandings, should kneel down in private, without any borrowed Form of Prayer, saying only what comes then into their own Heads.

Theoph. It would be very wrong, *Academicus*, to condemn a Manual *as such*, or to tell any People, learned or unlearned, that they ought not to make any Use of it. This would be quite rash and silly: But it cannot be wrong, or hurtful to anybody, to show, that Prayer is the natural Language of the Heart, and, as such, does not want any Form, or borrowed Words. Now all that has been said of Manuals of Prayers, only amounts to thus much; that they are not necessary, nor the most natural and excellent Way of praying. If they happen to be necessary to any Person, or to be his most excellent Way, it is because the natural, real Prayer of his Heart is already engaged, loving, wishing, and longing after, the Things of this Life; which makes him so insensible of his spiritual Wants, so blind and dead as to the Things of God, that he cannot pray for them, but so far as the Words of other People are put into his Mouth. If a Man is blind, and knows it not, he may be told to pray for Sight; if he is sick, and knows nothing of it, he may be told to pray for Health: So if the Soul is in this State, with regard to its spiritual Wants, a Manual may be of good Use to it, not so much by helping it to pray, as by showing it, at what a miserable Distance it is from those Tempers which belong to Prayer.

But when a Man has had so much Benefit from the Gospel, as to know his own Misery, his want of a Redeemer, who he is, and how is he to be found; there everything seems to be done, both to awaken and direct his Prayer, and make it a true Praying in and by the Spirit. For when the Heart really pants and longs after God, its Prayer is a Praying, as moved and animated by the Spirit of God; it is the Breach or Inspiration of God, stirring, moving and opening itself in the Heart. For though the earthly Nature, our *old Man*, can oblige or accustom himself to take heavenly Words at certain Times into his Mouth, yet this is a certain Truth, that nothing ever did, or can have the least *Desire* or *Tendency* to ascend to Heaven, but that which came down from

Heaven; and therefore nothing in the Heart can pray, aspire, and long after God, but the Spirit of God moving and stirring in it. Every Breath therefore of the true Spirit of Prayer, can be nothing else but the Breath of the Spirit of God, breathing, inspiring, and moving the Heart, in all its Variety of Motions and Affections, towards God. And therefore every time a good Desire stirs in the Heart, a good Prayer goes out of it, that reaches God as being the Fruit and Work of his Holy Spirit. When any Man, feeling his Corruption, and the Power of Sin in his Soul, looks up to God, with true Earnestness of Faith and Desire to be delivered from it, whether with Words, or without Words, how can he pray better? What need of any Change of Thoughts, or Words, or any Variety of Expressions, when the one Faith and Desire of his Heart made known to God, and continued in, is not only all, but the most perfect Prayer he can make? Again, suppose the Soul in another State, feeling with Joy its offered Redeemer, and opening its Heart for the full Reception of him; if it stands in this State of Wishing and Longing for the Birth of Christ, how can its Prayer be in an higher Degree of Request? Or if it breaks out frequently in these Words, 'Come, Lord Jesus, 'come quickly, with all thy holy Nature, Spirit, and Tempers 'into my Soul,' is there any Occasion to enlarge, or alter these Words into another Form of Expression? Can he do better, or pray more, than by continually standing from time to time in this State of wishing to have Christ formed in him? Nay, is it not more likely, that his Heart should be more divided and dissipated by a numerous Change of Expressions, than by keeping united to one Expression that sets forth all that he wants? For it is the Reality, the Steadiness, and Continuity of the Desire, that is the Goodness of Prayer, and its Qualification to receive all that it wants. Our Lord said to one that came to him, What wilt thou that I should do unto thee? He answered, 'Lord, 'that I may receive my Sight': And he received it. Another said, 'Lord, if thou wilt, thou canst make me clean': And he was cleansed. Tell me what Learning, or fine Parts, are required to make such Prayers as these? and yet what Wonders of Relief are recorded in Scripture, as given to such short Prayers as these! Or tell me what Blessing of Prayer, or Faith, or Love, may not now be obtained in the same Way, and with as few Words, as then was done? Every Man therefore that has any Feeling of the Weight of his Sin, or any true Desire to be delivered from it by Christ, has Learning and Capacity enough to make his own Prayer. For Praying is not speaking forth eloquently, but simply, the true Desire of the Heart; and the Heart, simple and plain in good Desires, is in the truest State of Preparation for all the Gifts and Graces of God. And this I must tell you, that the most simple Souls, that have accustomed themselves to speak their own Desires and Wants to God, in such short, but true Breathings of their Hearts to him, will soon know more of Prayer, and the Mysteries of it, than any Persons who have only their Knowledge from Learning, and learned Books.

Acad. You seem to me, *Theophilus*, to have much Truth in what you say, and yet to be in a Way by yourself. I cannot take you to be with those who place *all* in many and long Forms; and now I take you to be even more against those, who make much Account of what they call a *gifted Man*, and make that to be the *true Gift* of Prayer, when anyone is able to pray *extempore*, or with his own Words, for an Hour or two at a Time.

Theoph. I have shown you, *Academicus*, that Prayer is purely the Desire of the Heart; that it has not the Nature of praying, but so far as it is the true Language of the Heart. I have shown you the great Benefit that all People must receive from this true Prayer of the Heart. And to remove all Pretence of Want of Ability in the lowest Sort of People to pray from their own Hearts, I have shown, that the most *simple, short* Petitions, when truly spoken by the Heart, have all the Perfection that Prayer can have.

But mark, Sir, why or when I ascribe this Perfection to it. It is when the Heart stands continually in *this State* of wishing to have that, which is expressed in so few Words. It is then, that I said, there was no Occasion to *enlarge*, or *alter* the Words into another or longer Form, because the *Reality*, the *Steadiness*, and the *Continuity* of the Desire, is the Goodness and Perfection of the Prayer. Now, Sir, let us suppose two Men; the one is frequently an *Hour*, or two, or a whole Night, on his Knees, in silent Prayer, in high Acts of Love, and Faith, and Resignation to God, not outwardly spoken by his Mouth; the other is as long a Time pouring forth the Devotion of his Heart in a Variety of fervent Expressions. May not both these Men justly appeal to me, not only as not condemning, but as asserting, the Goodness of their *Length* and Manner of Prayer, since I make a short simple Petition to be only *then* a good Prayer, when it proceeds from a *steady, continued* Desire of the Heart? It is not therefore *Silence*, or a *simple* Petition, or a great *Variety* of outward Expressions, that *alters* the Nature of Prayer, or makes it to be *good,* or *better*, but only and solely the *Reality, Steadiness,* and *Continuity* of the Desire; and therefore whether a Man offers this Desire to God in the silent Longing of the Heart, or in simple short Petitions, or in a great *Variety* of Words, is of no

Consequence; but all of them are equally good, when the true and right State of the Heart is with them.

Thus you see, *Academicus*, that I am so far from being, as you said, in *a Way by myself*, that I am with every Man in *every Way*, whose Heart stands right towards God. But if you would know what I would call a true and great *Gift of Prayer*, and what I most of all wish for to myself, it is a *good Heart, that stands continually inclined towards God.*

Acad. I am not sorry, *Theophilus*, that I have made so unreasonable an Observation upon what you said, since it has occasioned you to give so good and just an Answer to it. But yet this *silent* Prayer you speak of, is what I never read nor heard anything of before; and it seems to me but like a *ceasing* to pray; and yet you seem to like it in its Turn, as well as any other Way of praying.

Theoph. All that I have said of Prayer, *Academicus*, has been only to this End, to show you its true and real Nature, whence it is to arise, where it is to be found, and how you are to begin, and become a true Proficient in it. If, therefore, you were at present to look no further, than how to put yourself in a State of beginning to practise a Prayer proceeding from your own Heart, and continuing in it, leaving all that you are further to know of Prayer, to be known in its own Time by Experience, which alone can open any true Knowledge in you, this would be much better for you, than to be asking beforehand about such things, as are not your immediate Concern.

Begin to be a Man of Prayer, in this easy, simple, and natural Manner, that has been set before you; and when you are faithful to this Method, you will then need no other Instructor in the Art of Prayer. Your own Heart thus turned to God, will want no one to tell it, when it should be *simple* in its Petitions, or *various* in its Expressions, or prostrate itself in *Silence* before God. But this Hastiness of knowing Things, before they become our Concern, or belong to us, is very common. Thus a Man that has but just entered upon the Reformation of his Life, shall want to read or hear a Discourse upon *Perfection*, whether it be absolutely attainable or not; and shall be more eager after what he can hear of this Matter, though at such a Distance from himself, than of such Things as concern the next Step that he is to take in his own proper State.

You, my Friend, have already rightly taken the *first Step* in the spiritual Life; you have devoted yourself absolutely to God, to live wholly to his Will, under the Light and Guidance of his Holy Spirit, intending, seeking nothing in this World, but such a Passage through it, as may tend to the Glory of God, and the

Recovery of your own fallen Soul. Your *next Step* is this, it is a looking to the Continuance of this first Resolution, and Donation of yourself to God, to see that it be kept alive, that everything you do may be animated and directed by it, and all the Occurrences of every Day, from Morning to Night, be received by you, as becomes a Spirit that is devoted to God. Now this *second Step* cannot be taken, but purely by Prayer; nothing else has the least Power here but Prayer: I do not mean you must frequently read or say a Number of Prayers (though this in its Turn may be good and useful to you) but the Prayer I mean, and which you must practise, if you would take this *second Step* in the spiritual Life, is *Prayer of the Heart*, or a Prayer of your own, proceeding from the State of your Heart, and its own Tendency to God. Of all things therefore look to this Prayer of the Heart; consider it as your infallible Guide to Heaven; turn from everything that is an Hindrance of it, that quenches or abates its Fervour; love and like nothing but that which is suitable to it; and let every Day begin, go on, and end, in the Spirit of it. Consider yourself as always wrong, as having gone aside, and lost your right Path, when any *Delight, Desire,* or *Trouble,* is suffered to live in you, that cannot be made a Part of this Prayer of the Heart to God. For nothing so infallibly shows us the true State of our Heart, as that which gives us either Delight or Trouble; for as our Delight and Trouble is, so is the State of our Heart: If therefore you are carried away with any Trouble or Delight, that has not an immediate Relation to your Progress in the Divine Life, you may be assured your Heart is not in its right State of Prayer to God. Look at a Man who is devoted to some *one Thing*, or has some one great worldly Matter at Heart, he stands turned from everything that has not some Relation to it; he has no Joy or Trouble but what arises from it; he has no Eyes nor Ears, but to see or hear something about it. All else is a Trifle, but that which some way or other concerns this great Matter. You need not tell him of any Rules or Methods to keep it in his Thoughts; it goes with him into all Places and Companies; it has his first Thoughts in the Morning; and every Day is good or bad, as this great Matter seems to succeed or not. This may show you how easily, how naturally, how constantly, our Heart will carry on its own State of Prayer, as soon as God is its great Object, or it is wholly given up to him, as its one great Good. This may also show you, that the Heart cannot enter into a State of the Spirit of Prayer to God, till that which I called the first *Step* in the spiritual Life is taken, which is the taking God for its *All,* or the giving itself up *wholly* to God. But when this Foundation is laid, the Seed of Prayer is sown, and the Heart is in a continual State of Tendency to God; having no other Delight or Trouble in Things of any kind, but as they help or hinder its Union with God. Therefore, *Academicus*, the Way to be a Man of Prayer, and be governed by its Spirit, is not to get a *Book* full of Prayers; but the best Help you can have from a Book, is to read one full of such Truths, Instructions, and awakening Informations, as force you to see and know *who*, and *what*, and *where*, you are; that God is your *All;* and that all is *Misery*, but a Heart and Life devoted to him. This is the best outward Prayer-Book you can have, as it will turn you to an inward Book, and Spirit of Prayer in your Heart, which is a continual longing Desire of the Heart after God, his Divine Life, and Holy Spirit. When, for the Sake of this inward Prayer, you retire at any time of the Day, never begin till you know and feel, why and wherefore you are going to pray; and let this *why* and *wherefore*, form and direct everything that comes from you, whether it be in Thought or Word. As you cannot but know your own State, so it must be the easiest Thing in the World to look up to God, with such Desires as suit the State you are in; and praying in this Manner, whether it be in one, or more, or no Words, your Prayer will be always sincere, and good, and highly beneficial to you.—Thus praying, you can never pray in vain; but one Month in the Practice of it, will do you more Good, make a greater Change in your Soul, than twenty Years of Prayer only by Books, and Forms of other People's making.

No Vice can harbour in you, no Infirmity take any Root, no good Desire can languish, when once your Heart is in this Method of Prayer; never beginning to pray, till you first see how Matters stand with you; asking your Heart what it wants, and having nothing in your Prayers, but what the known State of your Heart puts you upon *demanding, saying*, or *offering*, unto God. A Quarter of an Hour of this Prayer, brings you out of your Closet a new Man; your Heart feels the Good of it; and every Return of such a Prayer, gives new Life and Growth to all your Virtues, with more Certainty, than the Dew refreshes the Herbs of the Field: Whereas, overlooking this true Prayer of your own Heart, and only at certain Times taking a Prayer that you find in a Book, you have nothing to wonder at, if you are every Day praying, and yet every Day sinking further and further under all your Infirmities. For your Heart is your Life, and your Life can only be altered by that which is the real Working of your Heart. And if your Prayer is only a Form of Words, made by the Skill of other People, such a Prayer can no more change you into a good Man, than an *Actor* upon the

Stage, who speaks kingly Language, is thereby made to be a King: Whereas one Thought, or Word, or Look, towards God, proceeding from your own Heart, can never be without its proper Fruit, or fail of doing a real Good to your Soul. Again, another great and infallible Benefit of this kind of Prayer is this; it is the only Way to be delivered from the Deceitfulness of your own Hearts.

Our Hearts deceive us, because we leave them to themselves, are absent from them, taken up in outward Things, in outward Rules and Forms of Living and Praying. But this kind of Praying, which takes all its Thoughts and Words only from the State of our Hearts, makes it impossible for us to be Strangers to ourselves. The Strength of every Sin, the Power of every evil Temper, the most secret Workings of our Hearts, the Weakness of any or all our Virtues, is with a Noonday Clearness forced to be seen, as soon as the Heart is made our Prayer-Book, and we pray for nothing, but according to what we read, and find there.

Acad. O *Theophilus*, you have shown me, that it is almost as easy and natural a Thing to pray, as to *breathe;* and that the best Prayer in the World, is that which the Heart can thus easily send forth from itself, untaught by anything, but its own Sense of God and itself. And yet I am almost afraid of loving this kind of Prayer too much. I am not free from suspicions about it: I apprehend it to be that very *praying* by the *Spirit*, or as *moved* by the Spirit, or from a *Light within*, which is condemned as *Quakerism.*

Theoph. There is but one good Prayer that you can possibly make, and that is a Prayer *in* and *from* the Spirit, or as the Spirit of God *moves* you in it, or to it. This, this alone, is a Divine Prayer; no other Prayer has, or can possibly have any Communion with God. Take the Matter thus: Man is a *threefold* Being; he has three Natures; he partakes of the *Divine*, the *elementary*, and the *diabolical* Nature. Had he not these three Natures in a certain Degree in him, he could have no Communion with God, he could not enjoy the Elements, nor could the evil Spirits have the least Power of Access to him.

Now the *astral, elementary* Nature of Man, in this World, cannot have a Longing after the pure Deity; it cannot hunger, and thirst after the Divine Image, nor desire to be perfect as God is perfect; this is as impossible, as for the Beasts of the Field to long to be Angels. Therefore Flesh and Blood in us, can no more make a *Divine* Prayer, than in any other Animal of this World.

The *diabolical* Nature which is in us, can do nothing but that which the Devils do : It can only rise up in its *own* Pride, Envy, and Self-Exaltation, and only hate all the Goodness that is either in Heaven, or on Earth. And therefore it is a Truth of the greatest Certainty, that no Man ever did, or can send up a Divine and heavenly Prayer to God, or such a Prayer as can reach God, but *in* and *by* the Spirit of God in him. Our *astral, elementary* Man, and our proud, subtle, serpentine Nature, can read, or say a Prayer full of good Words and Wishes, as easily as *Satan* could use *Scripture-Language* in the Temptation of Christ ; but nothing can wish to be like God, or to *unite* with his Goodness and Holiness, but that Spirit in us, which partakes of his Divine Nature. Therefore to ridicule praying by the Spirit, or as moved by the Spirit, is ridiculing the *one only* Prayer that is Divine, or can do us any Divine Good ; and to reject and oppose it, as a vain Conceit, is to quench, and suppress all that is holy, heavenly, and Divine, within us. For if this Holy Spirit does not live, and move in us, and bring forth all the praying Affections of our Souls, we may as well think of reaching Heaven with our Hands, as with our Prayers.

Acad. I know not, *Theophilus*, how to deny anything that you have here said : Yet this Account seems to make no Distinction between *our own good* Spirit, and the Holy Spirit of God. I took the Inspirations, and Graces of the Holy Spirit to be something, that came into us from *without*, and to be as *distinct* from our own Good Spirit, as God is distinct from the Creature.

Theoph. The Holy Spirit of God is as necessary to our Divine Life, or the Life of Grace, as the *Air* of this World is necessary to our animal Life ; and is as *distinct* from us, and as much *without* us, as the *Air* of this World is *distinct* from, and *without*, the Creatures that live in it. And yet *our own* good Spirit is the *very Spirit* of God, moving and stirring in us. No Animal can unite with, or breathe the Air of this World, till it has first the Air of this World brought forth, as the *true Birth* of its own Life in itself; this is its only Capacity to live in the Spirit of this World ; and the Breath or Spirit that thus arises in its own Life, is the *very same* Breath, that is in outward Nature, in which it lives. It is strictly thus, with the Spirit of God in our Souls ; it must first have a Birth *within us*, arising from the Life of our Souls, and as such, is our only Capacity to have Life, and live in the Spirit of God himself, and is the *very Breath* of the Spirit of God, who is yet as distinct from us, as the Breath of our animal Life, that arises from our own Fire, is distinct from the Air of the World in which it lives. And thus, *Academicus*, our *own good* Spirit is the *very Spirit* of the Deity, and yet not God, but the Spirit of God, breathed or kindled into a creaturely

Form ; and this good Spirit, Divine in its *Origin*, and Divine in its *Nature*, is that alone in us, that can reach God, unite with him, co-operate with him, be moved, and blessed by him, as our earthly Spirit is, by the outward Spirit of this elementary World.

Acad. Indeed, *Theophilus*, you have, in few Words, so gone to the Bottom of this Matter, that nothing is left either for any further Doubt, or Inquiry about it. My own good Spirit is the Breath of God in me, and so related to God, as the Breath of my animal Life is related to the *Air*, or Spirit of this outward World. It is from God, has the *Nature*, the *Eternity*, the *Spirituality* of God, as the Breath of my Flesh and Blood, has the Grossness, the earthly, transitory Nature of the Spirit of this World. And as all my Communication with this World arises from the Breath of this World, kindled in my *own Life*, so all my possibility of Communication with God, arises solely from the Breath of his Holy Spirit *brought forth* in the Life of my Soul; and I can only live in God, by his Spirit having a Birth in me, as I can only live in this World, by having its Spirit born in me. This plain Truth sets all the Scripture-Doctrine, concerning the *Necessity*, *Power*, and *Operation* of the Holy Spirit, in the greatest and most edifying Degree of Clearness. Thus, what can be a more plain, sober, and palpable Truth, than when the Apostle says, ' They only are the Sons of ' God, who are led by the Spirit of God '? It is only like saying, that those Creatures only belong to this World, who live in, and by its Spirit. I shall here, Sir, only add, that my Gospel-Faith stands now upon a most solid, and comfortable Foundation ; my Heart is all delight, and Devotion to God, when I consider, *First*, That Christ my Redeemer is the first *Seed* of the *Woman*, or *Power of Salvation preserved in fallen* Adam ; *the Immanuel; the God within every Man ;* ' the Light that lighteth every Man ' that cometh into the World.' *Secondly*, That the Holy Spirit of God, the Breath of Eternity, has also *its Seed* of Life in my Soul ; for where the *Word*, or *Son* of God is, there is the Spirit of God in the *same State ;* if one is only a *Seed* of Life, a Spark of Heaven, the other is so also ; and these two, thus considered, are the glorious *Pearl* of Eternity, hidden in every Man's Soul, and so often spoken of before. And thus we understand, how the Whole of our Redemption (according to the plain Language of Scripture) is *inwardly* and *outwardly* solely the Work of the Light and Spirit of God, a Kingdom of God both *within* and *without* us, and to which we do not, cannot live, but so far as we are inspired, moved, and led, by the Spirit of God. Earnestly, therefore, to pray, humbly to hope, and faithfully to expect, to be *continually* inspired, and animated by the Holy Spirit of God has no more of *Vanity*, *Fanaticism*, or *enthusiastic* Wildness in it, than to hope and pray, to act in everything from and by a *good Spirit*. For as sure as the Lip of Truth hath told us, that there is but *One that is good*, so sure is it, that not a *Spark* of Goodness, nor a *Breath* of Piety, can be in any Creature, either in Heaven, or on Earth, but by that Divine Spirit, which is the *Breath* of God, breathed from himself into the Creature. The Matter is not about *Appearances* of Goodness, *Forms* of Virtue, *Rules* of Religion, or a *prudential Piety*, suited to Time, and Place, and Character; all these are Degrees of Goodness, that our old Man can as easily trade in, as in any other Matters of this World. But so much as we have of an *heavenly* and *Divine* Goodness, or of a Goodness that *belongs* to Heaven, and has the Nature of Heaven in it, so much we must have of a *Divine Inspiration* in us. For as nothing can fall to the Earth, but because it has the Nature of the Earth in it; so it is a Truth of the utmost Certainty, that nothing can ascend towards Heaven, or have the least Power to unite with it, but that very Spirit which came down from Heaven, and has the Nature of Heaven in it. This Truth, therefore, that the Kingdom of God is within us, that its Light is solely the *Lamb* of God, its Spirit solely the Spirit of God, stands upon a Rock, against which all Attempts are in vain. All that I now further desire to know, is only this; how I may keep free from all Delusions in this Matter, and not take my own natural Abilities, Tempers, and Passions, or the Suggestions of evil Spirits, to be the Working of the Spirit of God in me. Pray, Sir, tell me how I shall safely know when, and how far, I am led and governed by the Spirit of God?

Theoph. You may know this, *Academicus*, just as you know, when you are governed by the Spirit of Wrath, Envy, Guile, Craft, or Covetousness. Every Man knows this of himself, as easily, and as certainly, as he knows when he is hungry, pleased, or displeased. Now it is the same Thing with regard to the Spirit of God; the Knowledge of it is as perceptible in yourself, and liable to no more delusion. For the Spirit of God, is more distinguishable from all other Spirits and Tempers, than any of your natural Affections or Tempers are, from one another; as I will here plainly show you.

'God is unwearied *Patience*, a *Meekness* that cannot be pro-
'voked; he is an ever-enduring *Mercifulness;* he is unmixed
'*Goodness*, impartial, universal *Love;* his Delight is in the
'Communication of himself, his own Happiness, to everything,
'according to its Capacity. He does everything that is good,
'righteous, and lovely, for its own sake, because it is good,
'righteous, and lovely. He is the *Good* from which nothing but

'Good comes, and resisteth all Evil, *only* with Goodness.' This, Sir, is the *Nature* and *Spirit* of God, and here you have your *infallible* Proof, whether you are moved, and led by the Spirit of God. Here is a Proof that never can fail you; is always at hand; and is liable to no Mistake or Delusion. If it be the earnest Desire, and Longing of your Heart, to be *merciful* as he is merciful; to be full of his *unwearied Patience*, to dwell in his *unalterable Meekness;* if you long to be like him in *universal, impartial* Love; if you desire to communicate *every Good*, to every Creature that you are able; if you love and practise everything that is good, righteous, and lovely, for its *own sake*, because it is good, righteous, and lovely; and resist no Evil, but with *Goodness;* then you have the utmost Certainty, that the Spirit of God lives, dwells, and governs in you. Now all these Tempers are as capable of being known to every Man, as his own Love and Hatred; and therefore no Man can be deceived as to the Possession of them, but he that chooses to deceive himself. Now if you want any of these Tempers, if the *whole Bent* of your Heart and Mind is not set upon them, all Pretences to an *immediate Inspiration*, and *continual* Operation of the Spirit of God in your Soul, are vain and groundless. For the Spirit of God is *that* which I have here described; and where his Spirit dwells and governs, there all these Tempers are brought forth, or springing up, as the certain Fruits of it. What room, therefore, *Academicus*, for so much Uncertainty, or Fear of Delusion, in this Matter? Keep but within the Bounds here set you; call nothing a *Proof* of the Spirit or Work of God in your Soul, but *these Tempers*, and the Works which they produce; and then, but not till then, you may safely and infallibly say, with St. *John*, ' Hereby we know that he abideth ' in us by the Spirit which he hath given us.'

Acad. Indeed, *Theophilus*, you have given me a short, but very full and satisfactory Answer to my Question. I now perceive, that, as a spiritual Man, or one devoted to the Spirit of God, I am not to look after any *Extraordinaries*, any new Openings, Illuminations, Visions, or Voices, inward or outward, from God, as *Proofs* of the Spirit of God dwelling and working in me; but that all my Proof and Security of being governed by the Spirit of God, is to be grounded on other Matters: That the boundless Humility and Resignation of the Holy Jesus; the unwearied Patience, the unalterable Meekness, the impartial, universal Love of God, manifested in my Soul; are its only Proofs, that God is in me of a Truth. Thus far all is right and good.

But yet, Sir, surely it must be said with Truth, that the Spirit of God often discovers itself, and operates in good Souls in very extraordinary Ways, in uncommon Illuminations, and Openings of Divine Light and Knowledge, in the Revelation of Mysteries, in strong Impulses and Sallies of a wonderful Zeal, full of the highest Gifts and Graces of God : And that these have frequently been God's gracious Methods of awakening a sinful World.

Theoph. What you say, *Academicus,* is very true ; and almost every Age of the Church is a sufficient Proof of it. By the Goodness of God, the Church has always had its *extraordinary Persons*, highly gifted from above, made burning, and shining Lights, and carried into as uncommon Ways of Life, by the same Spirit, and for the same Ends, as *John* the *Baptist* was ; and as different from common Christians, as he was from the common *Jews.* But, my Friend, these extraordinary Operations of God's Holy Spirit, and the Wonders of his Gifts and Graces showing themselves at certain Times, and upon certain Persons, through all the Ages of the Church, are not Matters of common Instruction ; they belong not to our Subject ; it would be Ignorance and Vanity in me, to pretend to let you into the Secret of them ; it would be the same Thing in you, to think yourself ready for it.

Would you know the *Sublime,* the *Exalted,* the *Angelic,* in the Christian Life, see what the Son of God saith : ' Thou shalt love ' the Lord thy God with all thy Heart, with all thy Soul, with ' all thy Mind, and with all thy Strength ; and thy Neighbour ' as thyself. On these two, saith he, hang all the Law and the ' Prophets.' And without these *two Things*, no good Light ever can arise, or enter into your Soul. Take all the Sciences, shine in all the Accomplishments of the lettered World, they will only lead you from one vain Passion to another ; everything you send out from within you is selfish, vain, and bad ; everything you see or receive from without, will be received with a bad Spirit ; till *these two* heavenly Tempers have overcome the *natural Perverseness* of fallen Nature. Till then, nothing *pure* can proceed from within, nor anything be received in *Purity* from without.

Think yourself therefore unfit, incapable of judging rightly, or acting virtuously, till these two Tempers have the Government of your Heart. Then every Truth will meet you ; no hurtful Error can get Entrance into your Heart ; you will neither deceive, nor be deceived ; but will have a better Knowledge of all Divine Matters, than all the human Learning in the World can help you to.

Would you know what it is to love God with all your Heart and Soul, &c., you need only look back to that, which has been said of the *Nature* and *Spirit* of God.* For when with all your

---

* Page 140.

Heart and *Soul* you love, and long to have, that *Nature* and *Spirit*, to be wholly united to it, possessed and governed by it, then you love God with all your Heart and Soul, *&c.* And then you are first capable of loving yourself and your Neighbour rightly. For so much as you have of the Divine Nature and Spirit in you, just so much Power have you of loving yourself and your Neighbour aright ; that is, of loving only and equally, *that* in yourself and your Neighbour, which the Deity *only* and *equally* loves, both in you, and him. But it is time to part, when we have only told our silent Friend, *Humanus*, that if we live to meet again, we shall, with all our Hearts, receive him as a Speaker among us.—And so, Gentlemen, once more, Adieu.

FINIS.

THE
WAY
TO
DIVINE KNOWLEDGE:

BEING SEVERAL

DIALOGUES

BETWEEN

HUMANUS, ACADEMICUS, RUSTICUS, and THEOPHILUS.

As preparatory to a new Edition of the Works of JACOB BEHMEN; and the right Use of them.

By *WILLIAM LAW*, M. A.

LONDON:
Printed for J. RICHARDSON, in *Pater-noster-row*. 1752.

THE FIRST DIALOGUE

BETWEEN

Humanus, Academicus, Rusticus and *Theophilus.*

HUMANUS. Oh! *Theophilus*, I must yield, and it is with great Pleasure that I now enter into Conversation with you. You have taken from me all Power of cavilling and disputing. I have no Opinions that I choose to maintain, but have the utmost Desire of entering further into this Field of Light, which you have so clearly opened to my View. I shall not trouble you with the relation of what has passed in my Soul, nor what Struggles I have had, with that Variety of heathenish Notions which have had their Turn in my Mind. It is better to tell you, that they are dead and buried, or rather consumed to nothing by that new Light, which you have opened in so many great Points, that I was quite a Stranger to before. To reject all that you have said concerning the Fall of Angels, the Original of this World, the Creation and Fall of Man, and the Necessity of a Redemption, as great as that of the Gospel, is impossible ; nothing can do it, or stand out against it, but the most wilful and blind Obstinacy.

But these great Points cannot be received in any true Degree without seeing the vain Contention of all those, who either defend, or oppose the Gospel, without any true and real Knowledge of them. The one contend for, and the other oppose, not the Gospel, but a System of empty words, and historical Facts, branched into Forms and Modes of dividing one Church from another ; whereas the Gospel is no History of any *absent, distant*, or *foreign* Thing, but is a Manifestation of an *essential, inherent, real* Life and Death in every Son of *Adam ;* grounded on the Certainty of his first angelical Nature, on the Certainty of his real Fall from that, into an animal earthly Life of impure bestial Flesh and Blood, and on the Certainty of an inward Redemption from it, by the Divine Nature given again into him. These three great Points, with all the Doctrines, Duties, and Consequences, that are essentially contained in, or flow from them, are the

Gospel of *Jesus Christ*, to which, by your means, I am become a Convert. I am now, dear *Theophilus*, strongly drawn Two different Ways. First, I am all Hunger and Thirst after this new Light, a Glimpse of which has already raised me, as it were, from the Dead: and I am in the utmost Impatience to hear more and more of this Divine Philosophy, which, I so plainly see, opens all the Mysteries both of Nature and Grace, from the Beginning to the End of Time. What I have heard from you, when I was obliged to be silent, and what I have since found and felt by much reading the *Appeal*, and that *Dialogue*, obliges me to speak in this ardent Manner. They have awakened something in me which I never felt before, something much deeper than my Reason, and over which I have no Power; it glows in my Soul, like a Fire, or Hunger, which nothing can satisfy, but a further View of those great Truths, which I this Day expect from your opening to us the Mysteries of Heaven revealed to that wonderful Man, *Jacob Behmen*.

On the other hand, I find in myself a vehement impulse to turn Preacher amongst my former Infidel Brethren; which Impulse I know not how to resist: For being just converted myself, I seem to know, and feel the *true Place*, from whence Conversion is to arise in others; and by the Reluctance which I have felt in my Passage from one Side to the other, I seem also to know the *true Ground* on which Infidelity supports itself. And he only is able to declare with Spirit and Power any Truths, or bear a faithful Testimony of the Reality of them, who preaches nothing but what he has first seen, and felt, and found to be true, by a living Sensibility and true Experience of their Reality and Power in his own Soul. All other Preaching, whether from Art, Hearsay, Books, or Education, is, at best, but playing with Words, and mere trifling with sacred Things. Being thus divided in myself, I hope to have your Direction.

Theophilus. Dear *Humanus*, my Heart embraces you with great Joy, and I am much pleased with what you say of yourself. This *Hunger* of your Soul is all that I wish for; it is the *Fire* of God, the *Opening* of Eternity, the *Beginning* of your Redemption, the *Awakener* of the angelic Life, the *Root* of an omnipotent Faith, and the *true Seeker* of all that is lost. For all these Things, and much more, are the blessed Powers which will soon break forth, and show themselves to be the true Workings of this celestial Fire, that has begun to glow within you.

Your Business is now to give Way to this heavenly Working of the Spirit of God in your Soul, and turn from everything either within you, or without you, that may hinder the further Awakening of all that is holy and heavenly within you. For within you is that heavenly Angel that died in Paradise, and died no other Death, than that of being hid a while from your Sight and Sensibility.

For be assured of this, as a certain Truth, that corrupt, fallen, and earthly as human Nature is, there is nevertheless in the Soul of every Man, the Fire, and Light, and Love of God, though lodged in a State of Hiddenness, Inactivity, and Death, till something or other, human or Divine, *Moses* and the Prophets, *Christ* or his Apostles, discover its Life within us.

For the Soul of every Man is the Breath and Life of the Triune God, and as such, a Partaker of the Divine Nature; but all this Divinity is unfelt, because overpowered by the Workings of Flesh and Blood, till such time as Distress, or Grace, or both, give Flesh and Blood a Shock, open the long shut-up Eyes, and force a Man to find something in himself, that Sense and Reason, whilst at quiet, were not aware of. Wonder not therefore at this Conflict in your Soul, that you are eager after more Light, and impatient to communicate that which you have. For you must be thus driven; and both these Desires are only Two Witnesses to this Truth, that a heaven-born Spirit is come to Life in you.

Only remember this; Look well to the Ground on which you stand, keep a watchful Eye upon every Working of Nature, and take care that nothing human, earthly, private, or selfish, mix with this heavenly Fire: That is, see that your Mind be *free, universal, impartial*, without Regard to here or there, this or that, but loving all Goodness, practising every Virtue, for itself, on its own Account, because it is so much of God; neither coveting Light, nor longing to communicate it to others, but merely and solely for this Reason, that the Will of God may be done, and the Goodness of God brought to Life, both in you and them. For there is no Goodness but God's; and his Goodness is not alive, or fruitful in you, but so far, and in such a Degree, as the Good that you mean, and do, is done in and by that Spirit, by which God himself is good. For as there is but One that is good, so there is, and can be but One Goodness. And therefore it is, that we are called not to an human, worldly, prudential, partial Goodness, suitable to our selfish Reason, and natural Tempers, but to 'be perfect, as our Father in Heaven is 'perfect.' And the full Reason is expressed in the Words; for if our Father is in heaven, we must be there too in Spirit and Life, or we are not his Children; if Heaven is that for which we are made, and that which we have lost, it is not any human Goodness, but a heavenly Birth and Spirit of God's own Goodness, working in us, as it does in God, that can make us the heavenly Children of our Father in Heaven. You must love the

Light of God, as God loves it; you must desire that others may enjoy it, as God desires it. Now God is a free, universal, impartial Love, loving and doing every kind of Good, for its own Sake, because that is the highest and most perfect Working of Life; and because everything else but Goodness, for its own Sake, is imperfect, and a Degree of Evil, Misery, and Death. And no Creature can come out of its Imperfection, Misery, and Death, but by the pure, free, unmixed Goodness of God, being born in it. Though you had outwardly all Virtues, and seemed doing all that the Saints of God have done, yet unless the *same Spirit*, by which God himself is Good, brought forth your Goodness, all would be only an earthly Labour, that could have no Communication with Heaven.

Therefore, my Friend, set out right, and be assured of this Truth, that *Nature*, and *Self*, and every *particular View*, must be totally renounced; or else, be your Zeal what it will, ever so pleasing to yourself, or astonishing to the World, you are not working with God.

Here now you have the Test of Truth, by which you may always know, whether it be the Spirit of God, and the Love of God, that drives you. If your Zeal is after this *pure*, free, *universal* Goodness of God, then of a Truth the Spirit of God breatheth in you; but if you feel not the Love of this pure, free, universal Goodness, and yet think that you love God, you deceive yourself; for there is no other true Love of God, but the loving *that*, which God is.

But if you please, *Humanus*, pray tell me, in what manner you would attempt to make Converts to Christianity.

Humanus. I would not take the Method generally practised by the modern Defenders of Christianity. I would not attempt to show from *Reason* and *Antiquity*, the Necessity and Reasonableness of a Divine Revelation in general, or of the *Mosaic* and Christian in particular. Nor enlarge upon the Arguments for the Credibility of the Gospel-History, the Reasonableness of its Creeds, Institutions, and Usages; or the Duty of Man to receive Things above, but not contrary to, his Reason. I would avoid all this, because it is wandering from the true Point in Question, and only helping the Deist to oppose the Gospel with a Show of Argument, which he must necessarily want, was the Gospel left to stand upon its own Bottom.

And, on the other hand, should the Deist yield up such a Cause as this, and change Sides, he could only be said to have changed his Opinion about Facts, with any more altering or bettering his State in God, than if he had only altered his Opinion about Things in Dispute amongst the ancient Philosophers.

For since the *Fall* of Man, implying a real Change from his first State, or a total Death to his first created Life, since the Necessity of a new Birth of that lost Life, by the Life of God again restored to, or born in the Soul, are *two Points*, quite overlooked by those who defend the Truth and Reasonableness of the Christian Scheme, it may truly be said, that the *only Ground*, and *whole Nature* of the Gospel is quite dropped, and given up by those who thus defend it.

For the Gospel has but *one Ground*, or Reason, and that is the Fall of Man, it has but *one Nature*, and that is to help Man again to *all* that he had lost.

How unreasonable would it be, to offer the Christian Redemption to glorious Angels in Heaven? Could anything be more inconsistent with their heavenly, unfallen State? Yet just so unreasonable would it be to offer it to Man unfallen from his first created State.—For Man standing in that first Perfection of Life, which God breathed into him, and in that very outward State, or World, into which God himself brought him, wants no more Redemption, than the most glorious Angels do; and to preach to such a Man, in order to be reconciled to God, the Necessity of dying to himself, and the World he is in, would be as contrary to all Sense and Reason as to preach to Angels the Necessity of dying to themselves, their Divine Life and the Kingdom of Heaven, for which God had created them.

Thus does it appear, that the Fall of Man into the Life of this earthly World, is the sole Ground of his wanting the Redemption, which the Gospel offers.

Hence it is that the Gospel has only one simple Proposal of certain Life, or certain Death to Man; of Life, if he will take the Means of entering into the Kingdom of God, of death if he chooses to take up his Rest in the Kingdom of this World. This is the simple Nature, and sole Drift of the Gospel; it means no more, than making known to Man that this World, and the Life of it, is his Fall, and Separation from God, and Happiness, both here and hereafter: And that to be saved or restored to God and Happiness, can only be obtained, by renouncing all Love, and Adherence to the Things of this World. Look at all the Precepts, Threatenings, and Doctrines of the Gospel, they mean nothing, but to drive all Earthly-mindedness and carnal Affections out of the Soul, to call Man from the Life, Spirit and Goods of this World, to a Life of Hope, and Faith, and trust, and Love and Desire of a new Birth from Heaven.

To embrace the Gospel, is to enter with all our Hearts into its Terms of dying to all that is earthly both within us, and without us; and on the other hand to place our faith, and Hope, and Trust, and Satisfaction in the Things of this World, is to reject the Gospel with our whole Heart, Spirit and Strength, as much as any Infidel can do, notwithstanding we made ever so many verbal Assents and Consents to everything that is recorded in the New Testament.

This therefore is the one true essential Distinction between the Christian and the Infidel. The Infidel is a Man of this World, wholly devoted to it, his Hope and Faith are set upon it; for where our Heart is, there, and there only is our Hope and Faith. He has only such Virtue, such Goodness, and such a Religion, as entirely suits with the Interest of Flesh and Blood, and keeps the Soul happy in the Lust of the Flesh, the Lust of the Eyes, and the Pride of Life: This, and this alone, is *Infidelity*, a *total Separation* from God, and a Removal of all Faith, and Hope from him, into the Life of this World. It matters not, whether this Infidel be a *Professor* of the Gospel, a Disciple of *Zoroaster*, a Follower of *Plato*, a *Jew*, a *Turk*, or an Opposer of the Gospel-History: This Difference of Opinions or Professions alters not the Matter, it is the Love of the World instead of God, that constitutes the *whole Nature* of the Infidel.

On the other hand, the Christian renounces the World, as his horrid Prison; he dies to the Will of Flesh and Blood, because it is Darkness, Corruption, and Separation from God; he turns from all that is earthly, animal, and temporal, and stands in a continual Tendency of Faith, and Hope, and Prayer to God, to have a better Nature, a better Life and Spirit born again into him from above.

Where this Faith is, there is the Christian, the new Creature in Christ, born of the Word and Spirit of God: neither Time nor Place, nor any outward Condition of Birth, and Life, can hinder his Entrance into the Kingdom of God.

But where this Faith is not, there is the *true, complete* Infidel, the Man of the Earth, the Unredeemed, the Rejector of the Gospel, the Son of Perdition, that is *dead in Trespasses and Sins, without Christ, an Alien from the Commonwealth of Israel, a Stranger from the Covenants of Promise, having* no Hope, and without God in the World.

Here therefore I fix my true Ground of converting Men to Christianity; and how miserably, may I say, do they err, who place Christianity and Infidelity in anything else, but in the Heart either devoted to this World, or devoted to God!

He therefore that opens a Field of Controversy to the *Deist*, about Revelation in general, or the History of Facts, Creeds, and Doctrines of Churches, not only leads him from the Merits of the Gospel, but brings him into a Field of Battle, where he may stand his Ground as long as he pleases. This I can truly say from my own Experience, who have been twenty Years in this Dust of Debate; and have always found that the more Books there were written in *this Way* of defending the Gospel, the more I was furnished with new Objections to it, and the less apprehensive of any Danger from my not receiving it.

For I had frequently a Consciousness rising up within me, that the Debate was equally vain on both Sides, doing no more real Good to the one than to the other, not being able to imagine, that a Set of scholastic, logical Opinions about History, Facts, Doctrines, and Institutions of the Church, or a Set of logical Objections against them, were of any Significancy towards making the Soul of Man either an eternal Angel of Heaven, or an eternal Devil of Hell. And therefore it was, that I was often tempted rather to think, there was neither Heaven, nor Hell, than to believe that such a Variety of Churches, and Systems of Opinion, all condemning, and all condemned by one another, were to find the Heaven of God opened to receive them, but he who was equally led by Opinion to reject them all, was doomed to Hell. But you, Sir, (and how can I enough thank you for it?) have put a full End to all this vain Strife of Opinions floating in the Brain; You have dispersed the Clouds that surrounded my bewildered Mind; You have brought me home to myself, where I find Heaven and Hell, Life and Death, Salvation and Damnation at Strife within me; You have shown me the infinite Worth of Christianity, and the dreadful Nature of Infidelity, not by helping me to a new Opinion, for my *Reason* to maintain, but by proving to me this great and decisive Truth, that Christianity is neither more nor less, *than the Goodness of the Divine Life, Light and Love, living and working in my Soul;* and that Infidelity in its whole Nature, is purely and solely *the Heart of Man living in, governed by, and contented with the evil Workings of the earthly Life, Spirit, and Nature.*

This is the Infidelity that you have forced me to fly from, and renounce, and *that* is the Christianity, to which I am converted with all the Strength of my Heart and Spirit. Away then with all the Fictions and Workings of Reason, either for, or against Christianity! They are only the wanton Sport of the Mind, whilst ignorant of God, and insensible of its own Nature and Condition. Death and Life are the only Things in Question; *Life* is God, living and working in the Soul; *Death* is the Soul living and working according to the Sense and Reason of bestial Flesh and Blood. Both this Life, and this Death are of their own Growth, growing from their own Seed within us, not as busy Reason talks or directs, but as our Heart turns either to the one or the other.

But, dear *Theophilus*, I must now tell you, that I want to make haste in this new Road you have put me in. Time is short, I am afraid of leaving the World, before I have left all worldly Tempers, and before the first holy and heavenly Birth be quickened, and brought to Life in me.

An Angel my first Father was created, and therefore nothing but the Angel belongs to Man, and nothing but the Angel can enter into Heaven. Angelic Goodness, therefore, is the one Thing that Man must look up to God for, because it is the one Goodness that he has lost. Everything else, Flesh and Blood, Earth and all earthly Tempers, everything that had its Rise from the Fall of *Adam*, must be renounced, and given up to Death, and the first angelic Glory of the Life of God in Man may be again found in him.

Theophilus. Indeed, *Humanus*, you have made great Haste already; for all the Haste that we can make, consists in a total dying to all the Tempers and Passions which we have received from the Spirit of this World, by our Fall into it. And the more watchfully, earnestly, and constantly, we do this, the more Haste we make to our lost Country, and heavenly Glory.

It is no Extravagance, or overstraining the Matter, when we say, that our Goodness must be angelic; for no Goodness less than that, can be Divine and heavenly, or help us to a Life in Heaven. It is often said, that we are poor, infirm Men, and not Angels; and therefore must be content with the Poverty and Infirmity of human Virtues. That we are poor, infirm Men, is undeniable; but this is the one infallible Reason, why a Virtue that is according to our Nature, or of its own Growth, can do us no Good. We were not created poor and infirm Men by God, but have lost him, are separated from him; full of Misery, because we have changed our first State, and brought all this Poverty, Corruption, and Infirmity, upon ourselves. And therefore, as this Infirmity is from ourselves, so we must intend nothing less, or short of the total Removal of it, nor think that we have our proper Goodness, till we stand in that Degree of it, in which God created us. For, be assured of this great Truth, that nothing in us can be the Delight of God, but that very Creature, which he created. All therefore must be parted with, that God hath not created and brought to Life in us. And no Goodness but that of an Angel, can overcome the Evil that is in us, or do the Will of God on Earth, as it is done in Heaven, which is the only Goodness in and for which God created us.

Academicus. Pray, *Theophilus*, give me leave to say, that I should think it better, not to insist so much upon the Word *Angelic*, when you speak of the Goodness, that ought to be ours. For it seems to me too liable to Objection. We have not the high Faculties, and exalted Powers of Angels; and therefore our Goodness cannot rise up to an Equality with theirs.

Rusticus. Pray, *Academicus*, give me leave also to say, that if your Learning did not lead you to mind Words, more than Things, you could not have fallen into this critical Scruple. For our Call to angelic Goodness, does not suppose or require any high Stretch, or refined Elevation, of our intellectual Faculties and Powers. A *Shepherd* watching over his Flock, a poor *Slave* digging in the Mines, may each of them, though so employed to the End of their Lives, stand before God in a Degree of Goodness truly angelic. On the other hand, you may spend all your Time in high Speculations, writing and preaching upon Christian Perfection, composing Seraphic Hymns of heavenly Matters, with a Strength of Thought and Genius that delights both yourself and others, and yet, so doing to the Day of your Death, have only a Goodness like that of eating and drinking that which most pleases your Palate.

Would you know the true Nature of angelic Goodness, see how the Spirit of Christ speaks, ' Thou shalt love the Lord thy ' God with all thy Heart, Soul, and Strength, and thy Neighbour ' as thyself. I came into the World, not to do my own Will, ' not to seek my own Glory or Honour, not to have a Kingdom ' in this World, but to promote the Kingdom of God, and do ' the Will of my Father in Heaven. My Meat and Drink is to ' do the Will of him that sent me. When thou makest a Feast, ' call not thy rich Friends and Acquaintance, but the poor, the ' lame, and blind,' &c. ' Whether you eat or drink, or whatever ' you do, do all to the Glory and Praise of God.' Thus speaks the Spirit of Christ; and he that in this Spirit thus lives, is an Angel, whether he be in Heaven, or enclosed in Flesh and Blood. And all of us are in the Way of attaining to this angelic Goodness, as soon as we hate the selfish Tempers of our own earthly Life, and earnestly long, in the Spirit of Prayer, to have the Life of God brought forth in us. Now this Goodness we must have, or we have none at all; for there is but one *God*, one *Good*, and one *Goodness;* and it is rightly called Angelic, because nothing is capable of it, but the heavenly angelic Nature; nor can it have any Existence in Man, till the Workings of our earthly Nature are overcome, and brought into Subjection to *that* Spirit, which is not of Man, but from Heaven. For Flesh and Blood, in all its Workings, can work only for itself; Darkness can only be dark, it has no other

Nature; Coldness can only be cold; Earth can only be earthly; and the Works of Light can only proceed from Light. Flesh and Blood, or that Life which is only from the Stars and Elements of this World, can only work as the Stars and Elements work, only for Time, and a corruptible Life; it can only be bestial, and serve the Ends of a bestial Life; it is insensible and incapable of Divine Virtue, and is, and can be of no higher a Nature in a Man, than in a Beast, and must have the same End in both. It is quite incapable of entering into the Kingdom of God; and only for this Reason, because it is absolutely incapable of having any true and heavenly Goodness. It has then only its proper Goodness, when it has lost its Power of acting, and is governed by a Spirit superior to it; whilst it lives and rules, it can only live to itself; is nothing but an earthly own Will, own Love, own Honour, own Interest, never rising higher, doing better, or coming any nearer to Goodness, than its own Pride or Covetousness, Envy or Wrath, can carry it. For these Tempers, with all their lesser Subdivisions, are the *Atmosphere* that sets Bounds to the Breath of the earthly Life; they are essential to it, and as inseparable from it, as Hardness and Darkness are inseparable from a Rock of Stone. So long as the stony Rock lasts, so long is it hard and dark. And so long as earthly Flesh and Blood lives and acts, it can only live and act for itself; it can seek, love, like, or do no manner of Thing, but as its own Will, own Love, own Interest, is some way or other felt, and found in it. Would you know the true Ground and Reason of this? It is because no Life can go out of, or further than itself; nor can it will anything, but what its own Life is. This is absolutely true of every Life, whether it be Divine, earthly, or hellish; it can seek, love, and delight in nothing, but that which is according to its own Life.

See here, *Academicus*, the Folly of your quarrelling with the Word *Angelic*, since the Thing itself, angelic Goodness, is absolutely necessary; it is the Goodness of our first Creation, and must be the Goodness of our Redemption. The falling from it has brought forth all the Evils that we are surrounded with, and nothing can deliver us from the Death of our fallen State, but a true and full Resurrection of all that Purity and Goodness, which was living in the first Creation of Man. To be content with our Infirmities, is to be content with our Separation from God; and not to aspire after the one angelic Goodness, is to be *Carnally-minded*, which we are told, *is Death*, that is, Death to the one Divine Life.

A Virtue that is only according to the State of this earthly Life, is a Virtue of Art, and human Contrivance, a Fiction of

Behaviour, modelled according to Rule and Custom, or Education, that can go no deeper, nor rise higher, nor reach further, than the Sense and Reason, and Interests of Flesh and Blood, can carry it. But this can have no Communication with God and Heaven, because it is not born of them, but is a lower, separate State of Life, that at best can only bring forth a Civility of outward Manners, little better than such a new Birth as may be had from a Dancing-master. But the Goodness which we want, and which we were created to have, is the one holy blessed Life of God, and Christ, and Heaven, living in the Soul. For from Eternity to Eternity, there never was, or ever can be, any other heavenly Goodness in any Creature, but the Life, and Spirit, and Word of God, speaking, living, and breathing in it.

Bid the *Anatomist*, that can skilfully dissect an human Body, that can tell you the Names, Nature, and Offices of most of its Parts, that can show you how they all conspire to give Life, Strength, and Motion, to the living Machine: Bid him, I say, put Life into the dead Carcase.

Now learned Reason, when pretending to be a Master of Morality, is just as powerful as this very Anatomist. It can skilfully dissect a dead System of Morality, can separate all its Parts, tell you the Names, Nature, Distinctions, and Connections, of most kinds of Good and Evil. But when this is done, learned Reason, with all its Dictates, Distinctions, and Definitions, can do just as much Good to the Soul, that has lost its Goodness, as the Anatomist can do the Carcase that has lost its Life.

It is wonderfully astonishing, that you Men of Learning seldom come thus far, as to see and feel this glaring Truth, that Goodness must be a *living* Thing; but, blinded with the empty Sounds of Words in Variety of Languages, are as content and happy *with a Religion of Nature delineated,* or a Book of *Axioms, Maxims,* and *Deductions,* mathematically placed one after another, as if you had really found the Tree of Life. Whereas, in Truth, all this is no better than the Reading a Lecture upon the Use of the Heart, Liver, and Lungs, to a dead Carcase: For the Life of Goodness can no more be raised, or brought into the Soul, by this Art of Reasoning, than Life can be brought into the Carcase, by a Discourse upon the Heart, Liver, and Lungs, made over it.

Oh! *Academicus,* forget your Scholarship, give up your Art and Criticism, be a plain Man, and then the first Rudiments of Sense may teach you, that there, and there only, can Goodness be, where it comes forth as a *Birth of Life,* and is the free natural Work and Fruit of *that* which lives within us. For till

Goodness thus comes from a *Life* within us, we have in Truth none at all. For Reason, with all its Doctrine, Discipline, and Rules, can only help us to be so good, so changed, and amended, as a wild Beast may be, that by Restraints and Methods is taught to put on a Sort of Tameness, though its wild Nature is all the Time only restrained, and in a Readiness to break forth again as Occasion shall offer.

Thus far the Masters of Morality and human Discipline may go; they may tame and reform the outward Man, clothe him with the Appearance of many Images of Virtue, which will, some or all of them, be put off, just as Time, Occasion, and Flesh and Blood, require it. For the Goodness of a living Creature must be its own Life; it must arise up in it as its own Love, or any Passion doth; just as the Fierceness of the Tiger, and the Meekness of the Lamb, are the Birth of their own Life. And if Goodness is not our *natural* Birth from our natural Parents, we must of all Necessity be born again from a Principle above Nature, or no Goodness can be living in us. Now since Goodness is a Life, we have a Twofold Proof, that no Goodness can be living in us, till we are born again of the *Word* and Spirit of God: For Nature, as well as Scripture, assures us, that God is originally the *One Good*, and the *One Life;* and therefore no good Life can possibly be in us, but by the Word, Life, and Spirit of God, having a Birth in us. And from this Birth alone it is, that the free genuine Works of Goodness flow forth with the Freedom of the Divine Life, wherewith the Spirit of God has made us free; loving and doing all manner of Good, merely for Goodness-sake; virtuous in all kind of Virtue, purely for Virtue-sake: Then we are the natural true Children of our heavenly Father, and do the Works of Heaven with a cheerful and willing Mind. Then it is, that we are good in the Manner as God is good, because it is his Goodness that is born in us; we are perfect as he is perfect, we love as he loves, are patient as he is patient, we give as he gives, we forgive as he forgives, and resist Evil only with Good as he does.

This, *Academicus*, is angelic Goodness; and is the Goodness of those who are born again of the *Word*, and become new Creatures in the Spirit of *Christ*. This Goodness our first Father lost, when he chose to have the Eyes of Flesh and Blood, and the Spirit of this World, opened in him; and therefore our Redeemer, who well knew what we had lost, and must have again, has taught us in our daily Prayer, to ask for angelic Goodness in these Words; *viz.*, 'Thy Kingdom come; thy Will 'be done on Earth, as it is in Heaven.' But I have done, and I think you must have done, with your learned Scruple about the

Word *angelic*. And now, *Theophilus*, if you please, return to your Subject with *Humanus*.

Theophilus. Let me then tell you, *Humanus*, that I much approve of the Way that you intend to proceed in. You are come directly to the Truth and Heart of the Matter, and have hit upon the One only Method of putting *Deism* to a full Stand, by reducing Christianity to this One single great Point, which so evidently contains the whole Ground and Nature of it.

Now this One great Point consists of Two essential Parts; 1st, the Fall of Man from a Divine angelic Life, into an earthly, bestial, corruptible, miserable Life of this World. 2dly, The Redemption of Man, or his regaining his first angelic Perfection, by a new Birth of the Divine Nature, by the *Word* and Spirit of God. Stand steadily upon this true Christian Ground; and then you will not only stand safely yourself, but you will have left the Deist no Ground to stand upon. For here all the laboured Volumes of Infidelity, with which these last Ages have swarmed, are at once rendered useless, and cannot put so much as a little Finger into this Debate. Consult all, from *Hobbes* to the *Moral Philosopher*, and you consult in vain; their Works are as dead as themselves, and unable to give forth one Word against this Christianity. They had a much easier Task upon their Hands; for nothing can be easier than for Reason to object, and continue objecting, to the extraordinary Matters of the Old and New Testament. I do not mention this as an Accusation of the Deist, or to charge them with the crafty Contrivance of placing the Merits of the Cause where it is not. No, the Learning of the Christian World must bear the Blame of these fruitless Disputes: The Demonstrators of the truth and Reasonableness of Christianity have betrayed their own Cause, and left true Christianity unmentioned in their Defences of it. What a Reasonableness of Christianity have some great Names helped us to? Just as useful, and good to our fallen Souls, as the Reasonableness of consenting to the Death of *Pharaoh* and his Host in the *Red Sea*. But you, my Friend, being rightly converted to a Christianity that began before the Scriptures were written, and is as old as the Creation and Fall of Man, keep close to its true and real Ground; and, instead of showing the Reasonableness of believing a long History of Things, show the absolute Necessity of Man's dying to his present Life, in order to have a better from God. This is the Christianity that began with the Fall, and has been preached ever since to every Son of fallen Man, in every Corner of the World; and by the same Preacher that tells every Man, that he ought to be better than he is. For was not Man fallen from a better State than that he is now in, he could no more be ashamed or offended at anything that his Nature prompts him to do, than the Ox is ashamed at breaking into a good Pasture. Every Man therefore, from the Beginning of the World, has had Christianity and the Gospel written and preached within him; as it contains the Fall of Man, and his Want of being raised to a better State. But as we see, that the Truth and Reality of his Fall, and the Truth and Reality of his Redemption by a real Birth from above, can be lost, nay disowned, amongst those that are daily reading and expounding the Scriptures; so it is no wonder that the same should have happened to those, who had no Scriptures to read. Justly therefore, *Humanus*, are Churches and Creeds, Doctrines above and contrary to Reason, Miracles of the Old and New Testament, and all historical Facts and Matters, which are so great an Harvest to the Deists, justly, I say, are they removed by you out of the Debate; and the One great Point above-mentioned only insisted upon as the Whole of the Matter. For this One Point gained, all is gained; and, till this Point is cleared up, all the rest is but a Debate about nothing.

For if Man is fallen from a Divine Life, no one need to be told, that he can only be redeemed or saved from his Fall by having the same Divine Life born in him again, or a Second time. Nothing therefore touches the Truth of the Debate betwixt the Christian and the Infidel, but that which proves with Certainty, that Man has, or has not lost a Divine Life.

If he is thus fallen, has died this Death to a Divine Life, then the Nature and Necessity of the Christian New-birth sufficiently proves itself. But if it can be proved, that he is not thus fallen, but stands in that State and Degree of Life in which God created him; the Deists have reason enough to reject the Christian Scheme of Redemption.

Strange it is therefore beyond Expression, that every Man, whether Christian or Infidel, should not see, that here lies the Whole of the Matter; or that any learned Defender of Christianity should think of beginning anywhere, or in anything, but where the Redemption itself begins; or imagine there can be the least Ground to propose a Redemption to Man, till he shows *Why*, and from *What*, he is to be redeemed. Stranger is it still, if you consider, that Christians have nothing to excuse their wandering from this One great Point, since both the Testaments bear so open a Witness to it. 'In the day that thou eatest 'thereof thou shalt surely die;' says the Old Testament. 'Except a Man be born again from above, of the Word and 'Spirit of God, he cannot enter into the Kingdom of Heaven;' says the New Testament.

Thus do these Two Testaments begin with the most open Declarations of these Two Things; *viz.*, The Death of Man to his First created Life: 2dly, His Redemption only and solely by a real Birth of the Divine Life, received again from above. What Excuse therefore can be made for those who read the Scripture, and yet overlook that very One Point; not only so plainly declared, but which, in itself, is the One only Ground and Foundation upon which all the Scripture stands? For had not Man died, neither *Moses*, nor the *Prophets*, had ever been in Being. For Man not fallen, but abiding in his first created Perfection of Life, had been as free from any outward Law, as the Light is from Darkness. The keeping his own Nature, had been the keeping, and doing, and seeing, and knowing all that God required of him. So that neither Law, nor Prophecy, has any Ground or Reason, but because Man is dead to his first Life.

But seeing Man is dead to his first Life, and living only in an earthly bestial World, under the Power and Slavery of the evil Motions and Tempers of gross Flesh and Blood; therefore *Moses* must come with his Law, to set Sin before him, and give him Precepts of resisting and dying to all the Lusts of this new earthly Life, which he is fallen into : Therefore, to seek for any other Learning in or from *Moses*, than that of learning to resist and die to the Tempers and Passions of this earthly Life, is knowing nothing right of *Moses*, nor of ourselves.

Next after *Moses* came the *Prophets*, or the Spirit of Prophecy, with its *far-seeing Sight*, and Declaration of Glories to come. Now the Ground of Prophecy is this, it is because Man is to be *restored* to his first glorious State; and therefore the Spirit of Prophecy comes forth from God to awaken *Hope* and *Faith*, Expectation and Desire in Man; because these are the only Powers that can draw him out of the Mire of the earthly Life, in which he sticks, and carry him up to his first heavenly State again. Nothing therefore is to be sought for in or from the Prophets, but the Increase of our Hope, Faith, and Desire of the *New Birth* of that glorious Life which we have lost, and they foretold was to be had again.

Thus, my Friend, you see the Importance of this One Point; *Moses* and the Prophets have no Ground or Reason but this, that Man has lost his Divine Life; and that this same Divine Life is to be born again in him. Now seeing this is the Ground and Reason of the Scriptures, therefore is it the one unerring Key to the right Use of them. They have only this one Intent, to make Man know, resist, and abhor the Working of his fallen earthly Nature; and to turn the Faith, Hope, and longing Desire of his Heart to God: And therefore we are only to read them with this

View, and to learn this one Lesson from them. Whatever therefore occurs, that cannot be turned to this general End, but relates only to some temporal, occasional, or private Matter, is of no more Importance to us, than the Cloak and Parchments which St. *Paul* speaks of.

How many hundred Barns must there be, to hold all the learned Volumes, that had never been written, had Man looked upon the Scriptures as having no other View or End, but to teach him to renounce the Tempers of his fallen earthly Nature, and live unto God in Faith and Prayer; to be born again of the Divine Nature! But this one End being overlooked by learned Reason, *Hebrew* and *Syriac*, *Arabic*, *Greek*, and *Latin*, have been called in, to torture the Scriptures into a Chaos of confused Opinions, that has covered the Christian World with Darkness, and lost the only Good that was to be had from the written Word of God. Whereas, standing upon the Ground on which you stand, with only this one great Point at Heart, the Scriptures are a plain, easy, and certain Instruction; and no honest unlearned Heart stands in need of any Commentator, to help him to all the Benefit that can be had from Scripture, or secure him from any hurtful Error.

Humanus. Indeed, *Theophilus*, my own Experience can bear a full Testimony to the Truth of all that you have said. For upon my reading now the New Testament, with this Key in my Hand; *viz.*, of Man thus fallen, and thus called to a new Birth from Heaven; everything I read in it has Spirit and Life, and overflows my Soul with such an Unction, and Sensibility of sweet Doctrine, as I am not able to express. For whilst I consider it only as written to drive all earthly Tempers and Passions out of the Soul, and inflame the Heart with Love and Desire of the *Grace*, the *Spirit*, the *Light* and *Life* of the heavenly Nature, I can say, as the *Jewish* Officers did, Never Man spoke like *Christ* and his Apostles.

Why was the Son of God made Man? It was because Man was to be made again a Divine Creature. Why did Man want such a Saviour? It was because he was become earthly, mortal, gross Flesh and Blood. Now take *Christ* in this Light, and consider Man in this State, and then all that is said in the Gospel stands in the fullest Light.

Thus, 'Come unto me, all ye that are weary and heavy laden, 'and I will refresh you.' How poor, how mean, and uncertain a Sense is there in this, till you know, that Man has lost his Divine Nature, and is fallen into a World that is all *Labour*, *Burden*, and *Misery!* But as soon as this is known, then how easy, how plain, is the full and highest Sense of these Words,

'Come unto me, all that labour, are weary and heavy laden, and
'I will refresh you!'—I will bring to Life that first happy State
which you have lost. This is the *Note*, the *Paraphrase*, the
Expositor, the *Key* to the true Sense of every Doctrine of *Christ*;
which, though variously expressed to awaken the Heart, is only
one and the same Thing. Thus, 'Blessed are they that mourn,
'for they shall be comforted.' But why so? Because he that is
troubled at the Corruption, Vanity, and Impurity of his fallen
earthly State, has the Comfort of the heavenly Life ready for
him. Again, 'Blessed are they that hunger and thirst after
'Righteousness, for they shall be filled.' How plain and great is
the Sense here, as soon as we know, that *Christ* is our Righteousness: and that the righteous Life of *Christ* in the Soul, is that
Life which our first Father lost! Therefore, to hunger and thirst
after this Righteousness, is the one Way to be filled with that
Divine Life, that we had lost. Again, 'If any Man thirst, let
'him come unto me and drink: And out of his Belly shall flow
'Rivers of living Water.' What can the *Latin* or *Greek* Critic do
here? Nothing at all. He will only try to make some Excuse
for the Strangeness of the Phrase. But when these Words are
read by one who knows that he and all Mankind, have lost the
Divine Nature, he tastes and feels the glad Tidings which they
bring; and is in Love with these sweet Sounds, which promise
such an overflowing Return of Heaven into his Soul. Again,
'I beseech you,' says the Apostle, 'as Strangers and Pilgrims,
'abstain from fleshly Lusts, which war against the Soul,' &c. The
Critic looks into his Books, to see how *Latin* and *Greek* Authors
have used the Words *Stranger* and *Pilgrim*, and so some Sense
or other is given to the Apostle; but the Christian, who knows
that Man, wandering out of Paradise, a Colony of Heaven, was
taken Captive by the *Stars* and *Elements*, to live in Labour and
Toil, in Sickness and Pain, in Hunger and Thirst, in Heat and
Cold, amongst the Beasts of the Field; where evil Spirits, like
roaring Lions, seek to devour him; he only knows in what Truth
and Reality Man is a poor Stranger, and distressed Pilgrim upon
Earth. Again, 'To the Poor,' saith *Christ*, 'the Gospel is
'preached.' The Critic only considers the several kinds of worldly
Poverty. But the Christian, who knows that the real great
Poverty of Man consists in his having lost the Riches and Greatness of his first Life, knows, that to this poor Man the Gospel is
preached, because he only, who is sensible in this Poverty, can
hear and receive it. For to Man, insensible of his fallen State,
the glad Tidings of the Gospel are but like News from *Fairy
Land;* and the Cross of *Christ* can only be a Stumbling-block
and Foolishness to him, whether he be a Christian, a *Jew*, or a

Greek. Thus does it appear, that all the Doctrines and Sayings of *Christ* and his Apostles are full of a comfortable, Divine, and exalted Sense, or mere empty Words, just as the Fall of Man from a Divine Life, is either owned or disowned. But I have done.

Theophilus. Thus far then, *Humanus*, we are agreed, that the Fall of Man into the Life and State of this World, is the whole Ground of his Redemption; and that a real Birth of *Christ* in the Soul, is the whole Nature of it. Let me now only ask you, How you would endeavour to convince a Man of his fallen State?

Humanus. I would not begin with the Account that *Moses* gives of it, for several Reasons; but chiefly for these Two: *First,* Because the *Fall* is not an *historical* Matter; nor would a mere historical Knowledge of it be of any Use, or do any real Good to him. *Secondly,* Because *Moses's* Account is not the Proof of the Fall, and therefore not to be appealed to as such.

Moses is the first Historian of *natural Death,* and has recorded the Death of the First Man, and of many others who were born of him: But the *Proof* that Man is *mortal,* lies not in *Moses's* History of the Death of the First Man, but in the known Nature of Man, and the World from which he has his Life. Again, we do not want *Moses* to assure us, that there was a First Man; that he had something from *Heaven,* and something from the *Earth* in him; and must have come into the World in another Manner than all those who have descended from him. For every Man is himself the infallible Proof of this; *Moses* is only the Historian that has recorded the *When,* and *Where,* and *How* this First Man came into the World, and what was his Name. But the *Proof* and *Certainty* of the Fact, that such a First Man there must have been, lies not in *Moses's* Account, but stands proved to every Man from his own Nature and State in this World.

Thus it is with the *Fall;* we have no more Occasion to go to *Moses,* to prove that Man and the World are in a fallen State, than to prove that Man is a poor, miserable, weak, vain, distressed, corrupt, depraved, selfish, self-tormenting, perishing Creature; and that the World is a sad Mixture of false Goods, and real Evils; a mere Scene of all Sorts of Trials, Vexations, and Miseries; all arising from the Frame, and Nature, and Condition both of Man and the World. This is the full infallible Proof of the Fall of Man; which is not a Thing learnt from any History, but shows itself everywhere, and every Day, with such Clearness as we see the Sun. *Moses* is not the Prover of the Fact, that Man is fallen; but the Recorder of the *When* and *How,* and the *Manner* in which the Fall hath happened.

My First Attempt therefore, upon any Man, to convince him of the Fall, as the Ground of the Redemption, should be an Attempt to do that for him, which Affliction, Disappointments, Sickness, Pain, and the Approach of Death, have a natural Tendency to do ; *viz.*, to convince him of the Vanity, Poverty, and Misery of his Life and Condition in this World. For as this is the true Proof of the fallen State of Man, so Man can only be convinced of it, by having this Proof truly set before him. I would therefore appeal at first to nothing but his own Nature and Condition in the World ; and show him how unreasonable, nay, impossible it is, that a God, who has nothing in himself but infinite Goodness and infinite Happiness, should bring forth a Race of intelligent Creatures, that have neither natural Goodness, nor natural Happiness. The inspired Saints of God say thus, ' Man that is born of a Woman hath but a short ' Time to live, and is full of Misery.' Again, ' Man walketh in a ' vain Shadow, and disquieteth himself in vain.' Now if what is here truly said of Mankind, could be truly said of any Order of the Beasts and Animals of the Field, who could defend the Goodness of God in bringing such Creatures into such a State of Life ? Now though the Deist rejects the Scriptures, considered as a Volume of Divine Revelation, yet everything that he outwardly sees, and inwardly feels, demonstrates this *capital Truth* of Scripture, that Man is in this poor and miserable State of Life. And therefore, everything that we know of God, and everything that we know of Man, is a daily irresistible Proof, that Man is in a fallen State. Look at the human Infant just come out of the Womb, you can hardly bear the Sight ; it is a Picture of such Deformity, Nakedness, Weakness, and helpless Distress, as is not to be seen amongst the home-born Animals of this World : The *Chicken* has its Birth from no Sin, and therefore it comes forth in Beauty ; it runs and pecks as soon as its Shell is broken ; The *Pig* and the *Calf* go both to play, as soon as the Dam is delivered of them ; they are pleased with themselves, and please the Eye that beholds their frolic State and beauteous Clothing ; whilst the new-born Babe of a Woman, that is to have an upright Form, that is to view the Heavens, and worship the God that made them, lies for Months in gross Ignorance, Weakness, and Impurity ; as sad a Spectacle when he first begins to breathe the Life of this World, as when in the Agonies of Death he breathes his last.

What is all this, but the strongest Proof, that Man is the only Creature that belongs not to this World, but is fallen into it through Sin ? And therefore his Birth, in such Distress, bears all these Marks of Shame and Weakness. Had he been originally of this World, it is necessary to suppose, that this World had done the highest Honour to its highest Creature; and that he had begun his Life in greater Perfection than any other Animal, and brought with him a more beautiful Clothing than the finest Lilies of the Field have. But, to go on: When the human Infant is set upon his Legs, and begins to act for himself, he soon becomes a more pitiable Object than when crying in the Cradle. The Strength of his Life is a mere Strength of wild Passions; his Reason is Craft, and selfish Subtlety; he loves and hates only as Flesh and Blood prompt him, Jails and Gibbets cannot keep him from Theft and Murder. If he is rich, he is tormented with Pride and Ambition; if poor, with Murmuring and Discontent: Be he which he will, sooner or later, disordered Passions, disappointed Lusts, fruitless Labour, Pains and Sickness, will tear him from this World in such *Travail* as his Mother felt, when she brought forth the sinful Animal.

Now all this Evil and Misery, are purely the natural and necessary Effects of his Birth in the bestial Flesh and Blood of this World, and there is nothing in his *natural* State that can put a Stop to it; he must be evil and miserable *so long* as he has *only* the Life of this World in him. Therefore the absolute Certainty of the Fall, and the absolute Necessity of a New Birth, are Truths, independently of Scripture, plain to a Demonstration. Thus, God is in himself infinite Goodness, and infinite Happiness; but Man, in his present earthly Birth and Life, can neither have Goodness or Happiness; therefore his present State of Life could not be brought forth by a God who is all Goodness and Happiness. Thus every Man, that believes in a Creator infinitely perfect, is under a Necessity of believing the whole Ground of Christian Redemption, namely, that Man hath some way or other lost that Perfection of Life, which he had at first from his Creator.

But the Christian has yet an additional Proof of this Matter, because the Scriptures, which with him are infallible, so frequently and openly bear Witness to it.

Thus, 'Let us make Man in our Image, according to our Like-'ness.' How great, how Divine, is this Beginning of Man? How can there be any Evil or Misery, any Vanity or Weakness, in a Creature so brought forth? But now what is become of this Man? For if you look at Man just coming out of the Womb, the pitiable Object above described, what can be so absurd, as to call this Birth, his Creation in the Likeness and after the Image of God? Now what is said of the first Man, is not spoken of one Person, but of the human Nature; for the first Man, was only the first Instance of that which Mankind were to be. He had no Perfection peculiar to himself, but that of being the first Man ; and had he stood, all that came from him, had come to Life as he did, in the same Strength and Glory of Perfection, and not been born of a bestial Womb, like the wild Ass's Colt. Again, set the following Text against *Moses's* Perfection of the first Image of God, ' Man that is born of a Woman hath ' but a short time to live, and is full of Misery.'

Is not this a full Proof, that the first created Life of Man is quite dead, and that an earthly Life of Misery is risen up instead of it? Again, the Apostle saith, 'The natural Man knoweth ' not the Things of God ; they are Foolishness unto him.' Can this natural Man, the Man of earthly Flesh and Blood, that can have no Acquaintance with, or Knowledge of God, to whom the *Things of God are Foolishness;* can this be the Man first created in the Image and Likeness of God? What can be more absurd than such a Thought? Or what Excuse can be made for that Learning, which cannot see from so plain a Scripture, that human Nature, *now*, is not that human Nature, which it was at first created ; but is dead to that first Life, which it had in the Image and Likeness of God, or the Things of God could not possibly be *Foolishness* to it? But I will end this Matter with these borrowed Words, 'We were no more created to be in the ' Sorrows, Burdens, and Anguish of an *earthly Life*, than the ' Angels were created to be in the Wrath and Darkness of Hell. ' It is as contrary to the Will and Goodness of God towards us, ' that we are out of Paradise, as it is contrary to the Designs and ' Goodness of God towards the Angels, and some of them are ' out of Heaven, Prisoners of Darkness.

'The Grossness, Impurity, Sickness, Pain and Corruption of ' our Bodies, is brought upon us by ourselves, in the same manner, ' as the hideous, serpentine Forms of the Devils are brought ' upon them. How absurd, and even blasphemous would it be, ' to say with the Scripture and the Church, *That we are the* ' *Children of Wrath, and born in Sin*, if we had that Nature, ' which God at first gave us? What a reproach upon God, to ' say, that this World is a Valley of Misery, a Shadow of ' Death, full of Disorders, Snares, Evils, and Temptations, if this ' was an original Creation, or that State of Things for which God ' created us? Is it not as consistent with the Goodness and ' Perfection of God, to speak of the Misery and Disorder that ' unfallen holy Angels find above, and of the Vanity, Emptiness, ' and Sorrow of their heavenly State, as to speak of the Misery ' of Men, and the Sorrows of this World, if Men and the World ' were in that Order, in which God at first had placed them ? ' If God could make any Place poor and vain, and create any

'Beings into a State of Vanity and Vexation of Spirit, he might do so in all Places, and to all Beings.'*

Theophilus. You have put the Fall, *Humanus*, upon its right Proof, and shown great Judgment in your intended Method of converting anyone to the Belief of it. You have set the whole Matter in so just a Light, that I have nothing that I would add to it.

Humanus. Give me leave, Gentlemen, just to put in a Word or two concerning another plain Indication, that Man has lost that Life and Nature, in which he was first created. *Reason* has been my God, and is the vain Idol of modern Deism, and modern Christianity; and yet human *Reason* has no higher a Birth, than human *Ignorance*, *Infirmity*, and *Mortality;* they all began together; they are inseparable; they generate and are generated from one another; they are the Life of each other; and they must live and die together, and all bear the same Witness to the fallen State of Man. For no Creature can come from the Hands of God into a State of any Ignorance of anything, that is fit and proper to be known by it. This is as impossible, as for God to have an envious, evil Will. Now all right and natural Knowledge, in whatever Creature it is, is *sensible, intuitive,* and *its own Evidence.* But *Opinion, Reasoning,* or *Doubting* (for they are all but one Thing) can only *then* begin, when the Creature has lost its first right and natural State, and is got *somewhere,* and become *somewhat,* that it cannot tell what to make of. Then begins Doubting, from thence *Reasoning,* from thence *Debating;* and this is the high Birth of our magnified Reason, as nobly born, as *Groping* is, which has its Beginning in and from Darkness, or the Loss of Light. Hence we have a full Proof, that Man has lost his first natural State in which God created him. For Reasoning, Doubt, and Perplexity in any Creature, is the Effect of some Fall, or Departure from its first State of Nature, and shows, that it wants, and is seeking, something that its Nature would have, but knows not how to come at it. The *Beasts* seek not after Truth; a plain Proof, that it has no Relation to them; *has* no Suitableness to their Nature, nor ever belonged to them. Man is in Quest of it, in Perplexity about it, cannot come at it; takes Lies to be Truth, and Truth to be Lies; a plain Proof, both that he has it not, and yet *has* had it, was created in it, and for it; for nothing can seek for anything, but that which is lost, and is wanted; nor could it form the least Idea of it, but because it has belonged to it, and ought to be his.

---

* *Serious Answer to Dr. Trapp, on the Sin, &c., of being Righteous overmuch.*

The Beasts have no Ignorance of anything, that concerns them; but have all the sensible, intuitive Knowledge of everything that is the Good of their Nature. But man left to his Reason, is all over Ignorance, Doubt, Conjecture, and Perplexity in Matters of the highest Moment, about what he himself is, what is his chief Good, where he is to seek it, and how to obtain it. For to ask your Reason, how God is your God, how you are in him and from him, what he is in himself, and what he is in you, is but like asking your Hands to feel out the *Thickness*, or the *Thinness*, of the Light. To ask your Reason, whether the Soul of Man is immortal in its Nature, is to as good Purpose, is going no further out of the Way, than if you were to ask your *Eyes* to show you, where *Extension* begins, and where it ends. To ask your Reason, whether Man has anything of God, or the Divine Nature in him, is just as suitable to the Nature and Power of your Reason, as if you were to ask your *Nose*, whether this or that sweet, aromatic Smell in the Garden, has any *heavenly Power* mixed with, and opening itself in it.

Reason therefore, is so far from being able to help Man to that Knowledge, which his Nature and Condition want, that it can only help his Ignorance to increase and fructify in Doubts, Fictions, and absurd Debates. And the Thing cannot be otherwise; *Man* must *walk in a vain Shadow*, so long as Reason is his Oracle. For nothing can act suitably to Nature, find its true State in Nature, or answer the End of its Creation by the *Power* of Reason; because Reason is not the *Life*, the *Power*, or Former of Nature; and therefore has no more Power over Nature, than over the Powers and Principles of Vegetation, either in the Body of Man, or any other Creature. He therefore who turns to his Reason, as the true Power and Light of his Nature, betrays the same Ignorance of the whole Nature, Power, and Office of Reason, as if he were to try to smell with his Eyes, or see with his Nose. For as each of these Senses has only its *one Work* or Power which it cannot alter, or exceed; so Reason has only its *one Work* or Power, which it cannot alter, or exceed; and that one Work is, to be a bare Observer and Comparer of Things that manifest themselves to it by the Senses. This is as much its one only Power, as Seeing is the only Power of the Eyes. When therefore Reason takes upon it to determine on Things not manifested to it by the Senses, as to judge about a Divine new Birth, a Divine Faith; or how the Soul wants, or does not want God, *&c.*, it is then as much out of its Place and Office, as the Eye that takes upon it to smell; and its true Name and Nature is, *Whim, Humour, Caprice, Conjecture, Opinion, Fancy*, and every other Species of Blindness, and Passion.

Now suppose a Man to come thus into the World, with this chief Difference from other Creatures; that he is at a Loss to find out what he is, how he is to live, and what he is to seek, as his chief Happiness; what he is to own of a God, of Providence, Religion, &c. Suppose him to have Faculties that put him upon this Search, and no Faculties, that can satisfy his Inquiry; and what can you suppose more miserable to himself, or more unworthy of a good Creator? Therefore, if you will not suppose a God, that has been good to all Creatures, and given every Animal its proper Light of Nature, except Man, you must be forced to own, that Man has certainly lost the true Light and Perfection of his Nature, which God at first gave him.

But I believe *Academicus* wants to say something, and therefore I have done.

Academicus. I was only going to say, that every Attribute of God, everything that Sense and Reason force us to see, and know, and feel, both of ourselves, and the World, join with the Letter and Spirit of all Scripture in attesting, that Man has certainly had a Divine Life, to which he has certainly died. But yet I must own it is very difficult to conceive, how a Creature brought forth in so high Perfection, in such Enjoyment of the Life, Light, and Spirit of God, could either deceive himself, or be deceived by another.

Theophilus. All that we want to know, my Friend, is the Certainty of the Fact, and this is of the greatest Moment to us: For this is it, that takes us from the Herd of earthly Animals, and lays the Foundation of Religion, and Divine Virtue. For had not a Divine Life at *first* been in us, we should be *now* at the same Distance from all true Virtue and Goodness, and as incapable of forming the least Thought or Desire of it, as other Animals; and should have nothing to do, but to look to ourselves, live to our earthly Nature, and make the most of this World. For this is the only Wisdom and Goodness, that an earthly Nature is capable of, whether it be a Man, or a Fox. The Certainty therefore of the Fact, of our first Divine Birth, is all; nothing more need be inquired after. For on this Ground stands all our Comfort; hence it is, that, in Faith and Hope, we can look up to God as our Father, to Heaven as our native Country, and have the Honour to be accounted only as Strangers and Pilgrims upon Earth.

But however, to remove your Difficulty, I shall give you a little Sketch of the Possibility of Man's Falling, although created in the Perfection above-mentioned.

Now supposing God to have brought a new intelligent Creature into a new World, all the Attributes of God oblige us to suppose this Creature to be created in a perfect State both inwardly and outwardly. As intelligent, it must partake of the Divine Understanding; as living, it must have a Degree of the Divine Life in it; as good, it must have a Birth of the Divine Goodness in it; as an Offspring of Divine Love, it must have a Divine Happiness, for the Enjoyment of which the Love of God created it. Now there is but *one possible* Way for this intelligent Creature, thus endowed, to fall from, or lose the Happiness of its first created State. It cannot knowingly choose Misery, or the loss of its Happiness: Therefore it can only fall by *such* an Ignorance, or *Power* of falling, as is consistent with its perfect State. Now this Power lay wholly in the *Newness* of its Life: It only *began* to find itself an intelligent Being; and yet had a Power of Looking with the Eyes of its Understanding either inwards, or outwards; upwards, or downwards. It had a Power of acquiescing and rejoicing in *that*, which it found itself to be, and adoring that Power and Goodness which had brought it into the Possession of such a Nature: And it had a Power of *wandering* into Conjectures, and Reasons about *that*, which it *was not*. Now as a free, intelligent Creature, it could not be without this Power of thus turning its intelligent Eye; and yet as a beginning Creature that had no *Experience*, this Power could not be free from a *Possibility* of wandering; and therefore its Power of wandering was not a Defect, but a necessary Part of its first perfect State. Now in this *Possibility* of wandering with its intelligent Eye, looking where it ought not, and entering into Conjectures about *that*, which *it was not*, may be clearly seen the Possibility of its falling from a State of high Perfection.

This is the one only possible Way for a good, intelligent, *new* Creature, to lose its Happiness. And I think it may justly be affirmed, that the *Mosaic* Account of the Fall of Man is exactly this very Case; namely, how the Eye of his *new unexperienced* Understanding, beginning to cast a wandering Look into *that* which he *was not*, was by an unsuspected *Subtlety*, or Serpent, drawn into a *Reasoning* and Conjecturing about a certain *Good* and *Evil*, which were no Part of his own created State.

Which Inquiry, being given into, ended in the real Knowledge of this *Good* and *Evil*, the Sensibility of which became an immediate Death to his first Divine Life, destroyed the angelic Image in the Likeness of God, and set a gross, earthly, naked, ashamed, frightened, wretched Animal of bestial Flesh and Blood in its Place, the only Animal to which this new Knowledge of Good and Evil could belong.

Supposing therefore the Fall of Man, which is a Fact attested, and proved by every Thing we know of God, Ourselves, and the World ; the *Mosaic* Account of it has every Mark of Truth, Sobriety, and Justness, as being a plain and easy Description of the one only Way, by which a Creature so endowed could change or lose its first happy State.

Academicus. Truly, *Theophilus,* you have given a most natural and full Solution of my Difficulty, by which, I suppose, you mean as well to explain the Fall of Angels, as of Men. But, Sir, if that Pride, to which their Fall is charged, must have stolen upon them, in that same *unsuspected Way,* in which the Longing after the Tree of Good and Evil insinuated itself into Man ; *viz.,* from a wandering Look into *that,* which they were not, occasioned by the *Newness* of their untried Life, in which they had but just began to be ; suffer me then, to ask, Why the fallen Angels were not, at first, the immediate Objects of Divine Mercy and Goodness ? Why they are to be for ever Prisoners of a never-ending Hell ? Or, are you of Opinion, that Angels, as well as Men, will be at last brought back to their first State ?

Theophilus. Your Questions, *Academicus,* seem to have too much of Curiosity in them : But, as I hope you will not give way to this Temper, so I will, for once, comply with your Demands.

The *Fall* of Angels must be supposed to have been as soon after their Creation, as that of *Adam.* Had they stood any time in their new-created State, they had been in one and the same impossibility of Falling, as the Angels that are now in Heaven. For no pure, intelligent, good, and holy created Being, can possibly lose this Divine State of Perfection, but through the first Use of its untried State and Powers. The Manner of *Adam's* falling into the Life of this World, plainly shows the Manner how the Angels fell into Hell, namely, at first only by looking and conjecturing with their intelligent Eye into *that,* which they were not, which was not opened in them, but was hid in God. This Looking went on till it became a Lust and strong Longing after that *somewhat ;* just as it had done in *Adam,* who so gazed upon the earthly Good and Evil, till it opened itself in him. *Adam* looked only at that which was *Creaturely,* and in a *Life below* him ; and therefore only that *lower, creaturely, bestial* Life, was brought forth in him. But the Angel turning his wandering Look into that *Height* and Depth which was *not Creaturely,* but hid in God ; namely, into the *Might* and *Strength* of Eternity, that he might know *how* the creaturely Life was *kindled* by it ; and thinking himself by his exalted Nature, to be as near to this *great Power,* and as capable of *entering* into it, as *Adam* thought himself near to, and capable of knowing the Good and Evil of the earthly Life ; and as *Adam* thought to be like God in this

Divine Knowledge.

new Knowledge, so the Angels imagined to be like God, could he enter into *this Knowledge*, how the *Might* of God kindled the creaturely Life, for then he himself should have the Power of creating or kindling the creaturely Life; and as *Adam's* Imagination brought forth a Lust and longing, which could not be stopped, till the earthly Knowledge, and earthly Life, had opened itself in him; so the Angel's Imagination begot such a *Lust* and *Longing* to know the *Ground* and *Original* of Life, as would not be stopped till the *Ground* and *Original* of Life, namely, that *Depth of Darkness and Fire*, in and from which every creaturely Life must begin, was totally opened in him, and he as much swallowed up by Hell, as *Adam* was by the earthly Life. Thus you may see, how the same aspiring Imagination (but with regard to different Matters) rising in the same Manner, and from the same Cause in both these Creatures, and working itself up into a *Lust* and *Longing*, brought the one from Heaven into Hell, and the other from Paradise into a bestial World.

Now as the Lust of *Adam*, when it had obtained its Desire, opened all the Properties and Tempers of the bestial Life in him; so the Lust of the Angel, when it got what it wanted, *viz.*, the *Ground* and Original of the creaturely Life, which is *Darkness* and *Fire;* immediately opened all the dreadful Properties of Darkness and Fire in him, which at once swallowed up or extinguished the angelic Nature. Hence Wrath, Hatred, Pride, Envy, Malice, and every Enmity to Light and Love, are the *one only* Life of the fallen Angel; and he can will and act nothing else, but as these Properties of Darkness and Fire drive him.

To ask therefore, Why the fallen Angels continue in their State, is to ask, why *Darkness* is not made to be *Light?* For the *Root* and *Ground* of Nature is *unchangeable;* it keeps its *own Nature*, or it could not be the *Ground;* it must stand always in its *own Place*, and be only the Ground and Root; it cannot rise higher than the Root, no more than the Root of the Tree can be its Branches and Fruit. The Angels, therefore, being fallen into the Ground and Root of Nature, have only the working Life of the Ground and Root of Nature in them; and therefore seem to be as unchangeable, and incapable of having any other, as the Root itself is.

To ask therefore, why the fallen Angels were not helped by the Mercy and Goodness of God, as fallen Man was; is like asking, why the refreshing Dew of Heaven does not do that to *Flint*, which is does to the vegetable Plant? For as the Nature of the Flint is too hard, and too much compacted, to receive any Alteration from the sweet Softness of refreshing Water; so the fallen Angel, like the Flint, being shut up in the wrathful Working of its own hard Darkness and Fire, the Goodness of God can have no Entrance into it.

For what are we to understand by the *Mercy* and *Goodness* of God? His Mercy is his Patience. And his Goodness, is his *Light*, and *Word*, and *Holy Spirit*. Now every Creature has the Benefit of Divine Patience; but no Creature can have his *Goodness*, but that which is capable of receiving his *Light*, and Holy Spirit.

And his Light, and Holy Spirit, cannot enter into a Creature, as an external, additional Thing, that may be given to it, whether it will, or not, but must be brought forth as a Birth in it. For the Light, and Spirit of God, can be nowhere, but as a *Birth*, whether it be in God, or the Creature. And therefore the Goodness of God can be imparted to no Creature, but that which is capable of a *Birth* of the Light and Spirit of God, or, in the Words of Scripture, unless it be *born of the Word and Spirit of God*.

This therefore you may rest upon, as a certain Truth, that the *one only* Reason, why the fallen Angels have as *yet* had nothing of the Spirit or Light of God breathed into, or born in them, is, because they are as *yet* utterly incapable of such a Birth, or of being helped by the Divine Goodness. For as Flame cannot communicate itself to Flint, nor the Spirit of God to a Beast; because the Flint stands in the utmost Contrariety to Flame, and the Beast in a total Incapacity of Holiness; so the fallen Angel is in its working Life altogether incapable of receiving the Spirit and Life of God into it. Were it not thus, Angels had been helped, as early as Man: For the Goodness, or the Light and Spirit of God, loses no Time, but stands always in the same Fulness of Communication of itself to every Creature, that is capable of receiving it.

And therefore it is, that fallen Man was immediately helped, because he fell only into earthly Flesh and Blood, in which the *Light* of this World is kindled, which Light has something of Heaven in it, and was kindled by the Light of Heaven.

And therefore the Goodness of God, or his Light and holy Spirit, could come to Man's Assistance in the *Light of his Life*, and therein begin a Covenant of Redemption with him. For in this Light of his Life, which is a Ray of Heaven, the *inspoken Word* in Paradise could enter, and have Communion with it, and make itself to be a Beginning of Salvation to all those, who by Faith and Hope would lay hold of it, and endeavour after a new Birth from it. Thus stands the Ground and Reason why Men, and not Angels, were immediately helped at their Fall.

As to your last Question, whether I believe the final Restoration of all the fallen Angels? I shall only say, that neither ancient nor modern Writers, on either Side of the Question, have touched the true Merits of the Cause, or spoken to that Point, on which the Decision of the Matter wholly rests.

For it can neither be sufficiently affirmed, nor sufficiently denied, by any Arguments drawn either from the Divine Attributes, or Texts of Scripture; for they cannot come up to the Point in Question. But the true Ground and Merit of the Cause, lies solely in the *Possibility* of the Thing, which no one has attempted to prove, nor perhaps is anyone able to do it; namely, to show from a true Ground, that the diabolical Nature is possible to be altered. Darkness can by no Omnipotence be made to be Light; it can only be suppressed, or overcome by it, or forced to be hid under it, as Heaven hides or overcomes Hell; but still the Darkness has its first Nature, never to be changed.

Now if anyone can show, that the Devils are not *essentially* evil, as Darkness is essentially dark, but have only such an *accidental* Difference from Goodness, as *Ice* has from Water, or a Flint from transparent Glass; then their Restoration is possible, and they will infallibly have all their Evil removed out of them by the Goodness of God.

But unless it could be shown from a true Ground in Nature, that the fallen Angels must have something of the heavenly Life in them, though shut up in a thousand times harder Death, than Fire is in the dark Flint, no Length of Time, or anything else, can produce any Alteration, or Cessation of their evil Nature.

For Time cannot alter the Nature or Essence of Things; it only suffers that to come to pass which is possible, and consistent with the Nature of Things. No Length of Time can make a *Circle* to have, or give forth, the Properties of a *right Line*.

Now if the fallen Angels have nothing heavenly in them, but stand in as full a Contrariety to all that is heavenly, as the Circle does to the Properties of the *right Line;* then Goodness is as impossible to be ever awakened in them, as in a Beast. The Beast must always be what it was at first; and for this Reason, because nothing but the bestial Nature is in it: If therefore the fallen Angel is totally hellish, as the Beast is bestial, it must always be what it is.

But we have launched far enough in a Deep that does not belong unto us; and which cannot be sufficiently affirmed, or denied, but from the known Possibility, or the known Impossibility of the Thing, which does not yet appear. If it is possible, I am heartily glad of it; and am also sure enough, that it will then come to pass in its own Time. For if he could not be thought to be a good Man, who did not do all that he could to make Sinners become holy and happy in Goodness, we may be sure enough that the boundless Goodness of God, will set no Bounds to itself, but remove every Misery from every Creature that is capable of it. But let me now return to *Humanus,* and ask him, That supposing he could not convince a Man of the Certainty of his fallen State, how he would further proceed with him.

Humanas. Truly, *Theophilus,* I would proceed no further at all; and for this good Reason, Because I should then have nothing to proceed upon. Did I certainly know of an infallible Remedy for every Disorder of the Eyes, only to be had by going to *China* for it, I should not attempt to persuade a Man, who believed his Eyes to be sound and good, to leave all that he had, and go to *China* for this infallible Remedy for bad Eyes.

Now to press a Man to deny himself, and to leave all that he hath in the Enjoyments of Flesh and Blood, in order to be reconciled to God, who believes himself to be in the *same good* State, in which God created him, seems to be as wild a Project, as to desire him who is well pleased with the Goodness of his Sight, to go to the *Indies* to be helped to see.

And indeed, I very well know, from former Experience, that all Discourses about the Reasonableness of Christianity, the Doctrine of the Cross, the exceeding Love of God in giving so great a Saviour, with many more Things of the Like Nature, were mere empty Sounds, heard with the greatest Indifference, and incapable of raising the least Seriousness in me, merely because I had not the least Notion or Suspicion of the Truth and Greatness of my fallen State, and therefore was not the Man who had any Fitness to be affected with these Matters. And thence it was that *Christ* said, 'Come unto me, all ye that 'labour, and are heavy laden, and I will refresh you'; as plain as if he said, No one else can come to me, nor anyone else be refreshed by me.

Here therefore, in my humble Opinion, should all *begin,* who would propagate Christianity, or make true Converts to it, and *here stop,* as *Christ* did. It is only the weary and heavy laden, that are fitted to be Converts, or refreshed; and therefore we can no way help a Man to be a Christian, or fit him to be refreshed by *Christ,* but by bringing him into a full Sensibility of the Evil, and Burden, and Vanity of his natural State. And if he cannot be made sensible of this, we are to leave him to himself in his natural State, till some good Providence awakens him out of it; and not make Proposals to him of the Reasonableness of believing the Holy Trinity, the Incarnation of the Son of God, and the Necessity of his Sufferings and Death, *&c.,* for this Method is full as absurd, as to enter into solemn Debate with a confessed Atheist, about the Reasonableness of worshipping God in Spirit and Truth ; for, as the Existence of a God is the only Ground of proving that he ought to be worshipped in Spirit and in Truth, so the Certainty and belief of our fallen State, is the only Ground for showing the Reasonableness of the Mysteries of Redemption. And he that disowns the fall of Man from a Divine Life, has all the same Reasons for rejecting the Mysteries of our Salvation, as the Atheist has to reject the Doctrines of a spiritual Worship of God. Therefore, to expose the Mysteries of our Salvation, to the Wrangle of a Debate with an Unbeliever of the Fall of Man, which Mysteries have no other Ground to stand upon, is not only helping him to an easy Triumph over you, but is the most likely Method to prevent his ever being a Christian. For seeing how easily he can ridicule Mysteries, which, to him in his present State, can have no Reasonableness in them, he is put into the most likely Way of living and dying in a hardened Contempt of them. Whereas if you stick close to the One true Ground of Christianity, and only proceed as that proceeds, and make the Unbeliever no Offers of any other Christianity, but that which is to begin with the acknowledged Sensibility of the Fall of human Nature from its first Divine Life ; you stop where you ought to stop, and rob him of all Power and Pretence of meddling with the other Mysteries of Salvation.

The One Business then upon his Hands, if he will hold out against you, must be to deny his Reason and Senses, and maintain, in spite of both, that Man is not fallen, but is by Nature holy, just, good, and happy both in Body and Soul ; and that Mankind, and the World they are in, have all that Goodness and Happiness, which they could be supposed to have from an infinitely good and happy God ; and who can will nothing in the Creature but Goodness and Happiness. Here you bring the Deist to his proper Work, and all the Contradiction to Sense and Reason will lie on his Side : You set Christianity upon its true Ground ; and whoever thus defends it, as it ought to be defended, not only does Justice to the Christian Cause, but acts the most kind and friendly Part towards those who oppose it, merely through a Misunderstanding of its *true Ground and Nature ;* which I will venture to say is the Case of all the sober well-meaning Deists. For *Deism* has no natural Foundation, or Ground of its own, to stand upon ; it does not grow from any Root or Strength within itself, but is what it is merely from the *bad State* of Christendom, and the *miserable Use* that heathenish Learning, and worldly Policy, have made of the Gospel. If it (Deism) seems to itself to be *strong and well-grounded*, it is merely because it can so easily object to Church-doctrines, and scholastic Opinions: If it seems to itself to be *good*, it is because it can so easily lay open the Evils which Christians and Churches bring upon one another: If it seems to itself to be *highly rational*, its Reason is, because it is free from that Number of Absurdities and Contradictions, which Christian Churches lay to the Charge of one another. Lastly, if it keeps off all fearful Forebodings of the Consequences of not receiving the Gospel, it is because it so plainly sees, that Christians say, *Hail, Master*, kiss the Gospel, and then break every Part of it.

 This is the true Height, and Depth, and total Strength of Deism or Infidelity, it never had any other Support in myself but this; nor did I ever converse with a Deist, who carried the Matter higher or further than this, to support the Cause. Hence it is, that you made so speedy a Convert of me, by showing me such a Christianity as I never heard of before; and stripped of every Thing that gave me Power to oppose it. Had you proceeded in the Way practised by most Defenders of the Gospel, you had left me just as you found me, if not more confirmed in my old Way. But as you have justly removed all Controversy about Doctrines from the Merits of the Cause, and shown that it all lies in this one short, plain, and decisive Point, namely the Fall of Man; a Fall proved and demonstrated to all my Senses and Reason, by every Height and Depth of Nature, by every kind of Misery, Evil, and Sin in the World, by everything we know of God, Ourselves, and the World we live in; the Ground and Foundation of Christianity is undeniable, and no one can be too speedy a Convert to the Belief of it. And as you have also shown, that the whole Nature of the Gospel Redemption means nothing but the one, true, and only possible Way of delivering Man from his miserable State in this World; Christianity is shown to be the most intelligible and desirable Thing that the Heart of Man can think of. And thus, contrary to all Expectation, the Tables are quite turned; *Deism* can no longer *be founded on Argument*, and Christianity is as self-evident as our Senses; All Learning on both Sides, either for or against it, is insignificant; Christianity stands upon a Bottom quite superior to it, and may be the sure Possession of every *plain Man*, who has Sense enough to know whether he is happy or unhappy, good or evil. For this natural Knowledge, if adhered to, is every Man's *sure* Guide to that *one Salvation* preached by the Gospel. Which Gospel stands in no more need of Learning and critical Art *now*, than it did when *Christ* was preaching it upon Earth. How absurd would it have been for any Critics in *Greek* and *Hebrew*, to have followed *Christ* and his Apostles, as necessary Explainers of their hard Words, which called for nothing in the Hearers but penitent Hearts turned to God ; and declared, that they only who *were of God, could hear the Word of God!* How strange, that *Christ* should choose only illiterate Men to preach the Gospel of the Kingdom of God, if only great Scholars could rightly understand what they said ! Again, supposing learned Men to have only the true Fitness to understand the Word of Scripture, and that the plain Man is to receive it from them, How must he know which are the Scholars that have the right Knowledge? From whence is he to have this Information? For no one need be told, that ever since Learning has borne Rule in the Church, learned Doctors have contradicted and condemned one another in every essential Point of the Christian Doctrine. Thousands of learned Men tell the Illiterate, they are lost in this or that Church ; and Thousands of learned Men tell them, they are lost, if they leave it.

If therefore Christianity is in the Hands of Scholars, how must the plain Man come at it? Must he, though unable to understand Scripture, for want of Learning, tell which learned Man is in the right, and which is not? If so, the unlearned Man has much the greatest Ability, since he is to do that for Scholars, which they cannot do for themselves.

But the Truth of the Matter is this ; Christian Redemption is God's Mercy to all Mankind; but it could not be so, if every fallen Man, *as such*, had not some Fitness and Capacity to lay hold of it. It must have no Dependence upon Times and Places, or the Ages and several Conditions of the World, or any outward Circumstance of Life ; as the First Man partook of it, so must the last ; the learned Linguist, and the Blind, the Deaf and Dumb, have but one and the same common Way of finding Life in it. And he that writes large Commentaries upon the whole Bible, must be saved by *something* full as different from Book-knowledge, as they were, who lived when there was neither Book nor any Alphabet in the World.

For this Salvation, which is God's *Mercy* to the fallen Soul of Man, merely as fallen, must be something that *meets* every Man; and which every Man, as fallen, has *something* that directs him to turn to it. For as the Fall of Man is the Reason of this Mercy, so the Fall must be the Guide to it ; the Want must show the Thing that is wanted. And therefore the Manifestation of this one Salvation, or Mercy to Man, must have a Nature suitable, not to this or that great Reader of History, or able Critic in *Hebrew* Roots and *Greek* Phrases, but suitable to the common State and Condition of every Son of *Adam*. It must be something as grounded in human Nature, as the Fall itself is, which wants no Art to make it known; but to which the common Nature of Man is the only Guide in one Man, as well as another. Now this *something*, which is thus obvious to every Man, and which opens the Way to Christian Redemption in every Soul, is *a sense of the Vanity and Misery of this World; and a Prayer of Faith and Hope to God, to be raised to a better State.*

Now in this *Sensibility*, which every Man's own Nature leads him into, lies the Whole of Man's Salvation; here the *Mercy* of God and the *Misery* of Man are met together; here the *Fall* and the *Redemption* kiss each other. This is the Christianity which is as old as the *Fall;* which alone saved the First Man, and can alone save the last. This is it, on which hang all the Law and the Prophets, and which fulfils them both; for they have only this End, to turn Man from the Lusts of this Life, to a Desire, and Faith, and Hope of a better. Thus does the whole of Christian Redemption, considered on the Part of Man, stand in this Degree of Nearness and Plainness to all Mankind; it is as simple and plain as the feeling our own Evil and Misery, and as natural as the Desire of being saved and delivered from it.

This is the Christianity which every Man must first be made sensible of, not from Hearsay, but as a Growth or Degree of Life within himself, before he can have any Fitness, or the least Pretence to judge or speak a Word about the further Mysteries of the Gospel. But here I stop.

Theophilus. Well, *Humanus*, I have now pushed the Matter with you, as far as I intended; and you have given me full Proof of the Truth and Solidity of your own Conversion, and your Ability to do good amongst your old Brethren. You must now enter the Lists with them; not to charge them with Ignorance, Ill-will, or Profaneness of Spirit, but only to try, in the Spirit of Love and Meekness, to undeceive them, in the Manner you have been undeceived; and to show them, that Christianity is by no means that Thing, which you and they have so long disliked.

Nothing can be more right than your Resolution not to enter into Debate about the Gospel Doctrines, or propose the Reasonableness of them to anyone, till he owns himself sensibly convinced of the forementioned Fall of Man; and stands in a full Desire to be saved, or delivered from it. And if that Time never comes, you must leave him, as in the same Incapacity to hear or judge of the Doctrines of the Holy Trinity, the Incarnation of the Son of God, the Operation of the Holy Spirit, as *Epicurus* would be. For every Man that cleaves to this World, that is in Love with it, and its earthly Enjoyments, is a disciple of *Epicurus,* and sticks in the same Mire of Atheism, as he did, whether he be a modern Deist, a Popish or Protestant Christian, an *Arian*, or an orthodox Teacher. For all these Distinctions are without any Difference, if this World has the Possession and Government of his Heart. For the Whole of the Matter lies solely in this, whether Heaven, or Earth, hath the Heart and Government of Man. Nothing divides the Worshippers of the true God from Idolaters but this: Where Earth possesses and rules the Heart, there all are of *one* and the *same* Religion, and worship one and the same God, however they may be distinguished by Sect or Party.

And wherever the Heart is weary of the Evil and Vanity of the earthly Life, and looking up to God for an heavenly Nature, there all are of the one true Religion, and Worshippers of the true God, however distant they may be from one another, as to Time or Place. But enough has been said of this Matter.

Let me now only, before we break up, observe to you the true Ground and Nature of *Gospel Christianity:* I call it so, by way of Distinction from that *original universal* Christianity, which began with *Adam;* was the Religion of the Patriarchs, of *Moses* and the Prophets, and of every penitent Man in every Part of the World, that had Faith and Hope towards God, to be delivered from the Evil of this World.

But when the Son of God had taken a Birth in and from the human Nature, had finished all the Wonders that belonged to our Redemption, and was sat down at the Right Hand of God in Heaven, then a heavenly Kingdom was set up on Earth, and the Holy Spirit came down from Heaven, or was given to the Flock of *Christ* in such a Degree of Birth and Life, as never was, nor could be given to the human Nature, till Christ, the Redeemer of the human Nature, *was glorified.* But when the Humanity of Christ, our Second *Adam*, was *glorified*, and become all heavenly, then the heavenly Life, the Comfort, and Power, and Presence of the holy Spirit, was the Gift which he gave to his Brethren, his Friends and Followers, which he had left upon Earth.

The Holy Ghost descended in the Shape of cloven Tongues of Fire on the Heads of those, that were to begin and open the new Powers of a *Divine Life* set up amongst Men. This was the Beginning and Manifestation of the whole Nature and Power of *Gospel Christianity,* a Thing as different from what was Christianity before, as the Possession of the Thing hoped for, is different from Hope, or Deliverance different from the Desire or Expectation of it. Hence the Apostles were new Men, entered into a new Kingdom come down from Heaven, enlightened with new Light, inflamed with new Love, and preached not any absent or distant Thing, but *Jesus Christ*, as the *Wisdom and Power* of God, felt and found within them, and as a Power of God ready to be communicated in the same Manner, as a new Birth from above, to all that would repent and believe in him. It was to this Change of Nature, of Life and Spirit, to this certain, immediate Deliverance from the Power of Sin, to be possessed and governed by Gifts and Graces of an heavenly Life, that Men were then called to, as true Christianity. And the Preachers of it bore Witness, not to a Thing that they had heard, but to a Power of Salvation, a Renewal of Nature, a Birth of Heaven, a Sanctification of the Spirit, which they themselves had received. Gospel Christianity then stood upon its own true Ground; it appeared to be what it was. And what was it? Why, it was an *awakened Divine Life* set up amongst Men; itself was its own Proof; it appealed to its proper Judge, to the Heart and Conscience of Man, which was alone capable of being touched with these Offers of a new Life.

Hence it was, that Sinners of all Sorts, that felt the Burden of their evil Natures, were in a State of Fitness to receive these glad Tidings. Whilst the rigid Pharisee, the orthodox Priest, and the rational Heathen, though at Enmity with one another, and each proud of his own Distinction, yet all agreed in rejecting and abhorring a Spiritual Saviour, that was to save them from their carnal selves, and the Vanity of their own rational Selfish Virtues. But when, after a while, Christianity had lost its first Glory, appeared no longer as a *Divine Life awakened* amongst Men, and itself was no longer its own Proof of the Power and Spirit of God manifested in it; then heathenish Learning, and temporal Power, was from Age to Age forced to be called the Glory and Prosperity of the Church of Christ; although in the *Revelation* of *St. John*, its Figure is that of a scarlet Whore riding upon the Beast.

Here therefore, my Friend, you are to place the true Distinction of Gospel Christianity from all that went before it, or that is come up after it. It is purely and solely a *Divine Life awakened*, and *set up amongst Men*, as the *Effect* and Fruit of Christ's *Glorification in Heaven;* and has no other Promise from him but that of his Holy Spirit, to be with it, as its Light, its Guide, its Strength, its Comfort, and Protection, to the End of the World. Therefore as *Gospel* Christians, we belong to the *new Covenant of the Holy Spirit*, which is the Kingdom of God come down from Heaven on the Day of *Pentecost;* and therefore it is, that there is no Possibility of seeing or entering into this new Kingdom, but by being born again of the Spirit. The Apostles and Disciples of Christ, though they had been baptized with Water, had followed Christ, heard his Doctrines, and done Wonders in his Name; yet as then, stood only *near* to the Kingdom of God, and preached it to be *at hand.* They had only seen and known Christ according to the Flesh; had followed him with great Zeal, but with little and very low Knowledge either of him or his Kingdom; and therefore it was, that they were commanded to stand still, and not act as his Ministers in his new glorified State, till they were endued *with Power from on high:* Which Power they then received, when the Holy Ghost with his cloven Tongues of Fire came down upon them, by which they became the illuminated Instruments, that were to diffuse the Light of an heavenly Kingdom over all the World. From that Day began *Gospel Christianity*, with its true Distinction from everything that was before it; which was the *Ministration of the Spirit;* and the Ministers of it called the World to nothing but Gifts and Graces of the same Spirit, to look for nothing but Spiritual Blessings, to trust, and hope, and pray for nothing but the Power of that Spirit, which was to be the one Life and ruling Spirit of this newly-opened Kingdom of God. No one could join himself to them, or have any Part with them, but by dying to the Wisdom and Light of the Flesh, that he might live by the Spirit, through Faith in *Jesus Christ*, who had thus called him to his Kingdom and Glory. Now this Christianity is its own Proof; it can be proved from nothing but itself; it wants neither Miracles, nor outward Witness; but, like the Sun, is only its own Discoverer.

He that adheres only to the History of the Facts, Doctrines, and Institutions of the Gospel, without being born of its Spirit, is only such a Christian, and is no nearer to Christ, than the Jew, who carnally adhered to the Letter of the Law. They both stand in the same Distance from Gospel Christianity.

It is in vain therefore for the modern Christian, to appeal to Antiquity, to History, and ancient Churches, to prove that he belongs to Christ; for he can only belong to him, by having the Power of Christ, and the Spirit of God living and dwelling in his renewed inward Man.

But a learned Christianity, supported and governed by Reason, Dispute, and Criticism, that is forced to appeal to Canons, and Councils, and ancient Usages, to defend itself, has lost its Place, stands upon a fictitious Ground, and shows, that it cannot appeal to itself, to its own Works, which alone are the certain and only Proofs, either of a true, or a false Christianity.

For the Truth of Christianity is the Spirit of God living and working in it; and where this Spirit is not the Life of it, there the outward Form is but like the outward Carcase of a departed Soul.

For the Spiritual Life is as much its own Proof, as the natural Life, and needs no outward, or foreign Thing to bear Witness to it. But if you please, Gentlemen, we will end for this time, and refer what remains to the Afternoon.

The End of the First DIALOGUE.

THE
SECOND DIALOGUE.

ACADEMICUS. I Must take the Liberty, Gentlemen, of speaking first this Afternoon; for though I have been much pleased with what passed betwixt *Humanus* and *Theophilus* in the Morning, yet I must own to you all, that I was quite disappointed; for I came in full Expectation of hearing everything, that I wish, and want to know concerning *Jacob Behmen,* and his Works. For though I have been reading, for more than two Years, some one or other of his Books, with the utmost Attention, and I everywhere find the greatest Truths of the Gospel most fundamentally asserted, yet presently I am led into such Depths, as I know not where I am, and talked to in such new, intricate, and unintelligible Language, as seems quite impossible to be comprehended. Sometimes I almost suspect, that the Author understood not himself: For I think, if I knew any Truths, though ever so deep or uncommon; yet, if I understand them plainly myself, I could set them before others in the same Plainness, that they appeared to me.

All my Acquaintance have the same Complaint that I here make; but some hope, and others say, that if you live to publish any of his Books, you will remove most of his strange and unintelligible Words; and give us Notes and Explications of such as you do not alter. Surely a kind of Commentary upon him, would reconcile many to the reading of him, who in the State he is in, cannot have Patience to puzzle their Heads about him.

Rusticus. Oh this impatient Scholar! How many Troubles do I escape, through the want of his Learning? How much better does my old Neighbour *John* the Shepherd proceed? In Winter Evenings, when he comes out of the Field, his own Eyes being bad, the old Woman his Wife puts on her Spectacles, and reads about an Hour to him, sometimes out of the Scriptures, and sometimes out of *Jacob Behmen;* for he has had two or three of his Books some Years. I sat by one Evening, when my old Dame, reading *Jacob,* had much ado to get on: *John,* said I, do you understand all this? Ah, says he, God bless the Heart of the dear Man, I sometimes understand but little of him; and mayhap *Betty* does not always read right; but that little which I often do understand, does me so much Good, that I love him where I do not understand him.

John, said I, shall I bring a Man to you, that knows the Meaning of all *Jacob's* hard Words, and can make all his high Matters as plain to you, as the plainest Things in the World? No, no, replied *John,* I do not want such a Man, to make a talking about *Jacob's* Words; I had rather have but a little of his own, as it comes from him, than twenty times as much at second-hand. Madam, the *Squire's Wife,* of our Town, hearing how *Betty* and I loved the Scriptures, brought us, one Day, a huge *expounding Book* upon the New Testament; and told us, that we should understand the Scripture a deal better, by reading it in that Book, than the Testament alone.—The next Lord's Day, when two or three Neighbours, according to Custom, came to sit with us in the Evening; *Betty,* said I, bring out Madam's great Book, and read the fifth Chapter of *St. Matthew.* When she had done that, I bid her read the fifteenth Chapter of the first Epistle to the *Corinthians.* The next Morning, said I to *Betty,* carry this *expounding Book* again to my Mistress, and tell her, that the Words of Christ, and his Apostles, are best by themselves, and just as they left them.

And, as I was that Morning going to my Sheep, thought I to myself, This great *expounding Book* seems to have done just as much Good to this little Book of the Testament, by being added to it, and mixed with it, as a *Gallon* of Water would do to a little Cup of *true Wine,* by being added to it, or mixed with it. The Wine indeed would be all there; but its fine Taste, and cordial Spirit, which it had, when drank by itself, would be all lost and drowned in the Coldness and Deadness of the Water.

When my *Betty* used to read this, or some such Words of Christ, 'Blessed are the Poor in Spirit, for theirs is the Kingdom 'of Heaven;' she used to stop a little, that my Heart might have time to be affected with them, to love the blessed Thing there spoken of, and lift up itself to God in Desire of it. But this great Book takes this good Work from my Heart; and only calls upon my Mind, to behold the *many Parts* which the Text may be split into, and the *many Meanings,* some better and some worse, some higher and some lower, that every Part has, and may be taken in by some Doctor of some Church or other. Therefore, *Rusticus,* I sent the great Book to Madam again; and am, for the same Reason, utterly against hearing your *Expounder* of *Jacob Behmen.* If *Jacob* has more Truths than other Folks, he is the best able to tell me what they are; and if he has some Matters too high for me, I do not desire any lesser Man to make them lower.

When he, like an *Elijah,* in his *Fiery Chariot,* is caught up into such Heights, and sees and relates such Things, as I cannot yet comprehend; I love and reverence him for having been where I never was; and seeing such Things as he cannot make me see: Just as I love and reverence *St. Paul* for having been caught up into the third Heaven, and hearing and seeing Things not possible to be uttered in human Words.

As I have but *one End* in hearing the Scriptures read to me, to fill me with the Love of God, and every Kind of Goodness; so every Part of Scripture, whether plain or mysterious, does me the same Good, is alike good to me, and kindles the same heavenly Flame in my Soul. Thus these plain Words, 'Learn of me, for 'I am meek and lowly of Heart; and ye shall find Rest unto your 'Souls;' give me, without any Expounder of their Meaning, such an Aversion and Dislike of all Vanity and Pride, fill me with such sweet Contentment in every Lowliness of Life, that I long to be the Servant of every human Creature. On the other hand, these lofty Words of Scripture,—' Behold, a Throne was set in Heaven; 'and he that sat thereon, was, to look upon, like a Jasper-stone; 'and there was a Rainbow round about the Throne; and four-'and-twenty Seats; and upon the Seats, four-and-twenty Elders 'in white Raiment, and Crowns of Gold upon their Heads: And 'out of the Throne proceeded Lightnings, and Thunders, and 'Voices: And before the Throne were seven Lamps of Fire, which 'are the seven Spirits of God: And before the Throne there was 'a Sea of Glass like unto Crystal: And in the midst of the Throne, 'and round about it, were four Beasts full of Eyes before and 'behind: And the first Beast was like a Lion, the second like a 'Calf, the third had a Face as a Man, and the fourth was like 'a flying Eagle: And the four Beasts had each of them six Wings, 'and were full of Eyes; and they rest not Day and Night, saying, 'Holy, holy, holy Lord God Almighty, which was, and is, and is 'to come. And when these Beasts give Glory, and Honour, and 'Thanks, to him that sat on the Throne, the four-and-twenty 'Elders fall down before him that sat on the Throne, and cast their 'Crowns before the Throne, saying, Thou art worthy, O Lord, to 'receive Glory and Honour, for thou hast created all Things,' *&c.**

Now these lofty and mysterious Words, instead of puzzling my Head, lay hold of my Heart, which, all inflamed with them, rises up with the Eyes and Wings of the Beasts in their Song of Praise and Honour; and bows down with the Elders that worship the high and mighty Lord of Heaven and Earth. And thus I want no *Hebrew* or *Greek* Scholar to tell me this or that, what are the seven Spirits of God, why four Kinds of Beasts, why neither more nor less than six Wings, who were the Elders, and why

---

* Rev. iv. 2, *&c.*

twenty-four; but the *whole Matter*, as if a Glance of the Majesty of Heaven had just passed by me, strikes my Heart with such good Transports of Wonder and Joy, as make me all Longing and Desire to be one of those, who are always singing the Praises and Wonders of the Majesty of God. And thus, *Rusticus*, all that the Scriptures give me to drink, whether high or low, is equally a Cup of Blessing to me, and equally helps forward the Growth of Heaven in my Soul.

Bring not therefore your cunning Man, that has Skill in Words, to me; for Words are but Words; and though they be spoken even by the Messengers of God, as Angels, or Prophets, or Apostles; when they do their best, they can only do, as *John the Baptist* did *bear Witness to the Light:* But the Light itself, which can only give Light to the Soul, is God himself. And therefore not he that can best speak with the Tongues of Men and Angels, but he that most loves God, that is, that most loves *the Goodness of the Divine Nature*, he has most of God, and the Light of God within him.

Thus ended honest old *John* the Shepherd. And now, *Academicus*, if your learned Curiosity could be as much affected with what he has said, as my ignorant Simplicity is, you would drop all that you had said, as the Effect of such Impatience, as is much fitter to bring Darkness than Light into your Soul. You own, that, in the Works of *Behmen*, the greatest Points of Christianity are most fundamentally opened. And how can you be more self-condemned, than by desiring more?

But the Truth is, you have only heard these fundamental Matters; you have only received them as good *Notions;* are content with the *Hearsay* of them; and are therefore impatient to have more of this hearsay Knowledge, that you may become more learned in high Matters; and more able to talk about the Ground and Depth of Christian Doctrines. You know, as well as I can tell you, that this is your Joy in *Jacob Behmen;* and thence it is, that you have no Patience, when you cannot come at his Meaning, so as to add it to your Number of Notions. And thus you forget how often he tells you, and how fundamentally he proves to you, that this *notional* Knowledge, the Treasure of *human Reason*, is the very Builder of *Babel.* Whilst you are under the Guidance of our own *Babylonian Reason*, you can have no Good either from the Scriptures, or the Writings of *Jacob Behmen;* but will be hunting after *Notes* and *Commentaries* to help you to Notions, which only delude your Mind with the empty Shadows of Knowledge. Would you know the Truths of *Jacob Behmen*, you must see that you stand where he stood; you must begin where he began, and seek only, as he tells you he did, the 'Heart of God, that he might be saved from the Wrath 'of Sin and Satan'; and then it was, that the Light of God broke in upon him. But you, full of Power of your own Reason, want to stand upon the Top of his Ladder, without the Trouble of beginning at the Bottom, and going up Step by Step. But I believe you had rather have *Theophilus* speak than me; and therefore I shall now leave you to him.

Theophilus. Truly, *Academicus*, I am much of the same Mind with honest *Rusticus*, though perhaps I might not have spoken it so bluntly as he has done. You seem to be in the same Error, that most of my learned Friends are in, with regard to *Jacob Behmen*, who, though they greatly admire him, yet, of all People, receive the least true Benefit from him. They have been trained up in Dispute and Controversy, accustomed to determine everything by the Light of their own Reason, and know no other Guide to Truth. And therefore, till, sooner or later, they come to know the Falseness of this Guide, they can have no Entrance into the Region of Divine Light; but must be forced to take their Part, not of Truth, but of some such System of Opinions, as their Birth and Education has placed *them* in. Thus, a learned *Papist* has one Creed, and the learned *Protestant* has another; not because Truth and Light have helped him to it; but because Birth and Education have given to the one Popish, to the other Protestant Eyes. For *Reason*, which is the *Eye* or Light of both, finds as much to its Purpose, and as many good Tools to work with, in Popish, as in Protestant Opinions. *Learning* and *Criticism* are an open Field to both; and he only has the greatest Harvest, who is best skilled in Reaping.

Academicus. I perceive then, that I must renounce all my Learning and Reason, if I am to understand *Jacob Behmen*. I cannot say, that I am resolved to purchase it at so great a Price. I hope the Knowledge to be had from the Scriptures, will be sufficient for me, without his deep Matters. I did not expect to find you so great an Enemy to Learning.

Theophilus. Dear *Academicus*, be not so uneasy; I am no more an Enemy to Learning, than I am to that Art which builds Mills to grind our Corn, and Houses for ourselves to dwell in. I esteem the liberal Arts and Sciences as the noblest of human Things; I desire no Man to dislike or renounce his Skill in ancient or modern Languages; his Knowledge of Medals, Pictures, Paintings, History, Geography, or Chronology; I have no more Dislike of these Things in themselves, than of the Art of *Throwing* Silk, or making *Lace*. But then, all these Things are to stand in their proper Places, and everyone kept within its own Sphere.

Now all this Circle of Science and Arts, whether liberal or

mechanic, belongs solely to the *natural Man;* they are the Work of his *natural Powers and Faculties;* and the most wicked, sensual, unjust Person, who regards neither God, nor Man, may yet be one of the ablest Proficients in any or all of them. But now Christian Redemption is quite of another Nature; it has no Affinity to any of these Arts or Sciences? it belongs not to the outward natural Man, but is purely for the Sake of an *inward, heavenly* Nature, that was lost, or put to Death, in Paradise, and buried under the Flesh and Blood of the earthly, natural Man. It breathes a Spark of Life into this inward, hidden, or lost Man; by which it feels and finds itself, and rises up in new awakened Desires after its lost Father, and native Country.

This is Christian Redemption; on the one side, it is the *Heavenly Divine Life offering itself again to the inward Man, that had lost it.* On the other side, it is the *Hope, the Faith, and Desire of this inward Man, hungering, and thirsting, stretching after, and calling upon this Divine and Heavenly Life.*

Now, whether this awakened, new Man, breathes forth his Faith and Hope towards this *Divine Life*, in *Hebrew, Greek,* or *English* Sounds, or in no one of them, can be of no Significancy: A Man that can do it only in one, or in all these Languages, is neither further from, nor nearer to, this *redeeming Life of* God. Or can you think, that the *heavenly* Life must more willingly enter into, and open itself in, a Man that has many Languages, than in him, who knows only one? Or, that a Man, who can make *High Dutch, Welsh,* or *Greek Grammars,* must have a stronger Faith, a more lively Hope, and a more continual Thirst after God, than he who can but poorly spell in his Mother Tongue? But now, if this is too absurd to be supposed; then, my Friend, without the least Injury done, or the least Enmity shown to *Learning, Science, Reason,* and *Criticism,* you must place them just where I have done, amongst the Things and Ornaments of this earthly Life, and such Things as, in their own Nature, are as easy to be had, and as highly enjoyed, by Men that despise all Goodness, as by those who fear God, and eschew Evil.

And therefore, Sir, no Truths concerning the *Divine and Heavenly Life* are to be brought for Trial before this learned Bar, where both Jury and Judges are born and bred, live and move and have their Being in another World, which have no more Power of feeling the Divine Life, than an *Eagle's* Eyes can look into the Kingdom of God. If you, my Friend, having read many old *Greek* and *Latin* Books, should intend to publish *Homer,* or *Cæsar's Commentaries,* with critical Notes, I should have nothing to object to your Ability; you might be as well qualified by such Means for such a Work, as one Man is to make *Baskets,* or another *Traps* to catch Flies. But if, because of this Skill in old *Greek* and *Latin*, you should seem to yourself, or others, to be well qualified to write Notes upon the Spirit and Meaning of the Words of Christ, I should tell you, that your Undertaking was quite unnatural, and as impossible to be free from Error, as when a blind Man undertakes to set forth the Beauty of different Colours.

For the Doctrines of Redemption belong no more to the natural Man, than the Beauty of Colours to him, that never saw the Light. And from this unnatural Procedure it is, that the Scriptures are as useful to the *Socinian* or *Arian*, the *Papist* or the *Protestant;* and they can as easily, by the Light of Reason, charge one another with Absurdities, and confute each other's Opinion, as two blind Men can quarrel, and reject each other's Notions of *Red* and *Green.*

Jesus Christ is the Light of that heavenly Man that died in Paradise ; and therefore nothing in Man, but that awakened Seed of Life, that died in Paradise, can have the least Sensibility or Capacity for receiving the redeeming Power of *Jesus Christ.* But *Light* and *Life* have no Dependence upon Words or Phrases ; they both can only proceed from a *Birth*, whether it be the Light and Life of God, or the Light and Life of this World. How absurd would it be, to suppose, that a Man, naturally blind, must be taught Grammar or Logic, to fit him for the Reception of the Light of the Sun, and the Knowledge of Colours? Yet not less absurd, than to think, that Skill in *Hebrew* and *Greek* Words can open the Light of God and Heaven in the Soul. If you now, *Academicus*, can set this Matter in a juster Light, I am ready to hear you.

Academicus. Standing upon the Ground, that you, *Theophilus*, stand upon, all that you have said of *Reason, Science, historical Knowledge*, or critical Skill in Words, is unanswerable. For what can all these Things avail, if Redemption is purely a Birth of the Divine Nature, Light, and Spirit of God, offered to fallen Man ; which Birth can only be received by the Faith, Hope, and Desire of *that* inward Man, which is Divine in us ? For nothing else can have any Hunger or Thirst after the Divine Nature, but *that* which is itself born of it.

Now this true Ground of the Christian Redemption, gives the greatest Glory to God, and Comfort to Man. It explains the Fact, why plain and simple Souls, having their inward Man kindled into Love, Hope, and Faith in God, are capable of the highest Divine Illumination ; whilst learned Students, full of Art and Science, can live and die without the least true Knowledge of God and Christ, and Slaves to all the Lusts of the Flesh.

For thus, this Redemption belongs only to one Sort of People, and yet is common to all. It is equally near, and equally open, to every Son of Man. There is no Difference between Learned and Unlearned, between *Jew* or *Greek*, Male or Female, *Scythian* or Barbarian, Bond or Free; but the same Lord is God over all, and equally nigh to all that call upon him. It is told us, as the Glory of the Divine Goodness, that *it giveth Fodder to the Cattle; and feedeth the young Ravens that cry unto it.* What Cattle? Surely not only to the Cattle of *Jacob;* or only to the young Ravens that cry in the Land of *Judah.* Yet this would be much more consistent with the Goodness of the One universal God, than to hold, that only the Sons of *Jacob,* or the Children of the Circumcision, were in the Covenant of God's Redemption.

But now, though this one Ground of Christian Redemption stands in the highest Degree of Plainness from Scripture, and is absolutely certain from the very Nature of the Thing; yet, till I met with honest *Rusticus,* I never conversed with any Man, or read any Book, that gave me the least Hint of it. When I had taken my *Degrees,* I consulted several great Divines, to put me in a Method of studying Divinity. Had I said to them, 'Sirs, 'What must I do to be saved?' they would have prescribed *Hellebore* to me, or directed me to the Physician as a vapoured Enthusiast. And yet I am now fully satisfied, that this one Question ought to be the sole Inquiry of him, who desires to be a *true Divine.* And was our Saviour himself on Earth, who surely could do more for me than all the Libraries in the World, yet I need have asked no more Divinity-Knowledge of him, than is contained in this one Question.

It would take up near half a Day, to tell you the Work which my learned Friends have cut out for me. One told me, that *Hebrew* Words are all; that they must be read without Points; and then the old Testament is an opened Book. He recommended to me a Cart-load of Lexicons, Critics, and Commentators, upon the *Hebrew* Bible. Another tells me, the *Greek* Bible is the best; that it corrects the *Hebrew* in many Places; and refers me to a large Number of Books learnedly writ in the Defence of it. Another tells me, that Church-History is the main Matter; that I must begin with the first Fathers, and follow them through every Age of the Church, not forgetting to take the Lives of the *Roman* Emperors along with me, as striking great Light into the State of the Church in their Times. Then I must have recourse to all the Councils held, and the Canons made, in every age; which would enable me to see with my own Eyes the great Corruptions of the Council of *Trent.* Another, who is not very fond of ancient Matters, but wholly bent upon *rational* Christianity, tells me, I need go no higher than the *Reformation;* that *Calvin* and *Cranmer* were very great Men; that *Chillingworth* and *Locke* ought always to lie upon my Table; that I must get an entire Set of those learned Volumes wrote against Popery in King *James's* Reign; and also be well versed in all the Discourses which Mr. *Boyle's* and Lady *Moyer's* Lectures have produced: And then, says he, you will be a Match for our greatest Enemies, which are the Popish Priests, and modern Deists. My Tutor is very Liturgical; he desires me, of all Things, to get all the Collections that I can of the ancient Liturgies, and all the Authors that treat of such Matters; who, he says, are very learned, and very numerous. He has been many years making Observations upon them, and is now clear, as to the Time, when certain little Particles got Entrance into the Liturgies, and others were by Degrees dropped. He has a Friend abroad, in Search of ancient Manuscript Liturgies; for, by the by, said he, at parting, I have some Suspicion that our Sacrament of the Lord's Supper is *essentially* defective, for want of having a little Water in the Wine, *&c.* Another learned Friend tells me, the *Clementine Constitutions* is the Book of Books; and that all that lies loose and scattered in the New Testament, stands there in its true Order and Form; and though he will not say, that Dr. *Clarke* and Mr. *Whiston* are in the right; yet it might be useful to me to read all the *Arian* and *Socinian* Writers, provided I stood upon my Guard, and did it with Caution. The last Person I consulted, advised me to get all the Histories of the Rise and Progress of Heresies, and of the Lives and Characters of Heretics. These Histories, he said, contract the Matter; bring Truth and Error close in View; and I should find all that collected in a few Pages, which would have cost me some Years to have got together. He also desired me to be well versed in all the casuistical Writers, and chief School-men; for they debate Matters to the Bottom; dissect every Virtue, and every Vice, into its many Degrees and Parts; and show, how near they can come to one another without touching. And this Knowledge, he said, might be useful to me, when I came to be a Parish-Priest.

Following the Advice of *all* these Counsellors, as well as I could, I lighted my Candle early in the Morning, and put it out late at Night. In this Labour I had been sweating for some Years, till *Rusticus*, at my first Acquaintance with him, seeing my Way of Life, said to me, Had you lived about Seventeen hundred Years ago, you had stood just in the same Place as I stand now. I cannot read; and therefore, says he, all these Hundreds of Thousands of disputed Books, and Doctrine-Books, which these Seventeen hundred Years have produced, stand not in my Way; they are the same thing to me, as if they had never been. And, had you lived at the Time mentioned, you had just escaped them all, as I do now; because, though you are a very good Reader, there were then none of them to be read.

Could you, therefore, be content to be one of the primitive Christians, who were as good as any that have been since, you may spare all this Labour. Take only the Gospel into your Hands; deny yourself; renounce the Lusts of the Flesh; set your Affections on Things above; call upon God for his Holy Spirit; walk by Faith, and not by Sight; adore the holy Deity of Father, Son, and Holy Ghost, in whose Image and Likeness you were at first created, and in whose Name and Power you have been baptized, to be again the living Likeness, and holy Habitation, of his Life, and Light, and Holy Spirit.

Look up to *Christ*, as your Redeemer, your Regenerator, your second *Adam;* look at him, as truly he is, the *Wisdom and Power of God*, sitting at his Right Hand in Heaven, giving forth Gifts unto Men; governing, sanctifying, teaching, and enlightening with his Holy Spirit, all those that are spiritually-minded; who live in Faith, and Hope, and Prayer, to be redeemed from the Nature and Power of this evil World. Follow but this simple, plain Spirit of the Gospel, loving God with all your Heart, and your Neighbour as yourself, and then you are Christ's Disciple, and have his Authority to 'let the Dead bury their Dead.'

God is a Spirit, in whom you live and move and have your Being; and he stays not till you are a great Scholar, but till you turn from Evil, and love Goodness, to manifest his holy Presence, Power, and Life, within you. It is the Love of Goodness, that must do all for you; this is the Art of Arts; and when this is the ruling Spirit of your Heart, then Father, Son, and Holy Ghost, will come unto you, and make their Abode with you, and lead you into all Truth, though you knew no more of Books than I do.

So ended *Rusticus*. It is not easy for me, *Theophilus*, to tell you, how much Good I received from this simple Instruction of honest *Master Rusticus;* for so I may well call him, since he, in so few Words, taught me a better Lesson of Wisdom, than ever I had heard before.

What a Project was it, to be grasping after the Knowledge of all the Opinions, Doctrines, Disputes, Heresies, Schisms, Councils, Canons, Alterations, Additions, Inventions, Corruptions, Reformations, Sects, and Churches, which 1,700 Years had brought forth through all the Extent of the Christian World! What a Project is this, in order to be a *Divine*, that is, in order to bear *true*

Witness to the Power of *Christ*, as a Deliverer from the Evil of Flesh and Blood, and Hell, and Death, and a Raiser of a New Birth and Life from above! For as this is the Divine Work of *Christ*, so he only is a *true* and *able Divine*, that can bear a faithful Testimony to this *Divine Work* of *Christ*.

How easy was it for me to have seen with *Rusticus*, that all this Labyrinth of learned Inquiry into such a dark, thorny Wilderness of Notions, Facts, and Opinions, could signify no more to me now, to my own Salvation, to my Interest in *Christ*, and obtaining the Holy Spirit of God, than if I had lived before it had any Beginning! But the blind Appetite of Learning gave me no Leisure to apprehend so plain a Truth. Books of Divinity indeed I have not done with; but I will esteem none to be such, but those that make known to my Heart the *inward Power* and *Redemption* of *Jesus Christ*. Nor will I seek for anything even from such Books, but *that* which I ask of God in Prayer; viz., how better to know, more to abhor and resist the Evil that is in my *own Nature;* and how to attain a *supernatural Birth* of the Divine Life brought forth in me: All besides this is *Pushpin*. The shipwrecked Man wants only to get to Shore. Did we see the Truth of our State as he does, we should have but one Want, and that would be, to get Possession of our first created State. There is no Misery but in the Evil that is in our own fallen State; this is our Shipwreck, and great Distress; nor is there any Happiness, but in having the first Life of God, and all Goodness, opened again in the Soul. He that is not intent upon this one Thing needful, is not a wise Christian, much less a *Divine*, or one qualified to make known to others the Mystery of the Power of *Christ* in the Work of Redemption.

But I now go back to that which I first spoke of; and though I give up all that I said of putting out *Jacob Behmen* in new Language, with Comments, *&c.*, yet I must still desire, that, some way or other, he may be made more plain and intelligible; call it by what Name you please.

Theophilus. Jacob Behmen may be considered, (1.) As a Teacher of the true Ground of the Christian Religion. (2.) As a Discoverer of the false Antichristian Church, from its first Rise in *Cain*, through every Age of the World, to its present State in all, and every Sect of the present divided *Christendom*. (3.) As a Guide to the Truth of all the Mysteries of the Kingdom of God. In these Three respects, which contain all that anyone can possibly want to know or learn from any Teacher; he is the strongest, the plainest, the most open, intelligible, awakening, convincing Writer, that ever was. As to all these Three Matters, he speaks to everyone, as himself saith, *in the Sound of a Trumpet*. And here to pretend to be an Explainer of him, or make him fitter for our Apprehension, in these great Matters, is as vain, as if a Man should pipe through a *Straw*, to make the Sound of a *Trumpet* better heard by us.

Further, he may be considered, (4.) As a Relater of Depths opened in himself, of Wonders which his Spirit had seen and felt in his *Ternario sancto*. Now in this respect he is no Teacher, nor his Reader a Learner; But all that he saith is only for the same End, as St. *Paul* spoke of his having been in the Third Heaven, and hearing Things not possible to be spoken in human Words. And yet in these Matters it is, that most of his Readers, especially if they are Scholars, are chiefly employed; everyone in his way trying to become Masters of them. Thus, when he first appeared in *English*, many Persons of this Nation, of the greatest Wit and Abilities, became his Readers; who, instead of entering into his *one only* Design, which was their *own Regeneration* from an earthly to an heavenly Life, turned *Chemists*, and set up Furnaces to regenerate *Metals*, in Search of the Philosopher's Stone. And yet, of all Men in the World, no one has so deeply, and from so true a Ground, laid open the exceeding Vanity of such Labour, and utter Impossibility of Success in it from any Art or Skill in the Use of Fire. And this must with Truth be affirmed of him, that there is not any possible Error, that you can fall into in the Use of his Books, but what he gives you Notice of beforehand, and warns you against it in the most solemn Manner; and tells you, that the Blame must be yours, if you fall into it. Neither is there any Question that you can put, nor Advice or Direction that you can ask, but what he has over and over spoken to; telling you, in the plainest Manner, what the *Mystery* is which his Books contain; *how*, and by *whom*, and for what *End*, they are to be read.

There are Two Sorts of People to whom he forbids the Use of his Books, as incapable of any Benefit from them, and who will rather receive Hurt, than any Good from them. The First Sort he shows in these Words: 'Loving Reader, if thou lovest 'the Vanity of the Flesh still, and art not in earnest Purpose on 'the Way to the New Birth, intending to be a New Man, then 'leave the above-written Words in these Prayers unnamed, or 'else they will turn to a Judgment of God in thee.'* *Again*, ' Reader, I admonish you sincerely, if you be not in the Way of 'the Prodigal, or lost Son, returning to his Father again, that 'you leave my Book, and read it not; it will do you Harm.—

---

* *Repentance*, page 42.

Divine Knowledge.

'But if you will not take Warning, I will be guiltless; blame 'Nobody but yourself.'*

In this Advice, so different from that of other Writers, he shows the Truth and Reality of his own regenerated State; and that the very same Spirit speaks in him, as formerly said, 'Re-'pent, for the Kingdom of Heaven is at hand.'—'Unless a man 'deny himself, and forsake all that he hath, he cannot be my 'Disciple.'—'No Man can come unto me, except the Father 'draweth him.'—'Except a Man be born again from above, he 'cannot see the Kingdom of God.'—'He that is of God, heareth 'God's Word.'—'Come unto me, all ye that labour, are weary 'and heavy-laden.' For all these Texts of Scripture say that very self-same thing that *Jacob Behmen* doth, when he absolutely requires his Reader to be in the Way of the returning Prodigal. It is not Rules of Morality observed, or an outward blameless Form of Life, that will do: For Pride, Vanity, Envy, Self-love, and Love of the World, can be, and often are, the Heart of such a Morality of Life. But the State of the *lost Son* is quite another thing; and must be the State of every Man: As soon as he *comes to himself* and has seeing Eyes, he will then, like him, see himself far from home; that he has lost his first Paradise, his heavenly Father, and the Dignity of his first Birth; that he is a poor, beggarly Slave in a foreign Land, hungry, ragged, and starving, amongst the lowest Kind of Beasts, not so well fed and clothed as they are: When thus finding himself, he saith, 'I will arise, and go to my Father,' *&c.*, then has he his first Fitness for the Mysteries opened in *Jacob Behmen's* Writings; for they are addressed to Man only in this supposed State; they have no Fitness to him but in this State; and therefore no one, whether *Jew*, Christian, or Deist, who does not find and feel himself to be the *very lost Son* described in the Parable, has any Capacity to receive Benefit from them; but they will be a continual Stumbling-block to him. And it is just thus with the Gospel itself; wherever it is received and professed, without something of this Preparation of Heart, without this Sensibility of the lost Son, there it can only be a Stone of stumbling, and help the earthly Man to form a Religion of Notions and Opinions, from the unfelt Meaning of the Letter of the Gospel.

Secondly, The other Sort of People, whom he excludes from his Books, and for whom he has writ nothing, are the Men of *Reason*, who give themselves up to the Light of Reason, as the true Touchstone of Divine Truths. To these he declares over

---
* *Three Principles.*

and over, that he has not his Light from Reason; and that he writes nothing to Reason. 'The rational Man,' saith he, 'under-'stands nothing in reference to God; for it is without, and not 'in God.' Again, 'The true Understanding must flow from the '*inward Ground*, out of the living Word of God. In which 'inward Ground, all my Knowledge concerning the Divine and 'natural Ground, hath taken its Rise, Beginning, and Under-'standing. I am not born of the School of this World, and am 'a plain simple Man; but by God's Spirit and Will am brought, 'without my own Purpose and Desire, into Divine Knowledge in 'high natural Searchings.'* Again, 'He that will learn to 'understand the true Way, let him depart from and *forsake his* '*own Reason*.'† 'If my Writings,' says he, 'come into your 'Hands, I would that you should look upon them as of a Child's, 'in *whom the Highest* has driven his *Work;* for there is that 'couched therein, which no Reason may understand or compre-'hend.'‡ Again, 'Reason must be blinded, *kept under, and not* '*allowed to* stir.'§ Again, 'Reason must yield up its own Hear-'ing and Life, and give itself up to God, that God may live in 'the Understanding of Man, else there is no Finding in the 'Divine Wisdom. All that is taught and spoken concerning 'God, without the Spirit of God, is but *Babel*.'|| Again, 'We 'must wholly reject our own Reason; it is not available to help 'us to the Light, but is a mere leading astray, and keeping us 'back. This we intimate to the Reader, that he may know what 'he reads. Let none account it for a Work of outward Reason.' Again, 'Speaking of the Mystery,'¶ he saith, 'Pray to God, the 'most High, that he would be pleased to open the Door of Know-'ledge, without which no Man will understand my Writings; for 'they surpass the astral Reason; they apprehend and compre-'hend the Divine Birth; and therefore only the like Spirit can 'understand them aright. No Reasoning or Speculating reacheth 'them, unless the Mind be illuminated from God, to the 'finding of which the Way is faithfully shown to the seeking 'Reader.'**

And now, *Academicus*, you may see how needless it is to ask me, or anyone else, to help you to understand his Works: He himself has given you all the Assistance that can be given: He has laid open before you, in the utmost Plainness, both the Nature of the *Mystery*, and the *one only* possible Way that you can partake of it.

---

* *Epistles*, page 121.   † Page 138.   ‡ Page 141.
§ Page 68. || Page 9.   ¶ *Three-fold Life*, pages 68, 88
** *Epistles*, page 138.

Academicus. You speak often of the *Mystery*: Pray, What am I to understand by it?

Theophilus. You are to understand by it, the *deep and true Ground* of all Things. A *Mystery*, in which the Birth and Beginning of *eternal Nature,* or the first Workings of the *inconceivable God,* opening and manifesting his hidden Triune Deity in an outward State of Glory, in the Splendour of united Fire, Light, and Spirit, all kindled and distinguished, all united and beatified by the *hidden Three.* In this eternal Nature, all inward Powers, all the *hidden* Riches of the incomprehensible Father, Son, and Holy Ghost, are from Eternity to Eternity brought forth into outward Majesty, and visible Glory. In which Triune Opening of heavenly Glory, Power, and Majesty, the Triune God beholdeth himself as in his *own Manifestation,* is clothed as with his *own Garment,* dwelleth as in his *own Habitation,* and worketh all his Wonders of Wisdom and Omnipotence, in and by, and according to, the *possible Powers* of this eternal Nature. For this eternal Nature is the *first Possibility* of all After-beings and Things; for before, or without this eternal Nature, all is an eternal, silent, still, unmovable, unperceivable Nothingness; and this eternal Nature is the first Manifestation, the first Opening of the Divine Omnipotence: and in it are included, in its own infinite Bounds, all the Height and Depth, and Extent, of the Divine Wisdom and Powers. All that God is, and can do, or bring forth from himself, is done in and by the Working of his Triune Spirit in this eternal Nature.

This is the great Scene of his eternal Wisdom and Omnipotence, in which new Wonders are eternally rising up, and declaring the fathomless Depths of the Riches of the invisible Triune Deity. And to say, that God can do no more, than what he can do through and by the possible Powers of this eternal Nature, is only saying, that he can do no more than what he can do by himself, because this eternal Nature is the eternal Manifestation of the total God, or an Out-birth of that which the Deity is, in its invisible Power and Deity.

Out of this transcendent eternal Nature, which is as universal and immense as the Deity itself, do all the highest Beings, Cherubims and Seraphims, all the Hosts of Angels, and all intelligent Spirits, receive their Birth, Existence, Substance, and Form. They are all so many different, finite, bounded Forms of the heavenly Fire and Light of eternal Nature, into which creaturely Beings, the invisible Triune God breathes his invisible Spirit, by which they become both the true Children and Likeness of the invisible Deity, and also the true Offspring of his eternal Nature; and are fitted to rejoice with God, to live in the

Life of God, and live and work, and have their Being, in that eternal Nature, or Kingdom of Heaven, in which the Deity itself liveth and worketh. And they are one, and united in one, God in them, and they in God, according to the Prayer of Christ for his Disciples ; 'That they, and he, and his Holy Father, might be united in one.'*

This is in Part, what you are first to understand concerning the Mystery.

But, *Secondly*, It is a *Mystery*, in which the Creation and Fall of Angels, with all its Consequences in them, and their Kingdom; in which the System of this visible Universe, *why*, and from *what*, and how it came to be as it is ; the Birth of the Sun and the Planets, why and how they come to have such Difference in Nature, Place, and Office, and also of all the Stars ; the Nature of every creaturely Life, and Ground of its vast Variety ; the Cause of every inanimate dead Thing ; a Mystery in which the Creation, Dignity, and Perfection, of the first angelic Man in Paradise ; the whole Kingdom of Nature, and Kingdom of Grace; their Connection, Difference, and mutually affecting and working upon one another under the Providence of the invisible Spirit of God, from the Beginning to the End of Time ; are all unfolded from their first Root and Cause.

Thirdly, It is a *Mystery*, in which the Ground of Christian Redemption, its whole Nature, absolute Necessity, and the working of all its Parts both in the Redeemer and in the Redeemed, are set forth in the utmost Degree of Clearness; where the whole Process of *Christ*, as incarnate, living, suffering, dying, rising from the Dead, ascending into Heaven, and sitting at the Right Hand of God, and governing his Church on Earth by his Holy Spirit ; and all the practical Duties of the Gospel, whether of Faith and Hope, or of Self-denial ; dying to this World, and strict Conformity to the Life and Spirit of Christ ; are all demonstrated, from the deepest Ground of the Nature of Things, to be absolutely necessary to the Recovery and Redemption of the fallen human Nature.

This, Sir, is, in some Degree, the *Mystery* which it has pleased the Spirit of God to open in this plain and unlearned Man.

Academicus. Well, *Theophilus*, I entirely consent to this Account you have given of it, and think it is sufficiently supported by what is to be found in his Books ; they seem to mean all these great Matters which you mentioned. But then, Sir, give me Leave to tell you, that I think it is impossible for you to defend what you have said above concerning *Reason*, or to show the

---

* John xvii.

Unreasonableness of my demanding *rational* Illustrations and *Comments*. For if this is the Truth, that his Works contain the *Ground* and *Philosophy* of all Nature, and all Creatures ; surely they must not only allow the Use of our Reason, but call for the highest and most acute Exercise of it. For what can enter into the Reasons and Philosophy of Things, but Reason ? Or what do all these great Matters appeal to, but to our Reason ? I see no Possibility of denying this ; and if this be granted, all that has been said about silencing our Reason, must be given up.

Theophilus. The Conclusion, my Friend, that you here think to be so just and strong, as not possible to be denied, is so far from being so, that it is a glaring Absurdity ; and the quite contrary to that one only true Conclusion, which you should have made, and which so easily and naturally flowed from what was said. For if the *Mystery is the deep Ground of* all Things, of all Nature, and all Creatures, *&c.*, then the one Conclusion that infallibly flows from it, is this, that no Acuteness or Ability of natural Reason can so much as look into it. For natural Reason is no older than Flesh and Blood ; it has no higher a Nature or Birth than *natural Doubting;* it had no Existence when Nature begun its first Workings, and therefore can bear no Witness to them. It was not present, had no Eyes, when Things first came forth ; it never stood in the Centre, from whence the Birth of everything must arise ; it never saw the Forming of the first Seeds of every Life : And yet the *Mystery*, you see, contains all this : And therefore the one plain and necessary Conclusion is this ; That natural Reason is, and must be, as incapable of entering into this Mystery, as Flesh and Blood is incapable of entering into the Kingdom of Heaven.

Behold, now, what a flagrant Proof you have given of the Vanity, Weakness, and Blindness of natural Reason in Divine Matters. Your Reason saw, with the utmost Certainty, that the Mystery must be an Appeal to Reason, merely because it contained such an Height and Depth of a Divine Philosophy ; and yet the Height and Depth of its Matters is the *one full* Proof, that Reason can have nothing to do with it. This may show you, by what means *Babel* has built itself all over the Christian World. For, by the Light of this *Babylonian* Reason, the Defenders and Opposers of Doctrines, confute one another with such a Certainty and Strength of Reason, as you saw, that Reason must be the only Judge of the Mystery, from which it is just as much excluded by its own Nature, as the *Mole* under ground is, by its Nature, excluded from the Flight and Sight of the towering Eagle.

Academicus. Pray then tell me, How a Man is to attain the Knowledge of the Mystery, or have any Share in the Light of it.

Theophilus. There is but one possible Way, and that is this: It must be born in you. All true Knowledge, either of God or Nature, must be born in you. You cannot possibly know anything of God, but so far as God is manifested in you; so far as his Light and Holy Spirit is born in you, as it is born in him, and liveth and worketh in you, as it liveth and worketh in him. A distant, absent, separate God, is an unknown God. For God can only manifest God, as Light can only manifest Light, and Darkness make Darkness to be known.

Again, you can have no real Knowledge of Nature, and its inward working Power, but so far as the Workings of Nature, and the Birth of Things, are Working and a Birth in yourself. Natural Reason may trade in the Outside of Things; it may measure, and make Draughts of Magnitude, Height, and Distance of Things on the Earth, and above the Earth; it may make many and fine Experiments of the Powers of every Element: But then this is going no further into the Ground of Nature, than when the *Potter* makes curious Vessels with his Clay and Fire.

To count the Stars, to observe their Places or Motions, is just the same Height of natural Knowledge, as when the Shepherd counts his Sheep, and observes their Time of Breeding.

This World, with all its Stars, Elements, and Creatures, is come out of the invisible World; it has not the smallest Thing, or the smallest Quality of anything, but what is come forth from thence; and therefore every Quality of everything, is what it is, and worketh *that* which worketh, by a secret Power and Nature in and from the invisible World. *Bitter, sweet, sour, hard, soft, hot, cold, &c.*, have all of them their first Seed and Birth in the invisible World, called eternal Nature. The irrational Animals of this World feel all these Things: The rational Man goes further; he can reason and dispute about their outward Causes and Effects: But the Mystery of eternal Nature must first be opened in Man, before he can give the Divine Philosophy of them. For as they all come from thence, have their Nature, Birth, and Growth, from thence; so no Philosophy, but that which comes from thence, can give the true Ground of them.

If Man himself was not all these Three Things; *viz.* (1) A Birth of the holy Deity; (2) A Birth of eternal Nature; and (3) Also a Microcosm of all this great outward World; that is, of everything in it, its Stars and Elements; and if the Properties of every creaturely Life were not in an hidden Birth in him; no Omnipotence of God could open the Knowledge of Divine and natural Things in him.

For God can only manifest *that*, which there is to be manifested; and therefore only open *that*, which before lay unopened, and as in a State of Hiddenness or Death. Nothing can come forth from Man, or any Creature, but that which first had its Seed in him; and to think, that any Knowledge can be put into him, but that which is a Birth of his own Life, is as absurd as to think, that the Tree and its Branches may first grow, and then be brought to the Root.

We are led into Mistakes about this Matter, from the common Practice of the World, which calls everything Knowledge, that the Reason, Wit, or Humour of Man, prompts him to discourse about; whether it be Fiction, Conjecture, Report, History, Criticism, Rhetoric, or Oratory: All this passes for Sterling Knowledge; whereas it is only the Activity of Reason, playing with its own empty Notions.

From this Idea of Knowledge it is, that when this *rational* Man turns his Thoughts to the Study of Divinity, he is content with the same Knowledge of Divine Matters, as he had in these Exercises of his Reason; and he proceeds in the same Manner, as when he studied History and Rhetoric.

He turns his Mind to Hearsay, to Conjecture, to Criticism, and great Names; and thinks he is then a Member of the true Church, when he knows it as plainly, as he knows the ancient Commonwealth of *Rome*. His Knowledge of the Being of God stands upon the same Bottom, and is made known to him by the same Means and Methods of Proof, as he comes to be assured, that once upon a Time there was a *First* Man, and his Name was *Adam*. His Knowledge of the Kingdom of Heaven is looked upon to be sufficient, as soon as he knows it, as he knows that there is such a Place as *Constantinople*. When he turns his Inquiries into the Mysteries of Christian Redemption, he looks as much out of himself, as when he is searching into the Antiquities of *Greece;* and appeals to the same Helps for this Knowledge, as when he wants to know the inward Structure of *Solomon's* Temple, and all its Services, *&c.*

This is the great Delusion which has long overspread the Christian World; and all Countries, and all Libraries, are the Proof of it. It is this Power and Dominion of Reason in religious Matters, that *Jacob Behmen* so justly calls the *Antichrist in Babel;* for it leads Men from the Life and Truth of the Mysteries of *Christ*, to put a carnal Trust in a confused Multitude of contrary Notions, Inventions, and Opinions. And the thing is unavoidable, it cannot be otherwise with *Reason ;* it cannot do more Good with, or make a better Use of Gospel Doctrines; it is *Antichrist*, as soon as ever it is admitted to debate and state the Nature of any Divine Truth. And that for these Two great

Reasons: *First*, Because it has absolutely the same Incapacity for it, as the Man that is born blind hath for the Light. Wherein now lieth the Incapacity of the blind Man, to speak or think anything truly about Light? It is because he is born and bred in another World, where nothing of Light ever did or can enter; it is because there is the *Gulf* of a whole Birth betwixt him and the Light of this World; and therefore, though he lives ever so long, reasons ever so much, or hears ever so many Speeches about the Light, all that he gets by it is only more false Ideas of the unknown Thing.

Now this is strictly the Incapacity of Reason, to speak, or think anything truly of the Divine Life. It is because it is born and bred in another World, in the Darkness of Flesh and Blood, into which no Perception or Sensibility of God and Heaven can enter; it is because there is the *Gulf* of a whole Birth betwixt it, and the Light of God and Heaven; and therefore, let Reason, from Age to Age, hear, read, and dispute ever so much about the Light of God and Heaven, all that it can get by it, is only to be enriched with more and more Fictions and Falsities about the unknown Thing.

Secondly, Natural Reason, whenever judging, or ruling in Divine Matters, must be *Antichrist*, because it cannot make any other Use of the Mysteries of Religion, or do anything else with them, but in the *same Spirit*, and for the *same Ends*, that it receiveth and useth the Things of this World. It matters not, what are the Names or Natures of the Things, whether you call them spiritual or temporal: Natural Reason can make but one and the same Use of them; it can only turn them to an earthly Use, to worldly Prosperity, to private Interest, Honour, Power, or Distinction. And the Thing is unavoidable, it is impossible to be otherwise; it is not a Fault that Reason might amend, if it would: but is as much its own Nature, as it is natural to Flame to ascend. Now everything must act according to its Nature; every Kind of Life must be for itself, for its own Good. Now Reason has no higher a Birth and Nature, than the Spirit of this World; it must be as worldly as its Birth is, and cannot possibly have anything else but worldly Views, and the Interests of its own Flesh and Blood, in everything that it can make any use of. This is as essential to the natural Reason of Man, as to the natural Subtlety of every Beast; for they have both the same Original from the Light and Life of this World, have both the same earthly Nature, and can act only in an earthly Manner, to serve the same Ends of an earthly Life. The Reason of the one has no more of God and the Divine Nature in it, than the Subtlety of the other. And hence it is, that Man, following only the Cunning of his natural Reason, is often more mischievous than the worst of Beasts. And thus, you see how Reason, ruling in Divine Things, is, and must be *Antichrist:* First, As it turns the living Mysteries of God into lifeless Ideas, and vain Opinions: and, *Secondly,* As it sets up a worldly Kingdom of Strife, Hatred, Envy, Division, and Persecution, in Defence of them. And therefore it is a fundamental Truth, that Man has no Capacity for Divine Knowledge, till the Particle of Divine Life, lost in the Fall, is awakened; in which alone, the Mystery of God and the Divine Nature can have a Birth.

Academicus. You have carried your Point, *Theophilus*, with a high Hand, and I rejoice in seeing this Matter so well proved.— But still I would ask you something, that I know not how to express; I would fain understand more clearly, how this Mystery of God, and eternal Nature, is to be *born* in me.

Theophilus. Everything, *Academicus*, is, and must be, its *own Proof;* and can only be known from and by itself. There is no Knowledge of anything, but where the Thing itself is, and is found, and possessed. Life, and every Kind and Degree of Life, is only known by Life; and so far as Life reaches, so far is there Knowledge, and no further. Whatever Knowledge you can get by the Searching and Working of your own active Reason, is only like that Knowledge, which you may be said to have got, when you have searched for a Needle in a Load of Straw, till you have found it.

For nothing that is brought into the Mind from *without*, or is only an Idea beheld by our reasoning Faculty, is any more *our Knowledge*, than the seeing our natural Face in a Glass, is seeing our *own Selves.* And all the Ideas or Images that your Reason can form of any absent, unpossessed Thing, is no more a Part of your own Knowledge, than your drawing a Picture of your own Hand is making a Member of your own Body. It is therefore a vain and fruitless Inquiry, to be asking beforehand for the Knowledge of any *unpossessed* Matters; for Knowledge can only be yours, as *Sickness* and *Health* is yours, not conveyed into you by a Hearsay Notion, but the Fruit of your own Perception and Sensibility of that which you are, and that which you have in yourself. How often have you been warned against this Procedure, in Words like these? 'Therefore let the Reader be
' warned, not to dive further into these very deep Writings, nor
' Plunge his Will deeper, than so far as he *apprehendeth:* He
' should always rest satisfied with his *Apprehension;* for in his
' Apprehension, he standeth yet in that which hath its Reality;
' and therefore he erreth not, how deep soever the Spirit leadeth
' him: For to one more will be given than to another. And this

'is the *only Mark* to be observed, that everyone continue stead-
'fast in Humility towards God, and submit himself, that he may
'make the Will and the Deed as he pleaseth. When you do
'that, you are in yourself as dead; for you desire nothing but
'God's Will, and the Will of God *is your Life*, which goeth
'inward even to the Opening of the highest Mysteries.'*

One would have thought, *Academicus*, that this Advice, if only from the uncommon Nature of it, should have had more Effect upon you. For it is not only new to you, but to every Reader; there being nothing like it, either for the Sense, the Sobriety, or the Depth of its Matter, ever given by the wisest of Philosophers to their Readers.

Truth, my Friend, whatever you may think of it, is no less than the *Saviour* and Redeemer of the World.

Hear therefore its own Language: 'If any Man will be my 'Disciple, let him deny himself, and take up his Cross, and come 'after me.' He does not say, Let him get a clear and distinct Idea of me, what, and how I am God and Man in the Unity of my Person; he only tells him what he is to part with, what he must put off, to be made a Child of the Light. Search and look where you will, this Denial of Self is the one only possible Way to the Truth. For nothing has separated us from Truth, nothing stands betwixt us and Truth, but this Self of an earthly Life, which is not from God, but from our wandering out of our first created State.

God created us in and for the Light; and had *Adam* kept his first State, he had not been an ignorant, blind Pilgrim in the Darkness of this World, but the illustrious Opener of all its Wonders in the Light of God. But as this Light and Knowledge was lost in *Adam*, so it can only be recovered by him who came to restore all that was lost, and who justly called himself *the Light of the World*. Would you therefore be a Disciple of Truth you must not, with *Pilate*, ask, *What is Truth?* or consult the Schools, how you shall form an Idea of it: But you must alter your Life, put a Stop to all earthly Lusts, renounce all that you are, and have from Self; give up all the Workings of your own Reason, and your own Will; and then, and then only, are you fitted for that *Unction from above*, which can teach you all Things. But till Christ, who is the one Fountain of Life and Light, be opened in you; it is in vain, that you rise up early, and late take Rest, in Quest of Truth; for he himself hath said, 'Without me, ye can do nothing.' And every Son of earthly *Adam*, however naturally enriched with the Spirit, and Light, and Arts

---

* *Threefold Life*, page 158.

of this World, is born, and must remain, a *Spirit in Prison*, till Christ is found to be an inward Preacher, and Light within him. As he is the one Resurrection from the Dead, so is he the one Deliverer from everything that has the nature of Death, Darkness, and Ignorance. And to expect seeing Eyes, hearing Ears, and Sensibility of Heart, from anything but that *eternal Word*, by which we were at first made, is robbing God and Christ of more Honour, is a more idolatrous Departure from the true Worship and Dependence upon him, than if we sometimes hoped to have Good from this or that Saint's praying for us. For this is a Truth, that admits of no Restriction, but reaches from one End of the Earth to the other, that as no Man can come unto the Father, but through the Son ; so no one can come at any Divine Knowledge, either in Grace or Nature, but through him alone.

The *Schools* of this World are of no higher a Nature, than the *Markets* of this World ; and when rightly used, serve only to the Ends of this earthly Life. But as Markets and Traffic seldom keep within their just Bounds, but become serviceable to Vanity, earthly Lusts, and all the Luxury of Life ; so it mostly happens in our learned Labours ; we grow old and blear-eyed, in Studies that nourish Pride and Envy, Division and Contention ; and only help our old Man to be content with the Riches of his fallen Nature, and feel no Necessity of being born again.

Would you therefore be a *Divine* Philosopher, you must be a *true Christian ;* for Darkness is everywhere, but in the Kingdom of God ; and Truth nowhere to be found by Man, but in a *New Birth* from above. Man was created in and for the Truth ; that is, he was created in the Truth of the Divine Light, to see and hear, to taste and feel, to find and enjoy, all Things in the Truth of the Divine Life brought forth in him. And therefore it is, that for fallen Man there is but one Remedy ; it is only *the Truth* that can make him free. Truth is the only *Resting-place* of the Soul ; it is its *Atonement* and *Peace* with God ; all is, and must be Disquiet, a Succession of lying Vanities, till the Soul is again in the Truth, in which God at first created it. And therefore said the *Truth, Learn of me ; for I am meek, and lowly of Heart ; and ye shall find Rest unto your Souls.*

Academicus. Pray *Theophilus*, stop a while : Surely your Zeal carries you too far. All Ages of the World have seemed to agree in this, that the Gospel teaches purely the Simplicity of a godly Life ; calls no Man to be a Philosopher, nor gives the smallest Instruction in Matters that relate to Philosophy.

Theophilus. All this, *Academicus*, is very true ; but then, this very Simplicity and Plainness of the Gospel, turning Man only from this World, to a Faith, and Hope, and Desire of God, is the *one* Reason, and *full Proof*, that it alone is a true Guide into the highest School of Divine Wisdom and Philosophy; not only because Goodness is our greatest Wisdom, but because the Mysteries of God, of Grace, of Nature, of Time and Eternity, can no other possible way be opened in Man, but by this Simplicity of a godly Life taught in the Gospel; because *only* the godly Life hath Knowledge of God; just as the creaturely Life hath only Knowledge of the Creature, and the painful Life hath Knowledge of Pain. The Scripture saith, *that only the Spirit of God knoweth the Things of God.* And indeed, how can it possibly be otherwise? For since the Spirit of God is the Spirit and Life that goeth through all Nature and Creature, and only openeth its *own hidden* Powers therein; since it is that which is the Former of everything; that which makes everything to have the Life that it hath, and to work as it worketh; nothing but the Spirit of God, can possibly know the Things of God: And therefore, of Necessity, this Spirit of God must be in Man, and work in Man, as it is in Nature, and worketh in Nature, before Man can enter into the Knowledge and Working of God in Nature. And therefore here you have two immutable, and fundamental Truths: (1) That all our Ignorance of God and Nature is, and must be, purely and solely, the *Want of the Spirit and Life of God in us:* And, (2) That therefore the one only Way to Divine Knowledge, is the Way of the Gospel, which calls and leads us to a New Birth of the *Divine Nature brought forth in us.*

Academicus. I have nothing that I can, or would object to what you have said. But still I must say, that I do not enough apprehend, how the *Spirit and Life of God* must thus, of all Necessity, be born in us; nor indeed, do I entirely comprehend how it is done. Human Reason, or human Instruction, I see plain enough, cannot help me to any Divine Light. But suppose God should send an Angel to instruct me, and that frequently, would not Divine Knowledge be then imparted to me? And yet this would not be a Birth of God in me. Or, will you say, that God cannot sufficiently instruct me, even by the highest of his Angels?

Theophilus. An Angel, Sir, may instruct you, as the Scriptures instruct you; but it is only such an Instruction, as may direct you where and how to obtain that Light, which neither the Letter of Scripture, nor the Voice of an Angel, can bring forth in you. The highest Angel neither hath, nor ever can have, any more of a redeeming Power in it, than the dead Paper on which the Scriptures are written. But you are to observe, and mark it well, that you cannot have Divine Light from any other

Thing, but that which hath full Power to redeem you: For Light is not only Life, but the Perfection, and highest State of it; and therefore nothing can bring forth Light, but that which can bring forth the Truth and Perfection of Life.

Every other Thing, besides the Life and Light of God, stands only in a State of *ministerial Service* towards you: Whether it be Words of a Message from God, written on paper, engraven on tables of Stone, or spoken by the Mouth of an *Angel*, a *Prophet* or *Apostle;* be it which it will, it is only a creaturely Thing; and its creaturely Service can rise no higher, nor go any further, than to show the true Way to Him, who only himself can be the Truth, the Life, and the Light in you. For the Light of God cannot, even by God himself, be communicated to you by any Creature; and the Reason is, because the Light of God is God himself: It is the Light of his own Life: And therefore only himself can bring it forth wherever it is; and no Creature can possibly partake of his Light, but by having a Birth in and from the Divine Nature: For the Light of God can never be separate from the Divine Nature, or be anywhere but where the Divine Birth is. And thus you fully see, that all that can be divinely known, either in Heaven, or on earth, can only be known in that *one Way*, and by that *one Means*, by which fallen Man can be saved; namely, by a New Birth of the Light and Spirit of God within us. And therefore the simple Way of the Gospel, is the one only Way to attain all the Knowledge of all that, which can be known of God and Nature: For nothing can manifest God and Nature, but the Spirit of God working in Man, as he worketh in Nature, which can only be done by a New Birth of the Divine Nature, brought forth in Man: But when Man is thus born again of God, then the Life and Spirit of God is in him, and worketh in him, as it doth in Nature. And thus it is, that Man can only be a Divine Philosopher, when Christ, who is the Light of God, and the Light of Nature, is revealed in him. Then he is in that living *Word*, and that living Word is in him, by which all Things were at first made; and which maketh, createth, and worketh in him, as it worketh in all Things, both in Heaven and Earth.

Academicus. I never expected to have seen the Gospel New Birth proved to be the only open Gate to all that *Divine Knowledge*, which any Son of *Adam* ever had, or can have. But you have proved it to be so, beyond all Possibility of Denial. And I now only want to have you go on in this Doctrine of the New Birth; for I am persuaded, you can still add something to *that*, which has already been said upon it, both as to the Ground, and Nature, and Fruits of it.

Theophilus. You must remember, *Academicus*, that all that I can by Discourse, from the Beginning to the End of this Matter, do for you, amounts only to thus much : It is like giving you a full Assurance of a wonderful Pearl of glorious Virtues, hidden in the Ground of a certain Field, and showing you every Step of the Way you must take to find it. Now, if from Month to Month, you should be inquiring and hearing of some new Powers and Virtues of this heavenly Pearl ; what Good does all this Discourse and Hearsay do you ? You are just as far from the Pearl itself, and have no more of it, than when you first heard of it ; and would be in the same Distance from it, though you were always, to the End of your Life, loving to hear and talk about it. I have had no other End in all that is said of the New Birth, but to assure you of the Truth of the Thing, and the true Way to it. Now the Way to the New Birth lies wholly in your Will to it ; and every Step that you can take, consists in a continual Dying to the selfish corrupt Will, which you have from Flesh and Blood. Nothing can make any Change in you, but the Change of your Will. For everything, be it what it will, *is a Birth of that Will*, which worketh in you. You have nothing therefore to inquire after, nor anything that you can judge of yourself by, but the State of your Mind, the Working of your Will and Desire. These will give you more Light, than all the Men or Books in the World can give you : Where these are, there are you ; and what these are, that are you : There you live, and to that you belong ; and there you must have all the Good or Evil that can be called yours.

For nothing leads or carries you anywhere, nothing generates either Life or Death in you, but the Working of your Mind, Will, and Desire. If your Will is angelic, you are an Angel, and angelic Happiness must be yours. If your Will is with God, you work with God ; God is then the Life of your Soul, and you will have your Life with God to all Eternity. If you follow an earthly Will, every Step you take is a Departure from God, till you become as incapable of God, and the Life of God, as the Animals of this World. If your Will worketh in Pride and Self-exaltation, in Envy and Wrath, in Hatred and Ill-will, in Deceit, Hypocrisy, and Falseness, you work with the Devil, you are generating his Nature within you, and making yourself ready for the Kingdom of Hell. And thus it is, that *our Works follow us ;* and that *everyone will be rewarded according to his Works ;* and none can reap anything else but that which he hath sown. And the Seed of everything that can grow in us, is our Will. The Will maketh the Beginning, the Middle, and the End of everything ; it is the only Workman in Nature ; and everything

Divine Knowledge.

is its Work. It has all Power; its Works cannot be hindered; it carries all before it; it creates as it goes; and all Things are possible to it. It enters wherever it wills, and finds everything that it seeks; for its seeking is its finding. The Will over-rules all Nature, because Nature is its Offspring, and born of it; for all the Properties of Nature, whether they be Good or Evil, in Darkness or in Light, in Love or in Hatred, in Wrath or in Meekness, in Pride or Humility, in Trouble or Joy, are all of them the Offspring or Birth of the Will; as that liveth, so they live; and as that changeth, so they change. So that whatever you are, or whatever you feel, is all owing to the working and creating Power of your own Will. This is your God or your Devil, your Heaven or your Hell; and you have only so much of one, or the other, as your Will, which is the first Mover, is either given up to the one, or to the other.

For where the Will of Man is not, there he hath nothing; and where his Will is, there is all that *Something* which he hath, be it of what Kind it will; and it is inseparable from him, till his Will worketh contrary to it.

Academicus. Whence hath the Will of Man this mighty Power that it can have nothing, but that which itself hath willed?

Theophilus. You might as well ask, why a *Circle* must be perfectly round, or a straight Line free from every Degree of Crookedness. For as it is not a Circle till it is perfectly round, nor a straight Line till it is free from Crookedness, so the Will is not in Being, but so far as it is free, is its own Mover, and can have nothing but that which it willeth. *Secondly*, The Will is not a made Thing, which is made out of something, or that came out of some different State, into the State of a Will. But the free Will of Man is a true and real Birth from the free, eternal, uncreated Will of God, which willed to have a creaturely Offspring of itself, or to see itself in a creaturely State. And therefore the Will of Man hath the Nature of Divine Freedom; hath the Nature of Eternity, and the Nature of Omnipotence in it; because it is what it is, and hath what it hath, as a Spark, a Ray, a genuine Birth of the eternal, free, omnipotent Will of God. And therefore, as the Will of God is superior to, and ruleth over all Nature; so the Will of Man, derived from the Will of God, is superior to, and ruleth over all his own Nature. And thence it is, that as to itself, and so far as its own Nature reacheth, it hath the Freedom and Omnipotence of that Will from which it is descended; and can have or receive nothing, but what itself doth, and worketh, in and to itself.

And herein consisteth the infinite Goodness of God, in the Birth of all intelligent Creatures; and also the exceeding Height,

Perfection, and Happiness of their created State: They are descended from God, full of Divine Power; they can will and work with God, and partake of the Divine Happiness. They can receive no Injustice, Hurt, or Violence, either from Nature or Creature; but must be only that, which they generate, and have no Evil or Hurt, but that which they do in and to themselves. All Things stand in the Will, and everything, animate or inanimate, is the Effect and Produce of that Will, which worketh in it, and formeth it to be that which it is. And every Will, wherever found, is the Birth and Effect of some antecedent Will; for Will can only proceed from Will, till you come to the first working Will, which is God himself.

And here, my Friend, you have an easy Entrance into the true Meaning of many important Passages in the Books of *Jacob Behmen*, like those that follow: 'All,' says he, 'is magical; the 'Eternity is magical:—Magic is the Mother of all Things.—I 'speak from a magic Ground.—Here the Reader must have 'magical Eyes.—This hath a magical Understanding,' *&c.* Vulgar Reason is offended at these Expressions, because the Word *Magic* has, for many Ages, been mostly used in a bad Sense. But do not you be frightened at the Sound of these Words; they are not only innocent, but truly good and wise, and deeply founded on the Truth of Things. They have the most Christian and Divine Meaning; are strictly conformable to the Spirit of the Gospel, as shall be shown by-and-by; and are used for the best of Ends; namely, to open the true Ground of eternal and temporal Nature, and the Birth of Creatures in each of them. They are to show how the hidden, invisible Deity acteth and worketh all its Wonders in both these Worlds, in one and the same uniform Way; as also, how everything in Religion, whether it be a Mystery of God, a Grace of God, or a Duty of Man, hath its whole Ground, and Nature, and Efficacy, therein.

Now *magic Power* meaneth nothing but the *Working of the Will*, whether it be the Divine, or the creaturely Will; and everything that is the Work of the Will, and is produced by it, is called its magic Work, which only means, that it is generated by and from the Will, as a Birth brought forth by it. The Will is the Workman, and the Work is that, which it bringeth forth out of itself. So that by these Words, you are always to understand these two Things, the *Working, and the Work of the Will.* And now, you may already sufficiently see, that their Meaning is not only innocent and good, but as necessarily, and divinely, to be ascribed to God, as the Power of bringing Things into Existence by the Working of his Will. For here you have the true Ground and Original of the creating Power of God; how everything that is not God, is yet come from him, and out of him, as so many Births of his invisible Power, breaking forth into Visibility, and sensible Qualities of an outward Life.

The first Manifestation of the invisible God is that which is called, and is, *Eternal Nature;* which is the Eternity of all possible Powers and Qualities of Life, the first Source of every natural Power that can be in any Creature. All these Qualities of Life, in their eternal Birth, and rising from one another by the working Will of God, are the Out-birth, or outward Glory of God, in which he manifests his Triune, invisible Deity in a threefold Life of Fire, Light, and Spirit; which are the Ground of all the Qualities of Life, Sensibility, Power, and Spirit, that ever were, or can be found in any Creature. Everything that exists, or thinks, or moves, or finds itself in any Kind or Degree of Sensibility, is from, and out of, this glassy Sea of these united Powers of Life. And this whole Manifestation of all the possible Powers, and Perfection of Life and Glory, is called that Kingdom of Heaven, in which God dwelleth; and is, as it were, his Divine Workhouse, out of which he is perpetually giving forth new Works, and Forms of Wonder.

This Manifestation of God, is a *magic Birth* from the Triune *working* Will of the hidden Deity, which willed to see itself in this opened, outward Show of all the possible Powers of Life and Glory; and from whence new Worlds of finite Divine Beings, as so many living Images of God, might have a Possibility of coming forth. For without Nature, God must be by himself, and continue an unmanifested God. For no *Form* or Creature can be, unless there be something antecedent to it, that can be *formed.* *Life* must be, before there can be any finite living Creatures; just as *Light* must be, before there can be any *seeing* Eyes. And therefore the Manifestation of God in an outward Glory of all the possible Powers, Qualities, and Perfections of Life, called eternal Nature, must be, or there could be no Possibility for the Existence of any Creature.

Now this same working Will of the Triune Deity, which manifested itself in an eternal Nature, manifesteth itself in creaturely Forms, all generated from, all enlivened and animated with, that same Trinity of Fire, Light, and Spirit, that constitutes eternal Nature. So that all intelligent Creatures are that in their finite Being, which eternal Nature is in its infinite State. And thus all of them are from God, and from Heaven, live in God, and may work with God, as God is in Heaven, and Heaven in him; one Life, one Power, one Will, and one Happiness with God.

Now everything that is not God, but after him, and distinct

from him, must be that which it is, from the working Will of the Deity. For since it cometh into Being, only because it is *willed* to be, it can have nothing in it, or be any other Thing, but that which the working or creating Will brought forth. And as all Things began in and from this working Will, so all Things must go on in it; and there can be no other Creator, Worker, or Former of Things to all Eternity, but the working Will of God, either mediately or immediately. Nor can there be any other Nature in anything, but that which is the Birth, or magic Effect, of a working Will within it. And everything that is done by the Creature, everything which it seeks and likes, or abhors and resists, is all driven on by a working Will, or magic Power, which stirs, and generates, and works within it.

Would you know now the true Ground of all this? It is this: It is because *Will* is the first Original of all Power, and the Omnipotence of God consisteth in nothing else but his *working Will;* and therefore no Power ever was, or ever can be, anywhere else, but as it is in God; and if the Creature hath any Power, it must have it, as God hath it, in the working Will. For since all Nature, with all its Qualities, Births, and Creatures, are all brought into Being by the working Will of God, it evidently follows, that every Creature, with every Quality, Power, and Property in it, is magically born, and therefore must have a magic Nature, that is, a Nature that cometh from, and standeth in a working Will.

And now, Sir, you are come into a full View of the most important Matter of the Mystery of all Things; a Matter which, if rightly apprehended in the inward Ground of your Soul, puts an entire End to all the Jargon of a false Philosophy, and to all those Fictions of Doctrines and Disputes, which Reason has built upon the written Word of God.

For nothing is effected by Fiction and Invention, by any contrived Arts or Searchings of rational Inquiries; all this is nothing, because it toucheth not Nature, but leaveth it to itself; which carrieth on its own Works by its own Power, and can only work in its own Way; and must bring forth its own Births, independent of everything but its own working Life. But all lieth in the Will and working Desire of the Soul, because *Will* began and brought forth all that Nature that lives in the Soul, and is the only Life in it; and this Life can work and grow from nothing else, but that which first brought it forth. Hence you see the full Meaning of these Words of our Author, 'All is magical; and 'that Magic is the Mother of all Things;' and consequently, the only Opener of all Divine Knowledge. All which Expressions only imply thus much, that the *Will*, whether in God, or the

Creature, is the Ground and Seed of every Thing; is the generating working Power, which maketh and worketh all Things to be in that State and Condition which they are; and that every Thing begins, goes on, and ends, in the Working of the Will; and that nothing can be otherwise, than as its Will worketh; and therefore Eternity and Time are magical; and Magic is, and must be, the Mother of all Things.

Now here you see, in the utmost Degree of Clearness, how all true and false Religion divide from one another. For if nothing worketh but the Will, if nothing else carries on the Work of Nature, then all is false and vain in Religion, but the Working of the Will; and nothing is saving, or redeeming the Life of the Soul, but that which helps the Will to work towards God.

Hence it is, that our Author so often tells his Reader, that when he sees and finds this magic Birth of Things, he is *delivered from Babel;* not by running from one Place to another, or from one System of Opinions to another, but by *inwardly leaving* all the Workings of earthly Self, all the Paper-Buildings of natural Reason, and turning to God with the whole Will and working desire of his Heart. This is the right coming out of our own *Babel* of vain Opinions into the *Truth and Reality of Nature,* where the living God of Nature is found; not in Notions, but in the living Working of the Soul, and worshipped in Spirit and in Truth.

I said, into the *Truth and Reality of Nature,* because Nature is the Standard of Truth, and all is *Babel* but that which worketh with Nature; that is, with eternal Nature; for as eternal Nature is the Manifestation of the unchangeable God, so it must be as unchangeable in itself, and its own Workings, as God is; because it hath nothing in it, but what is in and from the unchangeable God. And therefore, God cannot be manifest, or work in any Creature, but as he is manifest, and worketh in eternal Nature; and therefore all that the Creature doth, is Labour lost, and a vain Beating of the Air, but that which it worketh with, and according to eternal Nature. Because God never was, nor ever can be, or be found, anywhere else but in his own Heaven, or eternal Nature. And no Soul can by any one possible thing find, or be found by God, but by standing before him in the same Will and Working as eternal Nature doth. And therefore all is Fiction and *Babel* but the Working of the Will, because nothing but the Will can work with Nature; and that for this Reason, because all Life, and all Nature, eternal and temporal, is what it is, merely and solely, from the Working of the Will. All things in Heaven and in Earth stand in this magic Birth; and nothing can change its State, either for better or worse, but as the Working of its Will changes. Justly therefore is it said, that where this Truth is found, there is a full and true Deliverance from *Babel*, that is, from all Strife, and Zeal, and Division about Opinions, Sects, and Churches; since the *one Thing* that works either to Life, or to Death, the one Thing that alone opens Heaven or Hell for us, is with every *individual Man*, in every Place, and in every Age of the World; and that one Thing is the *Working of the Will*. And when, in any such Man, his Will is turned from his own earthly Self, and this earthly Life, and worketh with its Desire to God, then all these Sayings of the Scripture are true of him; *viz.*, 'That he is redeemed from this 'evil World—that he has his Conversation in Heaven—that he 'is of God, and heareth God's Word—that he is saved by Faith— 'that Christ is revealed to him—that he is Christ's, and Christ is 'his—that Christ is in him of a Truth—and that he is led by 'the Spirit of Christ.' All these Texts would be true of him though he had never seen, nor heard, a Syllable of the written Word of God.

For the *Word* of God which saveth and redeemeth, which giveth Life and Light to the Soul, is not the Word printed on Paper, but is that eternal, *ever-speaking Word*, which is the Son of God, who in the Beginning was with God, and was the God by whom all Things were made. This is the universal Teacher and Enlightener of all that are in Heaven, and on Earth; who from the Beginning to the End of Time, without Respect of Persons, stands at the Door of every Heart of Man, speaking into it not human Words, but *Divine Goodness;* calling and knocking, not with outward Sounds, but by the *inward Stirring* of an awakened Divine Life. And therefore, as sure as that is true, which St. *John* saith, That this eternal Word 'is the Life of 'Men, and the Light that lighteth every Man that cometh 'into the World,' so sure is it, that our Saviour and Salvation, our Teacher and Enlightener, from whom we have every good Thought, is *Christ within us;* not within this or that Man, but in every Man wherever born, and in whom the Light of Life ariseth. And indeed how can it be otherwise? For if God is the God of all Men; and the *Word* of God the Life and Light of all Men; and all Men are capable of Goodness; and all Goodness can only be from God; and no Goodness can belong to Man, but that which is *within* him, then every Man must have the *Word*, or *Christ* of God within him, and can have it nowhere else. All Teachers therefore, who teach Men to look for Life or Salvation in anything but the *Word* and Spirit of God within them, stand chargeable with the Blood and Death of Souls; because, in all the Possibility of Things, nothing can overcome that Death which is in the Soul, but the *Word*, or *Christ* of God, living and working in it. For observe, Man must have Goodness in the same Way as God hath Goodness, that is, from the Divine Nature; for Goodness is nowhere else, neither is anything else capable of it; and therefore, if Goodness is to be in Man, the Divine Nature must, of all Necessity, be first brought to Life *within him*. But this cannot be, till the working Will of our Heart turns and gives up itself wholly to the Word and Spirit of God *within us*. For we can have nothing but that, towards which the Earnestness of our Will goeth.

Again, see here in a still higher Degree of Proof, the absolute Necessity, and unspeakable Benefit of the *Spirit of Prayer;* how it does, and must, in spite of all Opposition, raise the fallen Soul out of the Poverty of Flesh and Blood, into the Riches of an heavenly Nature brought forth in it. For since all Things in Heaven and Earth stand in a magic Birth, or Working of the Will; the Will is that, which hath all Power; it unites all that is united in Heaven or on Earth; it divides and separates all that is divided in Nature; it makes Heaven, and it makes Hell; for there is no Hell, but where the Will of the Creature is turned from God; nor any Heaven, but where the Will of the Creature worketh with God. Therefore, as we pray, so we are; and as our Will-Spirit secretly worketh, so are we either swallowed up in the Vanity of Time, or called forth into the Riches of Eternity. And therefore the Spirit of Prayer is most justly conceived, and most simply expressed, when it is said to be the Rising of the Soul out of the Vanity of Time into the Riches of Eternity: For all the Vanity which the Soul hath, is from its living in, and loving the Things of Time; and therefore it can only come out of the Vanity of its State, by loving and living in the Truths, which are the Riches of Eternity: For the Spirit of Prayer is the Hunger of the Soul; and as every Hunger is, so it eats; it always eateth that which it hungereth after, and hath a Life suitable to the Nature, State, and Condition, both of its Hunger, and its Food. If it hungereth after the Things of Flesh and Blood, it eateth nothing else, and only groweth in the bestial Life; and of the Flesh must reap the Corruption that belongs to Flesh: And if it hungereth after God, it eateth the Food which giveth Life to the Angels; it eateth the Bread that is come down from Heaven; namely, the real heavenly Body and Blood of *Christ*, which surely may be called the Riches of Eternity.

All the Mysteries of Religion, and the Necessity of the whole Process of *Christ* in our Redemption, have all of them their Ground, and Necessity, and Efficacy, in this *magic Nature* of Things, and are all of them only for this one End, to help fallen

Man to have a *working Will* towards that first Life, which he has lost. And therefore no one joins with the Mysteries of Redemption, or can have any Share in them, but he whose Will turns wholly from this World, and hath all its Working towards God and Heaven. And now, Sir, you see the plain, and easy, and certain Deliverance from all Perplexity and vain Labour in the Disputes and Divisions of Religion. It is but opening your natural Eyes, that is, letting simple Nature work with its own Power, and all Difficulties are removed; and the Way to God and Goodness is as natural, and as free from all Perplexity, as the opening our Eyes to see the Light of the Sun. For what is so natural to Man as the Working of the Will; And yet he can have nothing, or be anything, different from that, to which his Will worketh.

Nor does this at all too much exalt the human Will, or make our Salvation not to be the *pure Grace and Gift* of God to us, but quite the contrary. For the Will here spoken of, is not the Will of Flesh and Blood, but that heavenly Will, which is the only Spark of the Deity in us, given by the free Grace of God to all Mankind, as soon as fallen, and called in Scripture the *inspoken* Word of God in Paradise; which was the Beginning of the Redemption, when God first entered into a Covenant of Salvation with *Adam*, and all his Posterity. This *inspoken Word* is *Christ*, or the Spark of the Divine Nature, which is the Light that lighteth every Man that cometh into the World. And here, in this *Christ in us*, lieth the *Will* that hath the *Power* of Salvation in it; and all its Salvation is the Salvation of *Christ*. For it is the Will of this heavenly Nature, hid in every Man, that is the working Will, that bringeth forth the New Birth of Heaven in us; and therefore is the *pure free* Salvation of *Christ*, given to be a Redeemer within us. So that all our Salvation, though wrought out by this working Will within us, is, from the Beginning to the End, the pure Grace of God to us, and no Salvation of our own.

And thus, Sir, you see, that every Soul of Man is partly human, and partly Divine; and is united to an earthly and an heavenly Nature; and so not only can, but must, always work either with one or the other, and has nothing else to work with; and must and can be, or have nothing else, but as he followeth or worketh with either of these Wills. So that, infallibly to know both your present and future State, what you are, and to what you belong, you need only to see, what you cannot help seeing, *how*, and *where*, and to *what*, your Will worketh.

And thus, from this Knowledge of the magic Nature of Things, which all are that which they are, solely from the Working of the Will in everything, you are delivered from all vain Labour and Party-Zeal; and are brought back to that true and safe Ground; on which God has placed you to work out your own Salvation, without any Hindrance from any Builders of *Babel*, of whatever Denomination.

The Short is this: The whole Matter of Religion relates only to *Life and Death*. But Life and Death are both of them immutable, and founded in the unchangeable Nature of Things. Nothing can alter them, or invent a new Way, either to or from either of them. To what purpose then, is all this dividing into so many Parties? Why all this Strife and Zeal about Opinions? Death and Life go on their own Way, carry on their own Work, and stay for no Opinions. Does the *Stone* stop, or alter its Tendency towards the Earth? Do the Sparks and Flame cease to fly upwards, because Philosophers dispute and quarrel about the Reasons of one or the other? No; Nature goes on in its own Way, let Reason say what it will. Now *Death* and *Life* have their own unchangeable Nature and Working in and from themselves; and are just as distinct from, and independent of, all Opinions of Men about them, as the Things just now mentioned: So that to will and work, as *Life* willeth and worketh, and to will and work, as *Death* willeth and worketh, is the one only possible Way to partake either of Life or Death. What a Delusion is it therefore, to grow grey-headed in balancing ancient and modern Opinions; to waste the precious uncertain Fire of Life in critical Zeal, and verbal Animosities; when nothing but the kindling of our working Will into a Faith, that overcometh the World, into a steadfast Hope, and ever-burning Love, and Desire of the Divine Life, can hinder us from falling into eternal Death!

Academicus. Oh! *Theophilus*, you have led me into a Depth, that I never thought of seeing into.

For this magic Power of everything, that works in all Nature and Creature, shows me everything in a new View. You might well say, that Reason has no Power in this Mystery; that nothing is proposed to it: For since Life and Death have their own Working within themselves, and must at last, when Time is at an End, divide and take Possession of everything, according as its Will has worked either with one or the other, it signifies no more to them what Reason has been all this time discoursing about, than in what Language a Man used to talk. But before you go any further, I beg a Word or Two on these Matters. *First*, How I am to understand our Author, when he says, 'Here the 'Reader must have magical Eyes;' and, 'This or that hath a 'magical Understanding.' And, *Secondly*, That you would, as you promised, show, how the speaking thus of this magical Power of Life, is strictly conformable to the Spirit of the Gospel.

Theophilus. As to your First Matter, concerning *magical Eyes;* I should have thought the Thing plain enough already. But you may understand it thus. When a *Carpenter* cuts Timber into various Shapes and Forms, and then joins one Piece to another, till it is formed into the Shape of a House; this is no magical Work, because one Part does not grow from the other, till the Whole is brought forth, and therefore there is no need of magical Eyes to see what this Work is. But when an Oak groweth from an Acorn, or a Plant from a Seed in the Ground, here the Work is magical; that is, it is a Birth or Product generated from the working Will in the Acorn and Seed, from whence the Stem, and all its Branches and Fruits, grow forth; which working Will continueth, till the Plant or Tree hath reached its Limit, that is, till the working Will in the seed hath spent itself. Now all this is a magical Work, and therefore can only be seen by such magical Eyes, as can see into the Beginning, and go on with the Working of that which works and generates in the Tree or Plant.

As to your other Matter, How this Language of the magical Working of the Will, is 'entirely conformable to the Spirit of the 'Gospel;' the Answer is easy, because the Thing is plain. For the first possible Beginning of the Christian Life, is, by the Founder of it, expressly laid in a *New Birth* from above, and therefore plainly declared to be a magical Work, and to have no other Nature; because a generating Work, and a magical Work, are only different Expressions for the same Thing. And as the Beginning, so every following Advancement in the Christian Life, is as really and truly only a Growth of Life, or magical Birth from the Powers of Father, Son, and Holy Ghost, upon the working Will in the Soul, as the Plant, from its first Stirring in the Seed, to its last State, is only a Growth from the Powers of the Sun, Stars, and Elements, upon the working Will in the seed.

Everything that is outward in Religion, whether it be *Men* or *Things, planting* or *watering,* is only for the sake of this inward Birth; either to direct Man to it, to help him to work in it, or warn him of that eternal Death, which the Will, working according to Flesh and Blood, must inherit as its own genuine Fruit. And whoever fancies the Christian Life to be anything else than a Birth growing up in God, till it comes to the Perfection of the Divine Life, by the same Way of a gradual Growth, and in the same Reality, as the finished Flower has all its Perfection by way of a gradual Growth from the Seed, has not a Syllable in the Gospel, nor an Instance in Nature, to plead in Excuse of his fanciful Error.

For nothing worketh in all Nature or Grace, but what worketh as a Birth, or magical Growth of Life. For nothing can come from the living God but Life, nor for any other End, but to manifest some Kind or Degree of Life. There are no dead Forms, or lifeless Inventions to be found, till you come to the mechanic Works of Men's Hands, and the cobweb Schemes of dead Knowledge, brought forth by human Reason. For Reason is the old Serpent called Subtlety, the first and the last grand Deceiver of Mankind, that takes them from the powerful Workings of Nature, to follow the Shadows of empty Sounds, till all is swallowed up either by final Life or Death, which will at last reap everything into its own unchangeable Barn.

Again, *Faith*, and *Hope*, and *Love*, and *Desire* towards God, are the only Gospel Means of bringing forth the New Birth; and therefore all that the Gospel requires, is a magical Working of the Will.

For all these Powers, whether of Faith, Hope, Love, and Desire towards God and the Divine Life, are only so many different Powers of the Working of the Will, and have all their Efficacy, as so many Parts of it; and only alter, raise, and bring forth a New Life, because the Working of the Will is magical, and generates as it works, and unites with that which it willeth. And thus *Christ*, or the New Man in *Christ Jesus*, is formed in us, from a Seed of Heaven, which is the Will that can work towards God, till it becomes a godly Birth, as the Seed works towards the Sun, till it is changed into the Birth of a beauteous fragrant Flower.

Again, Hence it is, namely, from this magic Power of the Working of the Will, that our blessed Lord speaks so often of the Omnipotence of Faith; *viz*., 'That all Things are possible 'to him that believeth.—Whatsoever ye shall ask in Prayer, 'believing, ye shall receive.—If ye had Faith but as a Grain of 'Mustard-seed, ye Might say to this Tree, Be thou plucked up 'by the Root; and to this Mountain, Be thou cast into the Sea; 'and it should be done.—Thy Faith hath saved thee.—Accord-'ing to thy Faith, so be it done unto thee.'

Hence all these Truths plainly follow: *First*, That *Faith*, which is in itself only the Working of the Will, is the Source of all Power; and that all that is done in Nature is done by it alone; and that therefore all Nature standeth in a magic Working of the Will. For *all Things could not be possible to him that believeth*, but because Faith, or the Working of the Will, is the true Source of all Power in or over Nature. *Secondly*, Here is a full Demonstration of the high and powerful State, in which Man was at first created! A Lord over all this outward World; who could, by the Working of his Will, command the Obedience of all things about him.

This was the Dominion he had over all the Creatures on the Earth, in the Sea, and in the Air; not such a poor power as invented Weapons, or the Strength of his Hands and Feet, could help him to; but a Power here mentioned, of standing still, and, by the Faith or Will of his Mind, making every Creature to come or go, just as the faithful Disciple of *Christ* was, by his Faith, to have Power over every outward Thing of this World.

Now all this high State of his first Power, is undeniable from the Words of our Saviour. For it is not to be supposed, that he would turn Men's Thoughts to any such Powers, as to have *all Things obedient to their Faith*, or the working Will of their Minds, if this had not been Man's first created State, or such Powers as did then belong to it. For no Man or Creature can have any higher Power, than that which belongs to his first created State.

And therefore all Gospel Faith, however wonderful in its Power, can only have *somewhat* of that first powerful Faith, which Man had when he first came out of the Hands of God. And Faith *now* in a Redeemer, can only be the Means of obtaining Salvation, for this Reason; because Faith was *then* that original high Power in Man, which could have preserved him in his first Perfection and Glory of Life. Thus, when *Christ* saith, 'Thy Faith hath saved thee,' it is the same thing as if he had said, Faith had always such Power; that Faith was the *Strength* and *Glory* of the First Man, that could have saved him from falling under the Power of the Stars and Elements; that it was Faith alone which could and did put an End to his first paradisaical Glory, by turning its Strength and Desire into the Life of this World. *Again*, when our Lord saith, 'According to thy 'Faith, so be it done unto thee;' this was no new Thing, or new Operation in the Power of Faith, but was only a Declaration of a Truth as old as Nature and Creature, and was in Reality so much said of the powerful Faith of the First Man; and infallibly shows, that as *now*, so *then*, nothing was done to him in his Fall, but that which was done according to the Faith and Working of his Will. For this is God's immutable righteous Procedure with Man, that nothing but his own Works can follow him; and that, from first to last, whether standing or falling, according to his Faith, and working Will, so must it be done unto him. And therefore Man's Faith and working Will, was his Divine Power of living superior to, and independent of all the Stars and Elements of this World, in his own angelic Perfection of a Divine Life.

For if the Revival of Faith, in so small a Degree, as to be compared to a Grain of Mustard-seed, could bring forth in Man such a Divine Power over all the Things of this World, is it not a sufficient Proof of the high Power of his first lost Faith, which only thus coming again, as the smallest of Seeds, yet comes with such mighty Power over all outward Nature, the Flesh and the Devil? And thus, all that is said in the Gospel, of the Power of Faith, is, in the strictest Truth, so much said of the Power and Perfection of our first Father, over whom this earthly System had no Power: But whether he stood, or fell, or was to rise again, all was, and is, and must be done, by his Faith, or the Working of his Will.

And thus also, you see, that all that was said of the Nature and Extent of the *magic Power* of the Will, is not only conformable to, but is the *very Spirit* of the Gospel, and all the written Word of God. For from the first Promise made to *Adam*, to the last written Words of Scripture, Man is only called and directed to the true Exercise of these *magic, generating* Powers of the Will; namely, to *believe*, to *hope*, to *trust* in God; to *love, desire*, and *expect* the Renewal of a Divine Life from the Goodness of God.

Humanus. Give me leave only to add, that in these Words of our Saviour, 'According to thy Faith, so be it done unto thee,' and other such like Sayings, he has not only opened the true Nature and Power of Faith, but has discovered more of the true Philosophy of Nature, than ever was told the World before. Faith is generally considered as a speculative Thing, as an Assent of the Mind to the Credibility of Things related. This may sometimes, as well in the Scriptures, as in any other Books, be called Faith, as the same Word may be used in various Senses. But the Faith in Question, about which our Saviour speaks, and to which he ascribes so much Power, and which alone can do a Man any real Good or Harm, is quite of another Nature: I say, Good or Harm; because all that is good or bad proceeds from it, and carries its Power, which way it will: As it can work all Wonders, and overcome the World; so it alone has Power over Life and Heaven in the Soul, can drive them out, and set up the Kingdom of Hell and Death instead of them.

Now this Faith may be thus understood; it is that *Power by which a Man gives himself up to anything, seeks, wills, adheres to, and unites with it, so that his Life lives in it, and belongs to it.* Now to whatever the Soul gives itself up; whatever it hungereth after; and in which it delights, and seeks to be united; there, and there only, is *its Faith;* that Faith which can work either Life or Death, and according to which Faith, everything is, and must be done to Man.

Now this Faith is not a Matter of Choice, so that a Man may live without it, if he pleases; but essential to his Life, and altogether inseparable from it. For whatever the Life drives at, to whatever it is given up, there is its *living* and *powerful* Faith. Therefore, be a Man given up to what he will, seeking, delighting, and acquiescing in whatever it be, temporal or eternal, whether it be Christianity, Idolatry, Deism, or Atheism; this is a certain Conclusion, that every Man in the World is a Man of Faith, lives by Faith, and that equally so; because every Man's Life is equally given up to the seeking, and delighting in, and uniting itself to, something or other; and therefore every Man equally lives by Faith, and that in its highest Degree. It matters not, whether a Man delights and acquiesces in the Philosophy of *Epicurus*, or *Spinoza;* whether he be *given up* to Luxury and Sensuality, or to Syllogisms and Definitions, to Mysteries of Redemption, or Mysteries of Atheism: He is neither more nor less a Man of Faith for all this; but is equally under the Power of Faith, whether it be Divine, earthly, sensual, or devilish. For which way soever the Life of Man tends, or drives; to whatever he gives up himself; there he is, and lives by Faith, and that in its highest Degree; for no Faith can rise higher than this. Nor can a Man's Faith be anywhere, but where his Life is, and to which it belongs; nor can he be said to live to anything, but by Faith. For Faith is as much the one working Power of Life, as Thought is the one working Power of the Understanding; and the Understanding of Man may as easily proceed without being led by Thought, as the Life of Man go on without being led by *Faith;* that is, without *giving itself up to something,* or other, with which it would be united, and to which it would belong, as its desired Good; which, as I said before, is the highest Degree of the most living Faith.

The Debate therefore, set up by the Deists, about *Reason* and *Faith,* as two Principles of Life; the one appropriated to Christians, and the other to themselves, is founded on the grossest Ignorance of both their Natures; as great as that of supposing, that there are two Principles of seeing and smelling; *viz., Reason* and the *Senses.* And the Deist, who turns from all Faith, to have a Life of Reason, proceeds as much according to Nature, as if he were to leave it to Christians, to see and smell by their Senses; but himself and Brethren to see and smell by the Power of Reason. For Reason is no more the Power of Life, than it is the Power of the Senses; it can no more enter into, mix, or co-operate with *Life,* than with the Senses; but must stand below them both, and follow them both, in the same Degree of Inability to alter, increase, or lessen the natural Power of either of them, as the Eye hath to alter the Vegetation, or Colour, or Smell, of the Plant on which it looks. For Reason like the Eye, is only an outward Looker on; and can no more form, or model, or alter the Life of the Soul, than it can alter the Life and Vegetation of the Body. But this Saying, 'According to thy Faith, so 'be it done unto thee,' contains the unchangeable Ground, and true Philosophy of *Life*, and the Power of Life. And this Saying takes in every Individual of human Nature; and the Deist may as well think of turning Death over to the Christians, and reserving Immortality for himself, as to think of being anything else, either here or hereafter, but purely and solely that, which his Faith has brought to pass in him. He may, indeed, easily enough keep himself free from all Christian Faith; but, whether he will or no, a Faith must do all in him, and for him, just in the same Degree, as it does for the Christian. Let him make ever so many Declarations against the Superstition and Blindness of Faith; ever so many Encomiums upon the Beauty of Axioms, Syllogisms, and Deductions of Reason; his Life is just as far from being a Life of Reason, as the Christian's is, who declares only for a Life of Faith. For as the *Eye* and the *Nose* have just the same Nature, Office, and Power, in a Man, whether he be Deist, or Christian; and he cannot, as such, have either more or less from them, or be more or less helped by them; so Reason and Faith have just the same Nature, Office, and Power in a Man, and are always in him, and will always do the same for him, whether he be Christian or Deist. And was the Deist to change Sides, he would be neither more nor less a Man of Faith and Reason, than he was before; nor have got or lost any Power either of Faith or Reason. He would only be under a Divine, instead of an earthly and sensual Faith; and his Reason would not have changed its State, or Office, or Power, but only be the Servant of a better Master; that is, of a Divine Faith.

Now, was not Faith the Power of Life in *every* Man, no Man could live by Faith, nor could it be the Principle or Power of Life in *any* Man. But seeing every Man, whether earthly or heavenly, is that which he is, by Faith; and Faith will and must have its Work in every Man; and he cannot live without it, or free from it; hence is the absolute Necessity of the *one right* Faith, in order to Salvation, and the Impossibility of anything else to avail in the stead of it. Thence also it is, that Christianity applies not to the Reason of any Man, because Reason is not the Principle of Life, or the Former of it; but it calls the Heart to a right Faith, because Man is only lost and separate from God and Heaven, by his Faith in the Things and Powers of this World. And therefore all Salvation does, and only can, arise from a Faith turned to God ; and also all Damnation from Faith in the Things of this World. And no Man can turn either to God, or to this World, but by Faith ; that is, by giving up himself either to the one, or the other ; which is the *highest* Act or Power of Faith. For there is nothing that works either to Life or Death, in any Man, but *that* to which he is given up, by *Faith* in it. And Reason never had, nor ever can have, or do anything else, but one and the same *Under-work*, or Office, let Faith take which way it will.

The Delusion of the Deist lies here : He refuses an Assent to the *History of Facts and Doctrines* of the Gospel ; and this is *his Proof* to himself that he lives by Reason, and that it is the real Principle of his Life. On the other hand, he that assents to the History of Facts and Doctrines of the Gospel, is, by the Deist, reckoned to be a Man of Gospel Faith, and that lives by it. But this is all Mistake on both Sides. For this Assent on one Side, and Dissent on the other, touches not the Matter either of Reason or Faith. For both these Persons, notwithstanding this Difference of assenting, may not only be equally governed by Faith ; but have strictly one and the same Faith. For if the Things of this World have the Heart of both of them, which very easily may be, then they have but *one* and the same Faith, and are equally governed by it ; for they both equally *live by a Faith* in this World.

The Deist therefore hath no other possible way of showing, that he is not as much a Man of Faith, as any Christian can be, but by showing that he has no Will, no Desire, no Inclination of Heart left in him ; that his Life drives no way, is given up to no one thing, as its End and Good ; but that Reason, without *Affection*, carries him only from Syllogism to Syllogism, in Quest of nothing. Then it is, that he may deem himself to be a Man of Reason, but not till then ; for if he has any Heart that hath any Inclination to be *united with or belong to anything*, then he becomes a Man of Faith, and he lives by Faith in that, to which he is given up, as much as any Christian does, who is given up to the Mysteries of Christian Redemption.

I could not help saying thus much on this Delusion, in which I have been so long ensnared myself, and therefore have the utmost good Will and Earnestness to help others out of it. And, to this End, I shall add the following Passages, taken from a Book, where this whole Matter is justly said to be examined to the Bottom. 'We have no Want of Religion, but *so far* as we ' want to *better our State* in God ; or so far as we are *unpossessed* ' of God, or less possessed of him than we might be, and our ' Nature requires. This is the true and only Ground of Religion ;

'*viz.*, to alter our State of Existence *in God*, and to have more
' of the Divine Nature and Perfections communicated to us.
' Nothing therefore is our *Good* in Religion, but *that* which *alters*
' our State of Existence in God for the better, and puts us in
' Possession of *something* of God; or makes us Partakers of the
' Divine Nature, in such a Manner and Degree as we wanted it.
' Everything that is in Life, has its Degree of Life in and from
' God; it lives and moves and has its Being in God. This is as
' true of Devils, as of the highest and most perfect Angels.
' Therefore, all the Happiness or Misery of all Creatures consist
' only in this; *viz.*, as they are *more* or *less* possessed of God, or
' as they differently partake of the Divine Nature or according
' to their *different State* of Existence in God. But if this be a
' Truth (and who can deny it?) then we have the Certainty of
' Demonstration, that nothing can be *our Good* in Religion, but
' that which *communicates* to us *something* of God, or the Divine
' Nature, or that which *betters* our State and Manner of Existence
' in God.

' For if Devils are what they are, because of their State and
' Manner of *Existence in God;* if blessed Angels are what they are,
' because of their State, and Manner of Existence in God; then
' it undeniably follows, that all that is betwixt Angels and Devils,
' all Beings, from the Happiness of the one, to the Misery of the
' other, must and can have no other Happiness or Misery, but
' according to their *State* and Manner of Existence in God, or
' according as they have more or less of the State of Angels, or
' the State of Devils, in them. Therefore nothing can be our
' *Good* in Religion, but that which *alters* our State and Manner
' of Existence in God, and renders us possessed of him in a
' different and better Manner.

' Now, if you were to send to the fallen Spirits of Darkness all
' the Systems of your *Religion of Reason*, that have been pub-
' lished, to let them know that they have the Power of their own
' Restoration and Happiness within themselves; that they need
' seek to nothing, but their own natural Reason and Understand-
' ing, and the Strength and activity of their own Powers, to raise
' them to all the Happiness they are capable of; such a Religion
' would be so far from altering or mending their State of Exist-
' ence in God, or doing them any Good, that it would add Strength
' to all their Chains; and the more firmly they believed and relied
' upon it, the more would they be confirmed and fixed in their
' Separation from God. And yet, a Religion that must neces-
' sarily keep them in Hell, is the *only Religion*, that you will have
' to carry you to Heaven. May God deliver you from this Error!

' Hence it sufficiently appears, that your Way of *natural*

'*Reason*, cannot be the Way of Salvation; because the Want of
' Salvation is nothing else, but the wanting to have *our State and
' Manner of Existence in God altered for the better*, or to have
' *something* of God communicated to us, which we *want*, and are
' capable of receiving. But if this is, and must be, the Nature
' of Salvation; then no Religion can *save* us, or do us our proper
' Good, or supply our proper Want, but that which has Power to
' *alter* our State of Existence in God, or to *communicate* to us
' that of God, which we want, and are capable of. And there-
' fore, nothing but that same Power of God, which created us,
' which gave us our State and Manner of Existence in God, and
' communicated to us that which we possess in him, can redeem
' us, or help us to that State and Manner of Existence in him,
' which we have lost, and are in Want of.

'There never could have been any Dispute, about the Possi-
' bility of saving ourselves by our own natural Faculties, had not
' Men lost all true Knowledge both of God and themselves. For
' this Dispute cannot happen, till Men suppose God to be some
' *outward Being;* that our Relation to him is some *outward Rela-
' tion;* that Religion is an *outward Thing*, that passes between
' God and us, like Terms of Behaviour between Man and Man;
' that Sin hurts, and separates us from God, only as a Misde-
' meanour hurts, and separates us from our Prince; that an offended
' God either gives or refuses Pardon to us, as an angry Prince does
' to his Subjects; and that, what gives or forgives to us, is some-
' thing as distinct or different from himself, as when a Prince, sit-
' ting upon his Throne, gives or forgives something to an Offender,
' that is an hundred Miles from him.

'Now all this is the same total Ignorance of God, what he is
' in himself, and what he is in relation to us, and the Manner of
' his being *our Good*, as when the old Idolaters took Men to be
' Gods. And yet nothing is more plain, than that your Religion
' of Reason is *wholly founded* upon all these gross and false
' Notions of God. You have not an Argument in its Defence,
' but what supposes, that our Relation to God is an *outward
' Relation*, like that of Subjects to their Prince; and that what
' we do to and for God, as our Service to him, is, and must be
' done, by our own Power, as that which we do to and for our
' Prince, must be done by our own Power. And from these
' Errors it is, that you draw this false Conclusion, that if our own
' Reason and natural Power were not sufficient to obtain for us
' all that we want, and God requires of us; God must be less
' good than a good earthly Prince, who requires no more of us,
' than that which we have a natural Strength to do, or can do by
' our own Power. And yet all this is pure Absurdity, and has

'all the Grossness of Idolatry in it, as soon as you know, that
'God is no *outward* or *separate* Being; but that we are what we
'are, have what we have, and do that which we can do, because
'he has brought us to this State of Life, Power, and Existence
'in *himself;* because he has made us, so far as we are made,
'Partakers or Possessors of a Life *in him,* and has communi-
'cated to us, such a Life in himself; or in the Words of Scrip-
'ture, because, *in him we live and move and have our Being,* and
'consequently have no Life, Motion, or Being, *out of* him. For
'from this State of our Existence in God, it necessarily follows;
'*First*, That, by the Nature of our Creation, we are only put
'into a Capacity of *receiving* Good. A Creature, as such, can
'be in no other State; it is impossible for him to enrich himself,
'or communicate more Good to himself, as it was to create
'himself. *Secondly*, That nothing but God can do us any Good.
'*Thirdly*, That God himself cannot do us any Good, but by the
'Communication of himself, in some manner, to us. Hence it is
'plain, that your Religion of Reason, which suppose, that we have
'natural Powers, that can put us in Possession of that which we
'want to be possessed of in God; or, that we need no more
'Divine Assistance to recover what we have lost of God, than
'to obtain a Pardon from a Prince; or, that God need communi-
'cate no more of himself to us in our Reconcilement to him,
'than a Prince communicates of himself to his pardoned Sub-
'ject; has all the *Mistakes, Error,* and Ignorance of God, that is
'in *Idolatry,* when it takes God to be something that he is not;
'and has all the false Devotion that is in Idolatry, when it puts
'the same Trust in, and expects the same Benefit from, its own
'Powers and Faculties, which Idolaters did in and from their
'Idols. Your Religion of Reason, therefore, which you esteem
'as the modern Refinement of the human Mind, and more excel-
'lent and rational, than the Faith and Humility of the Gospel,
'has all the Dregs of the grossest heathen Idolatry in it; and
'has changed nothing in Idolatry, but the Idol; and only differs
'in such a Degree of Philosophy, as the Religion of worshipping
'the *Sun,* differs from the Religion of worshipping an *Onion*.

'For as soon as it is known and confessed, that God is all in
'all; that in him we live and move and have our Being; that
'we have nothing *separately,* or at a *Distance,* from him, but
'everything in him; that we have no Degree of Being, nor any
'Degree of Good, but in him; that the Almighty can give us
'nothing, but that which is *something* of himself; nor any De-
'gree of Amendment or Salvation, but in such Degree as he
'communicates *something more* of himself to us; as soon as this
'great immutable Truth is known, then it is known with the

'utmost Certainty, that to put our Trust in the *Sun,* or an *Onion,*
'or our *own Reason,* if not equally absurd, is yet equally idola-
'trous, and equally prejudicial to our Salvation.'*

And now, *Theophilus,* if you please, you may proceed in the Matter you were upon.

Theophilus. We have discoursed long enough for this time. Let Silence, Recollection, inward and outward Retirement, have their Work for a few Days. They purify the Heart; they weaken and disarm Self; they strengthen the Spirit of Prayer, and help us not only to pray, but to find, to love, and live in God. Let us all desire such an Interval as this; and then we shall be fitter to meet again for our mutual Benefit. My Friends, adieu.

The End of the Second DIALOGUE.

---

* *A Demonstration of the Gross and Fundamental Errors of a late Book,* entitled, '*A plain Account of the Sacrament,*' &c., page 82, &c., &c.

THE
THIRD DIALOGUE.

Academicus. If you please, *Theophilus*, pray go on, just where you left off at our last Meeting. For this Mystery seems to be at Daybreak with me; and the Approach of its Light leaves me no Power to be content without it.

Theophilus. You have seen, that all Nature begins and stands in a *magic* Birth; and is only a large Display of its working Power in every kind of Creature. You now want to see further into this Mystery, how Eternal Nature begins; and how God, the first, hidden, imperceptible Cause of all After-Things, manifests himself in the Properties of a visible and working Nature. Now I would, to the best of my Power, gladly assist you in this Matter, if I could find out a Way of doing it, by opening in your Heart a Knowledge of God, of Nature, and yourself, without helping you to a *mere Opinion*, or increasing your Thirst after Ideal Speculation. Tell me, therefore, what you propose by the Gratification of this Desire; or what Effect you expect from such Knowledge, as you here seek.

Academicus. All that I desire by it is, to strengthen and confirm the Ground on which I stand; that, seeing the true Philosophy of Religion, I may have nothing to fear from all that Variety of Attacks which now, more than ever, are made upon it by infidel Reason. I hope, therefore, it is no vain Curiosity, to desire to enter into the Depth of this Mystery, since I only desire thereby Strength to resist all the Enemies of Religion.

Theophilus. All this is right, and very well; provided you do but know who, and what, are the great and powerful Enemies of Religion. But this, perhaps, you do not so well apprehend, as you may imagine. Your own Reason, born, and bred, and governed, by your own Flesh and Blood, is the most powerful Enemy of Religion that you have to do with, and whom you have the most to fear from.

The Men of speculative Reason, whom you seem most to apprehend, are powerless Enemies, that cannot strike at your Religion with the Strength of a Straw. Did you but rightly see what their Power is, you would see it as ridiculous, as that of a few Water-Engines trying to quench the fiery Globe of the Sun: For Reason stands in the same Inability to touch the Truth of

Religion, as the Water-Engines to affect the Sun. Nay, its Inability is much greater; for could the Water, thrown from the Engine, be made to reach the Sun, it would have some, though an insignificant Effect upon it; but Reason can no more affect the Truth of Religion, than *Nothing* can affect *Something*. If Reason seems to have any Power against Religion, it is only where Religion is become a dead Form, has lost its true State, and is dwindled into Opinion; and when this is the Case, that Religion stands only as a well-grounded Opinion, then indeed it is always liable to be shaken; either by having its own Credibility lessened, or that of a contrary Opinion increased. But when Religion is that which it should be, not a Notion or Opinion, but a *real Life growing up in God*, then Reason has just as much power to stop its Course, as the barking Dog to stop the Course of the Moon. For true and genuine Religion is *Nature*, is *Life*, and the *Working* of Life; and therefore, wherever it is, Reason has no more Power over it, than over the Roots that grow secretly in the Earth, or the Life that is working in the highest Heavens. If therefore you are afraid of Reason hurting your Religion, it is a Sign, that your Religion is not yet as it should be, is not a *self-evident Growth of Nature and Life within you*, but has much of mere Opinion in it.

Observe the Word *self-evident;* for there lies the Truth of the Matter; for you have no more of the Truth of Religion, than what is *self-evident* in you. A blind Man may be rich in Notions and Opinions about the Nature, Power, and Good of Light; and in this Case, one blind Man may perplex another, and unsettle his Notions; but when the Light manifests itself, and is become *self-evident*, then he is at once delivered from an Uncertainty about it. Now Religion is Light and Life; but Light and Life can only manifest themselves, and can nowhere be known, but where they are *self-evident*.

You can know nothing of God, of Nature, of Heaven, or Hell, or yourself, but so far as all these Things are *self-evident* in you. Neither could any of these Things be of any Concern to you, but because they can all of them be *self-evident* in you. For the bare History, or Hearsay of any one thing, signifies no more to you, than the Hearsay of any other thing. And if God and Heaven, Hell and the Devil, the World and the Flesh, were not all of them *self-evident* in you, you could have no more Good or Hurt from any Hearsay about them, than from the Hearsay of pleasant Gardens, and dismal Prisons, in the World of the Moon.

Let it be supposed, that your ingenious Reason should suggest to you, that there are no Devils or Hell, and therefore no Occasion to believe that Revelation that gives an Account of *them:*

In this Case, do but turn to that which is *sensible* and *self-evident* in you, and then you must know, in the same Certainty as you know yourself to be alive, that there is *Wrath, Self-torment, Envy, Malice, Evil-will, Pride, Cruelty, Revenge, &c.* Now say, if you please, there are no other Devils but these, and that Men have no other Devils to resist; and then you will have said Truth enough, have owned Devils enough, and enough confessed, that you are in the Midst of them; that you are everywhere tempted by them; and that Flesh and Blood is too weak to resist them, and therefore wants some kind of Saviour, of so contrary a Nature, as has Power to destroy these Works of the Devil in you.

Now this is the only Knowledge that you can possibly have of an outward Hell, and outward Devils; and this Knowledge is as *self-evident* in you as your own Thoughts, and is as near to you as your own Life. But to see and know an outward Hell, or outward Devils, that are outward living Creatures, can never be your own Case, till all that is Divine and human in you is extinguished; and then you will have Knowledge enough, how Hell is a Place, and how the Devils of Rage, Wrath, Envy, and Pride, *&c.*, are living Creatures.

Again, Let it be supposed, that your sceptic Reason had brought you into Doubt about the Being and Providence of God in you: you have no Occasion to consult the Demonstrations which heathen Philosophers, School Divines, Deists, or Atheists, have produced about it, from the Existence of Things; all concluding, as well Christians, as Deists and Atheists, that there must be some eternal first Cause from which all has proceeded.

For what a God is this, that is only proved to be, because something now is, and therefore something must always have been, an infinite, eternal Something, with infinite Power to bring forth all that is come into Being? What a God, I say, is this, which the *Arian*, the Deist, the Atheist, is as willing to own as the Christian; and which is as serviceable to the Cause of *Arianism*, Deism, Idolatry, and Atheism, as it is to Christianity? For the Atheist has his omnipotent, eternal, first Cause, as well as all the Disputers for a God.

But now, if you turn from all these idle Debates and Demonstrations of Reason, to *that* which is *sensible* and *self-evident* in you, then you have a *sensible, self-evident* Proof of the true God of Life, and Light, and Love, and Goodness, as manifest to you as your own Life. For with the same self-evident Certainty, as you know that you think, and are alive, you know that there is *Goodness, Love, Benevolence, Meekness, Compassion, Wisdom, Peace, Joy, &c.* Now this is the *self-evident* God, that forces himself to be known, and found, and felt, in every Man, in the same Certainty of Self-evidence, as every Man feels and finds his own Thoughts and Life. And this is the God, whose Being and Providence, thus self-evident in us, call for our Worship, and Love, and Adoration, and Obedience to him: And this Worship, and Love, and Adoration, and Conformity to the Divine Goodness, is our *true Belief* in, and *sure Knowledge* of, the self-evident God. And Atheism is not the Denial of a first omnipotent Cause, but is purely and solely nothing else but the disowning, forsaking, and renouncing the Goodness, Virtue, Benevolence, Meekness, *&c.*, of the Divine Nature, that has made itself thus self-evident in us, as the true Object of our Worship, Conformity, Love, and Adoration. This is the *one true God*, or the Deity of Goodness, Virtue, and Love, *&c.*, the Certainty of whose Being and Providence, opens itself to you in the self-evident Sensibility of your own Nature; and inspires his Likeness, and Love of his Goodness, into you. And as this is the only true Knowledge that you can possibly have of God and the Divine Nature, so it is a Knowledge not to be debated, or lessened by any Objections of Reason, but is as self-evident as your own Life. But to find or know God in reality, by any outward Proofs, or by anything but by God himself made manifest and self-evident in you, will never be your Cause either here or hereafter. For neither God, nor Heaven, nor Hell, nor the Devil, nor the World, and the Flesh, can be any otherwise knowable in you, or by you, but by their own Existence and Manifestation in you. And all pretended Knowledge of any of these Things, beyond or without this self-evident Sensibility of their Birth within you, is only such Knowledge of them, as the blind Man hath of that Light, that never entered into him.

And as this is our only true Knowledge, so every Man is, by his Birth and Nature, brought into a certain and self-evident Sensibility of all these Things. And if we bring ourselves by Reasoning and Dispute into an Uncertainty about them, it is an Uncertainty that we have created for ourselves, and comes not from God and Nature. For God and Nature have made that which is our greatest Concern, to be our greatest Certainty; and to be known by us in the same Self-evidence, as our own Pain or Pleasure is. For nothing is Religion, or the Truth of Religion, nothing is good or bad to you, but that which is a self-evident Birth within you. So that if you call that only God, and Religion, and Goodness, which truly are so, and can only be known by their self-evident Powers and Life in you, then you are in the Truth, and the Truth will make you free from all Doubts; and you will no more fear or regard anything, that talkative Reason can discourse against it, than against your own seeing, hearing, or sensible Life. But if you turn from *Self-Evidence,* to *Reason* and *Opinion,* you turn from the *Tree of Life,* and you give yourself up to certain Delusion.

Wonder not therefore, my Friend, that though the Mystery under Consideration contains the greatest of Truths, yet I am unwilling to help you to reason and speculate upon it ; for if you attempt to go further in it, than Self-evidence leads you, you only go so far out of it, or from it. For the End of this Mystery, is not to furnish new or better Matter for Reason and Opinion, but to bring Man home to that *Sensibility,* which is self-evident in himself, and to lead him only by self-evident Principles, to see, and find, and feel the Difference between true and false Religion, in the same Degree of self-evident Certainty, as he sees and feels the Difference between Fire and Water. This, I say, is the great Intent of this Mystery, to bring Man into a Sensibility of God and Nature, to know and feel, that Good and Evil, Life and Death, are a self-evident Growth and Birth of Nature in Man, according as his Will enters into, and works with that which is unchangeably good, or unchangeably evil, in the Working of Nature. Now as the Workings of Nature are unchangeable in their Effects, and that which is naturally good or evil, must be always so; and seeing Man's Life standeth in Nature, and must work with it, must have only that Good or Evil which is unchangeable in Nature ; and seeing his State in Nature, whether good or evil, is, and can be, *only that,* which the sensible, self-evident Powers of his own Life manifest to him ; then you see the Fitness and Necessity of your keeping steadily to that, which is *self-evident* in you, as the very *Tree of Life,* the Criterion of all that Truth and Goodness that belongs to you. *Secondly*, you see with what good Reason *Jacob Behmen* so often tells you, That all that he has written, was only to 'help Man to seek and 'find himself,' to see and know his *Place* and *State* in Nature, and how to co-operate with God and Nature in generating a Birth of Heaven within himself. *Thirdly,* you may see how you and I should abuse this blessed Mystery, should we, instead of only and truly seeking and finding its Birth within us, make it a Matter of Reasoning and Opinion.

Academicus. I have neither Power nor Inclination to object to anything that you have said. But still I must desire you to assist me, in your own Way, and such as you judge to be suitable to the Intention of this Mystery. I plainly see, that the whole Ground of Religion lies in the Knowledge of what God is in himself, as distinct from Nature ; what Nature is in itself; what I have from God, and what I am in and from Nature ; and how

I am to work with it, as God himself is and worketh in Nature. For if this Knowledge can be opened in me, then the *Why*, and the *How*, of every Mystery of Redemption must be seen to the Bottom.

Theophilus. By Nature are Meant, *all the working, stirring Properties of Life*, or all the various Sensibilities which Life is capable of finding and feeling in itself. And therefore you need only look at the working Sensibilities of your own Life, the several Kinds and Ways of feeling and finding your own State, to know by a *self-evident* Certainty, what Nature is in itself. And thus also, in the same self-evident Certainty, you may know, that Nature is not God. For as you find, that Nature is opened in you; that all its Properties have their Existence in you; and yet that none of these Properties of Life are their own Happiness, or can make themselves to be happy, full of Peace, Delight, and Joy, and free from every Want; so you have a full self-evident Proof, that God is not Nature but entirely distinct from, and superior to Nature; and that, as considered in himself, he is *That* which alone can make Nature happy, free from Want, and full of all delightful Satisfaction. And thus you know, not from Hearsay, but from a self-evident Certainty in yourself, that God, considered as in himself, is the *Happiness*, the *Rest*, the *Satisfaction*, the *Joy*, the *Fulfilling* of all the Properties and Sensibilities of Nature; and also that Nature, in itself, is that working Life of various Properties and Sensibilities, which *want* to be made happy, which *reach* after something that they are not, and have not, and which cannot be happy or fulfilled, till something of an higher Nature than themselves be united with them; that is, the Working of Nature must be in Want, in Pain, and Dissatisfaction, till God (the Blessing and Fulfilling of Nature) is manifested, found, and enjoyed in it.

Now suppose you knew no more of what God is in himself, distinct from Nature, and what Nature is as thus distinguished from God, than is already opened in you, you would know enough to be a Key to all that which *Jacob Behmen* speaks of God, and of Nature; and enough also to show you how to co-operate with God and Nature, in bringing forth a New Birth of the Divine Life within you. For as soon as you know, that Nature in itself is only a working Life of various Sensibilities, which wants something distinct from itself, and higher than itself, to make it happy, then you have a self-evident Certainty of these following Truths: *First*, That God, considered as in himself, is the Blessing, the Satisfaction, the Heaven, and Happiness, of all and every Sensibility of Nature. *Secondly*, That therefore, as the Gospel teaches, only the *Word*, the *Light*, the Son of God, or *Jesus Christ*, can redeem fallen Nature, restore it to its first State of Blessedness in God. Thirdly, That therefore, as the Gospel teaches, you have but *one Thing* to do, and *that* one Thing absolutely necessary to be done; *viz.*, to *deny yourself;* that is, to turn this fallen Nature from itself, from all its own Wills and Workings in the Vanity of this Life, to give up itself in Faith, in Hunger and Thirst after that Light, Word, Son, or *Jesus Christ* of God, who is the Fulness, the Satisfaction, the Joy, and Blessedness, of all Nature; who alone can turn every Working and Sensibility of Nature into a Participation of heavenly Satisfaction and Joy. Now what can you desire, or need you to know of God, of Nature, and the Mystery of Christian Redemption, more than this? And yet all this is a self-evident Knowledge, born within you as soon as you turn to it.

Academicus. Oh! Sir, you quite transport me with this short, easy, and yet full Explication of so great a Matter, which has often perplexed me. But now I shall never be at a Loss, how to understand the Distinction between God and Nature, and also the absolute Necessity of it; which, when rightly known, sets all the Doctrines and Mysteries of Christian Redemption upon such a Ground, as cannot be removed. But still I must beg of you, to help me to the same Self-evidence of the Birth and Generation of the Properties of Nature, as they are set forth by *Jacob Behmen*, especially of the Three first Forms, which I perceive to be the Ground of all; and yet their Birth and Generation, their Union with, and Distinction from, one another, I do not enough comprehend, as he sets them forth. Thus, the first *Form* of Nature is said to be *Desire;* which is the Ground and Foundation of all Things. This Desire (the first Property) he saith, is 'astringing, drawing, shutting up, compressing, hardening,' *&c.* Now all this is evident enough; for I have a sufficient Sensibility, that this is the Nature of Desire; that, in its spiritual Way, it attracts, draws, compresses, and would shut up, or inclose, *&c.* But then, it is immediately said, that the Second Property is 'Attraction, Drawing, Sting, and Motion,' *&c.* Now if the First is *Attraction* and *Drawing,* how can the Second be different from it, and yet be Attraction and Drawing?

Theophilus. The Desire is not one *Property*, but is in itself all the Properties of Nature; it is the Ground in which they all dwell, and the Mother out of which they are all born: So that all that is said of the Three First Forms of Nature, is only so much said of Three Forms or Properties of the Desire. For the Desire is not the First Property of Nature; but every Property hath all that it hath in and from the Desire. The First Property of the Desire, or that which is the Peculiarity of its Nature, as distinguished from the Second, is, to *compress, inclose, shut up, &c.* whence cometh *Thickness, Darkness, Hardness, &c.* But no sooner does the Desire begin to compress, shut up, but it brings forth its own greatest Enemy, and the highest Resistance to itself: For it cannot *compress* or *thicken*, but by drawing or attracting; but drawing and attracting is quite contrary to shutting up, or compressing; because drawing or attracting is *Motion*, and every Motion is contrary to shutting up or compressing together.

And thus your Difficulty is removed : Attraction or Drawing is rightly ascribed to the Desire, and rightly called its Second Property, because it is born of it; and yet is directly contrary to that which is the Desire's First Property or Intention ; *viz.,* to *compress,* to *hold in Stillness, &c.*

Now as these Two Properties are Two Resistances, not in Two different Things, but are one and the same Thing in this Contrariety in and to itself, as they are inseparable, generate each other, are equal in Strength, and can neither of them overcome the other, so as to go one Way, but each of them stops the other in the same Manner ; and seeing this Desire cannot cease to be these Two contrary Things ; *viz.,* a *Holding-fast,* and *Moving-away,* a *Shutting-in,* and a *Going-out,* both in the same Degree of Strength ; neither able to shut up, nor to go out, nor able to cease from either ; these Two Contrarieties become a *whirling Anguish* in itself, and so bring forth a *Third Property* of *Nature.* And in these Three Properties lies the true Ground of all Sensibility of Life and also of every created Thing. Matter, Motion, Darkness, Fire, and every natural Power or Quality of anything, has its Beginning from them. Considered in themselves, they are the working Powers of that great and strong creaturely Life, which cannot be broken, because it begets itself, and every Property is included in, and generates each other. It is a Band or Knot of Life, that can never be loosed ; nor is capable of Annihilation, because it is a Birth of eternal Nature, which is as unchangeable as God himself. And as it arises from no outward Thing, but is generated in and from itself, its Work is eternal, and can never be made to cease. For as one Property has no Power over the other, but that of *forcing* it to exist ; as one Property does not weary the other, but always gives Strength to it ; so there can be no Cessation of their working, but they must do, as they do, to all Eternity.

Now the Life of these Three Properties, is a Life of Three contrary Wills, equally strong and powerful against each other ; and therefore is a Life of the highest Disquiet, Torment, and Anguish, full of the most horrible Sensibility. It is a Life that can feel nothing but its own tearing Contrariety, that reigns within it. And this is the Life of Nature separated from God; it is the Life of Hell, and the Devils; and is that Life of dark, raging Distraction, which every living Creature must be in, whose first Properties of Life are not softened and quieted, either by the Light of God, or the Light of this World, dwelling and making Peace in them. And he that will only seek to his Reason, to cool the Flame of these raging first Properties of Life, acts as wisely as he, whose House being on Fire, would only have it extinguished, by reading a Lecture upon the Nature of Water to it.

And now, Sir, you have seen plainly enough the Birth, Nature, and Difference of these three first Properties. But let it be supposed, that you have no feeling, or inward Sensibility, of these Three Properties, in the Manner they have been here described, according to *Jacob Behmen;* yet you have no Reason to be troubled at it, or put your Brain upon the Rack how to conceive it, or fear that you must want the Benefit of this Knowledge, till you have it as above described; for you have in yourself a most self-evident Proof, that the Thing is really so; and that Desire hath *all that* in it which he so deeply declares, from its first Seed, or Root.

For it is a Thing self-evident to you, that every Desire, as such, is in itself a restless Torment; that it hath Pain, Disquiet, and Anguish, in itself; and, as to itself, consists of nothing else. Now, whether you can, with *Jacob Behmen*, divide this restless, anguishing Desire into its Three essential Parts, of which it consists, matters not, as to the Reality of the Thing itself; for you have Sensibility enough, that the Desire is made up of Pain and Anguish, till the thing desired is obtained: And therefore you have all the Certainty and Benefit of this Knowledge, and it serves the same End, as if you knew the Ground of it, with the same Exactness as he has set it forth.

You have yourself for a Proof, that Desire and Pain begin together; and this is a full Proof of what was said; *viz.*, that Desire Begins with *Two Properties* that resist and strive against one another. Again, you have the same Evidence in yourself, that the Desire, left to itself, that is, without the least Glimpse of any Possibility of having that which it desires, is a Degree of Hell, and quite intolerable to itself: And this is a self-evident Proof of what was said; *viz.*, that the Third and last Property of the Desire, is that whirling Anguish, brought forth by the Two first Properties: For these Three Properties are the Whole of the Desire; it has nothing more in it. And when your Desire cannot cease, and yet has nothing but itself, without the least Mixture or Feeling of Hope in it, then you have a full Self-evidence of *all that* which the Desire is, in its Three essential, inseparable

Properties, and that strictly according to the Letter of *Jacob Behmen*.

Now all that is Nature, or natural Life within you, is only the working of Desire in this painful State; and *that* which can set this painful Life at Rest in you, is so much of God, or the Divine Nature, manifested in you, and changing your restless Properties of Life into Peace and Happiness. And as the working Properties of Desire are your natural Life, so the same working Properties are the Life of eternal Nature; from whence, as out of the Womb, your natural Life is brought forth, and hath neither more nor less in it than that which is in eternal Nature.

And if the working Properties, which constitute the Life of eternal Nature, could be supposed to be without God in them, eternal Nature would be a mere eternal Hell: But as the eternal Desire, with all its working Properties, is brought forth by the magic Power of the Divine Will, only for this End, that the holy Deity may manifest a Heaven of Glory in them; so eternal Nature always was, and always must be, a Kingdom of Heaven, or the unchangeable Manifestation of the invisible God in an outward Sensibility of Life, Happiness, Glory, and Majesty.

Academicus. I am fully satisfied as to this Point; and all that you have said, has the Evidence of Light at Noon-day. And I hope you will now go on in the Birth of the Four remaining Properties; and show me, in the same Degree of Evidence, how these Three Properties bring forth the Four following ones, which turn Nature into a Kingdom of Heaven.

Theophilus. These Three Properties of Nature, cannot bring forth the Four following ones. They can bring forth nothing but themselves to all Eternity, nor can ever be anything else in themselves, but what they were at first. Nature can rise no higher than this painful State; and its painful working Contrariety must always be the Ground of all Life, and all Sensibility of Life. For if (1) This Shutting-up, or Compressing; and (2) This Resistance to it; and (3) This Whirling arising from both, was ever to cease, there Life, and all Sensibility, must cease with them; and therefore these Three Properties must always do as they do, as the only possible Ground of every Kind and Degree of every creaturely Life, both in Heaven, and on Earth.

But if Life is to be happy, something else must come into them, not to destroy their natural Working, but to make every Contrariety in them a strife of Joy, and delightful Sensibilities. Thus, (1) Compressing, or Shutting-up, must find itself only to compress and keep in Light and Love; (2) The Attraction or Drawing-motion, must find itself to be the Drawing and Motion

Divine Knowledge. 241

of Love; and, (3) The whirling Anguish must whirl still, but as a *Transport of Joy*, unavoidably brought forth from the Strife of Love in the Two Properties of which it is born. And thus Nature remains in its full Strength; it compresses, it attracts, and it whirls, as it did at first; and nothing is lost, or taken from it, but its Hatred, Wrath, and Misery. Now here you are to observe, that every Thing or Creature, either in Heaven, Hell, or this World, hath its Substance, or all that is Substantially in it, solely from these Three First Properties of Nature. The creaturely Substance of an Angel, a Devil, or a dead Flint, all stand in these Three First Forms of Nature. And all the Difference betwixt high and low, spiritual and material, in the Creatures, arises from their different Participation of the Four following Forms of Nature. But the Four following Forms cannot exist, or manifest themselves, but in the Three first; and therefore the Three First are, and must be, as well in the highest as in the lowest of Creatures: They are the first *Something*, or *Substantiality* of Nature, in which the Light, and Love, and Spirit of God could manifest itself; for Spirit cannot work without something to work in and upon, and in which it may be found; nor could *Light* shine, unless there was *something* in Nature *thicker* than itself, to receive and reflect it: And therefore, *Thickness* or Darkness is, and must be, as eternal as the *visible* or *shining* Light. Darkness is so far from being a mere *Negation*, or only an *Absence* of the Light, that it is the *first* and *only* Substance, and the Ground of all the possible Substantiality in Nature, and the substantial Manifestor of Light itself, which could have no *Visibility, Shine*, or *Colour*, but in, and through, and by the Substantiality of Darkness or Thickness. This Darkness, Thickness, or Substantiality, is not co-existent with, or independent of God, but is the *compressing, astringing, thickening* Work of the first Property of the Desire; which Desire comes eternally from God, only as a magic Birth from the Will of the Deity, which willeth to come out of its Hiddenness, into an outward Visibility of a working Life. And therefore the Desire is the Beginning of Nature; it compresses and thickens. But what does it compress and thicken? Why, Nothing but itself; *viz.*, its own Three Properties. And these Three Properties thus brought forth, tied and bound in one another, are, from Eternity to Eternity, all the Substantiality and thickness, that is or ever can be in Nature, or any Creature, from the Highest to the Lowest. And they are thus brought forth, in this indissoluble Band in and by the Desire, that the invisible Light and Life of the hidden Deity, may have its *Something* to move and shine in; his hidden Spirit have *Something* to work and manifest itself in;

his hidden Love have *Something* into which it may give itself; and his hidden Life have Something in which it can open itself in a Variety of Births of Life. And *this Something* is the *working compressing Desire*, which includes in itself, (1) A continual Thickening, which is Darkness and Substantiality; (2) Motion or Resistance to this Thickening, which is the Ground of all Sensibility; And, (3) A restless State of Whirling from these two Properties, which is the very Nature and Power of Life. And thus these three Properties of the Desire, are that *sufficient Something*, in which the Deity, by entering into it, can manifest his hidden Power in all the Substances and working Properties of Nature, by turning them all in their different Workings, into an endless Variety of delightful Forms and Sensibilities of the creaturely Life.

Now this first Thickness, Darkness, or Substantiality, brought forth in the Desire, though it is not Matter, as Matter is seen and found in this World; yet these two Things must be affirmed of it: *First*, That it stands in the same Place, answers the same Ends, and is distinguished from Light and Spirit in the eternal World, just as Matter in this World stands distinguished from the Light and Spirit of this World. *Secondly*, That all the *Darkness*, Thickness, and Matter of every Kind in this World, is nothing else in itself, but the first Thickness, Darkness, and Substantiality in the Desire, brought down by various Steps into such Kinds of Materiality as are here to be seen. Look at what Kind of Materiality you will in this World; it is, in its whole Nature, nothing else but the Darkness or Thickness of the eternal World, brought into a further Degree of Thickness and Compression. And now we are come to see the true Ground; (1) How the Angels could destroy their Kingdom, or lose all the Light and Happiness of Heaven in it: And, (2) How also, their wasted, spoiled, darkened Habitation in the divided Properties of Nature, could be turned, and created by God, as it is, into this new Form of a material World.

The first Three Properties of Nature were never to have been seen or known, as they are in themselves, by any Creature; their Thickness, Strife, and Darkness, were brought forth by God, in Union with the Light, and Glory, and Majesty of Heaven; and only for that End, that the holy Deity might be made manifest in them. And therefore their own Nature, as they are in themselves, without God in them, could only then be first known, when the Angels turned their Desire backwards, to search and find the Ground and Original of Life, which could not be found, till these Properties were found, in which the original Ground of Life lay hid. This turning of their Desire into the Origin of

Life, was their whole turning from the Light of God; and therefore they found themselves where they had turned their Desire; that is, in the Centre of Nature; *viz.*, in the first Properties of Nature, which is the *Dark Centre*, or Ground of Life, which never should have been known or manifest to any Creature. For by the Centre of Nature, or the *Dark Centre*, you are always to understand these three first Properties; which, when without or separate from the Light and Goodness of the Deity in them, are in themselves only the Thickness, and Rage, and Darkness, of an omnipotent *Compressing*, an omnipotent *Resistance* to it, an omnipotent *Whirling* from these two omnipotent Contrarieties. I call them all omnipotent, because they cannot be stopped, but do all that they would; and though they are contrary to one another, yet each of them gives Strength to the other; so that the Omnipotence of the one, is the Omnipotence of the other.—And this is the boundless, incessant, strong Rage, Darkness, and Strife, of the hellish Life, which only is that, which these Three properties of Nature, when left to themselves, can feel or find. Now the Angels, which turned their Desire into this Centre of Nature, fell into the Life and working Power of these Three Properties: they felt nothing else in themselves, but these Properties; they had no other Will or Power of Working, but as these Properties worked; and therefore, as living and active Creatures, they could only live, and act, and co-operate, or unite with that Ground of Nature without them, which was the *same* and *one* with their own Nature; and therefore, all that they could do, was to stir up, awaken, call forth, and act with that Thickness and Darkness, and Strife, that was hidden in Nature, just as the Toad, in a fine Garden, only sucks the Poison that is hid in a good Herb. So the fallen Angels, though in Heaven, having only the Centre of Nature in themselves, could only find and work with that Centre and Root of Darkness, on which the heavenly Glory stood. But from this Power which they had of working in the Centre of Nature, hence came forth a *dark, wrathful Substantiality*, separated from the Light and Glory of the holy Deity; and thus a *new Kind* of Substantiality appeared in their Kingdom; and their outward Habitation was like their inward Life; *viz.*, a *Manifestation* of Nature fallen from God. And here now, you clearly see, how the First Thickness or Compression of the First Property of Nature, which was only the *hidden Substantiality* of the Light and Glory of Heaven, came into a *more outward* State, and made its first Approach or Step towards *Matter*, as you now see it. For there was now a *Thickness*, a *Darkness*, and Hardness which never had been before; for the Light being lost, then the First Property of

Nature lost its beatified State of Meekness, Transparency, and spiritual Fluidity; and became stiff, rigid, dark, and hard; and this, as I said, was its *first* Step or Descent towards the Hardness and Darkness of the Matter of this World, till it came to be Earth and Stones, by the creating Power of God. And thus it came to pass, as *Moses* speaks, *that Darkness was upon the Face of the Deep.* A State, that had no Possibility of Existence, till the Sin of Angels had manifested the hidden Centre of Nature, in the Working of its Three Properties, without the Light of God in them.

Now as a new Thickness of Darkness, Hardness, or Substantiality, was manifested by the strong working Powers of the Angels in the Centre, or the first Properties of fallen Nature; so God, to Manifest his Wisdom and Goodness towards this fallen Nature, took all these Properties in their own working Way; and made them in their own way of Working, to stop and overcome the Evil that was brought forth by them. For the Will of God joining with the wrathful *Astringency* of the first compressing Property of Nature, became the *Divine Fiat*, which increased this compacting Property to such a Degree, as created or compacted the darkened Substantiality into a Globe of Earth and Stones. And this same Divine *Fiat*, or creating Power, which coagulated the Grossness into Earth and Stones, compressed or coagulated all that was substantial, or belonged to Substantiality through their whole Kingdom, as well the heavenly as the earthly Part of it; so that all their Kingdom, as to its Substantiality, lost its Spirituality, and entered into a new created or compacted State of Thickness, as well the spoiled, as the unspoiled Part of their Kingdom. And as soon as this was done, the Angels lost all their Power in it, and over it. They could kindle no more Wrath in its heavenly Part, nor make any Use of that which they had spoiled, because all was shut up together in this new Compaction, with which the Spirituality of their Nature could have no Communication. And so they were left prisoners in their own Chains of Darkness, unable to stir up Wrath anywhere but in themselves. All this was done in the first Day of the Creation, when the *Fiat* of God compressed or created their whole Kingdom into a Heaven and Earth. Hence it is; *viz.*, from a Compaction of their whole Kingdom into a new-created Heaven and Earth; that all Things in this World, all its Elements and Stars, are a Mixture of Good and Evil, have something of the Goodness of Heaven, and something of the Wrath and Evil of Hell in them. Hence is the great Variety of metallic Ores and precious Stones in the Earth; the good and bad Qualities in Fire, Air, and Water. It is because the Divine

Fiat, or compacting Power, came at once in the utmost Swiftness upon their whole Kingdom, as the Good and Evil stood in Strife against each other, and compressed all into a State of Cessation and Conjunction with one another, as in the Prison of this new-created Materiality. And thus the heavenly and hellish Part of their Kingdom, Light and Darkness, Fluidity and Hardness, Meekness and Wrath, Good and Evil, were all shut up together in the same sudden Compaction; in which they lay, as in a State of Death, till the Divine *Fiat* should awaken a Life in it.

Now the Three First Properties of Nature; the First, a *Shutting* up; the Second, a *Running* out; and the Third, a *Whirling;* were by the Divine *Fiat*, in the three first Days of the Creation, become the Ground of an earthly, a watery, and airy Materiality, all according to the working Nature of the Three Properties; and all of them having something of an heavenly Nature shut up in them, which wanted to be delivered from its Bondage. Hence this threefold Materiality of Earth, Water, and Air, became a Subject fit for the Birth of the fourth Property of Nature. And therefore, on the fourth Day of the Creation, the Divine *Fiat* kindled in this *anguishing* Materiality, out of that very *Fire* and *Light* that was compacted and hid in it, the fourth Property of Nature (the eternal Fire) as a Globe of Fire and Light, which was to stand as an Out-birth of the eternal Fire, in the midst of this new-created Materiality, and become the Opener of all the astral Life and Light in this World. And as the eternal Fire, the fourth Property of eternal Nature, is not a moveable Thing that can change its Place, but must be always in the Place of its Birth, standing for ever, as a Birth, in the Midst of the seven Properties, for ever changing the three first Properties of Nature into the three last Properties of the Kingdom of Heaven; so the Sun, the true Out-birth of the eternal Fire, and having the same Birth and Office in this material World, as the eternal Fire hath in eternal Nature, is not, cannot be, a *moveable* Thing, or be in any *other Place* in this World, than where it is; but is, and must be, the *Centre* or Heart of this whole System, ever separating the three first Properties of this material World, from the three that follow, and ever changing the three first Forms of material Wrath, into the three following Forms of terrestrial Life, Light, and all delightful Sensibilities; in strict Conformity to that, which the eternal Fire does in eternal Nature, changing the Root, or first Properties of Nature, into a Kingdom of God, and heavenly Glory. For the *Sun* is not a Body of Fire brought into the Place where it is; but the *kindled Place* is its Body and Birth; and therefore it is as immoveable as Place is, and must be as it is;

viz., a Place giving forth Fire and Light till all material Nature is dissolved. The Place is kindled, not by any foreign Fire, but thus : In the first Compaction of the whole angelic Kingdom into this new Materiality, the good and bad Part, that is, the spoiled and unspoiled Substantiality of their whole Kingdom, was shut up in this new Compression or Materiality, in one and the same State of Death. *Secondly*, In the Beginning of the Creation, God said, ' Let there be Light, and there was Light ;' not a *shining* Light, for that came first from the Birth of the Sun, but a Power or Virtue of heavenly Light, not yet in a *visible, material Shine,* but as an *uncreated* Power of Light, entering into this whole Materiality, to stir up, and awaken the good Part of the heavenly Substantiality, that was shut up in the Compaction of this new Materiality.

Without these two Things, material Nature must have continued in its Darkness, and no fourth Form of Fire could ever have come forth in it. But from these two Things, *viz.*, the heavenly Substantiality, stirred up by the Power of Light entering into it, the three first Properties of Darkness were brought into a mere anguishing State ; from whence, by the Divine *Fiat*, the fourth Form of material Nature kindled itself, as a Fire, and *broke forth* in the Place of the Sun, and must be ever burning and flaming in the Midst of the material System ; because it is born of the three first Properties of Darkness, and brings forth the three last Properties of Light, and Life, and the Joy of Nature ; and therefore must always be in the Midst of the six Properties of Nature, itself making the Number to be seven. And thus the Sun, as the fourth Form of Nature, must always stand in the Midst of the whole material System. And this proved, not as *Copernicus* has proved it, from reasonable Conjectures, and outward Arguments, but from the internal Nature of its Birth, the first Root from which it proceeds, and the absolute Impossibility of its being otherwise. And thus it is, that the Truth and Depth of Nature is opened by the Spirit of God, in the Mystery made known to our illiterate Shoemaker. And thus you have a short Sketch, how this World came to be as it is. It is descended as an Out-birth of the eternal World, and all the seven Properties of eternal Nature work in it, as they work in Eternity; and the Eternity is manifested in the temporary Working of a new World, which is only to stand in this State of Thickness or Compaction for a time, till the Goodness of God towards fallen Nature has been sufficiently manifested thereby.

For as this material System of Things may, in a good Sense, be said to be an unnatural State, occasioned by the Disorders which the Fall of Angels brought into Nature ; and as it had no Beginning, but from the Will of God, commanding the first Property of Nature to coagulate and compress their disordered Kingdom into a new Thickness or Materiality, only as a Remedy to stop, remove, and overcome the Evil in Nature; so when this Remedy shall have had its Trial, and the Will of God shall no longer will this compressing together; then all that has been brought together by it, must fall back again into its first Eternity. And then, without any Possibility of being otherwise, every Birth in this World, that belongs to the Root or Centre of Nature, and has worked with it, must fall down into that eternal Abyss of Darkness, on which the Light of God for ever stands, unknown to it. And every Life that is born of Heaven, and has worked with it, must ascend into the Kingdom of God, or Abyss of Divine Glory and Majesty.

Oh *Academicus!* Look now (whilst these Thoughts are alive in you) at worldly Greatness, fleshly Wisdom, and earthly Schemes of Happiness; and tell me, if you can, what a Nothingness, what a Folly and Delusion, there is in them? Look again at the Apostle's Pilgrim, abstaining from worldly Lusts, desiring to know nothing but Christ, and him crucified; living in the Spirit of Prayer, and Thirst after God; striving in everything after the fullest Conformity to the Tempers, Spirit, Life, and Behaviour of Christ in this World ; and then tell me, whether Heaven and Earth, God and Nature, and all that is great, and wise, and happy, does not call upon you to be this Pilgrim.

Academicus. Truly, Sir, I enough see, that all worldly Wisdom, and ambitious Views of a Glory of Life in the Things and Concerns of this World, are no better than vain Attempts to be blessed and happy from the Ruins of the angelic Kingdom. For this World is only a Thickness and Materiality of the bestial Life, built upon the Ground of Hell ; that is, upon the first Properties of fallen Nature, brought into a harder, more compacted State of Existence than they have in Hell, and kindled into an astral, terrestrial, bestial Life, by the Power of the Sun. The bestial Life, therefore, is the highest Good and Happiness in it ; and the Creatures of this World have nothing that they seek for further in it. But Man being not created for it, but by Sin fallen into it, is the only Creature that makes an unnatural Use of it, and seeks for that in it, and by it, which cannot be found in it. Man, having been wise, great, and happy in his Creation, though they are all lost, has yet some remaining Sensibility of them, though fallen into a World, that cannot help him to them. Hence it is, that he would be wise, and great, and happy in a World, that has no Happiness but for Beasts; and can only help Man to know, that he is poor and miserable, and banished from his true native Country.

But, instead of learning this one Lesson of Truth, from the World he is in, which is all the Wisdom, Greatness, and Happiness, that can be had from it, he gives himself up to a Wisdom that is Foolishness, a Greatness that is all Meanness, and a Happiness that begins and ends in Torment and Delusion. Would you see all his greatness, Wisdom, and Happiness united, the Sum total of earthly Glory! It is, when he has in his Cap the Feathers of some Birds, wears a painted Riband, laced Clothes, is called by some new Name, and drawn from Place to Place by a Number of Beasts. Now, poor, and mean, and unnatural as this Fiction of earthly Glory is, yet this is the powerful Idol, that carries all before it! that destroys all Sense of Goodness, and Divine Virtue! and keeps the Heart of Man so earnestly devoted to it, that he has no Sense of the Eternity that is in him; that Eternity brought him forth, and Eternity will take him again!

Theophilus. It is true, *Academicus,* that the highest Good of this World is its bestial Life; and therefore it has no more, or other Happiness for a Man, than for a Beast; can give no more to one, than to the other; *viz.,* Food and Raiment; with which the bestial Life in Man ought to be content, as well as in the Beast. But seeing Man, in spite of the Nature of Things, will have an earthly Glory of Life; thence it is, that the Wisdom of this World is, and must be, Foolishness with God, and will be Foolishness with Man, as soon as he gets but a moderate Knowledge of himself. But give me leave just to observe, that though this material World has no higher Happiness than the bestial Life; yet God hath much higher Ends in creating it. For though the dark wrathful Properties of fallen Nature could only, in their Compaction, be made the Ground of a vegetable and bestial Life; yet you are to observe, that in the Creation of this World, *viz., in the Compaction of the whole angelic Kingdom,* the unspoiled heavenly Part thereof was shut up with that, in which the Wrath was kindled: And that for these two great Ends; *First,* That, by this Compaction, it might be taken out of the Power of the evil Angels, that they might not go on in kindling Wrath in it. *Secondly,* That this reserved good Part of their Kingdom, might be the Foundation and Ground of an heavenly paradisaical Life, and a new Host of heavenly Creatures, instead of the fallen Angels. Now, to do this, God created an human Angel, who was to call forth the paradisaical Life out of the compacted heavenly Substantiality, as the Sun opened a vegetable bestial Life, out of the gross Substantiality of the material World.

God breathed the Triune Spirit of the holy Deity into a Body taken out of the Earth, that is, into a Body of that *Heavenly Substantiality*, that was shut up in the Earth, as well as in every other Part of this material System ; and therefore his Body is rightly said to be taken or formed out of the Earth, because it was formed of that Substantiality, that was shut up in the Earth.

But when his wandering Eye had raised a longing Desire to know what the earthly Life was in its Good and Evil, and took the certain Means of knowing it ; then, as his Soul lost the Light and Spirit of God, so it lost also that heavenly luminous Body, in which the Light and Spirit of God could dwell, as it dwelleth in Heaven. And when this heavenly luminous Corporeity was lost, and shut up again in that earthly Bondage and Compaction in which it lay, before it was his Body ; then the poor fallen Soul was only clothed with the gross Corruptibility of bestial Flesh and Blood. You are to understand this Matter thus : When his Body was formed out of that heavenly Substantiality, that was in the Compaction of the Earth, it was not entirely separated from all earthly Materiality (because he was to have a Body of this World, as well as of the heavenly World), but its *State* in the earthly Materiality was *entirely changed*; it was till then shut up in the earthly Compaction, but now it is called out of that *earthly Death* into a State of Life; it is set free from the Power of the Earth, in a Superiority over it, to be its Happiness, and open its own Glory in it, and through it.

And thus you see the *Possibility*, the *Truth*, and the *Manner* of the Thing ; how his heavenly Body was taken out of the Earth at his Creation, set in Freedom from it, and in a living Superiority over it ; how, at the Fall, it was swallowed up, or compacted again in *its own first Earth ; viz.*, the earthly Body, or Materiality of *Adam :* For as it was not separated from this earthly Materiality, but only brought to Life in it, and Superiority over it ; so when the Divine Light, which was the Life of this Body, was lost, it then fell again into a State of Death in that gross Materiality, under which it lay before. And thus in the strictest Truth, the Body of *Adam* returned again to that very Earth, or Dust, from whence it was taken.

Now, when this happened, the fallen Angels entered again into some Power in their lost Kingdom. There was then something found, with which they could work, and join their own Power. For as the Soul of Man had lost the Light and Spirit of Heaven, so the same *dark Centre* of Nature, or the Three first wrathful Properties, were opened in it, as are opened in the fallen Angels. And thus they got Entrance into the awakened Hell in Man, and can work in it. For as often as Man stirred, followed, or worked with his Will according to these Properties, the Devil could enter into, and work with him; and so the first Son of fallen Man was made a Murderer. And hence it is, that Sin and Wickedness have known no Bounds; it is because it is the joint Work of fallen Angels, and fallen Man.

Stay a while, Sir, in View of these Truths: Here you see the Seat and Ground, the Birth and Growth, of all Sin and Evil; it lies in these Three dark, selfish, self-willed, wrathful, hellish Properties of the fallen Soul. This is the *dark Centre* of Nature, in which the Devils have all their own Power in themselves, and all their Power in you;—and till you resist this Hell within you, till you live in Contrariety to it, the Devils will not flee from you.

Here also you see, in a self-evident Light, the deep Ground, and absolute Necessity, of *that one* Redemption, which is called, and is, the *Meekness of the heavenly Blood of the Lamb of God*. For these Words in their true Ground, mean only the Changing of the Three first dark wrathful Properties of fallen Nature, into the Three last Properties of the heavenly Life, Light, and Love, which is the Life of God restored to the Soul, or the Light, and Spirit, or Word of God born again in it. Let me only add this one Word; Turn from Wrath of every Kind, as you would flee from the most horrid Devil; for it is his, it is he, and his Strength in you. Whether you look at Rage and Anger in a Tempest, a Beast, or a Man, it is but one and the same Thing, from one and the same Cause; and therefore your own Wrath is to be turned from, as the same with that of Hell; and which has its Birth and Strength from that Hell or Centre of Nature, which the Fall of Angels hath made known; and which only worketh thus differently, whether it be in a Man, a Beast, or the Elements of this World. And this must be, till the Centre of Nature is again in its Place of Hiddenness, by being wholly overcome by Heaven. Embrace therefore every Meekness of Love and Humility, with the same Eagerness as you would fall down at the Feet of *Jesus Christ;* for if it is his, it is he, and his Power of Salvation in you. Enter into no Strife, or Self-defence against anyone, that either reproaches you, or your Doctrine; but remember, that if you are to join with *Christ* in doing Good, your Sword of natural Wrath must be locked up in its own Sheath; no Weapons of Flesh are to be used; but you must work only in the Meekness, the Sweetness, the Humility, the Love and Patience of the Lamb of God; who, as such, is the only Doer of Good, the only Overcomer of Wrath, and the one Redemption of fallen Nature. If you are reproached as an *Enthusiast*, do not take Comfort in thinking, that it is the Truth of your own Piety, or the Want of it in others, that gives Occasion to the Charge ; for though both of these should happen to be the Case, yet they are not proper Reflections for you ; and if you take your Peace from them, it is not the Peace of God in you : But as in good Report, you are to be as though you heard it not, ascribe nothing to yourself from it ; so in evil Report, Self is just as much to be forgotten ; and both of them are to be used, only as an Occasion to generate Humility, Meekness, Love, and the Spirit of the Lamb of God, both in yourself, and all that speak either well or ill of you. For this is the Will and Working of Heaven ; it has but one Will, and one Work ; and that is, to change all the Wrath, Evil, and Disorder of Nature, into a Kingdom of God. And therefore he that would be a Servant of God, and work with Heaven, must will all that he willeth, do all that he doth, and bear all that he beareth, in that one Spirit, and one Will, with which Heaven ruleth over all the Earth.

You rejoice to think, that you know the true Ground of your Redemption ; how Heaven comes again into the fallen Soul, when that Property of Light and Love, which is called the *Fifth Property of Nature*, is generated in it. It is indeed a blessed Knowledge ; but its Blessedness is only then yours, when yourself are this *Fifth Property*, that is, when your Life is a Life of this Fifth Property ; when, whatever you do, wherever you go, or whatever you meet, you only do as this Fifth Property doth, give nothing but that which it giveth ; *viz.*, its gentle Light and Love to every Man, and every Thing, whether it be good or bad. For this Property hath nothing else to give, and yet is always giving; its Nature is, to communicate and impart itself, not here or there, but always and everywhere ; it has no other Will. When therefore this Property (the *Christ* of God, the Life of Heaven) is born in you, Friend and Foe will have the same from you ; you will have lost all Resentment ; you will love your Enemies ; bless them that curse you ; pray for them that despitefully use you ; and have but one Will towards every Man, and that is, that Light and Love may do that for him, which they have done for you.

Academicus. Oh ! *Theophilus*, you have given me more than I know how to contain ; and yet have increased my Thirst after more still. You have so touched the Cord of Love within me, that all my Nature stands in a trembling Desire after it ; I would fain feel nothing else but the gentle godlike Power of Love, living in my Heart. Pray *therefore*, of all Things, help me to understand how the Fire, the Fourth Property of Nature, is born ; and how it turns the Three first wrathful Forms into the Three following Forms of heavenly Joy, Triumph, and Happiness ; the

First of which Three Forms, is this *Fifth* of Light and Love: Therefore, help me here, I beseech you.

Theophilus. What a *Therefore* have you here drawn? That therefore, of all Things, I must needs help you to an *Opinion*, or *notional* Knowledge, *how* the Fire is born, and *how* it turns Nature into a Kingdom of God. For were I to join with you in forming Notions of *this How*, I should only help you to lose all, by being content with the Shadow, instead of the Substance.

You say, that your Nature stands in a *trembling Desire* after the Birth of this Light and Love: If so, you stand in the very Place of its Birth, and must stand there till it is born in you. It can be born nowhere else, nor in any other Manner; and all that *Jacob Behmen* has written, is only to direct and bring you to this Place of its Birth. He himself has given you all the hearsay Knowledge that you can have of it; for he can give you no more from the plainest Words. And therefore, to help anyone to work with his Brain for clear Notions, and rational Conceptions, of what he has written, is helping him to do and be that, which all his Works, from the Beginning to the End, absolutely declare against, as contrary to the whole Nature and End of them. Which speak, as he saith, with the Sound of a Trumpet; and chiefly to awaken Man out of the Dream and Death of rational, notional, and hearsay Knowledge; and to show him, that his own inward Hunger and Thirst after God, is that alone which can and must open the Fountain of Light and Divine Knowledge in him.

But to speak a Word or Two of the *Fire*, whose Birth you want to know. You know already, better than any Words can tell you, from a self-evident Knowledge, that *Nature is in you*; that it is not God, *but is* that which *wants* God, or its true Good; and must be an Emptiness, a Pain, and Want, till God is manifested in it. If you ask, Why Nature is only a State of Want and Disquiet, and unable to be content with itself? It is because the eternal, uncreated, incomprehensible Light, which no Creature can enter into, is that which gave Birth to all Nature, and from whence all Nature hath its Hungering, and State of Want. For Nature had never come into Being, but that the eternal, incomprehensible Light, longed to be manifested in an *outspoken* Life of Nature and Creatures, and in a *Visibility* and *Shine* of Glory: Therefore, as Nature came forth from this first Longing of the Light to be manifested in it, so Nature is in itself only a Want and Hungering, which the Light alone has raised, and can only satisfy.

Now from this Longing on both Sides, Nature wanting God, and God wanting to be manifested in Nature, the Union of both is effected; which is the Birth of that eternal Fire, or Fourth Form of Nature, which is always burning in the same Degree, that is, always doing the *same Thing; viz.*, always overcoming and shutting up the Three first Forms of Nature, and making them to be the hidden Root and Centre of Nature; and always bringing forth out of them the Three following Properties of Light and Love, and every joyful Sensibility of Life; that is, changing Nature into a Kingdom of Heaven. Now *that* which makes this Change in the Properties of Nature is, and is rightly called Fire, in the strictest literal Meaning of the Word; because all that we can conceive as Fire in this World, hath its whole Nature, Power, and Existence, from it. Not only the Fire of Life in Animals and Vegetables, but the Fire in the Kitchen, and the Candle, is each of them kindled as it is kindled, and doth all that it doth from this Fourth Property, or Fire of eternal Nature. The Thickness and Darkness in the Wood, and the Candle, have Fire kindled in them, and Light from that Fire, in no other Way, than as the Fourth Property is a Fire from the Thickness and Darkness of Nature, kindled by the Light of God entering into Union with it. Had the Wood, and the Candle, no *Water* or *Oil* in them, neither of them could give forth Fire and Light. Now Water and Oil have the Properties of Light in them: When therefore the Properties of Nature in the Wood, and the Candle, are put into Strife, and begin to work in Blackness and Darkness (which is the Beginning of every Fire), they by this Strife open an Entrance for the Properties of Light in the Water, and the Oil, to mix and unite with them; and by this Union of Darkness and Light, that Fire is kindled, which turns the Darkness of the Wood and Candle into a Shining and Light. And thus does every Fire kindled in this World, bear an infallible Witness to the *Kindling*, the *Nature*, and *Power*, of that eternal Fire, which, kindled by the Oil of Divine Light, changes the first dark Properties of Nature into the Light and Majesty of Heaven, Now what would you know more of Fire, or its Birth, than that it is, and only can be, kindled by the Light of God entering into, and uniting with, the first Properties of Nature in the Soul? Leave off therefore all working with your Reason in the Way of Notions; empty your Heart of all vain Satisfactions in earthly Things, that so the first Properties of Nature in your Soul, finding their Misery, and Want of God, may make you to be all Hunger, and Faith, and Desire of him. And then the Fire must kindle, nothing can hinder it; God will then infallibly come as a Fire and Light into your Soul, changing all the wanting, empty, restless Properties of your natural Life, into a Sweetness of a New Birth of Rest and Peace in him.

For nothing *works* either in God, or Nature, or Creature, but *Desire*. And as God created Angels and Men out of eternal Nature, only through a longing Desire of manifesting his own Goodness and Happiness in them, so every Angel and Man must find God, as a Life of Happiness and Goodness in him, as soon as Nature, either in Angel or Man, is become a Hunger after God. For Hunger does all in all Worlds, and finds all that it wants, and hungers after. Every Thing had its Beginning in it, and from it; and every Thing is led by it to all its Happiness.

Academicus. I am quite satisfied in all my Demands, and will ask for no more Help, as to the Use I am to make of our Author's Writings. Only tell me when they will all come forth in a new Edition, or which will be published first; for I want several of them, which I could never get.

Theophilus. If you have but Two or Three of his Books, it is enough; for every one of them has all in it that you need be taught, and sufficiently opens the Grounds of the whole Mystery of the Christian Redemption. He himself thought his Books to be too numerous; and expressed his Wish, that they were all reduced into one. As he wrote without any Art, and had no Knowledge of Regularity of Composition; so whatever particular Matter he occasionally entered upon, he always began again afresh from the same first Ground, and full Opening of the Mystery of Nature, from whence he explained and determined the Matter he was upon. And it was this frequent, and almost constant Repetition of one and the same Ground, that swelled his Writings into so many Volumes, though it may be said, that there is nothing separately in any of his Books, but what is to be found in almost every other, though not so largely set forth. You have no need therefore, to run with Eagerness through all his Books; but the Thing that you are to intend and look for, is the *Ground* and Foundation on which all his Doctrines are built, which contain the true Philosophy, or *fundamental Opening of all the Powers that work both in Nature and Grace;* and that by this Knowledge you may become a true Workman yourself; and know how to conform to, and concur with, all that the working Powers, either of Nature or Grace, require of you. Now this Ground and Foundation of all is (as far as Words can do it) opened to you in every one of his Books: And you have been already also sufficiently brought into the Knowledge of it, by what has been said of the *Birth* of Nature; what it is, how it works, how it came into Being, how it is distinct from God, how it wants God, how God is manifested in it, how every After-thing is from and out of it, is all that it is, and hath all that it hath, in it, and by it, and must have all its Happiness or Misery, according as it works with, or contrary to Nature. From this fundamental Ground, or Opening of the working Powers of Nature, you have seen how Angels could, and did, lose their first State in Nature; and how a Second new Creation could, and did, come out of their fallen State and Kingdom, all according to the Powers of fallen Nature, over-ruled, and governed, and put into a new Way by the good *creating Fiat* of God. You have seen how this new Creation, with Man its Lord, could, and did, lose also their First created State in Nature; and how God, over-ruling fallen Nature again, did, by his merciful *redeeming Fiat*, or by the Means of the holy *Jesus*, put this fallen new Creation in a State of Recovery, and all done according to the Powers, and Workings, and Possibilities of Nature. So that nothing is done arbitrarily, or by mere Will, but everything in Conformity to the unchangeable Workings and Powers of Nature; only directed, assisted, and helped, by the Mercy of his *redeeming Fiat*, so far as Nature was capable of being helped. This, Sir, is the true and fundamental Ground of all his Doctrines; and, standing upon this Ground, you stand in the Centre of Truth, whence everything that you need to know of God, of Nature, of Heaven, of Hell, of the Fall of Man, of his Redemption only and solely in and by the Word or Son of God, is known in such self-evident Certainty, as you find and know the Workings of your own Life: And also, that Happiness or Misery, Life or Death, can only be had, or not had, lost or found, solely as a *Birth in Nature*, brought forth by the Faith, or magic Power of the Will of Man, working either with, or contrary to, the *redeeming Fiat* of God.

To make therefore a right Use of his Writings, you should, for a sufficient Time, keep solely to that Part of them, which opens the Ground and Foundation of the Powers that work in Grace and Nature, till by a self-evident Sensibility it is opened in you, and your Heart stands in a Conformity to it, and true Working with it: For it is your own Heart, as finding the working Powers of Nature and Grace in itself, and simply given up in Faith to work with them, that is to be your Key and Guide to that Knowledge you are to have of them; whether it be from the Holy Scripture, or the Writings of this Author. For to this End, he tells you, he has written all; *viz.*, to help Man to *seek* and find himself; what is his Birth, his State and Place in Nature; what he is in Body, Soul, and Spirit; from what Worlds all these Three Parts of him are come; how they came to be as they are at present; what his Fall is, and how he must rise out of it. And therefore, if, in order to seek and find this Ground in yourself, you were, for some sufficient time, to read only to the 10th or 12th Chapter of his *Three Principles*, or to the 6th or 8th

Chapter of his *Threefold Life;* and proceed no further, till this Ground had made itself manifest in you, and your Heart stood in a strict Conformity to it, and Working with it; you would then be in a true Fitness to read further, and reap the full Benefit from any other of his Books, that should fall into your Hands; whether it was the *Way to Christ,* or the Book upon the *Incarnation.* But, above all Things, remember this Advice, as of the last Moment to you, *Be no Reasoner upon the Mystery;* seek for no Commentaries, or rational Explications of it, to entertain your Reason with: For, as soon as you do this; then, however true and good this Mystery may be in itself, it is, with regard to you, of no better Use than that very vain *Philosophy, and Science falsely so called,* condemned by the Apostle. It will only be the same Snare and Delusion to you, that other Learning and Philosophy is to other People. For if there is nothing good or Divine in you but the Faith, and Hope, and Love, and Desire of your Heart turned to God; if nothing can do any Good, be any Blessing or Happiness to this Faith, and Love, and Desire turned to God, but only God himself in his *holy Being;* and if nothing can communicate God to you, but God himself; and if God cannot communicate himself to you under a *Notion,* or an *Idea* of Reason, but a Degree of *Life, Good,* and *Blessing,* born or brought to Life in your Soul; then you see, that to give yourself up to Reasoning, and notional Conceptions, is to turn from God, and wander out of the Way of all Divine Communication.

Academicus. But if it be strictly thus, *Theophilus,* had it not been better, that these deep Matters had not been communicated to the World, since it is so natural to Man to make a wrong Use of them?

Theophilus. This Objection, *Academicus,* comes with the same Strength against the Scriptures themselves. For, excepting the *Seven thousands* unknown in every Age, as in the Days of *Elijah,* and a few spiritual Fathers and Writers in almost every Age of the Church, bearing faithful Witness to the truth and Mysteries of Religion, it must be said, that human Learning, governed by human Reason, hath, from Age to Age, to this very Day, not only mistaken the true End and Use of the Scriptures, but hath turned them into an Occasion of much Evil and Mischief. The Scriptures speak only to the Heart and Conscience of Man, not to amend or enlighten it with Notions and Opinions formed from the written Letter of the Word; but solely to make the *Being* and *Power* of God known and adored, and to awaken in Man a Sensibility of his Want of God; and to turn all the Power, and Strength, and Will of the Heart wholly to God, to receive Light, and Life, and Rest, in his *holy Being*.

But to speak now directly to your Objection: If I knew of any Person, who stood in the Faith and Simplicity of the first Christians, free from all carnal Adherence, or vain Trust, to Party-Notions, Doctrines, and Errors, brought forth by the Contention of Sects and Churches; whose Soul was dead to the earthly Nature, and all the Rudiments of this World, seeking only Light, Life, and Salvation, from God the Father, Son, and Holy Ghost, living and dwelling in him, redeeming and sanctifying his whole Body, Soul, and Spirit; To such a one I could freely say, this Mystery was needless; as having all that already, which this Mystery would do for him. For its only End is, to bring Man out of all the Labyrinths of false and notional Religion, to this very first State and Simplicity of the Gospel-Faith and Life.

And this may pass for a good Reason, why this Mystery was not opened by God in the first Ages of the Church; since there was then no Occasion for it. For Religion began, and went on, rightly, in its own true Way; it had the Faith and Heart of Man; it stood in its own proper Strength and Glory, and was an awakened Divine Life of Faith, simply given up with Joy and Gladness to the Mysteries of the Gospel; not wanting any *Whys* or *Wherefores*, because in the real Possession of all the *Good*, and *Blessing*, and *Power*, of every Mystery of Salvation.

But seeing a *worldly Spirituality*, called in Scripture the Whore riding upon the *Beast*, has had its Thousand Years in the Church; since not only every Kingdom, but almost every Corner of Christendom, has a *Babel* of its own, built upon some rational Interpretation of the Letter of Scripture; since learned Reason, *within* the Church, knows no other Use of Scriptures, but to reproach and condemn all other *Babels*, and to find Materials to strengthen its own; since Reason, *without* the Church, finds it as easy to reproach and condemn *all Revelation*, as it is to reproach all these *Babels* built upon it; since this is the finished Confusion, brought forth by the *Reason* and fleshly *Wisdom* both of those that defend, and those that oppose the Gospel; how adorable is the Goodness of God, in vouchsafing to these last Ages of the World such a Remedy (*viz.*, the Opening the Ground and Mystery of all things) as is suitable to the distressed and confused State of Religion in the World! And how easy is it also to see the greatest Reasons, why this Remedy was not afforded sooner! For as true Faith did not want it, and learned Reason, whilst pleased with itself, could not be in a Condition to receive it; so it was highly suitable to the Goodness and Wisdom of God, not to give forth this Mystery, till Reason, or fleshly Wisdom, had made Shipwreck of Faith; and had so filled up the Measure of its Folly, as to stand in its last and highest State of Distress,

Perplexity, and Confusion. For any Remedy is only then likely to be rightly received, when Distress and Perplexity make the Want of it to be sensibly felt.

Let not therefore the genuine, plain, simple Christian, who is happy and blessed in the Simplicity of Gospel-Faith, take Offence at this Mystery, because he has no Need of it. For it is God's Goodness to the distressed State of the Church, fallen from the Life and Power of Gospel-Faith, and groaning under the Slavery, Darkness, and Perplexity, of bewildered Reason and Opinions.

Neither let the orthodox Divine, who sticks close to the Phrases and Sentiments of Antiquity, reject this Mystery as heretical, because it opens a Ground of Man, and the Divine Mysteries, not known or found in the primitive Writers. For this is the very Reason, why he should thankfully receive it with open Arms, as having, and being that very Thing, which the distressed divided State of the Church now so greatly wants; and yet did not want, till it was fallen from its first Simplicity of Faith. For whilst Faith and Life defended the Mysteries of Religion, the Ground and Philosophy of it was not wanted. But when Orthodoxy had given itself up to Reason, and had nothing else for its Support but Reason and Argument from the Letter of Scripture, without the least Knowledge of the first Ground of Doctrines; then it could only be defended, as it is defended in every Sect and Division of the Christian World. For if Reason will defend the Mysteries of Redemption, without knowing the true Ground on which they stand, or why they must be as they are, from the Nature of the Thing; the more zealous and learned any Man is, the more Errors must he fall into in the Defence of them. For the greater the Strength is, that works without Light, the more Extravagancies it must produce. This is too visible in all the Controversies that have risen in the Church. Now, that learned Reason, as presiding in the Divinity-Schools, never yet had, nor could have, any Knowledge of the Ground of Man, and the Mysteries of Redemption, is plain from this one generally received Opinion, of every Age to this Day; *viz., That all Things were created out of Nothing.* For this Maxim entirely excludes *all Possibility* of giving any Account of the Ground and Reason of anything, either in the Nature of Man, or Religion; and is the same thing as saying, that Nothing has any Ground or Reason. For if that which begins to be, comes out of Nothing, it can only have the Nature of that out of which it comes; and therefore can have no more said about it, why it is this or that, than can be said of that Nothing, from whence it comes. And if the Mystery, or Life of

Divine Knowledge. 259

the human Nature, is out of Nothing, has no Reality of any antecedent Ground in it, out of which it came to be such as it is, and to have that which it hath; then it is most certain, that all the Mysteries of the Religion of Man must come forth from the *same Nothing*, and have no antecedent Ground from whence they come, that requires them to be as they are. For Man, created out of Nothing, cannot have a Religion that is of any higher Descent than himself, unless he is to have a Religion that is quite unnatural to him. But a Religion that has its Ground in Eternity, must be an unnatural Religion to Man that comes up in Time, and out of Nothing. If therefore you will hold Man to be out of Nothing, you must of all Necessity hold all the Mysteries of the Religion of Man to be also out of Nothing; and that therefore no possible Account can be given, either of the Ground of Man, or his Religion, or why there can be either Right or Wrong, Good or Evil, in either of them.

Hence you may see, why the Truth has always suffered in every Controversy of the Church; Thus, if you begin with that of St. *Austin* and *Pelagius*, about the Freedom of the human Will; do but suppose, what is Fact, that they both of them held the human Will to be created out of Nothing; and then you need not wonder at that Number of Volumes and Systems of Errors, which this Dispute has brought forth. For who can say, what the Will is, or is not; what Nature or Power it must have, if it is created out of Nothing? Whereas, if either of these Disputants had known, from a true Ground, what the human Will is; that it cannot be a made Thing, much less made out of Nothing; but that the Will of Angel or Man, is the eternal uncreated Will become creaturely, as a true direct Birth from the Divine Will, descended from it, born out of it, and from thence come into a creaturely State: then they had known, that the Will of Angel or Man, must have the Nature and Freedom of the eternal Will; and that its Freedom not only consisted in its Self-motion, but chiefly and most gloriously in this, that it could neither receive, nor have, nor be anything, as to its Happiness or Misery, but according to its own Working: And then all that Predestinarian Learning of Decrees, *&c.*, that has tormented the Church ever since the Time of St. *Austin*, had been prevented.

Look next at the *Socinian* Controversy. The *Socinians*, and their Opponents, met in the Field of Reason, to debate about the Fall, Original Sin, its Guilt, the vindictive Wrath of God, and the Necessity of satisfying the Divine Justice; the Necessity of the Incarnation, Sufferings, Death, and Satisfaction, of Christ, These were the great Points to be tried at the Bar of Reason. Now all these Disputants stood upon the old Ground; *viz.*, that

17—2

the Soul of Man, as well as all other Things, was created out of Nothing. And therefore they all stood absolutely excluded, from every Possibility of touching the true Ground or Reason of any one Doctrine in Debate. For the Soul, created out of Nothing, leaves no room to affirm, or even to suppose, that anything can be affirmed of the Ground and Reason of Christian Redemption. For surely, if the Soul of Man is created out of Nothing, it may and must with as much Sense be affirmed, that it may be *redeemed by Nothing;* and he that affirms the one, can have no Pretence to deny the other.

Just the same may be said of the present Controversy, betwixt the Christians and Infidels, concerning Christianity itself. You need not wonder, that so many learned Volumes have had so little Effect; or that the Defenders of Christianity seem to lose Ground, though the Infidels, at the same time, get no Advantage to their Cause, but that of increasing their Numbers. For as neither Side can go any higher, than a Creation out of Nothing; so neither Side can say anything from a true Ground, either for or against the Mysteries of the Gospel. If therefore Infidelity increases, it is not because it has got more Light, sees further into the Depths of Nature, or stands upon a more rational Ground; but merely because the Vanity and Blindness of the Dispute, has a natural Tendency to beget Indifference and Infidelity in the Hearts of Men.

Observe this Proposition; *viz.,* ' In God we live and have our ' Being.' Now, how easy is it for anyone to see, that no one can say anything as to the Ground and Reasons of the Mysteries of the Gospel, either for or against them, till he can go to the Bottom of this Proposition, and plainly show, either how we do, or do not, live and move, and have our Being, in God! For the Truth or Falseness of every Mystery of the Christian Redemption, plainly depends upon this Matter. If the Christian therefore will speak to the Purpose, in Defence of the Ground of the Gospel; he must be able to show, that we so are in God, so have our Life in him and from him, and so move in him, as to prove, from thence, the Ground, the Necessity, and Certainty, of the Christian Means of Redemption. On the other hand, the Deist cannot take one rational Step, or have any true Ground to stand upon, but so far as he can show, that we are not so from God, have not such a Nature in and from him, do not so live and move in him, as to have any *Want* or any *Fitness* for that Method of Redemption, which the Gospel teaches. But as neither Side did this, though the one Thing necessary to be done; so you also see, that neither Side had any Possibility of Doing it. For the Soul, created out of Nothing, allows of no Inquiry, whether anything of God be in it, or how it has its Life in him, or stands related to him. It admits of no searching after any Ground or Reason of its Good or Evil, or how it must have its Happiness or Misery from the Nature of the Thing. For if the *intelligent Life* itself must be supposed to come from no Ground, but to be created out of Nothing; then it is certain, that its Good and Evil, its Happiness or Misery, with everything else, must be supposed to have no Ground or Reason for being as it is, but to be created out of Nothing; and may go again into Nothing, just as the Creator pleaseth.

And now, Sir, you may enough see how all Controversy, both within and without the Church, has been so vain a thing. For Reason was to support Doctrines and Mysteries, without the least Knowledge of the Ground on which they stood; and Reason was to oppose them in the same Ignorance. You see also, why in these last Ages, where literal Learning has made so great a Figure, that the Matter has only been made worse, and Division and Error more triumphant. For as the Ground of the Truths was still wanted, and nothing appealed to, but the Letter and Phrase of Scripture; so the more artful and learned the Disputants were in Reasoning and Criticism, the more Absurdities must be defended on both Sides. Why is not the learned Papist shocked at Transubstantiation, or the Protestant at Predestination and Reprobation? Is it because each of them have enough of the *Truth* of Reason, and the *Goodness* of Criticism, to draw the Letter of Scripture to his Side. And this you may be assured of, that Reason, and literal Learning, have just as good Eyes in every other religious Matter, and will give just such an Account of every other Doctrine, when it comes into Dispute, as the Papist and Protestant have done in these two Points. And the thing cannot be otherwise: As the Deist and Christian both hold a Creation out of Nothing, they must both have only an arbitrary God, and arbitrary Religion, that has no antecedent Ground to stand upon, but is left to the arbitrary Proof or Reason of both of them. What Thanks, therefore, are due to the Goodness of God, for opening this great Mystery of all Things in our Author, wherein the Right and Wrong, the True and False, in Religion, is as manifest as any Thing can be to our Senses! Let no one therefore take Offence at the Opening of this Mystery, as if it brought anything new into Religion; for it has nothing new in it; it alters no Point of Gospel-Doctrine, nor adds any Thing to it, but only sets every Article of the old Christian Faith upon its true Ground, and in such a Degree of Light, as, when seen, is irresistible. It disturbs no one, who is in Possession of the Truth, because it points at nothing, drives to nothing, but to the opening the heavenly Life in the Soul. It calls no Man from any outward Form of Religion, as such; but only shows, that no outward Form can have any Good in it, but so far as it only means, and seeks, and helps, the renewed Life of Heaven in the Soul. 'A 'Christian,' says he, 'is of no Sect, and yet in every Sect'; a Truth which all Sects, as such, will dislike; and therefore a Truth equally wanted to be known, and equally beneficial to all Sects. For the chief Hurt of a Sect lies in this, that it takes itself to be necessary to the Truth; whereas the Truth is only then found, when it is known to be of no Sect, but as free and universal as the Goodness of God, and as common to all Names and Nations, as the Air and Light of this world.

Suffer me now, before we part, once more to repeat what I have so often said, that you would not receive this Mystery as a System of rational Notions; nor do with it, as the World has, for the most part, done with the Bible, only gather Opinions of Reason and Speculation from it. For it opens no Depth of Nature or Grace, but to help you to the Heart and Spirit of the returning prodigal Son, and to show you the Blindness and Vanity of Reason and Opinions; and that Truth can have no possible Entrance into you, but so far as you die to your earthly Nature. The Gospel saith all this to you in the plainest Words; and the Mystery only shows you, that the whole System of the Universe saith the same thing. To be a true Student or Disciple of the Mystery, is to be a Disciple of Christ; for it calls you to nothing but to the plain Letter of the Gospel; and wherever it enters, either into the Height or Depth of Nature, it is only to confirm the Truth of these Words of *Christ; viz.,* 'He that 'followeth not me, walketh in Darkness: And unless a Man deny 'himself, and forsake all that he hath, he cannot be my Disciple.' This is the Philosophy opened in this Mystery. It is not to lead you after itself, but to compel you, by every Truth of Nature, to turn to *Christ,* as the one Way, the one Truth, the one Life, and Salvation of the Soul; not as notionally apprehended, or historically known; but as experimentally found, living, speaking, and working, in your Soul. Read as long or as much as you will of this Mystery, it is all Labour lost; if you intend anything else by it, or would be anything else from it, but a Man dead to this World, that you may live unto God through *Christ Jesus,* in the Power of Faith, and the Spirit of Prayer. With these Words upon our Minds, my Friends, let us now end this Conversation.

The End of the Third DIALOGUE.

FINIS.

www.ingramcontent.com/pod-product-compliance
Lightning Source LLC
Chambersburg PA
CBHW060559230426
43670CB00011B/1886